The Taoist CEO

Navigating Business with Ancient Wisdom

Dr. David Leung

BY THE SAME AUTHOR

On a Happy Life: Designing Successful Organisations the Senecan Way

The Finite Advantage: Mastering Time and Leadership the Senecan Way

Bushido Leadership: The Immortal Code of Japan's Warriors

The Golden Mean: Leadership Lessons from Confucius' Doctrine

The Ripple Effect: Leadership Lessons from The Great Learning

Thirty-Six Stratagems: Ancient Chinese Wisdom for Modern Leadership

The Samurai Leader: Management Lessons from The Book of Five Rings

The Resilient Leader: Corporate Wisdom from the Book of Job

The Executive Prince: Adapting Machiavellian Strategies to Modern Leadership

Beyond the Sun: Ecclesiastes' Guide to Modern Leadership

The Hindu Leader: Applying the Bhagavad Gita to Contemporary Management

Wisdom from Proverbs: Biblical Principles for Modern Leadership

The Stoic Leader: Applying Meditations to Modern Management

Enlightened Leadership: Buddhist Principles for Business Success

The Confucian Leader: Transforming Modern Organisations with Classical Philosophy

The Taoist MBA: Leading with Softness, Stillness & Silence

The Art of War for CEOs: Sun Tzu's Timeless Strategies for Modern Business Strategy: A Blueprint for Business Warfare

Inside Accounting: The Sociology of Financial Reporting and Auditing

Research Methods for Accounting & Finance: A Guide to Writing Your Dissertation (ed.)

ABOUT THE AUTHOR

Dr. David Leung is a seasoned university lecturer with over 17 years of teaching experience. He holds a PhD and MSc in Science and Technology Studies from the University of Edinburgh, and an MBA from Durham University.

His journey, however, began far beyond the academic world. Before entering academia, he qualified as a Chartered Global Management Accountant with the Chartered Institute of Management Accountants (CIMA), gaining invaluable business experience across diverse industries—ranging from printing and property management to financial services, biotechnology, and tourism.

In 2024, Dr. Leung founded Dragon Business School (www.DragonBusinessSchool.com). This innovative institution aims to become a beacon of excellence, offering cutting-edge online business management courses designed to empower and inspire the next generation of business leaders.

PREFACE

In the complex and rapidly evolving landscape of modern business, leaders are constantly seeking ways to navigate challenges, inspire their teams, and drive sustainable success. While technological advancements and innovative strategies play crucial roles, the timeless wisdom of ancient philosophies can offer profound insights and guidance. Among these, the teachings of Lao Tzu, encapsulated in the *Tao Te Ching* (dào dé jīng 道德经/道德經), stand out as a beacon of simplicity, balance, and harmony.

The Taoist CEO: Navigating Business with Ancient Wisdom is an exploration of Book 1 of the *Tao Te Ching* through the lens of contemporary business leadership. This book delves into the principles of Taoism and their relevance to modern management practices, providing CEOs and leaders with a unique framework for fostering a balanced, ethical, and effective organisational culture.

Lao Tzu's *Tao Te Ching*, written over two millennia ago, offers timeless lessons that resonate with the core challenges and opportunities faced by today's business leaders. The concepts of non-action *(Wú Wéi* 無為/无为*)*, simplicity, humility, and living in harmony with the natural order provide a counterpoint to the high-pressure, target-driven environment that often characterises modern corporations.

This book aims to bridge the gap between ancient wisdom and contemporary business practices. Each chapter of Book 1 of the *Tao Te Ching* is meticulously analysed and interpreted to extract actionable insights that can be applied to leadership, strategy, and organisational development. The chapters are designed to inspire a shift in perspective, encouraging leaders to embrace a more holistic, mindful, and sustainable approach to business.

Key Themes & Applications

- *Non-Action (Wú Wéi):* Learn how the principle of effortless action can enhance decision-making, reduce stress, and foster a more innovative and adaptive organisational culture.
- *Simplicity:* Discover the power of simplicity in strategy and operations, leading to greater clarity, efficiency, and focus.
- *Humility:* Understand the value of humble leadership in building trust, respect, and loyalty within teams and across the organisation.
- *Harmony with Nature:* Explore how aligning business practices with natural rhythms and cycles can promote sustainability and long-term success.

The *Appendix* includes the original translation of Book 1 (chapters 1 to 37) of the Tao Te Ching, allowing readers to engage directly with the text and reflect on its profound insights.

As you embark on this journey through *The Taoist CEO*, I invite you to open your mind to the transformative potential of Lao Tzu's teachings, allowing this book to inspire you to lead with wisdom, compassion, and a deep connection to the natural flow of life. By embracing the wisdom of the *Tao Te Ching*, you will not only enhance your own leadership but also contribute to creating a more harmonious and sustainable world for future generations, finding the strength to lead with authenticity, the clarity to navigate complexity, and the balance to achieve lasting success.

David Leung
Edinburgh, 20 November 2024

CONTENTS

LAO TZU

EARLY LIFE

Lao Tzu *(Lǎozǐ 老子)* is traditionally believed to have been born around 604 BCE, during the Spring and Autumn period of Chinese history, in a village called Quren, located in the state of Chu. This area corresponds to present-day Luyi in Henan Province. There are various legends about his birth, with some accounts suggesting he was born with white hair, a sign of wisdom and venerability from a young age. His actual name was *Lǐ Ěr (李耳)*, and he was later honoured with the title *Lǎozǐ (老子)*, meaning 'Old Master.'

Lao Tzu's wisdom and intellectual prowess led him to serve as a royal archivist at the Zhou court in Wangcheng, which is in modern-day Luoyang. In this esteemed position, he had access to a vast array of ancient texts and historical records. His role involved preserving important documents, advising the court, and contributing to the intellectual and cultural life of the Zhou Dynasty. His profound understanding of history, literature, and philosophy made him a respected figure in the court.

Throughout his tenure at the Zhou court, Lao Tzu gained a reputation for his deep wisdom and extensive knowledge. Scholars and officials often sought his counsel on various matters, and he became known for his insightful observations on governance, ethics, and the nature of existence. His philosophical reflections were grounded in his understanding of the Tao *(The Way)*, emphasising harmony, balance, and the natural order of the universe.

Lao Tzu's teachings were characterised by a preference for simplicity, humility, and non-interference, which later became foundational principles of Taoism. His philosophical approach contrasted with the more structured and duty-bound Confucianism, leading to a rich intellectual exchange between followers of these different schools of thought.

ENCOUNTER WITH CONFUCIUS

The reputed encounter between Lao Tzu and Confucius is a legendary event in Chinese philosophical history, symbolising the meeting of two of the most influential thinkers of ancient China. Lao Tzu, the founder of Taoism, and Confucius, the progenitor of Confucianism, represented two distinct yet complementary philosophical traditions. While the historical accuracy of their meeting remains debated, the tale serves to highlight the rich intellectual exchange and the diverse perspectives that shaped Chinese thought.

According to legend, the encounter took place at the Zhou court, where Lao Tzu served as the royal archivist. Confucius, who was then a rising scholar and teacher, visited the court seeking knowledge and wisdom. Drawn by Lao Tzu's reputation for profound insight and learning, Confucius sought an audience with the elder sage.

The meeting between Lao Tzu and Confucius is often depicted as a significant exchange of philosophical ideas. Confucius, known for his teachings on morality, social order, and proper conduct, was reportedly impressed by Lao Tzu's deep understanding of the Tao *(The Way)*. The dialogue between them highlighted their differing yet complementary approaches to life, governance, and human nature.

Lao Tzu's Perspective: Lao Tzu emphasised the importance of living in harmony with the Tao, advocating for simplicity, humility, and naturalness. He stressed the value of non-action *(Wú Wéi*

無為/无为) and the need to let things unfold naturally without forceful intervention. Lao Tzu's philosophy focused on the inherent balance and flow of the universe, encouraging individuals to align themselves with this natural order.

Confucius' Perspective: Confucius, on the other hand, focused on the cultivation of virtue, proper conduct, and the maintenance of social harmony through ethical behaviour and adherence to rituals. His teachings underscored the significance of education, family loyalty, respect for elders, and the importance of moral integrity in governance and personal conduct.

While the details of their conversation are largely speculative, the encounter between Lao Tzu and Confucius is symbolic of the interplay between Taoist and Confucian thought. Their dialogue is said to have left a lasting impression on Confucius, influencing his views on certain aspects of governance and personal conduct.

Lao Tzu's Influence on Confucius: Some accounts suggest that Confucius came away from the meeting with a deeper appreciation for the virtues of humility and simplicity. Lao Tzu's emphasis on non-action and naturalness may have tempered Confucius' more structured and prescriptive approach, leading to a more nuanced understanding of balance and moderation.

Philosophical Divergence and Convergence: Despite their differing approaches, the philosophies of Lao Tzu and Confucius both contributed to the richness of Chinese thought. Taoism and Confucianism offered complementary perspectives that shaped the cultural, spiritual, and social fabric of China. Together, they provided a holistic understanding of life, ethics, and the cosmos.

AUTHORSHIP OF THE *TAO TE CHING*

Lao Tzu is traditionally credited with composing the *Tao Te Ching*. This foundational text of Taoism outlines the principles of living in harmony with the Tao *(The Way)*. The *Tao Te Ching* consists of 81 short chapters, each filled with profound and often paradoxical wisdom that encourages simplicity, humility, and naturalness. It is widely regarded as one of the greatest philosophical works in history, offering timeless insights into the nature of existence, leadership, and the human experience.

While Lao Tzu is traditionally credited with the authorship of the *Tao Te Ching*, modern scholarship suggests that the text may have been the work of multiple authors over time. This perspective is based on several factors:

Linguistic Analysis: Scholars have conducted linguistic analyses of the *Tao Te Ching*, examining the language, style, and terminology used in the text. These analyses suggest that the work may have been composed over an extended period, incorporating contributions from different authors.

Historical Context: The historical context in which the *Tao Te Ching* was written also supports the idea of multiple authorship. The text reflects various philosophical influences and cultural developments that occurred over centuries, indicating that it may have evolved through the collective input of several thinkers.

Manuscript Variations: Variations in ancient manuscripts of the *Tao Te Ching* further support the theory of multiple authorship. Different versions of the text have been discovered, each with slight variations in wording and structure. These differences suggest that the *Tao Te Ching* was a living document, subject to revisions and additions over time.

LATER LIFE

According to traditional accounts, Lao Tzu became increasingly disillusioned with the moral and political decay he observed in the Zhou Dynasty. The corruption and social strife of the time contrasted sharply with his vision of a harmonious life aligned with the Tao. Disheartened by the lack of interest in his teachings and the prevailing chaos, Lao Tzu decided to leave the Zhou court and seek solitude in the western wilderness.

As the legend goes, Lao Tzu embarked on a journey towards the western borders of China, intending to live out his remaining years in seclusion. He rode on an ox, symbolising simplicity and the harmonious relationship with nature that he espoused in his teachings. This journey itself became a metaphor for the Taoist ideal of retreating from worldly concerns to attain inner peace and wisdom.

Upon reaching the western frontier, Lao Tzu encountered a border guard named Yin Xi. Recognising the sage's wisdom, Yin Xi pleaded with Lao Tzu to write down his teachings before departing into seclusion. In response, Lao Tzu composed the *Tao Te Ching* in a single session, distilling his profound insights into the nature of existence, governance, and the Tao into 81 concise chapters. This act of writing down his wisdom ensured that his teachings would endure, even as he retreated from the world.

After completing the *Tao Te Ching*, Lao Tzu handed the manuscript to Yin Xi and continued on his journey, disappearing into the wilderness. The details of his later life remain shrouded in mystery, contributing to his legendary status. The story of his departure underscores the Taoist principles of detachment, simplicity, and the pursuit of harmony with the natural order.

HISTORICAL SIGNIFICANCE

The historical details of Lao Tzu's life remain obscure, largely due to the lack of concrete evidence and the passage of time. Much of what is known about Lao Tzu comes from traditional accounts and legendary narratives. Despite these uncertainties, his philosophical contributions have had a profound and lasting impact on Chinese thought and spirituality.

Lao Tzu's impact on Chinese thought and spirituality is undeniable. His teachings, encapsulated in the *Tao Te Ching*, have shaped the core principles of Taoism, one of the major philosophical and religious traditions in China. The emphasis on living in harmony with the Tao, the natural order of the universe, has resonated deeply with Chinese culture and has influenced various aspects of life, including governance, ethics, and personal conduct.

Taoism: As the foundational text of Taoism, the *Tao Te Ching* provides the philosophical framework for the tradition. Taoism advocates for simplicity, humility, and non-action *(Wú Wéi 無為/无为)*, principles that encourage individuals to live in accordance with the natural flow of life. The teachings of Lao Tzu have inspired countless followers and have been integrated into Taoist rituals, meditation practices, and ethical guidelines.

Confucianism: While Taoism and Confucianism are distinct traditions, Lao Tzu's philosophy has also been acknowledged by Confucian scholars. Confucianism, founded by Confucius, focuses on social harmony, ethical behaviour, and the cultivation of virtue. The interplay between these two traditions has enriched Chinese intellectual history, with Confucianism emphasising social order and Taoism advocating for natural harmony and spiritual freedom.

Buddhism: The arrival of Buddhism in China led to the development of Chán (Zen) Buddhism, which incorporates Taoist concepts of naturalness and spontaneity. Lao Tzu's teachings on the Tao and the importance of aligning with the natural order have found parallels in Buddhist thought, contributing to a syncretic blending of philosophical and spiritual ideas.

Lao Tzu is venerated as a philosopher by Confucians and as a saint or deity in popular religion. His wisdom and insights have earned him a revered status in Chinese culture, with many viewing him as a guide to living a balanced and harmonious life. Confucian scholars regard Lao Tzu as a philosopher who offered a unique perspective on life and governance, emphasising humility, simplicity, and non-action, which provides a valuable counterpoint to Confucian ideals of social responsibility and moral rectitude. In popular religion, Lao Tzu is often deified and worshipped as a spiritual figure who embodies the principles of Taoism. Temples dedicated to Lao Tzu can be found across China, serving as places of worship, meditation, and reverence, where people offer prayers and seek guidance from the venerable sage. These cultural and spiritual centres reflect the deep respect for Lao Tzu and his teachings, allowing followers to connect with his wisdom and principles.

During the Tang dynasty (618-907 CE), Lao Tzu was honoured as an imperial ancestor, reflecting the deep respect and admiration for his teachings. The Tang emperors, who claimed descent from Lao Tzu, elevated him to a position of great honour and incorporated Taoist principles into their governance. This recognition by the imperial family underscored the importance of Taoist philosophy in shaping the cultural and political landscape of China. The integration of Taoist principles into governance during the Tang dynasty highlighted the relevance of Lao Tzu's teachings in statecraft, as emperors who embraced Taoist ideals sought to govern with humility, simplicity, and a focus on harmony, aligning their policies with the natural order and the well-being of their subjects.

CHAPTER 1 – EMBRACING THE MYSTERY

Chapter 1 of the *Tao Te Ching* emphasises the concept of the Tao *(The Way)*, which is an ever-changing, elusive force that cannot be fully captured or named. This chapter can be profoundly insightful for modern-day strategic management in the following ways:

EMBRACING FLEXIBILITY & ADAPTABILITY

The Tao that can be trodden is not the enduring and unchanging Tao.

In the realm of strategic management, the principle that 'The Tao that can be trodden is not the enduring and unchanging Tao' emphasises the necessity of embracing flexibility. Just as the true Tao is fluid and ever-evolving, so too must an organisation's strategies be adaptable to survive and thrive in an ever-changing business landscape.

Rigid adherence to a single strategy can stifle innovation and hinder an organisation's ability to respond to unforeseen challenges and opportunities. Effective leaders recognise that no single plan can account for all variables and must be willing to pivot when circumstances shift. This flexibility enables organisations to remain agile and responsive, turning potential obstacles into opportunities for growth and advancement.

Modern business environments are characterised by rapid technological advancements, shifting consumer preferences, and unpredictable market conditions. In such a dynamic context, a static strategy is often rendered obsolete. Leaders must foster a culture of adaptability, where change is not feared but embraced as an integral part of the organisational process. This involves continuously monitoring external and internal environments, gathering insights, and being prepared to adjust plans accordingly.

Strategic pivots are not merely reactive but can be proactive measures to capitalise on emerging trends and innovations. Leaders should encourage a mindset of continuous learning within their teams, promoting an openness to new ideas and an eagerness to experiment. This could involve regular strategy reviews, scenario planning, and fostering a culture where feedback is valued and used to inform decision-making.

Resilience in business is closely linked to the ability to adapt. Organisations that are flexible can better withstand economic downturns, competitive pressures, and other disruptions. Flexibility allows for the reallocation of resources, the reorganisation of teams, and the reassessment of priorities to navigate through turbulent times effectively.

Diverse teams bring a wide range of perspectives and ideas, which are crucial for adaptability. By leveraging the collective intelligence of a diverse workforce, leaders can foster innovative solutions and more robust strategies. Collaboration across departments and functions can break down silos and ensure that the organisation can pivot smoothly and efficiently.

Leaders play a crucial role in setting the tone for adaptability. They must exemplify a willingness to change and demonstrate resilience in the face of uncertainty. This includes being transparent about challenges, communicating changes clearly, and involving team members in the process. By modelling adaptable behaviour, leaders can inspire their teams to embrace change and remain committed to the organisation's goals.

BEYOND LABELS & DEFINITIONS

The name that can be named is not the enduring and unchanging name.

This profound line from the Tao Te Ching suggests that any name or label we assign is inherently limited and cannot fully capture the true essence of reality. In the context of business, this has significant implications. Job titles, roles, and even company identities are often used to define and categorise, but they should not become rigid constraints. Recognising the limitations of labels allows organisations to stay dynamic and responsive to change.

In the ever-evolving business landscape, a flexible organisational structure is crucial. Leaders should avoid rigidly confining employees to predefined roles and instead encourage a more fluid approach where individuals can explore various aspects of the business. This flexibility can lead to greater innovation and creativity, as employees feel empowered to bring their unique skills and perspectives to different challenges and projects.

Rigid roles can create silos within an organisation, hindering communication and collaboration. By promoting cross-functional collaboration, leaders can break down these barriers. Employees should be encouraged to work on projects across different departments, sharing knowledge and skills. This approach not only enhances innovation but also builds a more cohesive and versatile team.

A growth mindset is essential for continuous improvement and flexibility. Leaders should cultivate an environment where learning and development are prioritised. This involves encouraging employees to seek new opportunities for growth, whether through formal training programmes, mentoring, or hands-on experiences. By doing so, organisations can adapt more readily to changing market conditions and new challenges.

Just as labels for individuals can be limiting, so too can rigid company identities. Organisations should be open to evolving their brand and identity to stay relevant and resonant with their audience. This might involve rebranding, shifting focus, or expanding into new markets. By staying flexible and adaptive, companies can better navigate the complexities of the modern business environment.

Empowerment is key to unlocking creativity and innovation. Leaders should create a culture where employees feel trusted and valued, with the autonomy to explore and experiment. This empowerment fosters a sense of ownership and accountability, driving employees to contribute their best efforts towards the organisation's success.

Diversity in thought, experience, and background enhances the richness of ideas within an organisation. By embracing diversity and avoiding the constraints of rigid roles and labels, leaders can tap into a wider range of insights and solutions. This inclusivity is not just about having diverse teams but also ensuring that all voices are heard and valued.

INNOVATION & ORIGINATING NEW IDEAS

(Conceived of as) having no name, it is the Originator of heaven and earth.

This line from the *Tao Te Ching* emphasises that the most profound and creative forces often emerge from the undefined and the unnamed. In a business context, innovation frequently springs from thinking beyond conventional boundaries and exploring uncharted territories. Just as the Tao represents the indefinable origin of all things, so too can groundbreaking ideas emerge from a space of open possibility and creativity.

Strategic leaders play a crucial role in fostering an environment where innovative ideas can thrive. By encouraging out-of-the-box thinking, leaders can inspire their teams to challenge assumptions and envision new possibilities. This involves creating a safe space where creative thinking is not only allowed but celebrated. Techniques such as brainstorming sessions, innovation labs, and design thinking workshops can help facilitate this creative exploration.

To tap into the originative potential, organisations must cultivate a culture that values exploration and experimentation. This means supporting initiatives that may not have immediate returns but hold the potential for significant breakthroughs. Encouraging a trial-and-error mindset, where failures are seen as learning opportunities rather than setbacks, can foster a more innovative and resilient organisation.

Innovation is often sparked by diverse perspectives and interdisciplinary collaboration. By bringing together individuals with different backgrounds, experiences, and viewpoints, organisations can generate a richer pool of ideas. Leaders should actively seek to build diverse teams and promote an inclusive culture where all voices are heard and valued.

Innovation thrives in environments where continuous learning is prioritised. Leaders should invest in the professional development of their teams, providing access to new knowledge, skills, and technologies. This ongoing education keeps employees engaged and equipped to contribute novel ideas and solutions. Additionally, fostering curiosity and a growth mindset encourages employees to stay ahead of industry trends and advancements.

For innovative ideas to flourish, employees need both the resources and the autonomy to experiment. This includes providing access to necessary tools, time for creative projects, and the freedom to pursue new approaches. Leaders should empower their teams by removing barriers and offering support, allowing them to take risks and innovate.

Recognition and reward are powerful motivators for fostering innovation. Leaders should celebrate successes, both big and small, and acknowledge the efforts of individuals and teams who contribute innovative ideas. This recognition not only motivates those involved but also signals to the entire organisation the value placed on creativity and forward-thinking.

BALANCING DESIRE & CONTENTMENT

> *Always without desire we must be found, If its deep mystery we would sound; But if desire always within us be, Its outer fringe is all that we shall see.*

This passage from the *Tao Te Ching* highlights the delicate balance between desire and contentment. It suggests that while ambition and goals are essential drivers of progress, an excessive focus on desire can cloud one's judgment and lead to a superficial understanding of deeper truths. In the business world, this translates to the importance of balancing ambition with an appreciation for the present state and a long-term vision.

Ambition fuels innovation, drives progress, and pushes individuals and organisations to achieve their goals. It is a critical component of strategic management, as it motivates leaders and teams to strive for excellence and reach new heights. However, unchecked ambition can lead to short-sighted decisions, increased stress, and a relentless pursuit of success at the expense of well-being and sustainability.

Overemphasis on desire can result in a narrow focus on immediate gains, neglecting long-term consequences and holistic success. Leaders who are overly driven by desire may prioritise short-term profits over sustainable growth, leading to decisions that could harm the organisation in the long run. It is essential for leaders to maintain a broader perspective, considering the long-term impact of their actions and fostering a culture of sustainable growth.

Contentment involves appreciating the present state and recognising the value of current achievements. Strategic leaders should foster a culture where success is celebrated, and employees are encouraged to appreciate their contributions and progress. This sense of contentment can create a positive work environment, enhancing employee satisfaction, loyalty, and overall well-being.

Balancing ambition and contentment requires a strategic approach that integrates both elements into the organisational culture. Leaders can set ambitious goals while also promoting a sense of contentment by:

- *Setting Realistic Goals:* Establishing achievable and meaningful goals that align with the organisation's long-term vision.
- *Celebrating Milestones:* Regularly acknowledging and celebrating achievements, both big and small, to foster a sense of accomplishment and motivation.
- *Encouraging Mindfulness:* Promoting mindfulness practices that help employees stay present and appreciate the moment, reducing stress and enhancing focus.
- *Fostering a Growth Mindset:* Encouraging continuous learning and development, viewing challenges as opportunities for growth rather than threats.
- *Promoting Work-Life Balance:* Implementing policies that support work-life balance, ensuring employees have time to recharge and maintain overall well-being.

A balanced approach to desire and contentment ensures that leaders maintain a long-term vision, focusing on sustainable growth rather than quick wins. This involves:

- *Strategic Planning:* Developing long-term strategies that prioritise sustainability, innovation, and resilience.
- *Ethical Leadership:* Making decisions that align with ethical principles and social responsibility, fostering trust and integrity.
- *Resilience and Adaptability:* Building a resilient organisation capable of adapting to changes and uncertainties while maintaining core values and objectives.

EMBRACING THE MYSTERY & COMPLEXITY

> *Under these two aspects, it is really the same; but as development takes place, it receives the different names. Together we call them the Mystery. Where the Mystery is the deepest is the gate of all that is subtle and wonderful.*

The business environment is inherently complex, characterised by a multitude of interconnected variables and unpredictable factors. Accepting this complexity rather than trying to oversimplify or control every aspect allows leaders to develop a more holistic and realistic approach to management. Embracing the mystery means recognising that not all elements can be fully understood or predicted, and that some degree of uncertainty is a natural part of the business landscape.

Leaders who are comfortable with ambiguity are better equipped to navigate uncertainty. This involves developing a mindset that views uncertainty not as a threat, but as an opportunity for discovery and innovation. By embracing the unknown, leaders can foster a culture that is more resilient and adaptable to change. This confidence in the face of uncertainty can inspire and reassure team members, encouraging them to take calculated risks and think creatively.

In the intricate dance of business dynamics, subtle and nuanced factors often hold significant influence. Leaders who pay attention to these subtleties can uncover insights that lead to competitive advantages. This involves being perceptive and attentive to the finer details of market trends, customer behaviours, and internal organisational dynamics. By appreciating these subtleties, leaders can make more informed and strategic decisions.

A key aspect of embracing mystery and complexity is fostering a learning organisation. This means creating an environment where continuous learning and curiosity are valued. Encouraging employees to explore new ideas, question assumptions, and learn from both successes and failures helps the organisation adapt and grow. Leaders should promote open communication and knowledge sharing, ensuring that insights and experiences are leveraged for collective growth.

Diverse perspectives are crucial for understanding and navigating complexity. Leaders should actively seek input from individuals with different backgrounds, experiences, and viewpoints. This diversity enriches the decision-making process and helps the organisation to see challenges and opportunities from multiple angles. By integrating these perspectives, leaders can develop more nuanced and effective strategies.

Embracing complexity requires strategic agility and flexibility. Leaders should be willing to pivot and adjust strategies as new information and circumstances arise. This involves being proactive in identifying potential disruptions and opportunities, and being prepared to respond swiftly and effectively. Agile organisations are better able to thrive in dynamic environments, leveraging their ability to adapt to maintain a competitive edge.

Modern technologies and data analytics can help leaders navigate complexity by providing deeper insights and more accurate predictions. By leveraging these tools, leaders can better understand trends, model scenarios, and make data-informed decisions. However, it is also important to recognise the limitations of data and avoid over-reliance on quantitative metrics alone. Balancing data-driven insights with qualitative understanding is key to managing complexity.

Mindful leadership is about being present and fully engaged in the moment, while also maintaining a broader perspective on long-term goals. This approach helps leaders stay grounded and make thoughtful, balanced decisions. Mindfulness practices can enhance leaders' ability to manage stress, maintain clarity, and foster a positive work environment.

CHAPTER 2 – INTERCONNECTEDNESS

Chapter 2 of the *Tao Te Ching* speaks to the interconnectedness of opposites and the natural flow of processes. This chapter can offer valuable insights for modern-day strategic management in the following ways:

UNDERSTANDING INTERDEPENDENCE & BALANCE

> *All in the world know the beauty of the beautiful, and in doing this they have (the idea of) what ugliness is; they all know the skill of the skilful, and in doing this they have (the idea of) what the want of skill is.*

In the realm of strategic management, acknowledging the interdependence of opposites is crucial for developing a comprehensive understanding of the business landscape. The presence of one quality inherently defines its opposite, highlighting the intrinsic balance within all aspects of business operations. For example, the recognition of beauty presupposes an understanding of ugliness, just as identifying skill requires an awareness of its absence. This principle can be applied to various elements of strategic management, such as strengths and weaknesses, opportunities and threats, and successes and failures.

A holistic approach to strategic management involves recognising and balancing both strengths and weaknesses. While it is important to leverage an organisation's strengths to gain a competitive edge, it is equally vital to address and mitigate its weaknesses. By doing so, leaders can develop more robust strategies that are resilient to internal and external challenges. This balanced perspective ensures that the organisation is well-prepared to navigate both favourable and adverse conditions.

Challenges and opportunities are two sides of the same coin, often emerging from the same circumstances. Strategic leaders must be adept at identifying and balancing these elements. For instance, market disruptions can pose significant challenges, but they also present opportunities for innovation and growth. By maintaining a balanced view, leaders can seize opportunities while effectively managing risks, ensuring the organisation remains agile and competitive.

Success and failure are integral parts of the business journey, each offering valuable lessons. Leaders should foster a culture where both successes and failures are embraced as learning opportunities. Celebrating successes boosts morale and motivation, while analysing failures provides insights into areas for improvement. This balanced approach encourages continuous learning and development, driving long-term success.

Effective strategic management requires holistic decision-making that considers the interconnectedness of various factors. Leaders should evaluate the potential impact of their decisions on all aspects of the organisation, including financial performance, employee well-being, customer satisfaction, and social responsibility. By recognising the interdependence of these elements, leaders can make more informed and balanced decisions that support sustainable growth.

Resilience in strategic management stems from the ability to balance and adapt to changing circumstances. Leaders who understand the interdependence of opposites can better anticipate and respond to fluctuations in the business environment. This resilience allows the organisation to weather challenges and capitalise on opportunities, ensuring long-term stability and success.

The concept of interdependence also involves embracing paradoxes. In business, seemingly contradictory elements can coexist and complement each other. For example, fostering a culture of innovation may require both creative freedom and structured processes. By embracing these paradoxes, leaders can create a dynamic and adaptable organisation that thrives in complexity.

Various strategic frameworks and tools, such as SWOT analysis (Strengths, Weaknesses, Opportunities, Threats), are designed to help leaders recognise and balance interdependent elements. These tools provide a structured approach to identifying and analysing key factors, enabling leaders to develop more comprehensive and balanced strategies.

EMBRACING DUALITIES IN DECISION-MAKING

Existence and non-existence give birth the one to (the idea of) the other; that difficulty and ease produce the one (the idea of) the other.

In the realm of strategic management, recognising the interconnected nature of dualities is crucial. The presence of one element inherently defines and gives rise to its opposite. Difficulty and ease, risk and reward, short-term gains and long-term sustainability—these pairs are not isolated but are interdependent. Understanding this relationship allows leaders to navigate complex business scenarios with greater insight and adaptability.

Every business decision entails a balance between difficulty and ease. Challenging situations often give rise to significant opportunities for growth and innovation. By embracing difficult circumstances and viewing them as opportunities for learning and improvement, leaders can cultivate resilience and drive progress. Conversely, periods of ease should be leveraged for strategic planning and capacity building, ensuring that the organisation remains prepared for future challenges.

Risk and reward are two sides of the same coin in strategic decision-making. Higher risks can lead to greater rewards, but they also require careful management and mitigation strategies. Leaders should develop a balanced approach to risk-taking, where potential rewards are weighed against possible downsides. This involves conducting thorough risk assessments, implementing robust contingency plans, and maintaining a risk-aware culture within the organisation.

Short-term gains and long-term sustainability are often perceived as conflicting goals, but they can be integrated through strategic planning. Leaders should focus on achieving immediate objectives while keeping an eye on the bigger picture. This involves investing in initiatives that yield quick wins without compromising the organisation's long-term vision and stability. By balancing short-term and long-term priorities, leaders can ensure sustainable growth and success.

Dualities in business scenarios also include the interplay between opportunities and challenges. Strategic leaders must be adept at identifying and leveraging opportunities while simultaneously anticipating and preparing for potential challenges. This dynamic approach ensures that the organisation remains agile and can pivot effectively in response to changing circumstances.

Embracing dualities requires fostering a culture of flexibility and adaptability within the organisation. Leaders should encourage their teams to approach problems with an open mind, considering multiple perspectives and solutions. This involves promoting a growth mindset, where employees are motivated to innovate and explore new possibilities, even in the face of uncertainty.

Holistic strategies take into account the dualities present in business scenarios, ensuring that decisions are well-rounded and consider all relevant factors. Leaders should integrate various aspects of their strategy, such as financial performance, employee well-being, customer satisfaction, and social responsibility, to create a balanced and resilient organisational framework.

Leaders who are comfortable with paradoxes and ambiguity are better equipped to navigate the complexities of the business environment. By accepting that dualities often coexist and complement each other, leaders can develop a more nuanced understanding of strategic challenges and opportunities. This acceptance fosters innovative thinking and the ability to thrive in uncertain conditions.

Embracing dualities involves a commitment to continuous learning and adaptation. Leaders should regularly review and adjust their strategies based on new insights and changing circumstances. This iterative approach ensures that the organisation remains responsive and can capitalise on emerging trends and opportunities.

LEADING WITH SUBTLETY & INFLUENCE

> *Therefore the sage manages affairs without doing anything, and conveys his instructions without the use of speech.*

Effective leadership often involves guiding and influencing without overt control. Leaders should empower their teams, create an environment of trust, and lead by example. This approach encourages autonomy and fosters a culture of innovation and collaboration. Just as the sage leads without overt actions, strategic leaders can achieve results through subtle guidance and empowerment.

This passage from the *Tao Te Ching* highlights the power of subtlety and influence in leadership. True leadership is not about exerting overt control or issuing direct commands but about guiding and influencing through presence, example, and trust. Just as the sage leads without overt actions, effective leaders can achieve profound results through subtle guidance and empowerment.

Empowering teams is a cornerstone of subtle leadership. By trusting and enabling employees to take ownership of their tasks and decisions, leaders foster an environment where individuals feel valued and motivated. This empowerment boosts morale and encourages a culture of self-sufficiency, where team members are inspired to innovate and take initiative. Empowered teams are more likely to collaborate effectively and contribute to the organisation's success.

Trust is fundamental to effective leadership. Leaders who build trust within their teams create a safe and supportive environment where employees feel confident to express their ideas and concerns. This trust is nurtured through transparency, consistency, and open communication. When employees trust their leaders, they are more likely to be engaged, loyal, and committed to the organisation's goals.

Leading by example is a powerful way to influence without overt control. Leaders who embody the values and behaviours they wish to see in their teams set a standard for others to follow. This approach fosters a culture of integrity and accountability, as team members are inspired to align their actions with the leader's example. Leading by example also builds credibility and respect, enhancing the leader's ability to influence others.

Autonomy is crucial for fostering a culture of innovation and collaboration. Leaders should provide their teams with the freedom to explore new ideas and approaches, without micromanaging or imposing rigid controls. This autonomy encourages creativity and allows employees to experiment and learn from their experiences. When team members have the freedom to innovate, they are more likely to develop innovative solutions and drive the organisation forward.

Subtle guidance involves influencing through actions rather than words. Leaders can guide their teams by creating an environment that supports desired behaviours and outcomes. This might include setting clear goals, providing resources and support, and recognising and rewarding positive contributions. By subtly shaping the environment, leaders can steer their teams toward success without the need for direct intervention.

Innovation and collaboration thrive in environments where subtle leadership principles are practised. By empowering teams, fostering trust, and encouraging autonomy, leaders create a fertile ground for creative problem-solving and teamwork. This collaborative culture enables the organisation to leverage diverse perspectives and skills, driving innovation and achieving superior results.

While subtle leadership often involves less direct communication, effective leaders still understand the importance of clear and meaningful interactions. This includes active listening, providing constructive feedback, and maintaining open lines of communication. By being attentive and responsive, leaders can ensure their teams feel heard and supported, further enhancing trust and collaboration.

While subtlety is a powerful tool, there are times when direct action and clear communication are necessary. Effective leaders know when to step in and provide explicit direction, balancing subtle influence with decisive leadership. This balanced approach ensures that the organisation remains agile and responsive to changing circumstances.

FOSTERING ORGANIC GROWTH & DEVELOPMENT

All things spring up, and there is not one which declines to show itself; they grow, and there is no claim made for their ownership.

In business, organic growth and development are crucial. Leaders should focus on nurturing their teams and fostering an environment where ideas and innovations can emerge naturally. This involves providing resources and support without micromanaging or claiming ownership of every success. When employees feel empowered and valued, they are more likely to contribute creatively and drive the company's growth.

This passage from the *Tao Te Ching* emphasises the natural and unforced development of all things. In the context of business, fostering organic growth means creating conditions where ideas and innovations can emerge and flourish naturally. It involves providing the necessary resources and support for growth while allowing employees the freedom to explore and develop their ideas without undue interference.

Leaders play a crucial role in creating an environment that nurtures growth and development. This involves providing the resources, tools, and support that employees need to succeed. Just as a gardener ensures that plants have the right soil, water, and sunlight, leaders should ensure that their teams have access to training, technology, and a supportive work culture. This nurturing environment allows creativity and innovation to thrive organically.

Empowerment is at the heart of fostering organic growth. When employees feel valued and trusted, they are more likely to take initiative and contribute creatively. Leaders should empower their teams by delegating authority, encouraging autonomy, and recognising individual contributions. This empowerment not only boosts morale but also encourages a sense of ownership and accountability, driving the company's growth.

Innovation often arises from the freedom to experiment and explore new ideas. Leaders should cultivate a culture that encourages experimentation and accepts failures as part of the learning process. By providing a safe space for innovation, leaders can inspire their teams to think outside the box and develop groundbreaking solutions. This innovative spirit is essential for staying competitive in today's fast-paced business environment.

Micromanagement stifles creativity and hampers growth. Leaders should avoid micromanaging their teams and instead focus on setting clear goals and providing the necessary support. By stepping back and allowing employees the freedom to execute their tasks, leaders enable them to take ownership of their work and develop their potential. This approach leads to more engaged and motivated teams, contributing to the organisation's success.

As the *Tao Te Ching* suggests, true growth happens without claiming ownership. Leaders should celebrate the successes of their teams and give credit where it is due. Recognising and appreciating the contributions of employees fosters a positive work culture and reinforces the value of collaboration. When employees see that their efforts are acknowledged and rewarded, they are more likely to stay committed and motivated.

Continuous learning and development are vital for organic growth. Leaders should invest in training and development programmes that help employees enhance their skills and knowledge. By providing opportunities for growth, leaders can ensure that their teams remain adaptable and capable of meeting new challenges. This commitment to learning fosters a culture of continuous improvement and innovation.

While providing structure and guidance is important, leaders should also allow for flexibility. This balance ensures that employees have a clear direction while retaining the freedom to explore and innovate. Flexibility allows teams to adapt to changing circumstances and seize new opportunities as they arise.

Collaboration and teamwork are essential for fostering organic growth. Leaders should encourage cross-functional collaboration, where employees from different departments and backgrounds come together to share ideas and solve problems. This collaborative approach leverages diverse perspectives and skills, leading to more innovative and effective solutions.

ACHIEVING WITHOUT ATTACHMENT

> The work is accomplished, and there is no resting in it (as an achievement). The work is done, but how no one can see; 'Tis this that makes the power not cease to be.

This passage from the *Tao Te Ching* emphasises the importance of achieving goals without becoming attached to them or allowing ego to take over. In the context of strategic management, this means that while it is crucial to celebrate successes, leaders should avoid becoming complacent or overly fixated on past achievements. Non-attachment encourages a continuous focus on growth and improvement, ensuring the organisation remains dynamic and forward-thinking.

Celebrating successes is important for maintaining morale and recognising the hard work of teams. It fosters a positive work environment and motivates employees to continue striving for excellence. However, these celebrations should be balanced with an understanding that success is part of an ongoing journey. By celebrating achievements without becoming complacent, leaders can inspire their teams to keep pushing forward and seeking new challenges.

Complacency can be detrimental to an organisation's growth and innovation. When leaders and teams rest on their laurels, they risk falling behind in a competitive and rapidly changing market. To prevent complacency, leaders should cultivate a mindset of continuous improvement. This involves regularly evaluating performance, setting new goals, and encouraging a proactive approach to problem-solving and innovation.

Continuous improvement is the practice of constantly seeking ways to enhance processes, products, and services. Leaders should instil a culture where feedback is valued, and employees are encouraged to identify areas for improvement. This iterative approach ensures that the organisation adapts to changes and remains competitive. Tools such as Kaizen, Lean, and Six Sigma can be implemented to systematically drive continuous improvement.

By emphasising the importance of the process rather than the end result, leaders can promote a culture of excellence. This involves recognising the value of effort, learning, and growth that occurs during the pursuit of goals. When employees are encouraged to focus on the quality of their work and the learning opportunities it presents, they are more likely to stay engaged and committed to the organisation's long-term success.

Empowering teams to take ownership of their work and decisions is crucial for achieving sustainable success. Leaders should delegate responsibilities, provide autonomy, and support their teams in their pursuits. This empowerment fosters a sense of accountability and motivation, driving employees to strive for continuous improvement and innovation.

A forward-thinking mindset involves looking ahead and anticipating future challenges and opportunities. Leaders should encourage strategic planning and scenario analysis to prepare the organisation for potential changes in the market or industry. By maintaining a long-term perspective, leaders can ensure that the organisation remains agile and adaptable.

Leaders play a pivotal role in modelling the behaviour they wish to see in their teams. By demonstrating non-attachment and a commitment to continuous improvement, leaders can inspire their teams to adopt the same mindset. This involves being open to feedback, acknowledging mistakes, and showing a willingness to learn and grow.

Innovation thrives in environments where non-attachment and continuous improvement are embraced. Leaders should create a culture that encourages experimentation and creativity, where employees feel safe to take risks and explore new ideas. By fostering a supportive and innovative environment, leaders can drive the organisation towards sustained success and growth.

CHAPTER 3 – SIMPLICITY & MODESTY

Chapter 3 of the *Tao Te Ching* offers profound insights into governance and leadership, emphasising simplicity, modesty, and the avoidance of inciting desires. These teachings can be effectively applied to modern-day strategic management in the following ways:

PROMOTING EQUALITY & REDUCING RIVALRY

> *Not to value and employ men of superior ability is the way to keep the people from rivalry among themselves.*

In the context of business, this passage from the *Tao Te Ching* suggests that placing excessive emphasis on individual talents can lead to unhealthy competition and rivalry within an organisation. While recognising and valuing individual skills and abilities is important, it is equally crucial to promote a culture where collaboration and teamwork are prioritised over individual accolades. This balance helps to create a more harmonious and productive work environment where all employees feel valued and motivated to contribute to the collective success.

Collaboration is at the heart of any successful organisation. Leaders should strive to create an environment where teamwork and mutual support are encouraged. This involves setting clear team goals, fostering open communication, and ensuring that all team members have the opportunity to contribute their unique skills and perspectives. By emphasising collective achievement over individual performance, leaders can reduce rivalry and build a cohesive, collaborative team.

One effective way to promote equality and reduce rivalry is to recognise and celebrate collective achievements. When leaders highlight team successes rather than focusing solely on individual accomplishments, it reinforces the importance of working together towards common goals. This collective recognition fosters a sense of unity and shared purpose, motivating employees to support one another and work collaboratively.

Inclusivity is essential for promoting equality within an organisation. Leaders should ensure that opportunities for growth, development, and recognition are accessible to all employees, regardless of their position or background. This involves implementing fair and transparent processes for promotions, rewards, and professional development. By providing equal opportunities, leaders can prevent feelings of resentment and rivalry, fostering a more inclusive and supportive workplace.

Peer support and mentorship programmes can play a significant role in promoting equality and reducing rivalry. By encouraging experienced employees to mentor and support their colleagues, leaders can create a culture of mutual respect and collaboration. Mentorship not only helps to develop individual skills but also strengthens team bonds and promotes a sense of shared responsibility for the success of the organisation.

Aligning individual and team goals with the broader organisational objectives can help to reduce rivalry and promote a sense of shared purpose. Leaders should communicate the organisation's vision and mission clearly, ensuring that all employees understand how their contributions align with the overall goals. This alignment creates a sense of collective ownership and motivates employees to work together towards common objectives.

To reinforce the importance of collaboration, leaders can implement team-based rewards and recognition programmes. By rewarding teams rather than individuals, leaders can encourage employees to prioritise teamwork and collective success. Team-based incentives, such as group bonuses or recognition events, can help to strengthen team cohesion and reduce competitive behaviour.

Constructive feedback is crucial for personal and professional growth. Leaders should provide regular, balanced feedback that recognises both individual and team contributions. This feedback should be focused on continuous improvement and development, rather than comparison and competition. By fostering a culture of continuous learning and growth, leaders can help employees to feel valued and supported, reducing feelings of rivalry and competition.

Leaders set the tone for the organisational culture. By demonstrating collaborative behaviour and valuing collective achievements, leaders can influence their teams to adopt the same approach. Leading by example involves recognising and celebrating team successes, supporting peer mentorship, and promoting inclusive opportunities. When leaders embody these values, they inspire their teams to embrace a culture of collaboration and mutual support.

FOCUSING ON ESSENTIAL NEEDS & AVOIDING EXCESS

Not to prize articles which are difficult to procure is the way to keep them from becoming thieves; not to show them what is likely to excite their desires is the way to keep their minds from disorder.

In the context of business, this passage emphasises the importance of focusing on what employees truly need to perform their roles effectively. Rather than offering excessive luxuries or perks that may create envy or distractions, leaders should ensure that fundamental needs are met. These essential needs include adequate resources, a supportive work environment, and opportunities for professional growth. By prioritising these necessities, leaders can help employees stay focused and motivated.

Ensuring that employees have the necessary resources to do their jobs effectively is crucial. This includes access to the right tools, technology, and information. By providing these resources, leaders enable employees to perform their tasks efficiently and achieve their goals. Adequate resources also reduce frustration and enhance job satisfaction, contributing to a more productive workforce.

A supportive work environment fosters collaboration, trust, and mutual respect among employees. Leaders should promote a culture where team members feel valued and supported. This includes providing a safe and inclusive workplace, encouraging open communication, and offering emotional and psychological support. When employees feel supported, they are more likely to be engaged and committed to their work.

Professional growth and development are essential for employee satisfaction and retention. Leaders should provide opportunities for continuous learning and career advancement. This can include training programmes, mentorship, and pathways for promotion. By investing in employees' development, leaders demonstrate their commitment to their teams' long-term success and well-being.

While perks and benefits can enhance the work experience, excessive luxuries can lead to envy and distraction. Leaders should carefully consider the types of perks offered, ensuring they align with the organisation's values and culture. Perks should enhance productivity and well-being rather than create competition or resentment among employees. Simple, meaningful benefits such as flexible working hours, wellness programmes, and recognition initiatives can be more effective than extravagant luxuries.

A sense of contentment within the workforce is crucial for maintaining stability and focus. Leaders should promote a culture of appreciation and gratitude, where employees feel recognised and valued for their contributions. Encouraging mindfulness and work-life balance can also help employees cultivate a sense of contentment and reduce stress. When employees are content, they are more likely to be motivated, engaged, and loyal to the organisation.

Recognition and rewards are important for motivating employees, but they should be balanced and equitable. Leaders should implement fair and transparent recognition programmes that celebrate individual and team achievements. This approach ensures that all employees feel valued and reduces the potential for envy and rivalry. Recognising efforts and achievements fosters a positive work culture and encourages continued high performance.

Aligning employees' work with the organisation's purpose and mission can help focus their efforts and reduce distractions. Leaders should communicate the organisation's goals and values clearly, ensuring that employees understand how their roles contribute to the bigger picture. This sense of purpose can be a powerful motivator, driving employees to work towards common objectives with enthusiasm and commitment.

Adopting minimalist principles in the workplace can help reduce excess and promote focus. This involves simplifying processes, eliminating unnecessary tasks, and decluttering workspaces. By creating a streamlined and efficient work environment, leaders can help employees concentrate on what truly matters and enhance overall productivity.

LEADING WITH HUMILITY & RESTRAINT

> *Therefore the sage, in the exercise of his government, empties their minds, fills their bellies, weakens their wills, and strengthens their bones.*

This passage from the *Tao Te Ching* emphasises the importance of leading with humility and ensuring that the basic needs of individuals are met. In the context of strategic management, humble leadership involves creating an environment where employees are well-supported, focusing on their essential needs without imposing excessive control or pressure. Leaders who practise humility and restraint can build a strong, resilient, and motivated team.

To lead effectively, leaders must ensure that their employees' basic needs are met. This includes providing adequate compensation, ensuring a safe and healthy work environment, and offering the necessary tools and resources to perform their jobs efficiently. When employees' fundamental needs are taken care of, they can focus on their work without unnecessary distractions or stress.

A supportive environment is crucial for employee well-being and productivity. Leaders should foster a culture of mutual respect, trust, and open communication. This includes being approachable, listening to employees' concerns, and providing constructive feedback. By creating a supportive atmosphere, leaders can help their teams feel valued and motivated to contribute their best efforts.

Micromanagement can stifle creativity, reduce motivation, and increase stress among employees. Leaders should avoid excessive control and instead empower their teams to take ownership of their work. This involves delegating tasks, trusting employees to make decisions, and providing autonomy. When employees feel trusted and empowered, they are more likely to be engaged and innovative.

Leaders should focus on providing opportunities for growth and development. This includes offering training programmes, career development initiatives, and pathways for advancement. By investing in employees' development, leaders demonstrate their commitment to their teams' long-term success. This fosters loyalty and encourages employees to stay with the organisation and continue contributing to its growth.

Humility in leadership involves recognising that leaders do not have all the answers and valuing the input and contributions of others. Humble leaders are willing to admit mistakes, seek feedback, and learn from their teams. This approach builds trust and respect and encourages a collaborative and inclusive work environment.

Leaders set the tone for the organisational culture through their actions and behaviours. By leading with humility and restraint, leaders can model the values they wish to see in their teams. This includes demonstrating integrity, showing appreciation for employees' efforts, and prioritising the collective good over individual accolades. Leading by example inspires employees to adopt similar behaviours and attitudes.

Effective leaders strike a balance between providing autonomy and offering support. While it is important to give employees the freedom to make decisions and take initiative, leaders should also be available to provide guidance and support when needed. This balance ensures that employees feel empowered but not abandoned, creating a sense of security and confidence.

Collaboration is key to a resilient and innovative team. Leaders should promote a culture of teamwork, where employees are encouraged to share ideas, collaborate on projects, and support one another. By fostering collaboration, leaders can leverage the diverse skills and perspectives of their teams to achieve better outcomes.

Resilience is the ability to adapt and thrive in the face of challenges. Leaders can build resilient teams by fostering a culture of continuous learning, encouraging flexibility, and supporting employees through difficult times. This involves recognising and celebrating successes, as well as learning from failures. A resilient team is better equipped to handle adversity and seize opportunities for growth.

ENCOURAGING SIMPLICITY & CLARITY

> He constantly (tries to) keep them without knowledge and without desire, and where there are those who have knowledge, to keep them from presuming to act (on it).

In the context of business, this passage from the *Tao Te Ching* can be interpreted as an encouragement to simplify and clarify processes and communications. Overcomplicating strategies and decision-making can lead to confusion, inefficiency, and misalignment within an organisation. By focusing on simplicity and clarity, leaders can create a more effective and cohesive work environment.

Effective communication is the cornerstone of any successful organisation. Leaders should strive to communicate their vision, goals, and strategies in a clear and straightforward manner. This involves using plain language, avoiding jargon, and ensuring that messages are easily understood by all team members. Clear communication helps to ensure that everyone is on the same page, reducing misunderstandings and increasing productivity.

Decision-making processes should be streamlined to avoid unnecessary complexity. Leaders can achieve this by establishing clear criteria for decisions, delegating authority appropriately, and minimising bureaucratic obstacles. Simplified decision-making processes allow for quicker, more efficient responses to challenges and opportunities, enabling the organisation to remain agile and competitive.

Simplicity in strategy means focusing on the core objectives of the organisation and avoiding distractions. Leaders should prioritise initiatives that align with the organisation's mission and goals, and eliminate or delegate tasks that do not contribute to these objectives. By keeping the focus on what truly matters, leaders can ensure that resources are used efficiently and effectively.

Clear guidelines and expectations help employees understand their roles and responsibilities. Leaders should provide detailed job descriptions, performance metrics, and standard operating procedures that outline what is expected of each team member. This clarity reduces ambiguity, enhances accountability, and ensures that everyone is working towards the same goals.

Streamlining processes involves identifying and eliminating inefficiencies within the organisation. Leaders should regularly review workflows, identify bottlenecks, and implement improvements that simplify operations. This can include adopting new technologies, automating repetitive tasks, and reorganising teams to enhance collaboration and efficiency.

Transparency in decision-making and communication fosters trust and alignment within the organisation. Leaders should openly share information about the organisation's performance, challenges, and plans for the future. This transparency helps employees understand the rationale behind decisions and feel more connected to the organisation's mission and goals.

Building a culture of clarity involves encouraging open dialogue and feedback. Leaders should create an environment where employees feel comfortable asking questions and seeking clarification. Regular team meetings, one-on-one check-ins, and feedback sessions can help ensure that everyone understands their role and how their work contributes to the organisation's success.

Overcomplicating strategies and processes can lead to confusion and reduced effectiveness. Leaders should resist the temptation to add unnecessary layers of complexity and instead focus on creating straightforward, actionable plans. Simplified strategies are easier to implement and more likely to be successful.

Encouraging simplicity and clarity is an ongoing process. Leaders should regularly assess their communication and decision-making practices, seeking opportunities for improvement. By fostering a culture of continuous improvement, leaders can ensure that the organisation remains efficient, effective, and aligned with its goals.

ACHIEVING STABILITY & ORDER THROUGH NON-ACTION

When there is this abstinence from action, good order is universal.

The principle of *Wú Wéi* (無為/无为), or non-action, is a central tenet of Taoist philosophy. It emphasises the importance of aligning with the natural flow of events and allowing processes to unfold organically. In the context of leadership and strategic management, *Wú Wéi* suggests that sometimes the best course of action is to step back and refrain from constant interference. By trusting in the abilities of their teams and fostering a supportive environment, leaders can achieve greater stability and order within their organisations.

Effective leaders recognise the strengths and capabilities of their teams. By trusting their employees to perform their roles without micromanaging, leaders empower their teams to take ownership of their work. This trust fosters a sense of responsibility and accountability, leading to higher levels of engagement and productivity. When employees feel trusted, they are more likely to rise to the occasion and deliver their best work.

A supportive environment is essential for enabling teams to operate autonomously and efficiently. Leaders should provide the necessary resources, tools, and guidance to help their teams succeed. This includes offering training and development opportunities, maintaining open lines of communication, and providing emotional and psychological support. When employees feel supported, they are better equipped to handle challenges and work collaboratively towards common goals.

Excessive interference from leaders can disrupt workflows and hinder progress. By stepping back and allowing processes to unfold naturally, leaders can create a more harmonious and efficient work environment. This approach involves setting clear expectations and goals, then allowing employees the freedom to determine the best way to achieve them. Leaders should intervene only when necessary, such as when obstacles arise or additional guidance is required.

Autonomy is a key factor in fostering innovation and creativity. When employees have the freedom to make decisions and take initiative, they are more likely to develop innovative solutions and improve processes. Leaders should encourage autonomy by delegating authority and empowering employees to take ownership of their projects. This autonomy not only boosts morale but also drives continuous improvement and organisational growth.

Patience is an essential aspect of *Wú Wéi*. Leaders should practise patience by allowing time for processes to develop and for their teams to find their own solutions. This patience helps to avoid rash decisions and promotes a more thoughtful and deliberate approach to problem-solving. By giving employees the space to explore and experiment, leaders can foster a culture of learning and resilience.

Achieving stability and order through non-action involves focusing on long-term goals rather than short-term fixes. Leaders should prioritise strategic planning and vision-setting, ensuring that the organisation remains aligned with its mission and values. This long-term perspective helps to create a stable foundation for sustainable growth and success.

Resilience is the ability to adapt and thrive in the face of challenges. By embracing the principle of non-action, leaders can build a more resilient organisation. This involves creating a culture of continuous learning, encouraging flexibility, and supporting employees through difficult times. A resilient organisation is better equipped to navigate uncertainties and seize new opportunities.

Leaders who practise *Wú Wéi* set a powerful example for their teams. By demonstrating restraint and trust in their employees, leaders can inspire similar behaviours throughout the organisation. This approach fosters a culture of mutual respect and collaboration, where employees feel empowered to contribute their best efforts.

While non-action is a valuable principle, it is important to balance it with timely and decisive action when needed. Leaders should remain vigilant and ready to step in when necessary, providing guidance and support to address challenges or seize opportunities. This balanced approach ensures that the organisation remains agile and responsive while maintaining stability and order.

CHAPTER 4 – EMPTINESS & HUMILITY

Chapter 4 of the *Tao Te Ching* emphasises the concept of emptiness, simplicity, and humility, offering profound insights for modern-day strategic management. Here's how these principles can be applied:

EMBRACING EMPTINESS & POTENTIAL

> The Tao is (like) the emptiness of a vessel; and in our employment of it we must be on our guard against all fulness.

In Taoist philosophy, the concept of emptiness is seen as a source of potential and possibility. Just as a vessel's usefulness comes from its empty space, so too does the potential for innovation and creativity arise from an open and unfilled state. In a business context, this translates to creating an environment that avoids unnecessary complexities and rigid structures, allowing space for new ideas and opportunities to emerge.

Innovation thrives in environments where there is room for creative thinking and experimentation. Leaders should ensure that their organisations do not become overburdened with rigid processes or excessive regulations that can stifle innovation. By maintaining flexibility and openness, businesses can adapt more readily to changes in the market and take advantage of new opportunities as they arise.

Complexity can create confusion and hinder productivity. Leaders should strive to simplify processes and remove unnecessary bureaucratic layers. This involves streamlining workflows, reducing redundant tasks, and eliminating barriers that prevent employees from focusing on their core responsibilities. Simplifying the organisational structure helps to create a more agile and responsive business.

A culture that values creativity and innovation is essential for long-term success. Leaders should encourage employees to think outside the box, take risks, and explore new ideas. This can be achieved by providing opportunities for brainstorming sessions, innovation labs, and creative workshops. By fostering an environment where creativity is valued and nurtured, leaders can unlock the full potential of their teams.

Flexibility and adaptability are key to navigating an ever-changing business landscape. Leaders should create policies and practices that allow for flexibility in how work is performed and encourage employees to adapt to new challenges. This might include flexible working hours, remote work options, and opportunities for continuous learning and development. By promoting a flexible work environment, leaders can help their organisations remain resilient and competitive.

Empowering employees involves giving them the autonomy to make decisions and take ownership of their work. When employees feel trusted and supported, they are more likely to contribute innovative ideas and solutions. Leaders should delegate authority, provide clear goals, and offer the necessary resources and support to enable employees to succeed. Empowered employees are more engaged, motivated, and capable of driving the organisation's growth.

An open mindset is crucial for embracing potential and innovation. Leaders should be open to feedback, new perspectives, and unconventional approaches. This involves creating channels for open communication, encouraging diverse viewpoints, and being willing to pivot when necessary. An openness to new ideas helps to ensure that the organisation remains dynamic and forward-thinking.

While some structure is necessary for coordination and efficiency, too much rigidity can stifle creativity. Leaders should find the right balance between providing clear guidelines and allowing freedom for exploration. This balance ensures that employees have a framework within which to operate, while also having the freedom to innovate and experiment.

Failure is an inevitable part of the innovation process. Leaders should create a culture where failures are seen as learning opportunities rather than setbacks. By celebrating attempts and learning from mistakes, organisations can foster a more resilient and innovative workforce. This approach encourages employees to take risks and pursue new ideas without fear of retribution.

Embracing emptiness and potential involves a commitment to continuous improvement. Leaders should regularly assess and refine their strategies, processes, and practices to ensure they remain relevant and effective. By adopting a mindset of continuous improvement, organisations can stay ahead of the curve and capitalise on emerging trends and opportunities.

SIMPLIFYING PROCESSES & REDUCING COMPLEXITY

> We should blunt our sharp points, and unravel the complications of things; we should attemper our brightness, and bring ourselves into agreement with the obscurity of others.

In this passage, Lao Tzu emphasises the importance of simplicity and clarity. The metaphor of 'blunting sharp points' and 'unraveling complications' suggests that reducing complexity and focusing on what truly matters can lead to greater harmony and efficiency. In the context of modern business, simplifying processes and reducing complexity can enhance organisational performance and agility.

Streamlining operations involves identifying and eliminating inefficiencies within the organisation. Leaders should regularly review workflows and processes to pinpoint areas where simplification can be achieved. This might include automating repetitive tasks, consolidating redundant functions, and eliminating unnecessary steps. By streamlining operations, organisations can reduce waste, improve productivity, and deliver better results.

Redundant processes can bog down an organisation and hinder its ability to respond quickly to changes. Leaders should conduct thorough audits to identify and remove these redundancies. This involves evaluating each process for its necessity and value-add, and retaining only those that contribute meaningfully to the organisation's goals. Simplifying the process landscape helps to create a more agile and responsive organisation.

To maximise efficiency, leaders should concentrate on activities that add real value to the organisation. This means prioritising initiatives and tasks that directly contribute to achieving strategic objectives and delivering customer satisfaction. By focusing on value-adding activities, leaders can ensure that resources are allocated effectively and that efforts are aligned with the organisation's mission.

Complex decision-making processes can slow down an organisation and create bottlenecks. Leaders should strive to simplify these processes by establishing clear decision-making frameworks and delegating authority appropriately. This involves setting clear criteria for decisions, empowering employees to make decisions within their scope, and reducing the layers of approval required. Simplified decision-making enables quicker, more effective responses to opportunities and challenges.

Clear and effective communication is essential for organisational efficiency. Leaders should prioritise straightforward and transparent communication, avoiding jargon and unnecessary complexity. This includes setting clear expectations, providing regular updates, and ensuring that information flows seamlessly across the organisation. Clear communication helps to align teams, reduce misunderstandings, and enhance collaboration.

Simplified processes and clear communication facilitate better collaboration among teams. Leaders should foster a culture of teamwork and open communication, where employees feel encouraged to share ideas and work together towards common goals. Collaborative tools and platforms can also support this effort, enabling seamless information sharing and project management.

Simplification is an ongoing process that requires continuous improvement. Leaders should encourage a culture of regular review and refinement, where employees are empowered to identify inefficiencies and suggest improvements. This involves soliciting feedback, conducting regular process audits, and implementing iterative changes. Continuous improvement ensures that the organisation remains efficient and adaptable.

Agility is the ability to quickly adapt to changes and respond to emerging opportunities. Simplified processes and reduced complexity contribute to greater organisational agility. By maintaining flexibility and avoiding over-complication, leaders can ensure that their organisations are better prepared to navigate the dynamic business environment. This agility allows organisations to stay competitive and responsive to market demands.

Leaders play a crucial role in promoting simplicity and reducing complexity. By modelling these principles in their own behaviour and decision-making, leaders can set a powerful example for the rest of the organisation. This includes making clear, straightforward decisions, communicating transparently, and prioritising value-adding activities. Leading by example inspires employees to embrace simplicity and efficiency in their own work.

PRACTISING HUMILITY & COLLABORATION

> *We should attemper our brightness, and bring ourselves into agreement with the obscurity of others.*

Lao Tzu's wisdom emphasises the importance of tempering one's brightness—symbolising ego and self-importance—and aligning with the humility of others. In the context of strategic management, practising humility means recognising that no single leader has all the answers and valuing the contributions of others. This approach fosters a collaborative environment where everyone's input is appreciated, leading to more effective decision-making and stronger team dynamics.

Leaders should actively recognise and value the contributions of their team members. This involves acknowledging individual efforts and celebrating successes, both big and small. By appreciating the diverse skills and perspectives of their employees, leaders can create a sense of belonging and motivate their teams to perform at their best. This recognition not only boosts morale but also reinforces the importance of each team member's role in achieving common goals.

Collaboration is key to achieving organisational success. Leaders should encourage a culture where teamwork and collective problem-solving are prioritised over individual accolades. This involves creating opportunities for cross-functional collaboration, where employees from different departments and backgrounds can come together to share ideas and work on projects. By fostering collaboration, leaders can leverage the collective intelligence of their teams, leading to more innovative and effective solutions.

Humility in leadership requires leaders to temper their own egos. This means being open to feedback, willing to admit mistakes, and ready to learn from others. By demonstrating humility, leaders can build trust and respect within their teams. Employees are more likely to feel comfortable sharing their ideas and concerns when they see that their leaders are approachable and open-minded. This openness creates a more inclusive and dynamic work environment.

Open communication is essential for fostering collaboration and mutual respect. Leaders should create channels for transparent and honest dialogue, where employees feel safe to express their thoughts and opinions. Regular team meetings, one-on-one check-ins, and feedback sessions can facilitate this open communication. By actively listening to their teams, leaders can gain valuable insights and address issues promptly, ensuring that everyone is aligned with the organisation's goals.

Mutual respect is the foundation of a harmonious work environment. Leaders should model respectful behaviour by treating all employees with kindness and fairness. This includes respecting diverse viewpoints, valuing different perspectives, and fostering an inclusive culture where everyone feels respected and valued. When mutual respect is prioritised, employees are more likely to collaborate effectively and work towards common goals.

The sharing of ideas is crucial for innovation and growth. Leaders should encourage employees to share their thoughts, suggestions, and innovations without fear of judgment. This can be facilitated through brainstorming sessions, innovation workshops, and collaborative platforms. By promoting the free exchange of ideas, leaders can tap into the creative potential of their teams and drive continuous improvement.

Collaboration and humility enhance decision-making by incorporating diverse perspectives and expertise. Leaders should involve their teams in the decision-making process, seeking input and feedback before making key decisions. This collaborative approach ensures that decisions are well-informed and consider multiple viewpoints, leading to better outcomes. It also fosters a sense of ownership and commitment among employees, as they feel their voices are heard and valued.

Leaders set the tone for the organisational culture through their actions and behaviours. By practising humility and collaboration, leaders can inspire their teams to adopt the same values. This includes being transparent, admitting when they do not have all the answers, and seeking input from others. Leading by example creates a culture where humility and collaboration are the norm, driving organisational success.

VALUING STILLNESS & REFLECTION

How pure and still the Tao is, as if it would ever so continue!

Lao Tzu's reflection on the stillness of the Tao highlights the importance of tranquility and introspection. In the context of modern business, taking time for stillness and reflection is crucial for effective leadership. In a world that is often dominated by constant activity and rapid decision-making, moments of stillness provide the opportunity for leaders to step back, gain clarity, and make more thoughtful and strategic decisions.

Stillness and reflection allow leaders to step back from the daily grind and view their organisation from a broader perspective. This bird's-eye view helps in assessing whether current strategies align with long-term goals and values. By regularly setting aside time for reflection, leaders can identify areas for improvement, recognise emerging opportunities, and ensure that their decisions are well-informed and aligned with the organisation's mission.

In the fast-paced business environment, decisions are often made under pressure, which can lead to reactive and short-sighted choices. By embracing stillness, leaders can slow down their decision-making process, allowing for more deliberate and thoughtful consideration. This reflective approach helps to mitigate impulsive decisions and fosters a more strategic and sustainable path forward.

The constant demands of leadership can lead to stress and burnout if not managed properly. Taking time for stillness and reflection provides leaders with the opportunity to recharge and reset. This practice can reduce stress levels, enhance mental clarity, and improve overall well-being. By prioritising self-care and mindfulness, leaders can maintain their energy and focus, enabling them to lead more effectively and sustainably.

Leaders can promote a culture of reflection within their organisations by encouraging their teams to take time for introspection and thoughtful analysis. This involves creating spaces and opportunities for employees to engage in reflective practices, such as mindfulness sessions, quiet workspaces, and regular team reflections. By fostering a reflective culture, leaders can help their teams develop deeper insights, enhance creativity, and improve overall performance.

Mindfulness practices, such as meditation, deep breathing exercises, and mindful walking, can support stillness and reflection. Leaders should encourage employees to integrate these practices into their daily routines, providing resources and opportunities for mindfulness training. Mindfulness helps individuals stay present, reduce stress, and improve focus, contributing to a healthier and more productive work environment.

While action and productivity are essential in business, balancing these with moments of stillness is key to long-term success. Leaders should recognise the value of pausing to reflect and ensure that their schedules include time for stillness. This balance allows for more thoughtful and strategic action, rather than constant busyness that may lead to burnout and inefficiency.

Leaders set the tone for their organisations. By demonstrating the importance of stillness and reflection in their own behaviour, leaders can inspire their teams to adopt similar practices. This includes taking regular breaks, engaging in reflective practices, and openly discussing the benefits of mindfulness and introspection. Leading by example creates a culture where stillness and reflection are valued and integrated into the organisational fabric.

Leaders should intentionally create time for reflection within their schedules. This might include setting aside a few minutes each day for quiet contemplation, scheduling regular retreats or reflection sessions, and incorporating reflective practices into team meetings. By making reflection a priority, leaders can ensure that it becomes a consistent and valuable part of their leadership approach.

Organisations that value stillness and reflection are better equipped to navigate challenges and adapt to change. Reflective practices enable leaders and teams to learn from experiences, anticipate future trends, and develop strategies that are both innovative and resilient. This reflective approach fosters a culture of continuous learning and improvement, driving long-term success.

RECOGNISING THE DEPTH OF THE TAO

I do not know whose son it is. It might appear to have been before God.

This line from the Tao Te Ching speaks to the infinite and unfathomable nature of the Tao. It suggests that the Tao is a fundamental principle that exists beyond human comprehension, predating even the concept of deities. In the context of strategic management, this can be interpreted as acknowledging the complexity and depth of the business environment. Leaders should approach their roles with a sense of humility and curiosity, recognising that there is always more to learn and understand.

Humility is crucial for effective leadership. It involves acknowledging that no one has all the answers and being open to new ideas and perspectives. Leaders who practise humility are more likely to seek input from others, listen actively, and appreciate the contributions of their team members. This openness fosters a collaborative and innovative environment, where diverse viewpoints can lead to better decision-making and problem-solving.

Curiosity drives continuous learning and improvement. Leaders should cultivate a curious mindset, constantly seeking to expand their knowledge and understanding of the business environment. This involves staying informed about industry trends, exploring new technologies, and being open to feedback and new ideas. A curious leader is better equipped to anticipate changes and adapt strategies accordingly, ensuring the organisation remains competitive and resilient.

The business environment is inherently complex, with numerous interconnected factors influencing outcomes. Recognising this complexity means understanding that simple solutions are rarely sufficient. Leaders should adopt a holistic approach, considering multiple variables and potential impacts when making decisions. This involves being comfortable with ambiguity and uncertainty, and developing strategies that are flexible and adaptable.

Staying open to new insights and perspectives is essential for navigating the complexities of the business world. Leaders should encourage a culture of open dialogue and continuous learning within their organisations. This includes creating opportunities for employees to share their ideas, providing access to training and development programmes, and fostering an environment where experimentation and innovation are valued. By staying open to new insights, leaders can uncover opportunities for growth and improvement that might otherwise be overlooked.

A learning organisation is one that continuously evolves and adapts based on new knowledge and experiences. Leaders should strive to build a learning organisation by promoting a culture of curiosity, experimentation, and reflection. This involves encouraging employees to take risks, learn from failures, and share their learnings with the team. By fostering a learning organisation, leaders can ensure that their business remains agile and responsive to changes in the market.

Recognising the depth of the Tao also means balancing stability with innovation. While stability provides a solid foundation for operations, innovation drives growth and keeps the organisation competitive. Leaders should create a stable environment that supports ongoing innovation, ensuring that their teams have the resources and support needed to experiment and develop new ideas. This balance helps to maintain operational efficiency while fostering a culture of continuous improvement.

Understanding the profound nature of the business environment involves leading with a sense of purpose. Leaders should clearly articulate the organisation's mission and values, ensuring that all team members understand and are aligned with the overarching goals. This sense of purpose provides direction and motivation, helping employees stay focused and committed to achieving the organisation's objectives.

Emotional intelligence is critical for navigating the complexities of leadership. Leaders should develop their emotional intelligence by cultivating self-awareness, empathy, and effective communication skills. This helps them build stronger relationships with their teams, understand and address employees' needs, and create a positive work environment. Emotionally intelligent leaders are better equipped to manage stress, resolve conflicts, and inspire their teams.

Reflecting on experiences and outcomes is key to gaining deeper insights and improving strategies. Leaders should regularly set aside time for reflection, both individually and with their teams. This involves reviewing past decisions, analysing successes and failures, and identifying lessons learned. Continuous reflection helps leaders refine their approaches and make more informed decisions in the future.

CHAPTER 5 – IMPARTIALITY & CLARITY

Chapter 5 of the *Tao Te Ching* provides profound insights on natural impartiality, the power of potential, and the importance of inner clarity. Here's how these teachings can be applied to modern-day strategic management:

EMBRACING IMPARTIALITY & OBJECTIVITY

> *Heaven and earth do not act from (the impulse of) any wish to be benevolent; they deal with all things as the dogs of grass are dealt with. The sages do not act from (any wish to be) benevolent; they deal with the people as the dogs of grass are dealt with.*

Lao Tzu highlights the impartial and objective nature of heaven and earth, which treat all things equally without favouritism or bias. This principle can be directly applied to strategic management, where leaders are called to make decisions based on rational analysis and fairness rather than personal biases or emotions. By striving for impartiality, leaders can create a more just and equitable organisation.

Rational decision-making involves analysing data, considering evidence, and evaluating options logically. Leaders should rely on objective criteria and systematic processes to guide their decisions. This includes gathering relevant information, assessing risks and benefits, and considering the potential impact on all stakeholders. By prioritising rationality, leaders can make decisions that are more likely to achieve desired outcomes and sustain long-term success.

Fairness is a cornerstone of effective leadership and organisational culture. Leaders should ensure that policies, practices, and decisions are applied consistently and equitably. This involves treating all employees with respect, providing equal opportunities for growth and development, and addressing any instances of bias or discrimination. Promoting fairness helps to build trust and loyalty among employees, enhancing overall organisational performance.

Personal biases can cloud judgment and lead to unfair decisions. Leaders should be aware of their own biases and take steps to mitigate their influence. This involves reflecting on personal attitudes and beliefs, seeking diverse perspectives, and being open to feedback. Implementing structured decision-making processes and using standardised criteria can also help to reduce the impact of biases.

A merit-based culture emphasises rewarding employees based on their performance, skills, and contributions rather than favouritism or subjective factors. Leaders should establish clear performance metrics, provide regular feedback, and recognise and reward achievements fairly. This approach motivates employees to strive for excellence and fosters a culture of accountability and high performance.

Impartial and objective decision-making fosters trust and a sense of equity within the organisation. When employees see that decisions are made fairly and transparently, they are more likely to trust their leaders and feel valued. This trust enhances collaboration, engagement, and morale, contributing to a positive and productive work environment.

Open dialogue and transparent communication are essential for impartiality and objectivity. Leaders should create channels for employees to voice their opinions, concerns, and suggestions without fear of retribution. Encouraging open dialogue helps to surface diverse viewpoints and ensures that decisions are well-informed and inclusive. This inclusivity enhances the quality of decisions and promotes a sense of ownership among employees.

To ensure fairness and impartiality, leaders should implement objective criteria for decision-making. This includes establishing clear guidelines for promotions, performance evaluations, and resource allocation. By using objective criteria, leaders can reduce the influence of personal biases and ensure that decisions are based on merit and evidence.

Unconscious biases can subtly influence decisions and behaviour. Leaders should provide training on unconscious bias to raise awareness and equip employees with strategies to mitigate its impact. This training helps individuals recognise and address their biases, fostering a more inclusive and equitable workplace.

Leaders set the tone for organisational behaviour. By consistently demonstrating impartiality and objectivity in their own actions, leaders can inspire their teams to adopt the same principles. This includes being transparent in decision-making processes, treating all employees fairly, and holding oneself accountable for maintaining high standards of integrity and fairness.

HARNESSING THE POWER OF POTENTIAL

> *May not the space between heaven and earth be compared to a bellows? 'Tis emptied, yet it loses not its power; 'Tis moved again, and sends forth air the more.*

Lao Tzu uses the analogy of a bellows to illustrate the concept of potential and latent power. A bellows, though seemingly empty, holds immense power when in use. In the business world, this analogy underscores the value of creating space and maintaining flexibility to harness untapped potential within the organisation. Leaders should recognise and leverage the latent resources and capabilities of their teams to drive innovation and productivity.

Creating space within an organisation involves providing employees with the freedom and flexibility to explore new ideas and approaches. This can be achieved by reducing unnecessary constraints and bureaucratic processes that stifle creativity. Leaders should foster an environment where experimentation and innovation are encouraged, allowing employees to unleash their full potential.

Innovation is the lifeblood of a successful organisation. Leaders should actively encourage creativity and innovation by providing opportunities for brainstorming, ideation sessions, and cross-functional collaboration. This includes creating dedicated spaces for innovation, such as labs or hubs, where employees can work on new projects and ideas without the pressure of their daily responsibilities. By promoting a culture of innovation, leaders can tap into the collective ingenuity of their teams.

Every organisation has untapped resources, whether in the form of employee skills, knowledge, or ideas. Leaders should identify and leverage these resources to enhance organisational performance. This involves recognising the unique strengths and capabilities of each team member and providing opportunities for them to contribute in meaningful ways. By valuing and utilising untapped resources, organisations can unlock new avenues for growth and success.

Rigid processes and excessive constraints can hinder innovation and limit an organisation's ability to adapt to change. Leaders should critically evaluate existing workflows and remove any barriers that impede flexibility and creativity. This might involve simplifying approval processes, reducing red tape, and empowering employees to make decisions. By minimising constraints, leaders create an environment where potential can flourish.

A growth mindset is essential for unlocking potential within an organisation. Leaders should encourage employees to embrace challenges, learn from failures, and continuously seek improvement. This involves providing regular feedback, recognising efforts, and celebrating successes. By fostering a growth mindset, leaders can inspire their teams to push boundaries and achieve greater heights.

Diversity and inclusion are powerful drivers of innovation and creativity. Leaders should promote a diverse and inclusive workplace where different perspectives and ideas are valued. This diversity can lead to more innovative solutions and a broader range of ideas. By embracing diversity, leaders can harness the collective potential of their teams and create a more dynamic and resilient organisation.

Continuous learning is crucial for maintaining flexibility and adaptability. Leaders should provide opportunities for professional development, such as training programmes, workshops, and access to online learning platforms. Encouraging employees to continually upgrade their skills and knowledge helps to keep the organisation competitive and prepared for future challenges.

Collaboration across departments and functions can unlock hidden potential within the organisation. Leaders should facilitate the creation of collaborative networks where employees can share knowledge, resources, and ideas. This can be achieved through regular interdepartmental meetings, collaborative projects, and the use of digital collaboration tools. By fostering a collaborative culture, leaders can break down silos and harness the power of collective intelligence.

Leaders should implement systems to identify, measure, and recognise potential within their teams. This involves using performance metrics, talent assessments, and recognition programmes to highlight and reward employees' contributions. By acknowledging and celebrating potential, leaders can motivate employees to continue striving for excellence and innovation.

THE IMPORTANCE OF CLEAR COMMUNICATION & INNER CLARITY

> *Much speech to swift exhaustion lead we see; Your inner being guard, and keep it free.*

Excessive communication and over-complication can lead to confusion and fatigue within teams. In strategic management, the key is to ensure that communication is clear, concise, and purposeful. Leaders should focus on delivering essential messages effectively and avoiding unnecessary details that might overwhelm employees. By simplifying communication, leaders can help teams stay focused and engaged.

Clear communication involves expressing ideas and directives in a straightforward and understandable manner. Leaders should use simple language, avoid jargon, and ensure that their messages are easily comprehensible. This clarity helps to prevent misunderstandings and ensures that everyone is on the same page. Clear communication also involves actively listening to feedback and responding to questions, further enhancing understanding and alignment.

Information overload occurs when too much information is shared, leading to confusion and decreased productivity. Leaders should prioritise the most important information and deliver it in a structured manner. This might involve summarising key points, using visual aids, and breaking down complex information into manageable chunks. By reducing information overload, leaders can help employees process information more effectively and maintain focus on their tasks.

Efficient communication is about being effective and economical with words. Leaders should encourage efficient communication practices within their teams, such as setting clear agendas for meetings, keeping discussions on track, and using concise language. This efficiency helps to save time, reduce frustration, and ensure that important messages are communicated effectively.

Inner clarity and mindfulness are essential for effective leadership. Leaders should regularly take time to reflect on their goals, strategies, and performance. This reflection helps to gain clarity and perspective, allowing leaders to make more informed and thoughtful decisions. Mindfulness practices, such as meditation and deep breathing, can help leaders stay focused, reduce stress, and maintain mental clarity.

Clear communication and inner clarity contribute to better decision-making. When leaders are clear in their thinking and communication, they can make decisions that are well-informed and aligned with the organisation's goals. This clarity helps to ensure that decisions are made with confidence and purpose, leading to better outcomes and long-term success.

Encouraging a culture of open but efficient communication helps to maintain a productive and harmonious work environment. Leaders should create channels for open dialogue, where employees feel comfortable sharing their thoughts, ideas, and concerns. This openness fosters a sense of trust and collaboration, allowing teams to work together more effectively. Regular team meetings, feedback sessions, and one-on-one check-ins can facilitate this open communication.

A healthy work environment is one where communication is clear and stress is minimised. Leaders should promote practices that support mental well-being and reduce stress, such as encouraging regular breaks, providing resources for mindfulness and relaxation, and fostering a supportive and inclusive culture. When employees feel mentally clear and supported, they are more likely to be productive, engaged, and satisfied with their work.

Effective leadership involves balancing communication with action. While clear communication is important, leaders should also ensure that their words are supported by meaningful actions. This involves setting clear expectations, following through on commitments, and demonstrating accountability. By aligning communication with action, leaders build credibility and trust within their teams.

Leaders set the tone for communication within their organisations. By practising clear and concise communication themselves, leaders can set a powerful example for their teams. This includes being transparent, actively listening, and encouraging open dialogue. Leading by example creates a culture where clear communication is valued and practised by everyone in the organisation.

CHAPTER 6 – THE VALLEY SPIRIT

Chapter 6 of the *Tao Te Ching* highlights the enduring and gentle power of the 'valley spirit' or the 'female mystery,' symbolising the essence of life and creation. This chapter can provide valuable insights for modern-day strategic management in the following ways:

EMBRACING ENDURING POWER & SUSTAINABILITY

The valley spirit dies not, aye the same; The female mystery thus do we name.

Lao Tzu's reference to the 'valley spirit' highlights the concept of an enduring and inexhaustible source of vitality. In strategic management, this analogy underscores the importance of sustainability and a long-term vision. Just as the valley spirit remains constant and unchanging, organisations should strive to build strategies that are resilient and sustainable over time, rather than focusing on quick wins or temporary solutions.

Sustainable growth involves creating strategies that balance immediate needs with long-term goals. Leaders should prioritise initiatives that ensure the organisation's ongoing viability and success. This might include investing in sustainable practices, such as environmentally friendly operations, ethical sourcing, and corporate social responsibility. By committing to sustainability, businesses can build a strong foundation for future growth and stability.

A long-term vision is essential for guiding an organisation towards enduring success. Leaders should clearly articulate the organisation's mission, values, and long-term goals, ensuring that these are communicated effectively to all stakeholders. This vision provides direction and motivation, helping employees stay focused on the bigger picture and align their efforts with the organisation's overarching objectives.

Short-termism, or the focus on immediate gains at the expense of long-term stability, can undermine an organisation's success. Leaders should resist the temptation to pursue quick wins that compromise sustainability. Instead, they should adopt a long-term perspective, considering the future implications of their decisions. This approach helps to ensure that strategies are not only effective in the present but also beneficial for the organisation's future.

Resilience is the ability to adapt and thrive in the face of challenges and change. Leaders should invest in building a resilient organisation by fostering a culture of agility, continuous learning, and innovation. This involves creating flexible processes, encouraging experimentation, and supporting employees through change. A resilient organisation is better equipped to navigate uncertainties and capitalise on emerging opportunities.

Ethical practices are fundamental to sustainability. Leaders should prioritise ethical decision-making, ensuring that their strategies are aligned with principles of integrity and social responsibility. This includes treating employees fairly, engaging in transparent business practices, and contributing positively to the community and environment. By embracing ethics, organisations can build trust and loyalty among stakeholders, enhancing their long-term viability.

Innovation is a key driver of sustainable growth. Leaders should create an environment that encourages creativity and experimentation, where employees feel empowered to explore new ideas and solutions. This involves providing resources for research and development, fostering cross-functional collaboration, and recognising and rewarding innovative contributions. By prioritising innovation, organisations can stay competitive and adapt to changing market conditions.

Investing in talent and development is crucial for long-term success. Leaders should prioritise the continuous growth and development of their employees, providing opportunities for training, career advancement, and skill-building. By nurturing talent, organisations can build a strong and capable workforce that is prepared to drive future growth and innovation.

Balancing profit with purpose involves aligning business goals with broader social and environmental objectives. Leaders should integrate sustainability into their core business strategy, considering the impact of their actions on the environment, society, and future generations. This balance ensures that the organisation not only achieves financial success but also contributes positively to the world.

Leaders play a pivotal role in setting the tone for sustainability within their organisations. By demonstrating a commitment to long-term vision and ethical practices, leaders can inspire their teams to adopt similar values. This includes making decisions that prioritise sustainability, communicating the importance of long-term goals, and holding oneself accountable to high standards of integrity and responsibility.

VALUING NURTURING & SUBTLE INFLUENCE

> *Its gate, from which at first they issued forth, Is called the root from which grew heaven and earth.*

Lao Tzu's metaphor of the 'gate' and 'root' emphasises the importance of beginnings and foundations. Just as the roots of a tree provide the essential support and nutrients for growth, nurturing the foundational aspects of an organisation is crucial for its long-term health and success. This approach focuses on building a strong base from which everything else can flourish.

In business, creating a supportive environment means providing the conditions necessary for employees to thrive. This includes offering resources, tools, and opportunities for growth. Leaders should ensure that their teams have the support they need to develop their skills and perform their roles effectively. This supportive environment fosters loyalty, engagement, and high performance.

Nurturing talent involves recognising and developing the potential within each employee. Leaders should invest in training and development programmes that help employees build their skills and advance in their careers. Mentorship and coaching are also valuable for guiding employees and helping them reach their full potential. By nurturing talent, leaders can build a capable and motivated workforce that drives the organisation's success.

Innovation is key to staying competitive and adapting to change. Leaders should create a culture that encourages creativity and experimentation. This means providing the space and freedom for employees to explore new ideas and take risks. Encouraging cross-functional collaboration and diverse perspectives can also stimulate innovation. By fostering a culture of innovation, organisations can discover new opportunities and drive continuous improvement.

Development is an ongoing process that involves continuous learning and improvement. Leaders should promote a growth mindset within their organisations, where employees are encouraged to seek out new knowledge and refine their skills. This can be supported through access to learning resources, opportunities for professional development, and a culture that values curiosity and growth.

Company culture is the root from which the organisation grows. Leaders should cultivate a positive and inclusive culture that reflects the organisation's values and mission. This involves fostering an environment of mutual respect, open communication, and collaboration. A strong company culture attracts and retains top talent and creates a cohesive and motivated workforce.

Employee well-being is fundamental to organisational health. Leaders should prioritise the physical, mental, and emotional well-being of their employees. This includes providing a safe and healthy work environment, offering wellness programmes, and supporting work-life balance. When employees feel cared for and supported, they are more likely to be engaged and productive.

Core values serve as the guiding principles of an organisation. Leaders should clearly define and communicate these values, ensuring that they are integrated into all aspects of the business. This alignment helps to create a sense of purpose and direction, guiding decision-making and behaviour. By reinforcing core values, leaders can build a strong and resilient organisation.

Subtle influence involves guiding and shaping the organisation without exerting overt control. Leaders should lead by example, demonstrating the behaviours and attitudes they wish to see in their teams. This approach encourages autonomy and empowerment, allowing employees to take ownership of their work. Subtle influence fosters a culture of trust and respect, where employees feel valued and motivated.

A strong foundation is essential for sustainable growth. Leaders should focus on establishing solid structures and processes that support the organisation's mission and goals. This includes clear policies, effective communication channels, and robust performance management systems. By building a strong foundation, leaders ensure that the organisation is well-equipped to navigate challenges and seize opportunities.

UTILISING GENTLE LEADERSHIP & INFLUENCE

Long and unbroken does its power remain, Used gently, and without the touch of pain.

Gentle leadership is about influencing and guiding without force or coercion. Strategic leaders should use their power and influence with care, focusing on empowering their teams and leading by example. This approach fosters a positive and collaborative work environment, where employees feel valued and motivated to contribute their best. Gentle leadership encourages innovation, creativity, and a sense of ownership among team members.

Lao Tzu's teaching highlights the strength and enduring nature of gentle influence. In the context of strategic management, gentle leadership involves guiding and influencing without resorting to force or coercion. It is about empowering others, leading by example, and fostering an environment where individuals feel valued and motivated. This approach not only nurtures a positive work environment but also drives innovation and ownership among team members.

Empowerment is a key aspect of gentle leadership. Leaders should trust their teams and delegate authority, allowing employees to take ownership of their tasks and decisions. By providing the necessary resources and support, leaders can enable their teams to perform at their best. Empowerment fosters a sense of responsibility and accountability, leading to higher levels of engagement and productivity.

Gentle leaders lead by example, demonstrating the behaviours and values they wish to see in their teams. This includes showing respect, integrity, and humility in all interactions. When leaders model these qualities, they set a standard for others to follow, creating a culture of trust and mutual respect. Leading by example also builds credibility and inspires team members to embody the same principles in their work.

A positive work environment is essential for employee well-being and productivity. Gentle leaders create an atmosphere where collaboration, open communication, and mutual support are encouraged. This involves recognising and appreciating employees' contributions, providing constructive feedback, and addressing issues promptly and fairly. A supportive environment helps to reduce stress and increases job satisfaction, leading to better overall performance.

Gentle leadership encourages a culture of innovation and creativity. Leaders should create opportunities for employees to explore new ideas, take risks, and experiment without fear of failure. This can be achieved by fostering a safe and inclusive environment where diverse perspectives are valued. Encouraging innovation not only drives continuous improvement but also empowers employees to contribute their unique insights and solutions.

When employees feel a sense of ownership over their work, they are more likely to be invested in the success of the organisation. Gentle leaders nurture this sense of ownership by involving employees in decision-making processes, seeking their input, and recognising their achievements. This approach builds a sense of pride and commitment, motivating employees to go above and beyond in their roles.

While gentle leadership emphasises a caring and supportive approach, it is also important to maintain firmness and clarity in expectations. Leaders should set clear goals and standards, and hold team members accountable for their performance. Balancing firmness with compassion ensures that employees understand their responsibilities while feeling supported and valued.

Active listening is a critical skill for gentle leaders. It involves fully engaging with and understanding the perspectives and concerns of others. Leaders should practise active listening by being present in conversations, asking open-ended questions, and reflecting on what is being said. This approach fosters open communication and trust, and helps leaders make informed decisions that consider the needs and insights of their teams.

Trust is the foundation of effective leadership. Gentle leaders build trust by being consistent, transparent, and reliable in their actions. They communicate openly, follow through on commitments, and show empathy and understanding. When employees trust their leaders, they are more likely to be engaged, loyal, and committed to the organisation's goals.

Collaboration is essential for achieving collective success. Gentle leaders promote a culture of teamwork, where individuals are encouraged to work together towards common goals. This involves creating opportunities for cross-functional collaboration, facilitating open dialogue, and recognising team achievements. Collaboration leverages the diverse skills and perspectives of employees, leading to more innovative and effective solutions.

CHAPTER 7 – SELFLESSNESS & SERVICE

Chapter 7 of the *Tao Te Ching* offers profound wisdom on the concepts of selflessness, endurance, and the natural order. Here's how these teachings can be applied to modern-day strategic management:

EMBRACING SELFLESSNESS & SERVICE

> *Heaven is long-enduring and earth continues long. The reason why heaven and earth are able to endure and continue thus long is because they do not live of, or for, themselves.*

Lao Tzu highlights the enduring nature of heaven and earth, attributing their longevity to their selfless existence. They do not act for their own benefit but for the greater balance and harmony of the universe. In the realm of strategic management, this principle of selflessness can be applied to leadership, where prioritising the collective good over personal gain can lead to more sustainable and harmonious organisational growth.

In strategic management, leaders should focus on serving the greater good of the organisation rather than pursuing personal interests. This involves making decisions that benefit the organisation as a whole, even if it means sacrificing personal accolades or short-term gains. By prioritising the needs of the team and the long-term goals of the organisation, leaders can foster a culture of trust and collaboration.

Trust is the foundation of any successful organisation. When leaders act selflessly and consistently prioritise the well-being of their employees and the organisation, they build trust within their teams. Trust encourages open communication, mutual respect, and a sense of security, allowing employees to perform at their best. A culture of trust also reduces turnover and increases employee loyalty, contributing to long-term stability and success.

Selflessness in leadership encourages collaboration over competition. Leaders should create an environment where team members feel comfortable working together towards common goals. This involves promoting teamwork, recognising collective achievements, and providing opportunities for cross-functional collaboration. A collaborative culture leverages diverse perspectives and skills, leading to more innovative and effective solutions.

Sustainability is about ensuring that the organisation can endure and thrive over the long term. Leaders should adopt strategies that balance short-term objectives with long-term goals, considering the impact of their decisions on future generations. This includes implementing sustainable practices, investing in employee development, and maintaining ethical standards. By fostering sustainability, leaders ensure that the organisation remains resilient and capable of adapting to change.

Leaders who embrace selflessness and service lead by example, demonstrating the behaviours and values they wish to see in their teams. This includes showing empathy, humility, and a commitment to the organisation's mission and values. When leaders model selfless behaviour, they inspire their teams to adopt similar principles, creating a cohesive and purpose-driven organisation.

Prioritising the well-being of employees is a key aspect of selfless leadership. Leaders should create a supportive environment where employees feel valued and cared for. This involves providing resources for mental and physical health, promoting work-life balance, and recognising and addressing the unique needs of each team member. When employees feel supported, they are more engaged, productive, and committed to the organisation.

Ethical decision-making is a hallmark of selfless leadership. Leaders should consider the broader implications of their actions, ensuring that they align with the organisation's values and ethical standards. This involves being transparent, honest, and fair in all dealings, and holding oneself accountable to high ethical standards. Ethical leadership builds trust and credibility, both within the organisation and with external stakeholders.

Servant leadership is a philosophy that emphasises the leader's role as a servant to their team. This involves focusing on the needs of others, empowering employees, and helping them achieve their full potential. By adopting a servant leadership approach, leaders can create a more inclusive and supportive work environment, where everyone feels valued and motivated to contribute their best.

A selfless leader maintains a long-term vision that guides the organisation towards enduring success. This involves setting clear and achievable goals, staying committed to the organisation's mission, and continuously evaluating and adjusting strategies to meet evolving needs. A long-term vision ensures that the organisation remains focused on sustainable growth and resilience.

LEADING WITH HUMILITY & PUTTING OTHERS FIRST

> *Therefore the sage puts his own person last, and yet it is found in the foremost place; he treats his person as if it were foreign to him, and yet that person is preserved.*

Lao Tzu's teachings emphasise the power of humility and the importance of putting others first. In the context of strategic management, humility is a key trait that enables leaders to build trust, foster collaboration, and create a positive organisational culture. By prioritising the needs of their team and organisation above their personal ambitions, leaders can cultivate an environment where everyone thrives.

Effective leaders understand that their success is intrinsically linked to the success of their team. By focusing on the development and well-being of their employees, leaders can create a supportive and motivated workforce. This involves recognising individual and team achievements, providing opportunities for growth, and offering the necessary resources and support to help employees excel in their roles.

A supportive work environment is one where employees feel valued and encouraged to contribute their best efforts. Leaders can foster this environment by demonstrating empathy, actively listening to their team's concerns, and addressing any issues promptly. When employees feel supported, they are more likely to be engaged, productive, and committed to the organisation's goals.

Humility in leadership promotes a culture of collaboration over competition. Leaders should encourage open communication and teamwork, where employees feel comfortable sharing ideas and working together towards common objectives. By facilitating cross-functional collaboration and recognising collective achievements, leaders can leverage the diverse talents and perspectives of their teams, leading to more innovative and effective solutions.

Putting others first does not mean neglecting one's own needs; rather, it involves balancing personal and organisational goals. Leaders who adopt a selfless approach often find that their own position and influence are strengthened as a result. By prioritising the long-term success of the organisation and the well-being of their team, leaders can build a resilient and sustainable enterprise.

Leaders who embody humility and selflessness set a powerful example for their teams. This involves showing integrity, admitting mistakes, and being open to feedback. By modelling these behaviours, leaders inspire their teams to adopt similar values and attitudes, creating a cohesive and aligned organisation.

A selfless approach to leadership can enhance a leader's influence and credibility. When employees see that their leader genuinely cares about their well-being and prioritises the organisation's success, they are more likely to respect and follow that leader. This trust and respect translate into greater influence, allowing the leader to guide the organisation more effectively.

While selflessness is important, it is also crucial for leaders to take care of their own well-being and maintain a healthy balance between personal and professional responsibilities. This balance ensures that leaders can sustain their energy and effectiveness over the long term. By managing their own needs alongside those of their team and organisation, leaders can achieve a harmonious and productive work environment.

Humility involves recognising that there is always room for improvement. Leaders should foster a culture of continuous learning and development, where employees are encouraged to seek out new knowledge and refine their skills. By providing opportunities for professional growth and creating a safe space for experimentation and innovation, leaders can drive continuous improvement and organisational excellence.

Selfless leadership helps to build strong, long-term relationships with employees, partners, and stakeholders. By demonstrating a commitment to the collective good, leaders can cultivate loyalty and trust, leading to more stable and fruitful collaborations. These relationships are essential for sustaining growth and navigating challenges in the dynamic business environment.

CREATING A PURPOSE-DRIVEN ORGANISATION

Is it not because he has no personal and private ends, that therefore such ends are realised?

Lao Tzu's reflection emphasises the idea that selfless leaders, who focus on a purpose greater than themselves, can achieve extraordinary results. In strategic management, creating a purpose-driven organisation means aligning the goals of the business with a clear mission and vision that transcends personal ambitions. This alignment inspires and unites teams, driving commitment, engagement, and overall success.

When leaders focus on a purpose greater than themselves, they inspire their teams to work towards common goals. This shared purpose fosters unity and collaboration, as employees understand that their efforts contribute to something meaningful and impactful. By articulating a compelling mission and vision, leaders can motivate their teams to strive for excellence and take pride in their work.

A clear mission and vision provide direction and focus for the organisation. Leaders should ensure that the organisation's goals are aligned with its core mission and vision, creating a coherent strategy that guides decision-making and actions. This alignment helps to ensure that all efforts are geared towards achieving the organisation's long-term objectives, fostering a sense of purpose and continuity.

Purpose-driven organisations tend to have higher levels of employee engagement and commitment. When employees see how their work contributes to the larger mission, they are more likely to be motivated and dedicated. Leaders can enhance this commitment by regularly communicating the organisation's purpose, celebrating milestones, and recognising individual and team contributions. This ongoing reinforcement helps to sustain engagement and drive performance.

A purpose-driven approach enables employees to achieve both their individual goals and the collective aspirations of the organisation. Leaders should provide opportunities for professional development, personal growth, and career advancement, aligning these opportunities with the organisation's mission. By supporting employees' individual aspirations, leaders can create a more fulfilling and motivating work environment.

A sense of shared purpose fosters a cohesive and motivated team. Leaders should encourage open communication, collaboration, and mutual support, creating an inclusive culture where everyone feels valued and heard. This cohesive environment promotes teamwork and innovation, driving the organisation towards its goals. A motivated team is more likely to go above and beyond, contributing to the overall success of the organisation.

Purpose-driven organisations are often more resilient and sustainable. A clear mission and vision provide a stable foundation that helps the organisation navigate challenges and adapt to change. Leaders should continuously reinforce the organisation's purpose, ensuring that it remains relevant and inspiring in the face of evolving circumstances. This resilience ensures long-term success and sustainability.

A purpose-driven approach enhances organisational culture by embedding core values and principles into everyday practices. Leaders should integrate the mission and vision into all aspects of the organisation, from hiring and onboarding to performance management and employee recognition. This integration ensures that the organisation's culture is aligned with its purpose, fostering a positive and cohesive work environment.

A clear and compelling purpose can stimulate innovation and creativity within the organisation. When employees are motivated by a meaningful mission, they are more likely to think creatively and seek innovative solutions. Leaders should provide the resources and support needed to encourage experimentation and risk-taking, leveraging the collective potential of the team to drive continuous improvement.

Authentic leadership is key to creating a purpose-driven organisation. Leaders should embody the organisation's mission and vision in their actions and decisions, demonstrating a genuine commitment to the greater good. This authenticity builds trust and credibility, inspiring employees to align their efforts with the organisation's purpose.

CHAPTER 8 – THE VIRTUE OF WATER

Chapter 8 of the *Tao Te Ching* emphasises the qualities of water, highlighting adaptability, humility, and the importance of virtue in various aspects of life. These teachings can offer valuable insights for modern-day strategic management:

EMBRACING ADAPTABILITY & FLEXIBILITY

> *The highest excellence is like (that of) water. The excellence of water appears in its benefiting all things, and in its occupying, without striving (to the contrary), the low place which all men dislike.*

In Chapter 8 of the *Tao Te Ching*, Lao Tzu uses the metaphor of water to illustrate the qualities of adaptability and flexibility. Water is one of the most powerful elements in nature, not because it strives or forces its way, but because of its ability to adapt, flow, and conform to its surroundings. In strategic management, leaders can learn a great deal from water's nature, applying these qualities to navigate and thrive in dynamic environments.

Adaptability is the ability to adjust to new conditions and respond effectively to changes. In the fast-paced world of business, adaptability is crucial for survival and success. Leaders who are adaptable can shift their strategies and approaches based on emerging trends, market conditions, and unforeseen challenges. This flexibility allows organisations to remain competitive and seize new opportunities as they arise.

Strategic leaders should continually assess their environment and be willing to adjust their strategies to align with changing circumstances. This might involve pivoting to new markets, adopting innovative technologies, or reevaluating business models. By staying attuned to the external environment and being open to change, leaders can ensure that their organisations remain relevant and effective.

Challenges are an inevitable part of any business journey. Leaders who embrace adaptability can navigate these challenges more effectively. This involves maintaining a flexible mindset, being willing to experiment with different solutions, and learning from failures. By approaching challenges with resilience and creativity, leaders can turn obstacles into opportunities for growth and improvement.

Opportunities often arise in unexpected ways. Leaders who are flexible and adaptable are better positioned to recognise and capitalise on these opportunities. This might involve exploring new markets, forming strategic partnerships, or innovating products and services. By being proactive and open to new possibilities, organisations can drive growth and achieve long-term success.

Flexibility in leadership means being open to different perspectives and approaches. Just as water takes the shape of any container it is placed in, flexible leaders can adapt their style to suit different situations and individuals. This might involve adjusting communication styles, being receptive to feedback, and fostering an inclusive environment where diverse ideas are valued. Flexibility enhances collaboration and drives better decision-making.

Water's ability to occupy the low places that others avoid is a metaphor for humility. Humble leaders recognise the value of every team member and are willing to listen and learn from others. This humility fosters a culture of respect and collaboration, where everyone feels empowered to contribute their best. By putting ego aside and focusing on the collective good, leaders can build stronger and more cohesive teams.

Leaders should foster a culture of adaptability within their organisations. This involves encouraging continuous learning, promoting flexibility in processes, and supporting a growth mindset. By creating an environment where employees feel safe to experiment and innovate, leaders can drive continuous improvement and keep the organisation agile.

While adaptability is important, it must be balanced with stability. Leaders should provide a clear vision and consistent values that guide the organisation, even as strategies and tactics evolve. This balance ensures that the organisation can adapt to change without losing its core identity and purpose. Stability provides a foundation from which flexibility and innovation can flourish.

Leaders set the tone for adaptability and flexibility within their organisations. By demonstrating a willingness to change and adapt, leaders can inspire their teams to embrace these qualities. This involves being transparent about challenges and changes, actively seeking input from others, and showing a commitment to continuous learning and improvement.

Adaptable and flexible organisations are more resilient in the face of change and uncertainty. By fostering a culture of adaptability, leaders can equip their teams with the skills and mindset needed to navigate and thrive in dynamic environments. This resilience ensures that the organisation can withstand disruptions and emerge stronger and more competitive.

PRACTISING HUMILITY & SERVING OTHERS

> The excellence of water... in its occupying, without striving (to the contrary), the low place which all men dislike.

Lao Tzu uses the metaphor of water to illustrate the virtue of humility. Water naturally seeks the lowest places, which are often overlooked or avoided by others, and in doing so, it benefits all things around it. In leadership, this principle of humility involves leaders being willing to take on less glamorous tasks and prioritise the needs of others above their own. This approach fosters respect, trust, and a strong sense of community within the organisation.

Servant leadership is a philosophy where leaders prioritise serving their team members and the organisation. Instead of seeking personal gain or recognition, servant leaders focus on the growth and well-being of their employees. This leadership style is grounded in empathy, listening, and stewardship. By embodying the qualities of water—humility and service—leaders can create a work environment that is supportive, collaborative, and high-performing.

Leaders who demonstrate humility and a willingness to serve others earn the respect and trust of their teams. When leaders put the needs of their team members first, they show that they value and care about their employees' well-being and success. This respect and trust are fundamental to building strong, effective teams that are committed to the organisation's goals.

A servant leadership approach fosters a collaborative work environment. Leaders who are willing to get involved in day-to-day tasks and support their team members set a tone of cooperation and mutual support. This approach encourages team members to work together, share ideas, and help one another, leading to increased innovation and productivity. Collaboration becomes a natural part of the organisational culture, driving better outcomes.

When leaders practise humility and serve others, it has a positive impact on team morale and productivity. Employees who feel supported and valued are more likely to be motivated and engaged in their work. High morale leads to increased job satisfaction, lower turnover rates, and a stronger commitment to the organisation's mission. Productivity improves as employees are more willing to go above and beyond in their roles.

Leaders who lead by example set a powerful standard for their teams. By demonstrating humility and a commitment to serving others, leaders inspire their employees to adopt similar behaviours. This creates a ripple effect throughout the organisation, where acts of service and collaboration become the norm. Leading by example also reinforces the organisation's values and mission, creating a cohesive and aligned team.

Servant leaders focus on the development and growth of their team members. By providing opportunities for learning, mentoring, and career advancement, leaders help employees achieve their full potential. This investment in personal and professional growth not only benefits the individuals but also strengthens the organisation as a whole. Employees who are continuously developing their skills are better equipped to contribute to the organisation's success.

A culture of humility and service is foundational to a strong, resilient organisation. Leaders should actively cultivate this culture by recognising and rewarding acts of service, promoting open communication, and creating an inclusive environment where everyone feels valued. A strong organisational culture enhances employee engagement, retention, and overall performance.

Humility enables leaders to handle challenges and setbacks with grace. Instead of reacting defensively or blaming others, humble leaders approach difficulties with a mindset of learning and improvement. They are open to feedback and willing to make necessary changes to benefit the organisation. This attitude fosters a culture of resilience and continuous improvement, helping the organisation navigate challenges effectively.

Humility and servant leadership extend beyond the organisation to relationships with external stakeholders. Leaders who prioritise service and humility build strong, positive relationships with customers, partners, and the community. These relationships are based on trust, respect, and mutual benefit, enhancing the organisation's reputation and creating opportunities for collaboration and growth.

ENSURING SUITABILITY & ALIGNMENT

The excellence of a residence is in (the suitability of) the place; that of the mind is in abysmal stillness; that of associations is in their being with the virtuous; that of government is in its securing good order; that of (the conduct of) affairs is in its ability; and that of (the initiation of) any movement is in its timeliness.

Lao Tzu's teachings in Chapter 8 emphasise the importance of suitability and alignment in various aspects of life and governance. In strategic management, leaders must ensure that their decisions and actions are well-aligned with the organisation's goals and values. This holistic approach includes considering suitability, maintaining mental clarity, building virtuous relationships, securing good order, and ensuring the ability and timeliness of initiatives.

Leaders should ensure that resources, talents, and strategies are well-suited to the current needs and future direction of the organisation by carefully assessing and allocating resources to areas where they can be most effective, understanding the organisation's priorities, and directing resources to support key initiatives. Matching the right people to the right roles is crucial, so leaders should recognise the strengths and potential of their team members and assign tasks that align with their skills and career aspirations. Developing strategies that are relevant to the organisation's current context and future goals ensures that efforts are focused and effective, so leaders should regularly review and adjust strategies to remain aligned with changing circumstances.

Maintaining a calm and focused mindset, even in the face of challenges, is crucial for effective leadership. A still mind allows leaders to think clearly and make rational decisions, essential for navigating complex situations and avoiding impulsive reactions. Practising mindfulness helps leaders stay present and focused, reducing stress and enhancing overall well-being through techniques such as meditation, deep breathing, and reflective practices. This mental stillness enables leaders to approach problems with a balanced perspective, considering multiple viewpoints and potential outcomes before taking action.

Building relationships with trustworthy and virtuous individuals is essential for strengthening an organisation's foundation, as cultivating a network of individuals who share similar values and ethical standards fosters trust, integrity, and mutual respect. Working with virtuous and competent partners encourages collaboration and innovation, so leaders should seek out alliances and partnerships that align with the organisation's mission and contribute to its success. Engaging with mentors and advisors who exemplify virtuous behaviour provides valuable guidance and support, helping leaders navigate challenges and make sound decisions.

Designing an effective organisational structure ensures clear roles, responsibilities, and communication channels, supporting efficient workflow and decision-making. Establishing robust processes and systems helps maintain order and consistency, and leaders should continuously evaluate and improve these processes to enhance efficiency and effectiveness. Implementing strong governance practices ensures accountability, transparency, and ethical behaviour, including setting policies, monitoring performance, and addressing any issues promptly, promoting stability and efficiency within the organisation.

Leaders must ensure that initiatives are executed effectively and at the right time by ensuring they are led by individuals with the necessary skills and expertise, investing in training and development to build a capable and confident workforce. Timing is critical for success, so leaders should assess the best time to launch new projects or make strategic decisions, considering external factors and organisational readiness. Effective execution involves careful planning, coordination, and monitoring, with leaders setting clear goals, allocating resources, and tracking progress to ensure initiatives are completed successfully.

By integrating these principles into their leadership approach, strategic leaders can create a well-aligned and thriving organisation. This involves continuously assessing and adjusting strategies, maintaining mental clarity, building ethical relationships, promoting good order, and ensuring the ability and timeliness of initiatives. Embracing these practices fosters a culture of excellence, resilience, and sustainable success.

LEADING WITHOUT EGO & CONFLICT

> *And when (one with the highest excellence) does not wrangle (about his low position), no one finds fault with him.*

Lao Tzu's wisdom in this passage underscores the importance of leading without ego and avoiding unnecessary conflicts. Leaders who prioritise the greater good over personal gain or status are more likely to cultivate a respectful and effective work environment. By minimising distractions and promoting cooperation, leaders can foster a culture of mutual respect and high productivity.

Ego-driven actions can undermine leadership and create a toxic work environment. When leaders focus on their own status or personal achievements, they can alienate their team members and create unnecessary conflicts. By putting aside their ego, leaders can make decisions that are in the best interest of the organisation and its people.

Leaders should prioritise the overall well-being and success of the organisation over personal ambitions. This means making decisions that benefit the entire team, even if it means sacrificing personal recognition or short-term gains. By focusing on the greater good, leaders can build trust and loyalty within their teams, creating a more cohesive and motivated workforce.

A harmonious work environment is one where employees feel valued, respected, and supported. Leaders who avoid conflicts and foster a spirit of cooperation contribute to a positive workplace culture. This involves addressing issues constructively, promoting open communication, and encouraging collaboration. A harmonious environment enhances employee satisfaction and drives higher levels of engagement and productivity.

Cooperation is key to achieving organisational goals. Leaders should create opportunities for teamwork and collaborative problem-solving, where employees feel empowered to contribute their ideas and skills. By promoting cooperation, leaders can leverage the diverse strengths of their team members, leading to more innovative and effective solutions.

Ego-driven conflicts can be a major distraction in the workplace, diverting attention away from important tasks and goals. Leaders who act without ego can minimise these distractions by addressing conflicts quickly and fairly, and by setting a tone of mutual respect and understanding. This approach ensures that the team remains focused on their objectives and can work together efficiently.

Respect is a fundamental aspect of effective leadership. Leaders who demonstrate humility and prioritise the needs of others are more likely to earn the respect of their team members. This respect fosters a culture of trust and collaboration, where employees feel comfortable expressing their ideas and concerns. By building mutual respect, leaders can create a more inclusive and dynamic work environment.

A culture of cooperation and mutual respect leads to higher productivity. When employees feel supported and valued, they are more motivated to perform at their best. Leaders who minimise conflicts and create a positive work environment can enhance overall productivity and drive organisational success. By focusing on the collective goals, leaders can ensure that everyone is working towards the same objectives.

Leaders who embody the principles of humility and ego-less leadership set a powerful example for their teams. By demonstrating these qualities in their actions and decisions, leaders inspire their employees to adopt similar behaviours. Leading by example creates a ripple effect throughout the organisation, fostering a culture of humility, cooperation, and mutual respect.

Ego-less leadership aligns with ethical behaviour and integrity. Leaders who prioritise the greater good and avoid personal gain demonstrate a commitment to ethical principles. This ethical approach builds trust and credibility both within the organisation and with external stakeholders. By encouraging ethical behaviour, leaders can create a more sustainable and reputable organisation.

CHAPTER 9 – THE PITFALLS OF EXCESS

Chapter 9 of the *Tao Te Ching* offers valuable insights on moderation, humility, and the dangers of excess. Here's how these teachings can be applied to modern-day strategic management:

EMBRACING MODERATION & BALANCE

> It is better to leave a vessel unfilled, than to attempt to carry it when it is full. If you keep feeling a point that has been sharpened, the point cannot long preserve its sharpness.

Lao Tzu emphasises the virtue of moderation and the dangers of excess. In strategic management, adopting a balanced approach is essential for sustainable success. By avoiding extremes and striving for equilibrium in various aspects of business, leaders can ensure that their organisations remain effective, resilient, and productive.

Allocating resources wisely is a key aspect of moderation. Leaders should ensure that resources—whether financial, human, or material—are distributed in a way that meets the organisation's needs without overextending any particular area. This involves careful planning and regular assessment to avoid wastage or shortages. Balanced resource allocation supports steady progress and helps prevent burnout and inefficiency.

An even distribution of workload is crucial to maintaining a healthy and productive work environment. Leaders should monitor team workloads to ensure that no one is overburdened. This might involve delegating tasks, providing support, and setting realistic expectations. By managing workloads effectively, leaders can prevent employee burnout, increase job satisfaction, and maintain high levels of performance.

Setting achievable and realistic goals is another important aspect of embracing moderation. Leaders should establish clear, attainable objectives that align with the organisation's mission and capacities. Overly ambitious goals can lead to stress and disappointment, while modest, incremental goals encourage continuous improvement and sustained motivation. A balanced approach to goal-setting fosters a positive and driven organisational culture.

Pushing for constant peak performance without allowing time for rest and recuperation can lead to burnout. Leaders should recognise the importance of work-life balance and encourage employees to take breaks, use their vacation time, and prioritise their well-being. By fostering a culture that values health and balance, organisations can maintain long-term productivity and employee satisfaction.

Moderation is key to achieving sustainable growth. Leaders should focus on steady, incremental progress rather than rapid, unsustainable expansion. This involves making strategic investments, carefully managing resources, and maintaining a long-term perspective. Sustainable growth ensures that the organisation can adapt to changes and continue to thrive over time.

Just as a point that is continually sharpened cannot maintain its sharpness, an organisation that is constantly pushed to its limits will eventually lose effectiveness. Leaders should allow time for reflection, learning, and recalibration. This might involve regular strategic reviews, employee development programmes, and opportunities for innovation and creativity. Maintaining focus and sharpness requires balancing periods of intense activity with times of rest and renewal.

A culture that values balance and moderation is essential for organisational health. Leaders should promote values such as fairness, inclusivity, and respect for diverse perspectives. This involves creating policies and practices that support equality and well-being, and encouraging behaviours that align with these values. A balanced organisational culture fosters trust, collaboration, and a strong sense of community.

Balanced decision-making involves considering multiple factors and perspectives before taking action. Leaders should avoid hasty decisions driven by pressure or bias and instead adopt a thoughtful, measured approach. This might involve seeking input from various stakeholders, analysing data, and weighing potential risks and benefits. By enhancing decision-making processes, leaders can ensure more effective and sustainable outcomes.

Leaders play a critical role in modelling balanced behaviour. By demonstrating moderation in their actions and decisions, leaders can set a positive example for their teams. This includes managing their own workload, taking time for self-care, and making balanced, thoughtful decisions. Leading by example reinforces the importance of moderation and balance within the organisation.

A balanced approach to leadership and management builds organisational resilience. By avoiding extremes and maintaining equilibrium, leaders can create an adaptable and robust organisation capable of navigating challenges and seizing opportunities. Resilience ensures that the organisation can sustain growth and success in the face of adversity.

AVOIDING THE PITFALLS OF EXCESS

When gold and jade fill the hall, their possessor cannot keep them safe. When wealth and honours lead to arrogancy, this brings its evil on itself.

Lao Tzu's teaching warns against the dangers of excessive accumulation and the arrogance it can breed. In the context of strategic management, this principle is particularly relevant. Leaders must be vigilant to avoid the pitfalls of wealth and accolades that can lead to complacency and a disconnect from the core values of the organisation.

Regardless of success, leaders should remain humble and grounded by recognising that achievements result from collective efforts and maintaining a mindset of gratitude and openness, making them more approachable and inspiring trust and loyalty among their teams. Staying grounded means staying focused on the core mission and values of the organisation, resisting the temptation to be swayed by external recognition, and remaining dedicated to the foundational principles that guide their organisation.

Complacency can be a significant risk when success leads to a false sense of security, so leaders should cultivate a culture of continuous improvement where the organisation consistently seeks ways to innovate and enhance performance, ensuring it remains competitive and dynamic. Encouraging a mindset of lifelong learning within the organisation helps combat complacency, so leaders should promote ongoing education and skill development to ensure employees at all levels continually grow and adapt to new challenges.

Ethical practices are the foundation of sustainable success, so leaders should prioritise integrity in all dealings, ensuring that decisions and actions align with ethical standards, which builds trust with employees, customers, and stakeholders. By embracing corporate social responsibility (CSR), organisations can align their success with positive contributions to society, so leaders should integrate CSR initiatives into their strategies, demonstrating a commitment to ethical practices and community engagement.

The well-being of employees should be a top priority for leaders, which involves creating a supportive work environment that promotes physical, mental, and emotional health, providing resources and initiatives that support work-life balance, stress management, and overall well-being. Recognising and appreciating the contributions of employees fosters a positive and motivated workforce, so leaders should implement programmes to celebrate achievements, offer constructive feedback, and provide support for personal and professional growth.

Leaders should balance the pursuit of material success with a strong focus on organisational values by making decisions that reflect the organisation's mission and principles, rather than being driven solely by financial gains. Ensuring that the organisation's activities and strategies are aligned with its core mission helps maintain focus and purpose, so leaders should regularly revisit and communicate the mission to keep everyone aligned and motivated.

Leaders should aim for sustainable growth that balances ambition with realistic expectations by setting achievable goals and avoiding the pressures of rapid, unsustainable expansion. Mindful management of resources ensures that the organisation does not overextend itself, so leaders should allocate resources judiciously, considering long-term needs and potential risks.

Leaders who exemplify humility, ethical behaviour, and a focus on continuous improvement set a powerful example for their teams, inspiring employees to adopt similar principles through their actions and decisions. Holding oneself accountable to high standards of conduct reinforces these values within the organisation, with leaders being transparent about their decisions and taking responsibility for their actions.

RECOGNISING THE VALUE OF COMPLETION & WITHDRAWAL

> When the work is done, and one's name is becoming distinguished, to withdraw into obscurity is the way of Heaven.

Lao Tzu emphasises the importance of knowing when to step back after achieving success. This principle is highly relevant in strategic management, where recognising the value of completion and withdrawal can lead to healthier and more sustainable organisational growth. By stepping back, leaders can prevent overdependence on any single individual and encourage the development of new leaders within the organisation.

When leaders consistently handle all major tasks and decisions, it can create an unhealthy reliance on their presence and abilities, but delegating responsibility helps distribute workload and ensures the organisation can continue to function smoothly in their absence. By stepping back, leaders give their team members the opportunity to take on more significant roles, building confidence and competence within the team and preparing them for future leadership positions.

Leaders should focus on mentoring and coaching their team members, helping them develop the skills and knowledge needed to lead, which prepares the next generation of leaders to take the helm when the time comes. Providing opportunities for employees to take on new challenges and responsibilities fosters their professional growth, so leaders should encourage team members to step out of their comfort zones and embrace leadership roles.

Once a project or milestone is completed, leaders should shift their focus to new challenges and opportunities, ensuring the organisation remains dynamic and forward-thinking. Stepping back allows leaders to create space for innovation, and when team members are given the freedom to experiment and explore new ideas, it can lead to breakthroughs and improvements that drive the organisation forward.

Recognising the value of completion and withdrawal helps maintain a healthy work-life balance for leaders, allowing them to avoid burnout and overextension and sustain their energy and effectiveness over the long term. An organisation that does not rely on a single individual is more resilient and adaptable, so by developing a diverse leadership pipeline and fostering a culture of shared responsibility, organisations can better withstand changes and challenges.

Leaders should recognise that success is a collective effort by stepping back and giving credit to the team, demonstrating humility and appreciation for their contributions. Cultivating a culture that values humility encourages all team members to contribute their best without seeking personal glory, fostering a collaborative spirit, mutual respect, and a strong sense of community within the organisation.

Having clear succession plans in place ensures a smooth transition of leadership, as leaders should identify and prepare potential successors, reducing uncertainty and disruption during leadership changes. Stepping back gradually and providing support during transitions helps ensure continuity, with leaders remaining available for guidance and advice while allowing new leaders to establish their own style and direction.

CHAPTER 10 – INTELLECT & INTUITION

Chapter 10 of the *Tao Te Ching* explores the themes of unity, mindfulness, selflessness, and the mysterious nature of the Tao. Here's how these teachings can be applied to modern-day strategic management:

INTEGRATING INTELLECT & INTUITION

> *When the intelligent and animal souls are held together in one embrace, they can be kept from separating.*

Lao Tzu's wisdom in this passage emphasises the importance of harmonising intellect (logical thinking) and intuition (gut feeling). In strategic management, integrating these two aspects can lead to more effective and well-rounded decision-making. Leaders who balance analytical skills with intuitive insights are better equipped to understand complex situations and make strategic choices that consider both facts and instincts.

Intellect involves the use of analytical skills to assess data, identify patterns, and evaluate options, enabling leaders to make informed decisions based on evidence and logical reasoning, ensuring that decisions are grounded in reality and supported by facts. Critical thinking is essential for assessing information objectively and making rational judgments, as leaders should cultivate their critical thinking skills to question assumptions, consider multiple perspectives, and anticipate potential outcomes, enhancing the robustness of decision-making. Intellect also plays a key role in strategic planning, where leaders analyse market trends, competitive landscapes, and organisational capabilities to develop long-term strategies; by using intellectual rigour, leaders can create well-structured and effective plans that guide the organisation towards its goals.

Intuition involves a deeper, often subconscious understanding of situations that goes beyond analytical reasoning, providing valuable insights that are not immediately apparent through analysis alone; therefore, leaders should trust their gut feelings, especially when data is incomplete or ambiguous. Closely linked to emotional intelligence, intuition helps leaders understand and manage their own emotions and those of others, enabling them to navigate complex interpersonal dynamics and make decisions that consider the human element of business. Furthermore, intuition fuels creativity and innovation by allowing leaders to think outside the box and explore unconventional solutions, helping them identify new opportunities and drive initiatives that set the organisation apart from competitors.

Integrating intellect and intuition leads to holistic decision-making that considers both rational analysis and instinctive understanding, enabling leaders to balance analytical tools and methods with their intuitive insights. This approach allows leaders to grasp the full picture in complex situations, making decisions that are well-informed and contextually appropriate. Furthermore, the combination of intellect and intuition enhances a leader's adaptability, equipping them to quickly assess situations using both analytical and intuitive approaches in rapidly changing environments, thereby responding effectively and seizing opportunities.

Mindfulness practices can help leaders become more aware of their intuitive insights and integrate them with their analytical thinking; techniques such as meditation and reflective journaling enhance self-awareness and improve decision-making. Encouraging input from diverse team members helps balance intellect and intuition, as different perspectives bring a range of analytical and intuitive insights, leading to more comprehensive and well-rounded decisions. Additionally, experience is a valuable teacher that enhances both analytical skills and intuitive understanding, so leaders should reflect on past decisions, learn from successes and failures, and continuously refine their ability to integrate intellect and intuition.

Leaders should model the integration of intellect and intuition in their own decision-making processes, demonstrating how to balance these aspects and inspiring their teams to adopt a similar approach, thereby enhancing their collective decision-making capabilities. Creating a culture that values both analytical rigour and intuitive insights encourages employees to develop and use both skills, which leaders can promote by recognising and rewarding decisions that reflect a balanced approach.

PRACTISING MINDFULNESS & FLEXIBILITY

When one gives undivided attention to the (vital) breath, and brings it to the utmost degree of pliancy, he can become as a (tender) babe.

Mindfulness involves being fully present and attentive to the current moment. In leadership, this means paying close attention to the immediate context, environment, and people involved, without distraction. Practising mindfulness allows leaders to respond more effectively to challenges and opportunities as they arise.

Mindfulness helps leaders clear mental clutter and focus on the task at hand, enhancing their ability to analyse situations accurately and make informed decisions. By staying present and not dwelling on past mistakes or future uncertainties, leaders can reduce stress and anxiety, fostering a calm and composed demeanour that positively influences the entire team. Mindful leaders are better equipped to consider all relevant factors and perspectives before making decisions, leading to more effective and sustainable outcomes through a thorough and balanced approach.

Flexibility is the ability to adapt to changing circumstances and respond effectively to new information. Leaders who are flexible can pivot their strategies and approaches as needed, ensuring that the organisation remains agile and resilient.

Lao Tzu's reference to becoming like a 'tender babe' symbolises openness, receptivity, and adaptability. Just as a child is open to new experiences and learns quickly, leaders should remain open to new ideas and changes.

In a rapidly evolving business environment, leaders must be ready to adapt their strategies and approaches by staying informed about industry trends, being open to feedback, and continuously reassessing goals and plans. Flexible leaders create an environment where innovation can thrive, driving continuous improvement and staying ahead of the competition by being open to new ideas and encouraging creative thinking. Flexibility also allows leaders to respond effectively to unforeseen challenges, adjusting their approach based on the situation to find the best solutions rather than rigidly adhering to a predefined plan.

Leaders should cultivate presence by practising mindfulness techniques such as meditation, deep breathing, and reflective journaling, which enhance self-awareness and help them stay grounded in the present moment. While having clear structures and plans is important, leaders should balance these with the ability to adapt, ensuring that the organisation remains focused yet agile, capable of seizing opportunities and navigating challenges. Mindful and flexible leaders are empathetic, understanding the needs and perspectives of their team members, which fosters a supportive work environment where employees feel valued and motivated.

Leaders should model mindfulness in their daily actions by demonstrating the benefits of being fully present and attentive through active listening, thoughtful communication, and maintaining focus during meetings and interactions. Additionally, leaders can inspire their teams by demonstrating flexibility in their decision-making and problem-solving processes, showing a willingness to adapt and embrace change, which encourages their teams to do the same.

Organisations that prioritise continuous learning are better equipped to adapt and innovate, so leaders should provide opportunities for professional development and encourage employees to expand their skills and knowledge. Open communication is key to fostering mindfulness and flexibility; therefore, leaders should create channels for feedback, ideas, and discussions to ensure all team members feel heard and valued. Additionally, a focus on well-being supports mindfulness and reduces stress, so leaders should implement wellness programmes, promote work-life balance, and create a supportive environment where employees can thrive.

CLEANSING IMAGINATION & CLARITY

When he has cleansed away the most mysterious sights (of his imagination), he can become without a flaw.

Lao Tzu's wisdom underscores the significance of mental clarity and the elimination of unnecessary distractions. For leaders, this means focusing on clearing their minds of biases, assumptions, and overcomplicated thoughts. By doing so, they can approach challenges with a fresh perspective and make better strategic decisions.

Biases can cloud judgment and lead to poor decision-making, so leaders should strive to identify and eliminate their own biases by seeking diverse perspectives and being open to feedback, ensuring decisions are based on objective analysis rather than preconceived notions. Assumptions can limit thinking and creativity, so leaders should question their assumptions and encourage their teams to do the same, fostering a culture of curiosity and critical thinking where assumptions are tested and validated before being accepted. Overcomplicated thoughts can create confusion and hinder clarity; therefore, leaders should aim to simplify their thinking by breaking down complex issues into manageable components, allowing for clearer analysis and more effective problem-solving.

Practising mindfulness can help leaders maintain a clear and focused mindset; techniques such as meditation, deep breathing, and mindfulness exercises enhance self-awareness and reduce stress, enabling leaders to stay present and attentive, thus improving their decision-making ability. Regular reflection allows leaders to clear their minds and gain insights by setting aside time for quiet contemplation or journaling to process their thoughts and emotions, which leads to greater clarity and understanding and provides opportunities to review past decisions and learn from experiences. Minimising distractions is key to maintaining focus, so leaders should create an environment that supports concentration through physical space arrangements or time management strategies, which may involve setting boundaries for uninterrupted work time, reducing digital distractions, and prioritising tasks effectively.

Encouraging diverse viewpoints within the team leads to more innovative and effective solutions, so leaders should promote an inclusive environment where different perspectives are valued and considered, enhancing the team's ability to approach challenges from multiple angles and develop well-rounded strategies. A beginner's mindset, which involves approaching problems with curiosity and openness, prevents complacency and fosters continuous improvement, so leaders should cultivate this mindset by being open to new ideas and willing to learn. Lifelong learning is essential for maintaining a fresh perspective; therefore, leaders should pursue ongoing education and professional development opportunities, staying informed about industry trends, new technologies, and best practices to adapt to changing circumstances and make more informed decisions.

Leaders should leverage analytical tools and methodologies, such as data analytics and scenario planning, to support clear and objective decision-making by evaluating options and assessing risks, thereby providing a solid foundation for making well-informed decisions. Effective decision-making involves balancing intuition with logical analysis, so leaders should trust their instincts while grounding their decisions in data and evidence, ensuring that decisions are both innovative and practical. Additionally, collaborative decision-making processes help build consensus and buy-in from the team, so leaders should facilitate open discussions, seek input from relevant stakeholders, and encourage constructive debate, ensuring that decisions are well-considered and supported by the team.

Leaders should model clarity in their communication and actions by being clear and concise, setting a standard for their teams to follow, which includes articulating goals, providing clear instructions, and avoiding ambiguity. Creating a culture that values clarity involves setting expectations for clear communication and decision-making; leaders should encourage transparency, provide training on effective communication, and recognise efforts to maintain clarity within the organisation.

LEADING WITH NON-ACTION (*WÚ WÉI* 無為/无为)

> *In loving the people and ruling the state, cannot he proceed without any (purpose of) action?*

Wú Wéi (無為/无为), a foundational concept in Taoist philosophy, translates to 'non-action' or 'effortless action.' It emphasises the idea of achieving goals by aligning with the natural order and flow of events rather than exerting force or imposing will. In strategic management, *Wú Wéi* means creating an environment where processes unfold naturally, and employees are empowered to act with autonomy and creativity.

Leaders practising *Wú Wéi* focus on creating conditions that allow work to flow naturally and smoothly by understanding and respecting the inherent dynamics of the organisation and the market, facilitating outcomes without constant intervention or micromanagement. Instead of pushing against obstacles, *Wú Wéi* encourages leaders to work with the natural currents, which might involve adjusting strategies to fit the changing environment, finding paths of least resistance, and leveraging existing strengths and opportunities.

Empowering employees is a key aspect of *Wú Wéi*; leaders should trust their team members and provide them with the autonomy to make decisions and take actions within their roles, fostering a sense of ownership and accountability that leads to higher motivation and performance. Additionally, leaders should focus on supporting the growth and development of their employees by providing the necessary resources, training, and mentorship, ensuring that the team is equipped to handle challenges independently.

Efficient and effective processes are the backbone of *Wú Wéi* in strategic management; leaders should strive to streamline operations by eliminating unnecessary steps, reducing bureaucracy, and implementing systems that facilitate smooth workflow, minimising friction and allowing the organisation to operate more seamlessly. Processes should also be designed to encourage innovation and creativity; leaders can achieve this by creating an environment that rewards experimentation and learning from failures, aligning with *Wú Wéi's* principle of allowing things to unfold naturally and fostering a culture of continuous improvement.

Leaders who practise *Wú Wéi* lead by example, demonstrating calm, confidence, and trust in their teams, setting a tone of effortless effectiveness and inspiring their teams to adopt similar behaviours. While practising non-action, leaders should still provide a clear vision and direction, serving as a guiding star to ensure all team members are aligned with the organisation's goals and mission. With this clarity, employees can navigate their roles independently, knowing their efforts contribute to a shared purpose.

Empowered employees are more engaged and committed to their work, and when team members feel trusted and valued, they are more likely to contribute their best efforts and take initiative. An environment that embraces *Wú Wéi* encourages creativity by removing the constraints of rigid control, allowing employees to explore new ideas and approaches, which leads to innovative solutions and continuous improvement. By aligning with the natural flow and reducing unnecessary interventions, organisations can achieve sustainable success, ensuring they remain adaptable and resilient in the face of change.

Cultivate a leadership style that prioritises trust and empowerment by delegating authority, encouraging autonomy, and providing support without micromanaging. Establish feedback loops for continuous learning and adaptation through regular check-ins and open communication channels, ensuring the organisation can respond to changing circumstances effectively. Practise mindful decision-making by taking time to reflect, gather input, and make thoughtful choices that align with the organisation's goals and values.

DEMONSTRATING SUBTLE LEADERSHIP

> In the opening and shutting of his gates of heaven, cannot he do so as a female bird? While his intelligence reaches in every direction, cannot he (appear to) be without knowledge?

Lao Tzu's analogy of a leader acting like a 'female bird' and appearing 'without knowledge' encapsulates the essence of subtle leadership. This style is characterised by facilitating and enabling success without seeking recognition or drawing attention. Subtle leaders guide their teams with a light touch, fostering an environment of trust and collaboration where everyone feels valued and empowered.

Subtle leaders facilitate rather than command by providing necessary resources, removing obstacles, and creating conditions for success; by stepping back and allowing their team to take the lead, they empower employees to take ownership of their work and achievements. Leaders who practise subtle leadership do not seek the spotlight but focus on the success of their team and organisation rather than personal accolades, building a culture of humility and collaboration where collective effort is celebrated over individual recognition.

Trust is the foundation of subtle leadership; leaders should demonstrate trust in their team's abilities by delegating tasks and giving employees the autonomy to make decisions, fostering a sense of responsibility and accountability that enhances overall performance and job satisfaction. Subtle leaders also encourage their team members to contribute their insights and ideas, creating an inclusive environment where everyone's voice is heard, promoting innovation and creativity. This collaborative approach ensures that the best ideas are brought to the forefront, leading to better decision-making and outcomes.

A key aspect of subtle leadership is promoting shared leadership by distributing responsibilities among team members based on their strengths and expertise, which encourages collaboration and mutual support as team members work together to achieve common goals. Subtle leaders recognise the contributions of their team members and provide opportunities for growth and development by offering constructive feedback, celebrating achievements, and supporting professional development initiatives. By investing in their team's growth, leaders ensure the organisation has a strong pipeline of future leaders.

Lao Tzu's concept of appearing 'without knowledge' emphasises humility, encouraging leaders to adopt a learner's mindset, remain open to new ideas, and admit when they do not have all the answers, which fosters an environment where team members feel comfortable sharing their expertise and perspectives. Active listening is a crucial skill for subtle leaders, as genuinely listening to their team members demonstrates respect and value for their input, helping leaders understand the needs and concerns of their team and enabling them to provide better support and guidance.

Leaders should model the behaviours they wish to see in their team, demonstrating humility, trust, and a collaborative spirit to set a positive example that inspires their team members to adopt similar behaviours. Open communication channels facilitate the free flow of ideas and feedback, so leaders should establish regular check-ins, team meetings, and feedback sessions to ensure that everyone feels heard and valued. Subtle leaders are adaptable and attuned to the dynamics of their team, adjusting their leadership style based on the needs and preferences of their team members to create a supportive and effective work environment.

Team members who feel valued and empowered are more engaged and committed to their work, with subtle leadership fostering a sense of ownership and pride, leading to higher levels of engagement and productivity. A collaborative environment encourages teamwork and mutual support, promoting a culture of shared responsibility where team members work together towards common goals. By focusing on the development and well-being of their team, subtle leaders create a strong and resilient organisation, ensuring sustainable success and preparing the organisation for future challenges and opportunities.

PRACTISING SELFLESSNESS & HUMILITY

> (The Tao) produces (all things) and nourishes them; it produces them and does not claim them as its own; it does all, and yet does not boast of it; it presides over all, and yet does not control them.

Lao Tzu highlights the Tao's qualities of nurturing without claiming ownership, acting without boasting, and guiding without controlling. Strategic leaders can draw inspiration from these principles, focusing on their role to support and nourish their teams. By practising selflessness and humility, leaders can create an environment where collaboration and mutual respect thrive, leading to greater innovation and empowerment.

Selfless leaders ensure that their teams have the resources they need to succeed, including access to tools, information, and support necessary for their roles. By prioritising the well-being and success of their employees, leaders create a foundation for sustainable growth. Additionally, leaders should invest in the personal and professional development of their team members by offering training opportunities, mentorship, and career advancement pathways, which not only enhances individual capabilities but also strengthens the overall team.

Leaders who do not seek credit for their actions build a culture of humility and collective achievement by celebrating team successes rather than individual accolades, fostering a sense of unity and shared purpose. Selfless leaders regularly acknowledge and appreciate the contributions of their team members, boosting morale and motivation as employees feel valued and respected for their efforts.

Collaboration is essential for innovation and problem-solving, so leaders should create opportunities for team members to work together, share ideas, and support each other, which builds trust and enhances the collective strength of the organisation. Leaders should also listen actively to their team members' ideas, concerns, and feedback, demonstrating respect and empathy to ensure that everyone feels heard and valued. Active listening provides valuable insights that can inform better decision-making.

Innovation flourishes in an environment where team members feel safe to share their ideas without fear of judgment, so leaders should foster a culture that encourages experimentation and learning from failures, driving continuous improvement and creative solutions. Empowering employees to take ownership of their work leads to higher engagement and innovation, so leaders should provide the autonomy to make decisions and pursue initiatives within their roles, which builds confidence and encourages proactive problem-solving.

Selfless leaders act as facilitators, guiding their teams without micromanaging, allowing employees to develop their skills and take initiative while providing support and direction when needed. Trust is the cornerstone of effective leadership, and by trusting their team members to perform their roles effectively, leaders create an environment of mutual respect and accountability. Trust-based leadership empowers employees and fosters a culture of ownership and responsibility.

Leaders should embody humility in their actions and decisions, demonstrating modesty and a focus on the collective good to set a powerful example for their teams, inspiring others to adopt similar values and attitudes. Humble leaders are open to feedback and willing to learn from their experiences, fostering a culture of continuous learning and adaptation by encouraging feedback from their team members and acting on it to enhance their effectiveness.

Selfless and humble leadership builds strong, trusting relationships within the team, forming the foundation for effective collaboration and long-term success. By focusing on the well-being and development of their team, leaders ensure sustainable growth for the organisation, leading to higher employee retention, increased engagement, and better overall performance. Teams led by selfless and humble leaders are more resilient and adaptable, as the culture of mutual respect, trust, and collaboration enables the organisation to navigate challenges and seize opportunities more effectively.

CHAPTER 11 – PRESENCE & ABSENCE

Chapter 11 of the *Tao Te Ching* emphasises the concept of emptiness and the essential role of space and absence in creating utility and function. Here's how these teachings can be applied to modern-day strategic management:

RECOGNISING THE VALUE OF EMPTINESS & SPACE

The thirty spokes unite in the one nave; but it is on the empty space (for the axle), that the use of the wheel depends.

Lao Tzu's metaphor of the wheel highlights the essential nature of empty space. Just as the utility of the wheel depends on the empty space for the axle, the effectiveness of strategic management can greatly benefit from recognising and valuing the concept of emptiness or space. This idea emphasises that space—both physical and mental—is crucial for fostering creativity, innovation, and effective problem-solving.

Allowing for unstructured time in schedules gives employees the freedom to think creatively and explore new ideas, which can lead to breakthroughs and innovations that structured schedules may not permit. Providing open and flexible work environments can stimulate creativity and collaboration by designing office spaces that encourage movement and interaction or implementing flexible work arrangements that allow employees to choose when and where they work best, helping them feel more comfortable and inspired, leading to higher productivity and creativity.

Innovation requires an environment where employees feel safe to experiment and take risks, so leaders should create a culture that encourages trial and error, viewing failure as a learning opportunity rather than a setback. By providing this space for experimentation, leaders can foster continuous improvement and innovation. Additionally, encouraging diverse perspectives within the team can lead to more innovative solutions, as leaders should promote an inclusive environment where different viewpoints and ideas are valued, leading to more creative and effective problem-solving.

Regular reflection is essential for personal and organisational growth, so leaders should allocate time for employees to reflect on their experiences, successes, and challenges, leading to deeper insights and a better understanding of how to improve processes and strategies. Providing space for professional development helps employees grow and advance in their careers, so leaders should encourage continuous learning through training programmes, workshops, and other educational opportunities, ensuring that the organisation remains competitive and capable of adapting to new challenges.

Overloading teams with tasks can lead to burnout and decreased effectiveness, so leaders should monitor workloads and ensure that employees have a manageable amount of work. By balancing workloads, leaders can maintain high levels of productivity and employee well-being. Prioritising tasks and projects helps prevent overwhelm and ensures that the most important work gets done, so leaders should provide clear guidance on priorities and support their teams in focusing on what matters most, creating a more organised and efficient work environment.

Space allows for better collaboration, so leaders should create opportunities for team members to work together, share ideas, and support each other, using both physical and virtual collaborative spaces to enhance communication and teamwork. Creating space for open communication and feedback builds trust within the team, fostering an environment where employees feel comfortable sharing their thoughts and concerns, which is essential for effective collaboration and innovation.

Leaders should model the importance of balance by demonstrating how to create space for creativity, reflection, and personal well-being, inspiring their teams to adopt similar practices and values. Recognising the value of downtime and rest is crucial for sustained productivity, so leaders should encourage employees to take breaks, use their vacation time, and maintain a healthy work-life balance, helping to prevent burnout and promote long-term well-being.

By creating space for creativity and innovation, organisations can continuously generate new ideas and solutions, which is essential for staying competitive in a rapidly changing market. An organisation that values space is better equipped to adapt to changes and navigate challenges, as the flexibility and openness fostered by recognising space contribute to greater resilience and adaptability. Providing space for reflection, development, and well-being leads to higher employee satisfaction and retention, as employees who feel supported and valued are more likely to be engaged and committed to the organisation.

FOSTERING INNOVATION THROUGH FLEXIBILITY

> *Clay is fashioned into vessels; but it is on their empty hollowness, that their use depends.*

Lao Tzu's analogy of clay vessels emphasises that the utility of objects often arises from their empty spaces. In the context of business, this principle translates to the significance of flexibility and adaptability in fostering innovation. By creating an environment where there is space for experimentation and the acceptance of failure, leaders can drive continuous improvement and cultivate a culture of innovation.

Innovation requires a willingness to take risks, so leaders should cultivate a culture where team members feel safe to explore new ideas without fear of failure by setting aside time and resources for experimentation and innovation projects. When employees know their creative efforts are valued, they are more likely to take initiative and think outside the box. Not every innovation effort will succeed, and that's okay; leaders should frame failures as valuable learning experiences. By analysing what went wrong and why, teams can gain insights that inform future efforts, shifting the mindset from fear of failure to embracing it as part of the innovation process, encouraging more bold and creative thinking.

Flexible work environments support innovation by allowing employees to adapt their workflows to suit their creative processes, which can include flexible work hours, remote work options, or collaborative spaces designed to inspire creativity, leading to greater productivity and innovation. Implementing agile methodologies can further enhance flexibility and responsiveness by involving iterative development, frequent feedback, and adaptive planning, allowing teams to quickly pivot and refine their ideas based on real-time feedback, making the innovation process more fluid and dynamic.

Innovation is often an iterative process, so leaders should encourage teams to develop, test, and refine their ideas in cycles, allowing for constant improvement and adaptation, leading to more robust and successful outcomes. Establishing regular feedback loops ensures that insights and suggestions are continuously gathered and integrated into the innovation process, so leaders should create channels for open communication where team members can share their experiences and ideas, fostering a culture of continuous improvement.

Empowered employees are more likely to innovate, so leaders should provide the autonomy and resources necessary for teams to explore new ideas, trusting them to take ownership of their projects and encouraging them to think creatively. Recognising and celebrating both successes and well-intentioned failures reinforces the value of innovation, so leaders should highlight and reward creative efforts, regardless of the outcome, to show that all contributions are appreciated and integral to the organisation's growth.

Leaders should model flexibility in their actions and decision-making by showing a willingness to adapt and embrace change, setting a powerful example for their teams and encouraging a similar mindset throughout the organisation. Additionally, leaders should demonstrate open-mindedness by actively seeking out new ideas and perspectives, being receptive to suggestions from all levels of the organisation, and fostering an inclusive environment where diverse viewpoints are valued.

Organisations that prioritise flexibility and innovation are better positioned to stay competitive in a rapidly changing market by continuously evolving and adapting, seizing new opportunities, and responding effectively to challenges. A flexible approach to innovation enhances organisational resilience, as teams accustomed to adapting and experimenting are more agile and capable of navigating uncertainty, ensuring the organisation remains robust and forward-thinking. Additionally, a culture that values innovation and flexibility leads to higher employee engagement and satisfaction, as employees who feel empowered to contribute their ideas and see their impact are more motivated and committed to the organisation's success.

DESIGNING FUNCTIONAL STRUCTURES

> *The door and windows are cut out (from the walls) to form an apartment; but it is on the empty space (within), that its use depends.*

Lao Tzu's metaphor emphasises that the utility of an apartment comes from its empty spaces, such as doors and windows, which enable functionality. Similarly, in strategic management, creating functional organisational structures involves designing spaces—both physical and metaphorical—that facilitate effective communication, collaboration, and innovation. These structures should be adaptable and supportive, allowing for interaction and flow without unnecessary constraints.

Designing office spaces that encourage teamwork can significantly enhance productivity and innovation, with open-plan layouts, collaborative zones, and flexible seating arrangements promoting interaction among team members, breaking down silos, and fostering a culture of collaboration. Shared workstations where employees can work together on projects foster collaboration and spontaneous idea-sharing, while breakout rooms provide small, private spaces for focused work or team meetings, ensuring a balance between open spaces and quiet areas. Flexibility in workspace design allows employees to choose the environment that best suits their task, including quiet zones for concentrated work, casual meeting areas for brainstorming sessions, and adaptable spaces that can be reconfigured as needed, supporting various work styles and activities and enhancing overall productivity.

Setting up communication channels that are open and transparent ensures that information flows freely within the organisation. This involves consistent communication through team meetings, newsletters, and updates to keep everyone informed and aligned with organisational goals. Encouraging an open-door policy where employees feel comfortable approaching leaders and colleagues with ideas, concerns, or feedback fosters trust and openness. Additionally, leveraging digital tools like Slack, Microsoft Teams, and Zoom facilitates communication in modern workplaces, enabling instant messaging, video conferencing, and collaborative workspaces, ensuring that remote and in-office teams stay connected and engaged.

Overly rigid or bureaucratic processes can stifle creativity and slow down decision-making, so leaders should strive to streamline processes by removing unnecessary steps and simplifying workflows. This involves adopting lean management principles to eliminate waste and optimise processes, ensuring that every step adds value, and granting employees the authority to make decisions within their roles to reduce bottlenecks and speed up project timelines. Agility in organisational processes allows teams to adapt quickly to changes and new opportunities, so implementing agile methodologies, such as Scrum or Kanban, enables iterative progress, flexibility, and rapid response to feedback, supporting continuous improvement and dynamic project management.

A culture of continuous improvement thrives on regular feedback, so leaders should create mechanisms for gathering and acting on feedback from employees at all levels, such as anonymous surveys, suggestion boxes, and regular feedback sessions or 360-degree reviews, to encourage open dialogue and foster a culture of transparency and improvement. Recognising and celebrating improvements, whether big or small, motivates employees to continue striving for excellence, so leaders should be open to adapting processes based on feedback and continuously seeking ways to enhance efficiency and effectiveness.

Just as empty spaces in an apartment are essential for its use, creating space within organisational structures is crucial for innovation. This involves providing dedicated spaces where employees can experiment with new ideas, technologies, and approaches without the constraints of their daily responsibilities, and organising events and workshops focused on creative problem-solving and innovation, encouraging employees to think outside the box and collaborate on new solutions.

Leaders should model open and transparent communication in their interactions by sharing information openly and encouraging dialogue, setting a standard for the rest of the organisation. Demonstrating flexibility in leadership style and decision-making encourages employees to adopt a similar approach, as leaders should be adaptable, open to new ideas, and willing to adjust strategies as needed.

BALANCING PRESENCE & ABSENCE

> Therefore, what has a (positive) existence serves for profitable adaptation, and what has not that for (actual) usefulness.

Lao Tzu's insight in this passage underscores the importance of balancing what is present with what is absent. In strategic management, this balance is crucial for creating an organisation that is both stable and adaptable. By understanding and leveraging the interplay between tangible resources (presence) and intangible potential (absence), leaders can develop more strategic and innovative approaches to business challenges.

The tangible assets of an organisation, such as financial capital, human talent, and technology, form its backbone, and effective management of these resources ensures smooth and efficient operations, so leaders should ensure that these resources are optimised and aligned with organisational goals. Organisational structures, including hierarchies, roles, and responsibilities, provide a framework for operations, streamlining processes, facilitating communication, and ensuring accountability, so leaders should design structures that support organisational objectives while allowing for flexibility and growth. Strategic plans and goals guide the organisation's direction and actions, providing clarity and focus, enabling the pursuit of its mission effectively, so leaders should develop strategies that are adaptable to changing circumstances and aligned with the organisation's core values.

Creating space within the organisation allows for creativity, reflection, and innovation, whether through unstructured time for brainstorming, flexible work environments, or open communication channels, fostering a culture of continuous improvement and new ideas. Flexibility involves the capacity to adapt to new information, changing conditions, and unexpected challenges, enabling organisations that prioritise flexibility to pivot quickly, explore new opportunities, and stay resilient in the face of uncertainty. Leaders should promote a flexible mindset and agile practices. The potential within an organisation represents its untapped opportunities and capacities for growth, so recognising and nurturing this potential involves investing in employee development, exploring new markets, and fostering an entrepreneurial spirit, with leaders identifying and leveraging the potential to drive innovation and progress.

Leaders should strategically allocate resources, structures, and strategies while ensuring there is enough space and flexibility for growth and adaptation through continuous assessment and adjustment to maintain balance. By creating an environment that values both presence and absence, leaders can encourage innovation, such as setting aside dedicated time for creative projects, promoting cross-functional collaboration, and rewarding innovative thinking. Additionally, fostering an inclusive culture that values diverse perspectives and encourages open dialogue allows leaders to create opportunities for all team members to contribute their ideas and insights, leveraging the collective potential of the organisation.

Incorporate both presence and absence into strategic planning by developing robust strategies while leaving room for flexibility and innovation, creating plans that are detailed yet adaptable for adjustments as needed. Implement feedback mechanisms that capture both current performance and future potential, with regular feedback loops enabling continuous improvement and identifying areas needing more space or flexibility. Leaders should practise mindful leadership, being aware of the present needs of the organisation while envisioning its future potential, allowing for balanced decision-making that considers both immediate and long-term goals.

Organisations that balance presence and absence are better equipped for sustainable growth, ensuring current operations are efficient while allowing for innovation and adaptation. The interplay between stability and flexibility builds organisational resilience, helping organisations navigate challenges more effectively and emerge stronger. Creating space for creativity and innovation leads to the development of new ideas and solutions, keeping the organisation competitive and forward-thinking. A balanced approach fosters a positive work environment where employees feel valued and empowered, leading to higher job satisfaction, productivity, and retention.

CHAPTER 12 — SENSORY OVERLOAD

Chapter 12 of the *Tao Te Ching* emphasises the distractions of sensory indulgence and the importance of focusing on essential needs. Here's how these teachings can be applied to modern-day strategic management:

AVOIDING SENSORY OVERLOAD & DISTRACTIONS

> *Colour's five hues from th' eyes their sight will take; Music's five notes the ears as deaf can make; The flavours five deprive the mouth of taste; The chariot course, and the wild hunting waste Make mad the mind; and objects rare and strange, Sought for, men's conduct will to evil change.*

Lao Tzu's passage highlights the negative impact of excessive sensory stimuli on our perception and judgment. In the context of business, sensory overload can lead to distractions, reduced productivity, and poor decision-making. Strategic leaders should recognise the impact of excessive stimuli and work towards creating environments that minimise unnecessary distractions, enabling teams to maintain focus on important tasks and goals.

Sensory overload can overwhelm employees, making it difficult for them to concentrate on their work, leading to mental fatigue and reduced productivity. Leaders should be aware of this and take steps to mitigate its effects. When surrounded by distractions, it becomes challenging to process information effectively and make sound decisions, so leaders need to ensure that their teams have the mental clarity required for critical thinking and decision-making by minimising unnecessary distractions.

Leaders should identify and minimise common sources of distractions in the workplace, such as reducing noise levels, managing visual clutter, and controlling the use of personal devices during work hours to create a calm and organised work environment that helps employees focus better. Establishing quiet zones or designated areas for focused work, free from noise and other distractions, can help employees concentrate on tasks that require deep concentration. Additionally, encouraging mindfulness practices, such as meditation and deep breathing exercises, can help employees manage stress and improve focus, so leaders can promote these practices by incorporating mindfulness sessions into the workday or providing resources for employees to practise on their own.

Encouraging regular breaks helps prevent mental fatigue and sensory overload, allowing employees to recharge and return to their tasks with renewed focus and energy. Offering flexible work schedules can help employees manage their workload and reduce stress, supporting a more balanced and effective work environment. Multitasking can lead to cognitive overload and decreased efficiency, so leaders should encourage employees to focus on one task at a time, prioritising quality over quantity to improve concentration and overall performance.

Implementing periods of digital detox, where employees disconnect from digital devices, can help reduce sensory overload, so leaders can designate specific times or days for digital detox, encouraging employees to engage in offline activities and interactions. Efficient communication tools and practices can help minimise unnecessary interruptions, so leaders should establish clear communication protocols, such as designated times for checking emails or using project management tools to streamline communication and reduce information overload.

Leaders should model focused behaviour by demonstrating effective time management and minimising their own distractions, setting a positive example to inspire their teams to adopt similar practices. Fostering a culture that values focus and concentration involves recognising and rewarding efforts to minimise distractions, so leaders should promote and support initiatives that enhance productivity and well-being, reinforcing the importance of maintaining focus.

By minimising distractions and managing sensory overload, organisations can achieve higher levels of productivity, as employees who are able to focus on their tasks are more likely to complete them efficiently and effectively. Reducing sensory overload and promoting a balanced work environment contribute to employees' overall well-being, leading to higher job satisfaction, lower stress levels, and better mental health. A focused and clear-minded workforce is better equipped to make sound decisions, so creating an environment that supports mental clarity enhances the quality of decision-making within the organisation. Organisations that prioritise focus and minimise distractions are better positioned for sustainable growth, ensuring that employees remain engaged, productive, and capable of driving the organisation towards its strategic goals.

PRIORITISING ESSENTIAL NEEDS OVER DESIRES

Therefore the sage seeks to satisfy (the craving of) the belly, and not the (insatiable longing of the) eyes. He puts from him the latter, and prefers to seek the former.

Lao Tzu's passage emphasises the importance of fulfilling essential needs rather than indulging in endless desires. In the context of strategic management, this means that leaders should focus on meeting the fundamental needs of their organisation and employees, such as job satisfaction, work-life balance, and professional development. By addressing these core needs, leaders can create a stable and motivated workforce, reducing the negative effects of constantly chasing after the latest trends or superficial gains.

Ensuring that employees find meaning and fulfillment in their work is crucial for maintaining motivation and productivity, so leaders should strive to create roles that align with employees' skills and interests, provide opportunities for challenging and engaging work, and recognise and reward contributions. Matching employees with tasks that utilise their strengths and passions can lead to higher job satisfaction, so leaders should regularly review job roles and responsibilities to ensure alignment with individual capabilities and interests. Providing opportunities for employees to tackle challenging and meaningful projects can boost engagement, so leaders should encourage innovation and creativity, allowing employees to take ownership of their work.

Maintaining a healthy work-life balance is essential for employee well-being and overall organisational health, so leaders should promote policies and practices that support this balance, such as flexible work schedules, remote work options, and time-off policies. Allowing employees to have flexible work hours or remote work options can help them manage their personal and professional responsibilities more effectively, leading to reduced stress and increased productivity. Encouraging employees to take regular breaks and vacations ensures that they have time to rest and recharge, so leaders should model this behaviour by taking their own time off and respecting employees' need for downtime.

Investing in employees' professional growth fosters a culture of continuous improvement and loyalty, so leaders should provide access to training, mentorship, and career advancement opportunities. Offering regular training sessions and educational opportunities helps employees develop new skills and stay up-to-date with industry trends, so leaders should support ongoing learning by providing access to courses, workshops, and conferences. Implementing mentorship programmes allows employees to learn from more experienced colleagues, receive guidance, and gain valuable insights into their career paths, so leaders should encourage mentorship relationships and recognise the contributions of both mentors and mentees.

Constantly chasing after the latest trends can lead to distraction and a lack of focus on what truly matters, so leaders should carefully evaluate new trends and technologies, adopting only those that align with the organisation's core values and strategic goals. Leaders should assess the potential impact of new trends on their organisation, considering factors such as relevance, feasibility, and long-term benefits to ensure that resources are allocated wisely and effectively. By staying true to the organisation's core values, leaders can avoid the pitfalls of superficial gains and make decisions with the long-term success of the organisation in mind.

Focusing on long-term goals rather than short-term gains helps create a stable and sustainable organisation, so leaders should develop and communicate a clear vision that guides the organisation towards its long-term objectives. A well-defined vision provides direction and purpose, helping employees understand the organisation's long-term goals and their role in achieving them, so leaders should regularly communicate this vision and ensure it is integrated into all aspects of the organisation. Developing strategies that prioritise long-term growth over short-term profits ensures the organisation's stability and resilience, so leaders should balance immediate needs with future opportunities, making decisions that support sustainable success.

Recognising and appreciating employees' efforts and achievements fosters a positive work environment and boosts morale, so leaders should implement regular recognition programmes and celebrate both individual and team successes. Implementing recognition programmes that highlight employees' contributions on a regular basis helps maintain motivation and engagement, so leaders should use various methods, such as awards, shout-outs, and team celebrations, to recognise achievements. Celebrating both small and large successes creates a sense of accomplishment and encourages employees to continue striving for excellence, so leaders should take the time to acknowledge milestones and express gratitude for their team's hard work.

Leaders who prioritise their employees' needs and well-being create a supportive and empowering work environment by being approachable, providing regular feedback, and offering support and resources to help employees succeed. Being approachable and accessible to employees fosters open communication and trust, creating an environment where employees feel comfortable sharing their ideas, concerns, and feedback. Offering support and resources to help employees overcome challenges and achieve their goals demonstrates a commitment to their success, with leaders actively listening to their team's needs and providing the necessary tools and assistance.

CHAPTER 13 – FAVOUR & DISGRACE

Chapter 13 of the *Tao Te Ching* explores the themes of favour and disgrace, honour and calamity, and the importance of selflessness in leadership. Here's how these teachings can be applied to modern-day strategic management:

MANAGING RECOGNITION & CRITICISM

Favour and disgrace would seem equally to be feared; honour and great calamity, to be regarded as personal conditions (of the same kind).

Lao Tzu's wisdom in this passage highlights the transient nature of both recognition (favour) and criticism (disgrace). In strategic management, it is crucial for leaders to understand that these external evaluations are temporary and should be approached with a balanced and composed mindset. By maintaining equanimity, leaders can navigate the highs of praise and the lows of criticism effectively, ensuring rational decision-making and consistent leadership.

Recognising that both praise and criticism are fleeting helps leaders maintain a balanced perspective, avoiding becoming overly attached to positive recognition or excessively distressed by negative feedback, thus allowing for steady and objective leadership. Managing emotions is key to maintaining equanimity, so leaders should develop strategies for emotional regulation, such as mindfulness practices, reflective journaling, or seeking support from mentors. By managing their emotional responses, leaders can remain calm and focused in the face of both praise and criticism.

While recognition can be gratifying, it is important for leaders to stay grounded and humble, acknowledging their team's contributions and sharing the credit for successes to reinforce a culture of collaboration and mutual respect. Instead of becoming complacent with praise, leaders should use positive feedback as motivation for continuous improvement, recognising areas of strength to build on successes and strive for greater achievements. Praise can sometimes lead to ego inflation, negatively impacting decision-making and relationships, so leaders should remain self-aware and avoid letting praise inflate their sense of self-importance, as humility fosters better team dynamics and more effective leadership.

Leaders should view criticism as an opportunity for growth and improvement, as constructive feedback provides valuable insights into areas that need attention. By approaching criticism with an open mind, leaders can identify ways to enhance their performance and the organisation's success. It is important for leaders to separate personal feelings from professional feedback, seeing criticism as a commentary on performance or actions, not a personal attack. This distinction helps leaders respond to feedback objectively and constructively. Leaders should embrace a learning mindset, using criticism as a catalyst for adaptation and growth, reflecting on feedback and making necessary adjustments to continuously evolve and improve their leadership approach.

A clear and consistent vision helps leaders stay focused on long-term goals, regardless of external praise or criticism, ensuring that their approach remains steady and purpose-driven by aligning decisions and actions with this vision. Leaders should anchor their actions and decisions in the organisation's core values, providing a stable foundation that guides them through both positive and negative feedback while maintaining integrity and consistency. Open and transparent communication builds trust and fosters a supportive environment, so leaders should communicate honestly with their teams about successes and challenges, reinforcing a culture of openness and continuous improvement.

Leaders should set aside time for regular reflection on their experiences, feedback, and decisions to gain insights, recognise patterns, and maintain a balanced perspective. Engaging with a diverse range of perspectives provides a more comprehensive understanding of feedback, so leaders should seek input from various stakeholders, including team members, peers, and mentors, to gain a well-rounded view. Building resilience helps leaders navigate the ups and downs of recognition and criticism, which involves developing coping strategies, maintaining a positive outlook, and learning from both successes and setbacks.

Leaders who manage recognition and criticism effectively are better positioned to sustain high performance by maintaining focus and motivation, driving continuous improvement, and achieving long-term success. A balanced and composed leader fosters a positive team environment where employees feel supported, valued, and motivated, leading to higher levels of engagement and collaboration. Equanimity in the face of praise and criticism enables leaders to make more rational and strategic decisions, ensuring that decisions are based on objective analysis and aligned with the organisation's goals.

UNDERSTANDING THE TEMPORARY NATURE OF SUCCESS & FAILURE

What is meant by speaking thus of favour and disgrace? Disgrace is being in a low position (after the enjoyment of favour). The getting that (favour) leads to the apprehension (of losing it), and the losing it leads to the fear of (still greater calamity).

Lao Tzu's passage emphasises that both success (favour) and failure (disgrace) are temporary states. For strategic leaders, this means not becoming overly attached to achievements or disheartened by setbacks. Recognising the transient nature of these experiences helps leaders maintain perspective, focusing on long-term goals and continuous improvement rather than being swayed by short-term fluctuations.

Success can be gratifying, but becoming too attached to it can lead to complacency and fear of failure, so leaders should celebrate achievements but remain grounded, understanding that success is not permanent, which encourages ongoing efforts to improve and innovate. Failure is an inevitable part of any journey, so leaders should view setbacks as opportunities for learning and growth rather than as permanent defeats. By understanding that failure is temporary, leaders can remain resilient, quickly recovering and adapting to new circumstances.

A clear, long-term vision helps leaders stay focused on what truly matters, acting as a guiding star that keeps the organisation aligned with its core mission and values, so leaders should regularly communicate this vision, ensuring that short-term successes and failures do not distract from long-term objectives. Embracing a mindset of continuous improvement means always seeking ways to enhance processes, products, and performance, so leaders should encourage their teams to learn from both successes and failures, fostering a culture of innovation and adaptability.

Emotional reactions to success or failure can lead to impulsive and short-sighted decisions, so leaders should strive to make decisions based on rational analysis and strategic thinking, considering long-term implications rather than immediate emotional responses. Utilising data and evidence-based decision-making helps leaders maintain objectivity, so by relying on facts and analytics, leaders can make informed choices that support sustained growth and resilience, regardless of short-term fluctuations.

Consistency in leadership fosters trust and reliability, so leaders should maintain a steady approach, providing clear guidance and support regardless of the organisation's immediate successes or challenges, creating a sense of security and confidence within the team. Open and honest communication helps manage expectations and maintain morale, so leaders should be transparent about both successes and failures, discussing lessons learned and plans for moving forward to reinforce a culture of trust and mutual respect.

Leaders should regularly reflect on their experiences, analysing both successes and failures to identify key takeaways, which helps maintain perspective and continuously improve their approach. Engaging with mentors and support networks provides valuable insights and guidance, offering perspective from those with more experience and helping navigate the highs and lows of their journey. Recognising achievements is important but should be balanced with an understanding of the broader context, so leaders should celebrate successes while also acknowledging areas for improvement and setting new goals.

By recognising the temporary nature of success and failure, leaders can maintain sustained motivation, encouraging ongoing effort and resilience to drive long-term performance and growth. Understanding transience helps leaders remain adaptable, ready to pivot and respond to changing circumstances, ensuring the organisation can navigate challenges and seize new opportunities. A culture that values continuous improvement and learning from experience fosters a positive and dynamic work environment, where employees feel engaged, supported, and motivated to contribute to the organisation's success. Leaders who prioritise long-term goals over short-term fluctuations can steer their organisations towards sustained success, ensuring efforts align with the organisation's mission and vision, driving meaningful and impactful outcomes.

PRACTISING SELFLESSNESS & HUMILITY

What makes me liable to great calamity is my having the body (which I call myself); if I had not the body, what great calamity could come to me?

Lao Tzu's passage highlights the critical role of selflessness in leadership. When leaders prioritise the needs of their organisation and team above their own personal gain, they can make more objective and effective decisions. By practising selflessness and humility, leaders reduce the fear of personal failure or disgrace, enabling them to take calculated risks and innovate confidently.

Leaders should focus on the long-term success and well-being of the organisation rather than seeking personal accolades, making decisions that benefit the collective good, even if it requires personal sacrifice. By keeping the organisation's mission and goals at the forefront, leaders can steer their teams towards sustained success. When ego is set aside, leaders can make decisions based on rational analysis and the best available information, allowing for more effective problem-solving and strategic planning, as decisions are not clouded by personal biases or desires for recognition.

Selfless leaders are more willing to take calculated risks because they are not driven by the fear of personal failure, fostering innovation and allowing the organisation to explore new opportunities and ideas. This openness to risk-taking encourages a culture where experimentation is valued, and failure is seen as a stepping stone to success. A selfless approach helps leaders view mistakes as learning opportunities rather than personal setbacks. By fostering an environment where team members feel safe to take risks and learn from failures, leaders can drive continuous improvement and creative problem-solving.

Humble leaders acknowledge the contributions of their team members and share credit for successes, building trust and morale as employees feel valued and appreciated for their efforts.

Regularly highlighting and celebrating team achievements reinforces a collaborative and supportive culture. Additionally, humble leaders actively seek input and feedback from their team members, leveraging diverse perspectives and expertise within the organisation for better decision-making and stronger outcomes. Creating channels for open communication and encouraging team members to share their ideas and insights is essential for fostering this inclusive approach.

Selfless leaders empower their employees by providing the autonomy and resources they need to succeed, fostering a sense of ownership and accountability, and motivating employees to take initiative and contribute their best efforts. Investing in the development and growth of team members demonstrates a leader's commitment to their well-being and success, so leaders should provide opportunities for professional development, mentorship, and career advancement, helping employees achieve their full potential.

A culture of selflessness and humility strengthens team dynamics by promoting mutual respect and collaboration, so leaders should encourage teamwork and create an environment where diverse perspectives are valued and leveraged for collective success. Organisations led by selfless and humble leaders are more resilient and adaptable, as this resilience comes from a shared commitment to the organisation's goals and a supportive culture that encourages learning and growth. By fostering resilience, leaders ensure that the organisation can navigate challenges and seize opportunities effectively.

Selfless and humble leadership drives sustainable growth by prioritising the organisation's long-term success over short-term gains, ensuring decisions are made with a focus on enduring impact and continuous improvement. A culture of selflessness and humility creates a positive and inclusive work environment, where employees are more likely to feel engaged, motivated, and loyal to the organisation, leading to higher retention and overall performance. By reducing the fear of failure and encouraging calculated risks, selfless leaders foster a culture of innovation, allowing the organisation to stay competitive and forward-thinking, continually adapting to changing market conditions.

LEADING WITH EMPATHY & RESPECT

> *Therefore he who would administer the kingdom, honouring it as he honours his own person, may be employed to govern it, and he who would administer it with the love which he bears to his own person may be entrusted with it.*

Lao Tzu's wisdom emphasises the importance of empathy and respect in leadership. Effective leaders understand that their team members deserve the same care and consideration they would want for themselves. By fostering a positive and collaborative work environment, leaders can ensure that employees feel valued and motivated. Demonstrating genuine concern for the well-being of the team builds trust and loyalty, ultimately leading to a more cohesive and productive organisation.

Empathy begins with active listening, so leaders should make an effort to listen to their team members' concerns, ideas, and feedback without interrupting or judging, demonstrating respect and showing that they value their employees' perspectives. Recognising and appreciating employees' hard work and contributions fosters a positive work environment, so leaders should regularly express gratitude and acknowledge their team members' efforts, whether through verbal praise, written notes, or public recognition. Leaders should also offer support to their team members in both their professional and personal lives, providing resources for professional development, offering flexible work arrangements to accommodate personal needs, and being available to discuss any challenges or concerns.

Collaboration is key to a successful organisation, so leaders should create opportunities for team members to work together on projects, share ideas, and support each other, encouraging innovation and enhancing overall team performance. Trust is the foundation of a strong team, and leaders can build trust by being transparent, reliable, and consistent in their actions and decisions. When employees trust their leaders, they are more likely to feel secure and committed to the organisation. An inclusive work environment values diverse perspectives and ensures that all team members feel welcome and respected, so leaders should actively promote inclusivity by encouraging diverse viewpoints and addressing any issues of discrimination or exclusion.

Leaders should recognise the importance of work-life balance and encourage employees to take care of their well-being by promoting the use of vacation time, supporting flexible work schedules, and creating a culture where taking breaks is encouraged. Providing opportunities for professional growth and development shows that leaders care about their employees' future, so they should support ongoing learning through training programmes, mentorship, and career advancement opportunities. When employees raise concerns, leaders should address them promptly and effectively, demonstrating that they take their team members' issues seriously and are committed to finding solutions.

Consistency in words and actions is crucial for building trust, so leaders should align their behaviour with the organisation's values and goals, demonstrating integrity and reliability. Empowering employees to make decisions and take ownership of their work fosters a sense of trust and confidence, so leaders should delegate authority and provide the necessary resources and support, allowing team members to thrive and contribute meaningfully. Celebrating both individual and team successes reinforces a sense of community and shared purpose, so leaders should create opportunities for team members to celebrate achievements together, whether through team meetings, social events, or recognition programmes.

When employees feel valued and respected, they are more likely to be engaged and motivated, leading to higher levels of productivity, creativity, and overall job satisfaction. A team that operates in a positive and respectful environment is more cohesive and collaborative, enhancing communication, problem-solving, and the ability to work together effectively towards common goals. Organisations known for their empathetic and respectful leadership are more likely to attract and retain top talent, extending this positive reputation to clients, partners, and stakeholders, thereby enhancing overall success. Leading with empathy and respect creates a strong foundation for long-term success, fostering a supportive and inclusive culture that ensures the organisation can navigate challenges, seize opportunities, and achieve sustainable growth.

CHAPTER 14 – THE FORMLESS TAO

Chapter 14 of the *Tao Te Ching* delves into the elusive and intangible nature of the Tao, emphasising the importance of recognising and embracing the subtle and formless. Here's how these teachings can be applied to modern-day strategic management:

EMBRACING THE INTANGIBLE & UNSEEN

> *We look at it, and we do not see it, and we name it 'the Equable.' We listen to it, and we do not hear it, and we name it 'the Inaudible.' We try to grasp it, and do not get hold of it, and we name it 'the Subtle.'*

Lao Tzu's passage highlights the significance of intangible and unseen elements. In the context of strategic management, it underscores the importance of acknowledging and valuing aspects of business that are not always visible or quantifiable. Elements such as company culture, employee morale, and brand reputation, though subtle, play a crucial role in the success of an organisation. Leaders should focus on these subtleties and work to cultivate a positive and supportive environment.

Company culture represents the shared values, beliefs, and behaviours that shape how employees interact and work together. A strong, positive culture fosters a sense of belonging and purpose, driving employee engagement and satisfaction. Leaders play a pivotal role in shaping and nurturing company culture by clearly articulating the organisation's values, leading by example, and fostering an inclusive environment where everyone feels valued and respected. Ensuring that company culture aligns with the organisation's mission and goals is essential, so leaders should regularly assess and refine the culture to support strategic objectives and enhance overall performance.

Employee morale refers to the overall outlook, attitude, satisfaction, and confidence that employees feel at work, with high morale leading to increased productivity, creativity, and retention, while low morale can result in disengagement and high turnover. Leaders can boost employee morale by recognising achievements, providing opportunities for growth, and ensuring a healthy work-life balance, regularly soliciting feedback and addressing concerns to maintain high morale. Prioritising employee well-being through supportive policies, mental health resources, and a positive work environment is crucial, as leaders should create a culture that values and promotes well-being, enhancing overall morale and performance.

Brand reputation is the perception of the organisation by its stakeholders, including customers, employees, and the public, with a strong, positive reputation building trust, loyalty, and competitive advantage. Leaders should cultivate trust by consistently delivering on promises, maintaining transparency, and demonstrating ethical behaviour, enhancing stakeholder confidence and loyalty through reliability and integrity. Protecting brand reputation involves effectively managing challenges and crises, so leaders must be prepared to address issues promptly, communicate openly, and take responsibility for resolving problems to maintain trust and credibility.

Open and transparent communication fosters a supportive environment where employees feel comfortable sharing ideas and concerns, so leaders should promote regular dialogue, provide constructive feedback, and actively listen to their team members. Empowering employees by giving them autonomy and responsibility enhances their sense of ownership and motivation, so leaders should provide the necessary resources, support, and opportunities for employees to succeed and grow. Collaboration drives innovation and collective success, so leaders should create opportunities for teamwork, encourage cross-functional projects, and celebrate collaborative achievements, fostering a culture of unity and cooperation.

By recognising and valuing intangible aspects, leaders can drive sustainable growth, as a strong culture, high employee morale, and a positive brand reputation contribute to long-term success and resilience. A supportive and inclusive environment fosters creativity and innovation, with employees more likely to share ideas and take risks when they feel valued and supported, leading to continuous improvement and competitive advantage. A positive culture and high morale lead to higher employee engagement and retention, with employees who feel connected to the organisation and its values more likely to stay and contribute their best efforts. A positive brand reputation enhances relationships with customers, partners, and other stakeholders, as trust and loyalty built through consistent and ethical behaviour strengthen the organisation's position and influence.

NAVIGATING AMBIGUITY & UNCERTAINTY

Its upper part is not bright, and its lower part is not obscure. Ceaseless in its action, it yet cannot be named, and then it again returns and becomes nothing.

Lao Tzu's passage underscores the reality that the business environment is often characterised by ambiguity and uncertainty. For strategic leaders, this means being comfortable with the unknown and adaptable to changing conditions. By embracing the fluid and ever-changing nature of the market, leaders can develop strategies that are both flexible and resilient, ensuring their organisations can thrive even in unpredictable times.

Markets are inherently unpredictable, influenced by factors such as economic shifts, technological advancements, and geopolitical events, so leaders must accept that not all variables can be controlled or predicted. Ambiguity often complicates decision-making processes, requiring leaders to rely on judgment and intuition as much as on data and analysis, especially when information is incomplete or conflicting. Change is a constant in business, whether it's evolving customer preferences, emerging competitors, or regulatory changes, so leaders must be prepared to navigate ongoing shifts in the landscape.

Leaders should develop adaptive strategies that allow for quick pivots in response to new information or changing circumstances, which can involve scenario planning where multiple potential futures are considered and contingency plans are developed for each. Implementing agile methodologies enables organisations to remain responsive and adaptable, as agile practices such as iterative development, frequent feedback loops, and incremental adjustments help teams quickly adapt to changes and continuously improve their processes and products. Innovation is key to navigating ambiguity, so leaders should foster a culture of experimentation and creativity, encouraging employees to explore new ideas and solutions, as being open to innovation allows organisations to better respond to unexpected challenges and seize new opportunities.

Diverse perspectives enhance an organisation's ability to navigate ambiguity, so leaders should create an inclusive environment where different viewpoints are valued and considered in decision-making processes, leading to more robust and innovative solutions. Continuous learning is essential for staying adaptable and resilient, so leaders should support ongoing education and skill development, ensuring that employees are equipped to handle new challenges through training programmes, workshops, and access to industry resources. Psychological safety allows employees to take risks and express their ideas without fear of negative consequences, so leaders should create a culture where team members feel safe to voice their opinions and experiment with new approaches, fostering creativity and adaptability.

Scenario planning involves anticipating a range of possible futures and developing strategies for each, so by considering various scenarios, leaders can prepare for different outcomes and be more agile in their response to changes. Effective risk management involves identifying potential risks, assessing their impact, and developing mitigation strategies, so leaders should regularly review and update their risk management plans, ensuring they are prepared for both foreseeable and unexpected challenges. Utilising decision-making frameworks, such as SWOT, PESTEL, OODA Loop, Six Thinking Hats, Eisenhower Matrix, Porter's Five Forces, Balanced Scorecard, and Vroom-Yetton Decision Model, can help leaders navigate ambiguity more effectively. These frameworks provide structured approaches for evaluating options, weighing risks and benefits, and making informed choices even with incomplete information.

Leaders should model flexibility and adaptability in their own behaviour by demonstrating openness to change and a willingness to pivot strategies, setting a positive example for their teams. Open and transparent communication is crucial during times of uncertainty, so leaders should regularly update their teams on developments, explain the rationale behind decisions, and provide clear guidance on next steps, building trust and helping employees navigate ambiguity with confidence. Empowering teams to make decisions and take action fosters a sense of ownership and accountability, so leaders should delegate authority and provide the necessary support and resources, allowing teams to respond quickly and effectively to changing circumstances.

Organisations that embrace ambiguity and uncertainty are more agile and capable of responding to changes, allowing them to stay competitive and innovative in a dynamic market. By developing flexible strategies and fostering a culture of adaptability, organisations become more resilient, able to withstand disruptions and continue to thrive even in the face of significant challenges. Navigating ambiguity often leads to strategic innovation, so organisations that are open to new ideas and willing to experiment are better positioned to identify and capitalise on emerging opportunities. Embracing ambiguity and uncertainty supports sustainable growth, as continuously adapting and evolving enables organisations to achieve long-term success and resilience.

UNDERSTANDING THE IMPORTANCE OF SUBTLE INFLUENCE

This is called the Form of the Formless, and the Semblance of the Invisible; this is called the Fleeting and Indeterminable.

Lao Tzu's passage highlights the significance of subtle influence and indirect action in leadership. Strategic leaders should recognise that not all effective leadership is overt and directive. Instead, they can guide their teams through inspiration, support, and by creating an environment where employees feel empowered to take initiative. This approach fosters a sense of ownership and creativity, leading to more innovative and effective outcomes.

Leaders can inspire their teams by clearly articulating a compelling vision and core values, which provide direction and purpose, while shared values create a strong foundation for collective action. When employees understand and connect with the organisation's mission, they are more motivated to contribute meaningfully. Leading by example is a powerful form of subtle influence, as leaders who embody the values and behaviours they wish to see in their team set a standard for others to follow. This authenticity builds trust and encourages employees to emulate positive behaviours. Sharing stories that illustrate the organisation's values, successes, and challenges can inspire and engage employees, making abstract concepts tangible and relatable, reinforcing the desired culture and motivating employees to strive for excellence.

Demonstrating empathy and understanding towards employees' needs and challenges is a subtle yet powerful way to influence, as leaders who show genuine concern for their team's well-being foster a supportive environment where employees feel valued and respected. Providing mentorship and coaching helps employees develop their skills and confidence, subtly influencing their growth and performance by offering guidance and support, empowering them to achieve their full potential. Ensuring that employees have the necessary resources and tools to perform their tasks effectively is another form of subtle support, as removing obstacles and providing the means for success creates an environment conducive to high performance.

Empowering employees with autonomy and trust encourages them to take initiative and ownership of their work, so leaders should delegate responsibility and provide the freedom to explore new ideas and approaches, fostering a culture of innovation and accountability. Creating open lines of communication where employees feel safe to express their ideas and concerns is crucial, so leaders should encourage dialogue, listen actively, and respond constructively, ensuring that employees feel heard and valued. Subtle yet consistent recognition and encouragement can significantly impact motivation and morale, so leaders should acknowledge employees' efforts and successes, reinforcing positive behaviours and promoting a culture of appreciation.

An environment that values subtle influence and indirect action fosters creativity and innovation, as employees are more likely to experiment and propose new ideas when they feel supported and empowered. When employees are trusted and given autonomy, they develop a stronger sense of ownership and accountability, leading to higher levels of engagement and commitment to the organisation's success. Subtle influence promotes a collaborative culture where employees feel safe to share their thoughts and work together towards common goals, enhancing problem-solving and driving collective achievements. Leaders who practise subtle influence build sustainable leadership by developing and nurturing the capabilities of their team members, ensuring the organisation remains resilient and adaptable to future challenges.

A culture built on subtle influence and support is more resilient and adaptable, as employees feel confident in their abilities and supported by their leaders, equipping them to handle change and uncertainty. Subtle influence fosters a mindset of continuous improvement, encouraging employees to seek out better ways of working, driven by intrinsic motivation and the desire to contribute to the organisation's success. A positive organisational climate, characterised by trust, respect, and collaboration, is the result of effective subtle influence, attracting and retaining top talent and contributing to long-term organisational growth and success.

APPLYING TIMELESS PRINCIPLES TO MODERN CHALLENGES

> When we can lay hold of the Tao of old to direct the things of the present day, and are able to know it as it was of old in the beginning, this is called (unwinding) the clue of Tao.

Lao Tzu's teachings, though ancient, offer timeless principles that can be effectively applied to contemporary strategic management challenges. By drawing on these foundational concepts, leaders can navigate modern complexities with a perspective grounded in balance, harmony, and adaptability. Integrating these principles allows leaders to develop strategies that are effective, sustainable, and aligned with the core values of their organisation.

Maintaining a work-life balance is crucial for employee well-being and productivity in today's fast-paced world, so leaders can apply the Taoist principle of balance by promoting policies that support flexible work hours, remote work options, and encouraging employees to take time off to recharge, which helps prevent burnout and fosters a healthier, more engaged workforce. Effective resource allocation involves balancing the distribution of financial, human, and technological resources to ensure optimal productivity and growth, so leaders should prioritise projects and initiatives that align with the organisation's strategic goals while ensuring that resources are not overextended, supporting sustainable development and efficient use of assets. Balanced decision-making requires considering both short-term gains and long-term impacts, so leaders should weigh the immediate benefits of a decision against its potential long-term consequences, ensuring that actions taken today support future goals, helping to build a resilient and forward-thinking organisation.

Harmony within teams is essential for collaboration and innovation, so leaders can foster harmonious relationships by promoting open communication, inclusivity, and mutual respect, encouraging team-building activities, and creating a supportive environment where everyone feels valued, enhancing teamwork and collective success. Conflicts are inevitable in any organisation, but how they are handled determines the overall harmony, so leaders should approach conflicts with empathy and seek win-win solutions that address the needs and concerns of all parties involved, maintaining a positive and cohesive work environment. A harmonious organisational culture is one where values, beliefs, and behaviours are aligned with the organisation's mission and goals, so leaders should actively cultivate a culture that reflects these values, ensuring consistency and harmony throughout the organisation and strengthening employee engagement and loyalty.

The ability to adapt quickly to changing circumstances is a key competitive advantage, so leaders should encourage a culture of innovation where employees feel empowered to explore new ideas and approaches. Implementing agile methodologies can help teams remain flexible and responsive to market shifts and emerging opportunities. Adaptability is enhanced by continuous learning and professional development, so leaders should provide opportunities for employees to acquire new skills and knowledge through training programmes, workshops, and access to industry resources, ensuring that the organisation remains capable and competitive. Building resilience involves preparing for and effectively managing change and adversity, so leaders should develop contingency plans, conduct regular risk assessments, and foster a culture of resilience where challenges are viewed as opportunities for growth. This adaptability ensures the organisation can navigate uncertainties with confidence.

Incorporating balance, harmony, and adaptability into strategic planning involves setting clear, long-term objectives while remaining flexible to adjust plans as needed, with leaders engaging in regular strategic reviews to ensure alignment with evolving goals and market conditions. Investing in leadership development ensures that future leaders are equipped with the skills and mindset to navigate modern challenges, with programmes that emphasise emotional intelligence, strategic thinking, and adaptability helping to cultivate leaders who can uphold and apply timeless principles in their roles. Building strong relationships with stakeholders, including customers, partners, and investors, requires a harmonious approach, so leaders should engage stakeholders through transparent communication, collaboration, and by demonstrating a commitment to shared values and goals.

Organisations that integrate balance, harmony, and adaptability into their strategies are more likely to achieve sustainable success, as these principles support long-term growth, resilience, and the ability to thrive in a dynamic environment. By fostering a positive and supportive work environment, leaders enhance employee satisfaction and retention, leading to engaged and productive employees who contribute to the organisation's overall success. Organisations that embody timeless principles such as integrity, respect, and adaptability build strong reputations, attracting top talent, loyal customers, and strategic partners, further strengthening their position. A culture that embraces innovation and continuous improvement drives ongoing success, as encouraging creativity and adaptability ensures that the organisation remains at the forefront of industry developments and trends.

CHAPTER 15 – SUBTLETY & DEPTH

Chapter 15 of the *Tao Te Ching* provides insights into the qualities of wise and skilful leaders, emphasising subtlety, humility, patience, and a deep understanding of the Tao. Here's how these teachings can be applied to modern-day strategic management:

EMBRACING SUBTLETY & DEPTH

> *The skilful masters (of the Tao) in old times, with a subtle and exquisite penetration, comprehended its mysteries, and were deep (also) so as to elude men's knowledge.*

Lao Tzu's teachings highlight the importance of a profound and nuanced understanding of the world. In strategic management, leaders should strive to cultivate such a deep and subtle comprehension of their business environment and organisational dynamics. This involves being observant, intuitive, and thoughtful in decision-making. Leaders who possess depth of insight can anticipate challenges, identify opportunities, and navigate complexities with greater ease.

Leaders should engage in active observation by paying close attention to the details of their environment, including market trends, competitor actions, and internal operations. This attentiveness allows them to identify subtle shifts and emerging patterns that may impact the organisation. Effective leaders listen not just to what is being said, but also to what is left unsaid, as being attuned to the nuances of conversations and non-verbal cues provides deeper insights into their team's sentiments and the broader organisational climate. Leveraging data and analytics to observe trends and patterns is crucial, so leaders should use both quantitative and qualitative data to inform their understanding of the business landscape, making data-driven decisions that are grounded in empirical evidence.

While data and rational analysis are important, intuition plays a critical role in decision-making, so leaders should learn to trust their gut feelings, especially when navigating ambiguous situations where not all information is available. Engaging in reflective practices such as meditation, journaling, or quiet contemplation can help leaders connect with their intuition, allowing for introspection and a deeper connection with one's inner wisdom. Intuition is often honed through experience, so leaders should reflect on past decisions and outcomes, learning from both successes and failures to refine their intuitive judgment.

Thoughtful decision-making involves taking the time to deliberate and consider all aspects of a situation before acting, so leaders should resist the urge to make hasty decisions, allowing space for reflection and careful consideration. Gathering input from a diverse range of perspectives ensures that decisions are well-rounded and informed, so leaders should seek advice from colleagues, mentors, and experts in various fields to gain a comprehensive understanding of the issues at hand. Effective decision-making requires a balance between rational analysis and emotional intelligence, so leaders should consider both the logical aspects of a decision and its potential emotional impact on stakeholders.

Leaders with depth of insight are proactive in identifying potential challenges and developing contingency plans, a forward-thinking approach that helps mitigate risks and ensures the organisation is prepared for various scenarios. Conducting scenario analysis involves envisioning different future states and their potential impact on the organisation, so leaders should explore various 'what-if' scenarios to anticipate challenges and opportunities, making strategic adjustments as needed. Regularly scanning the external environment for signs of change or disruption allows leaders to stay ahead of emerging trends and challenges, maintaining vigilance to help the organisation remain agile and responsive.

Cultivating a mindset of creativity and curiosity enables leaders to identify new opportunities, so they should encourage innovative thinking within their teams, fostering a culture where new ideas are explored and valued. Conducting thorough market analysis helps identify gaps and opportunities in the market, so leaders should stay informed about industry developments, customer preferences, and competitor strategies to seize new opportunities. Recognising and leveraging the organisation's strengths can uncover opportunities for growth and differentiation, so leaders should focus on areas where the organisation has a competitive advantage and build on those strengths.

Navigating complexities requires a systemic approach, understanding how different parts of the organisation and external environment interact, so leaders should consider the broader implications of their decisions, recognising the interconnectedness of various factors. Flexibility and adaptability are key to managing complexity, so leaders should be open to adjusting their strategies and approaches in response to changing circumstances, maintaining agility in the face of uncertainty. A commitment to continuous learning ensures that leaders stay informed and equipped to handle complexities, so they should seek out opportunities for professional development, staying abreast of new theories, technologies, and best practices.

Leaders with depth of insight can develop a more nuanced and strategic vision for the organisation, informed by a deep understanding of the business environment and internal dynamics. Thoughtful and intuitive decision-making leads to better outcomes, as leaders who embrace subtlety and depth are able to make more informed and effective decisions, benefiting the organisation as a whole. By anticipating challenges and identifying opportunities, leaders can build a more resilient organisation, allowing it to navigate uncertainties and adapt to change successfully. Leaders who cultivate subtlety and depth inspire confidence and trust within their teams, fostering a positive organisational culture and enhancing employee engagement and performance.

PRACTISING HUMILITY & SIMPLICITY

> Shrinking looked they like those who wade through a stream in winter; irresolute like those who are afraid of all around them; grave like a guest (in awe of his host); evanescent like ice that is melting away; unpretentious like wood that has not been fashioned into anything; vacant like a valley, and dull like muddy water.

Lao Tzu's depiction of humility and simplicity in leadership captures the essence of being genuine, unpretentious, and open to learning. Effective leaders should embody these qualities to create a collaborative and respectful work environment. By practising humility and simplicity, leaders can foster a culture where everyone feels valued and motivated to contribute.

Leaders should maintain an open-door policy, encouraging employees to approach them with ideas, concerns, and feedback, fostering trust and making employees feel heard and respected. Demonstrating active listening involves fully concentrating on the speaker, understanding their message, and responding thoughtfully, showing that leaders value their team members' input and perspectives. Being open to feedback, both positive and constructive, demonstrates humility, so leaders should seek feedback from their team and be willing to make changes based on that input, building a culture of continuous improvement.

Leaders should strive to be authentic, showing their true selves rather than projecting an image of infallibility, as authenticity builds credibility and trust, with employees appreciating leaders who are genuine and relatable. Humble leaders acknowledge their limitations and are not afraid to admit when they do not have all the answers, encouraging a collaborative approach to problem-solving where team members feel empowered to contribute their expertise. Recognising and sharing credit for successes with the team reinforces an unpretentious leadership style, so leaders should highlight the contributions of others and celebrate collective achievements rather than seeking personal accolades.

Leaders should model a commitment to continuous learning and personal growth by pursuing further education, attending workshops, or seeking mentorship, demonstrating a willingness to learn and inspiring their teams to do the same. Viewing mistakes as opportunities for learning rather than failures is a key aspect of humility, so leaders should be transparent about their own mistakes and the lessons learned, creating an environment where team members feel safe to take risks and learn from their experiences. Humble leaders encourage innovation by creating a safe space for experimentation and new ideas, fostering a culture of innovation and continuous improvement through openness to creative thinking.

Mutual respect is the foundation of a collaborative environment, so leaders should treat all team members with respect and encourage the same behaviour among employees, fostering positive relationships and effective teamwork. Encouraging collaboration and teamwork involves creating opportunities for team members to work together on projects and initiatives, facilitating cross-functional collaboration, and promoting a sense of unity and shared purpose. Inclusive leadership involves valuing and leveraging the diverse perspectives and experiences of all team members, so leaders should actively promote diversity and inclusion, ensuring that everyone feels valued and included in decision-making processes.

Employees are more likely to be engaged and motivated when they feel valued and respected by humble leaders, leading to higher levels of productivity and job satisfaction. A culture of humility and simplicity fosters collaboration and teamwork, with employees more willing to share ideas and support each other, leading to better problem-solving and innovation. Humble and approachable leadership creates a positive organisational culture where employees feel appreciated and motivated, attracting and retaining top talent and contributing to the organisation's long-term success. Leaders who practise humility and simplicity are better equipped to navigate challenges and uncertainties, with their openness to learning and collaboration enabling them to adapt and find effective solutions in the face of adversity.

By fostering a culture of continuous improvement and innovation, humble leaders support sustainable growth, ensuring the organisation remains dynamic and capable of evolving with changing market conditions. Humble and genuine leaders build strong relationships with their team members based on trust and mutual respect, enhancing communication, collaboration, and overall organisational effectiveness. Leaders who embrace humility and simplicity can quickly adapt to new information and changing circumstances, making them agile and responsive, which helps the organisation navigate complexities with ease.

VALUING PATIENCE & CLARITY

> Who can (make) the muddy water (clear)? Let it be still, and it will gradually become clear. Who can secure the condition of rest? Let movement go on, and the condition of rest will gradually arise.

Lao Tzu's passage emphasises the value of patience and the natural emergence of clarity and solutions over time. In strategic management, patience is a crucial quality that allows leaders to make well-informed and effective decisions. By allowing situations to settle and not rushing to conclusions, leaders can foster a calm and thoughtful approach within their organisations, ensuring that decisions are beneficial in the long run.

Leaders should resist the urge to make quick decisions in the face of uncertainty, taking the time to gather all relevant information and allowing the situation to unfold, thus gaining a more comprehensive understanding and making better choices. Patience involves taking the time to observe and reflect on the current state of affairs, creating space for reflection, and analysing the situation from multiple angles before arriving at a conclusion, which helps in identifying underlying issues and potential solutions. Trusting that clarity will emerge over time requires confidence in the decision-making process, so leaders should cultivate a mindset that values the natural progression of events, understanding that solutions often become apparent with time and careful consideration.

Leaders can foster a calm work environment by setting a tone of patience and composure, managing stress, promoting work-life balance, and encouraging a culture of mindfulness and focus, which enhances overall productivity and well-being. Encouraging thoughtful discussion and debate within the organisation helps uncover diverse perspectives and insights, so leaders should facilitate open dialogue, ensuring all voices are heard and considered before making decisions. This collaborative approach leads to more robust and well-rounded outcomes. While urgency can sometimes drive action, emphasising the importance of a thorough decision-making process ensures well-considered decisions, so leaders should prioritise the quality of decisions over the speed at which they are made, reinforcing the value of patience.

Implementing regular check-ins and progress reviews allows leaders to monitor the development of situations over time, providing opportunities to reassess and adjust strategies based on new information and evolving circumstances. Incorporating mindfulness practices, such as meditation and deep breathing exercises, helps leaders and employees cultivate patience and clarity, enhancing self-awareness, reducing stress, and improving focus. Leaders should encourage employees to take time for reflection, whether through journaling, quiet contemplation, or team debriefs, as reflection allows individuals to process experiences, gain insights, and make more informed decisions.

Patience enables leaders to make more informed decisions by allowing time for a thorough analysis of the situation, leading to more effective and sustainable outcomes. A calm and patient approach reduces stress and anxiety within the organisation, making employees feel more supported and less pressured to deliver immediate results, thus enhancing overall well-being and performance. Clarity often emerges when situations are allowed to settle, and by practising patience, leaders can uncover the root causes of issues and develop more effective solutions. Patience fosters better relationships within the organisation, as leaders who are patient and composed build trust and respect, creating a positive and collaborative work environment.

Organisations that value patience and clarity are more likely to achieve sustainable growth, as thoughtful decision-making and a calm work environment contribute to long-term success and resilience. Patience allows for strategic agility, with leaders better equipped to navigate uncertainties and adapt to changing circumstances, ensuring the organisation remains competitive and forward-thinking. A culture that values patience and clarity promotes a positive work environment, where employees feel valued and empowered to contribute thoughtfully, leading to higher engagement and job satisfaction. By fostering a patient and reflective approach, organisations can continuously improve their processes and outcomes, with a commitment to ongoing learning and development driving innovation and excellence.

AVOIDING SELF-CENTREDNESS

They who preserve this method of the Tao do not wish to be full (of themselves). It is through their not being full of themselves that they can afford to seem worn and not appear new and complete.

Lao Tzu's wisdom emphasises that true leaders should avoid self-centredness and focus on the needs of their team and organisation. By prioritising the well-being and development of their employees, leaders can build a stronger and more cohesive organisation. This selflessness fosters a supportive and collaborative culture where everyone is encouraged to grow and succeed.

Leaders should prioritise the physical, mental, and emotional well-being of their team members by creating a healthy work environment, providing access to wellness resources, and ensuring a balanced workload, showing genuine concern for their team's well-being to build a positive and supportive workplace. Professional development is key to employee growth and satisfaction, so leaders should offer opportunities for training, mentorship, and career advancement, investing in their team's development to enhance individual skills and strengthen the organisation's overall capabilities. Acknowledging and celebrating the contributions of team members is essential for fostering a sense of value and belonging, so leaders should regularly recognise achievements, both big and small, and express appreciation for their employees' efforts.

A selfless approach promotes a culture of collaboration, so leaders should encourage teamwork and create opportunities for team members to work together on projects, leading to better problem-solving, innovation, and a stronger sense of community within the organisation. Empowering employees means giving them the autonomy and resources they need to succeed, so leaders should delegate responsibilities, trust their team members to make decisions, and provide the necessary support for them to excel, resulting in increased motivation and job satisfaction. Open and honest communication is vital for building trust and cohesion, so leaders should maintain transparency in their actions and decisions, keeping team members informed and engaged, fostering a culture of trust and mutual respect.

Selfless leaders build trust with their team members by demonstrating that they prioritise the collective good over personal gain, which enhances relationships and contributes to a positive organisational climate. When employees feel valued and supported, they are more likely to be engaged and motivated, leading to higher levels of employee engagement, increased productivity, and job satisfaction. A supportive and collaborative culture encourages creativity and innovation, as employees are more likely to share ideas and take risks when they feel empowered and appreciated, leading to continuous improvement and growth. By focusing on the well-being and development of their team, leaders ensure the long-term success of the organisation, as a cohesive and motivated workforce is better equipped to navigate challenges and seize opportunities.

Leaders should conduct regular check-ins with their team members to understand their needs, concerns, and aspirations, staying connected and addressing any issues promptly. Demonstrating selflessness and humility in their actions and decisions sets a powerful example for others to follow, as leaders should model the behaviours they wish to see in their team, such as collaboration, transparency, and empathy. Leaders should actively seek feedback from their team members and be open to making changes based on that input, reinforcing a culture of continuous improvement and mutual respect. Instead of seeking recognition, leaders should focus on the impact of their actions on the team and organisation, prioritising collective success to create a more meaningful and fulfilling work environment.

Organisations led by selfless leaders are more likely to achieve sustainable growth, as the focus on well-being, development, and collaboration creates a strong foundation for long-term success. A culture of selflessness fosters a positive and inclusive work environment where employees feel valued, supported, and motivated, leading to higher retention and overall organisational effectiveness. Selfless leadership builds resilient teams that can navigate challenges and adapt to change, with strong relationships and trust enabling teams to work together effectively in any situation. Leaders who prioritise the needs of their team and organisation are better equipped to make strategic decisions that benefit the collective, ensuring strategic agility and the ability to respond to emerging opportunities and threats with confidence.

CHAPTER 16 – NOBILITY

Chapter 16 of the *Tao Te Ching* emphasises the principles of stillness, returning to one's roots, understanding unchanging rules, and cultivating a noble character. These teachings can offer valuable insights for modern-day strategic management:

EMBRACING STILLNESS & REFLECTION

The (state of) vacancy should be brought to the utmost degree, and that of stillness guarded with unwearying vigour.

Lao Tzu's wisdom emphasises the importance of stillness and reflection in leadership. In strategic management, prioritising moments of stillness allows leaders to think deeply about the organisation's direction, evaluate past actions, and plan for the future. By fostering a culture where reflection is valued, leaders can make more thoughtful and informed decisions, leading to more sustainable and effective strategies.

Leaders should set aside dedicated time for reflection, free from distractions and interruptions, which could involve scheduling regular quiet periods or retreats to contemplate and strategise. Incorporating mindfulness practices such as meditation, deep breathing, or yoga helps leaders cultivate a state of stillness, enhancing self-awareness, reducing stress, and improving focus, enabling them to approach decision-making with clarity and calm. Creating designated spaces for quiet reflection within the workplace encourages both employees and leaders to take moments of stillness, providing a sanctuary for deep thinking and contemplation, and fostering a reflective organisational culture.

Conducting post-action reviews after major projects or initiatives helps leaders and teams reflect on what worked well and what could be improved, involving analysing outcomes, identifying lessons learned, and documenting insights for future reference. Reflecting on past experiences allows leaders to understand the impact of their decisions and actions, acknowledging successes and failures to make more informed choices moving forward, avoiding past mistakes, and building on previous achievements. Leaders should encourage their teams to engage in reflective practices, with team debriefs and retrospective meetings providing opportunities for collective reflection, enabling teams to share insights, celebrate successes, and identify areas for improvement.

Setting aside time for strategic planning is essential for long-term success, so leaders should conduct regular planning sessions to assess the organisation's current position, envision future goals, and develop actionable strategies to achieve them. Visioning exercises help leaders and teams imagine the desired future state of the organisation, involving creative thinking and visualisation techniques that inspire forward-looking strategies and innovative solutions. Scenario planning involves exploring different potential futures and developing plans for various contingencies, a forward-thinking approach that helps leaders prepare for uncertainty and adaptability, ensuring the organisation remains resilient and agile.

Leaders should model reflective practices by demonstrating the importance of stillness and contemplation in their own routines, sharing their reflective processes and insights to inspire their teams to adopt similar practices. Creating an environment where open dialogue and thoughtful discussion are encouraged fosters a reflective culture, so leaders should facilitate conversations that allow employees to share their thoughts, experiences, and perspectives, enriching the collective understanding. Acknowledging and celebrating moments of reflection and the insights gained from them reinforces their value, so leaders should highlight examples of how reflection has led to better decision-making and strategic outcomes, promoting a culture that values deep thinking.

Reflective leaders make more informed and effective decisions, as the clarity and insights gained through stillness and contemplation lead to better strategic choices and outcomes. Thoughtful reflection helps leaders develop strategies that are sustainable and aligned with the organisation's core values, making them more likely to withstand challenges and support long-term success. Reflection fosters creativity and innovation by allowing leaders and teams to think deeply about new ideas and approaches, driving continuous improvement and keeping the organisation competitive. Leaders who prioritise stillness and reflection are more self-aware, empathetic, and resilient, enhancing their leadership effectiveness and their ability to inspire and guide their teams.

RETURNING TO CORE VALUES

> *When things (in the vegetable world) have displayed their luxuriant growth, we see each of them return to its root. This returning to their root is what we call the state of stillness; and that stillness may be called a reporting that they have fulfilled their appointed end.*

Lao Tzu's passage emphasises the necessity of returning to core values and foundational principles to maintain organisational integrity and purpose. For strategic leaders, this means regularly revisiting and reinforcing the organisation's mission, vision, and values. By ensuring that all actions and decisions are aligned with these core principles, leaders can foster a strong and cohesive culture that supports long-term success.

Leaders should regularly reflect on the organisation's core values, mission, and vision, ensuring these guiding principles remain relevant and central to operations and strategies, scheduling periodic reviews, such as quarterly or annual retreats, to revisit and refine these elements. The mission and vision statements encapsulate the organisation's purpose and long-term aspirations, so leaders should ensure they are clear, compelling, and regularly communicated to all employees, keeping the organisation aligned with its foundational goals. Conducting workshops or training sessions focused on core values helps reinforce their importance, engaging employees in discussions about their application in daily operations and exploring ways to better integrate them into the organisational culture.

Leaders should exemplify the organisation's core values in their actions and decisions, modelling integrity, transparency, and commitment to these principles to set a powerful example for their teams, reinforcing the importance of core values throughout the organisation. Incorporating core values into the decision-making process involves evaluating options and strategies through the lens of the organisation's values, ensuring choices align with the overarching mission and vision, fostering ethical and principled decision-making. Implementing recognition programmes that highlight and reward behaviours aligned with core values can reinforce their importance, so leaders should celebrate employees who exemplify the organisation's values, showcasing these individuals as role models for others.

Regular communication about the organisation's core values helps keep them top of mind for all employees, so leaders should incorporate discussions about values into meetings, internal communications, and performance evaluations, ensuring that values remain central to the organisational culture. Organisational policies and practices should reflect and support core values, so leaders should review and align policies, such as hiring practices, performance management, and employee development programmes, to promote and reinforce these values. Actively engaging employees in conversations about core values fosters a sense of ownership and alignment, so leaders should encourage employees to share their perspectives on how values are being lived out and invite suggestions for improvement, strengthening the organisational culture.

Core values provide a consistent foundation that guides the organisation through change and uncertainty, enabling leaders to create a stable and reliable environment where employees know what is expected and can navigate challenges with confidence. An organisation that consistently adheres to its core values builds trust and loyalty among employees, customers, and stakeholders, essential for maintaining positive relationships and fostering long-term commitment. When employees understand and believe in the organisation's core values, they are more likely to be aligned and motivated, enhancing collaboration, engagement, and overall performance, driving the organisation towards its strategic goals. Emphasising core values fosters an ethical and principled culture, where leaders who prioritise integrity and ethical behaviour create an environment that empowers employees to act with honesty and accountability, reinforcing the organisation's reputation and credibility.

Organisations that consistently return to and reinforce their core values are better positioned for sustainable success, as these values provide a guiding framework that supports long-term growth and resilience. A strong focus on core values contributes to a positive organisational climate where employees feel connected to a larger purpose and are more likely to experience job satisfaction and fulfillment. Core values serve as a compass that guides strategic decisions, ensuring that strategies align with foundational principles, allowing leaders to navigate changes and uncertainties with agility and confidence. An organisation known for its commitment to core values enjoys a strong reputation among customers, partners, and the broader community, attracting talent, fostering loyalty, and enhancing its overall impact.

UNDERSTANDING & APPLYING FUNDAMENTAL PRINCIPLES

The report of that fulfilment is the regular, unchanging rule. To know that unchanging rule is to be intelligent; not to know it leads to wild movements and evil issues.

Leaders should understand and apply fundamental principles that govern successful management and operations. These principles, such as ethical behaviour, clear communication, and effective resource management, provide a stable foundation for decision-making. By adhering to these timeless rules, leaders can avoid erratic and detrimental actions, ensuring consistent and reliable progress.

Lao Tzu's passage underscores the importance of understanding and adhering to fundamental principles that govern successful management and operations. These timeless rules provide a stable foundation for decision-making, ensuring consistent and reliable progress. Strategic leaders who understand and apply these principles can avoid erratic and detrimental actions, steering their organisations towards sustainable success.

Key Fundamental Principles

Ethical Behaviour: Upholding ethical standards is crucial for maintaining trust and credibility. Leaders should model integrity, honesty, and fairness in their actions and decisions. Ethical behaviour fosters a culture of accountability and respect, which is essential for long-term organisational success.

Clear Communication: Effective communication is a cornerstone of successful leadership. Leaders should ensure that information flows smoothly within the organisation, promoting transparency and understanding. Clear communication involves active listening, providing constructive feedback, and articulating goals and expectations clearly.

Effective Resource Management: Efficiently managing resources—whether financial, human, or technological—is vital for achieving strategic objectives. Leaders should allocate resources wisely, ensuring that they are used effectively to support the organisation's mission and goals. This includes budgeting, workforce planning, and technology investments.

Continuous Learning: Embracing a mindset of continuous learning and improvement helps organisations stay competitive and adaptive. Leaders should encourage ongoing education and professional development for themselves and their teams, fostering a culture of growth and innovation.

Strategic Planning: Developing and implementing strategic plans provides direction and focus. Leaders should engage in regular strategic planning sessions to assess the organisation's current state, set long-term goals, and develop actionable strategies. This forward-thinking approach ensures that the organisation remains aligned with its mission and can navigate changes effectively.

Collaborative Leadership: Promoting collaboration and teamwork enhances problem-solving and innovation. Leaders should create opportunities for cross-functional collaboration, encouraging diverse perspectives and collective efforts. This collaborative approach strengthens relationships and drives collective success.

Leaders should ensure that all decisions are aligned with the organisation's core values and principles, reinforcing the importance of these fundamental rules and supporting the organisation's mission and vision. Effective decision-making involves considering the long-term impact of actions, weighing the potential benefits and risks to contribute to sustainable success rather than short-term gains. Incorporating diverse perspectives into the decision-making process leads to more robust and well-rounded outcomes, so leaders should actively seek input from various stakeholders, including employees, customers, and experts. Continuous monitoring of decisions and their outcomes allows leaders to make necessary adjustments, ensuring strategies remain effective and aligned with the organisation's goals.

Adhering to fundamental principles provides a consistent framework for decision-making, ensuring stability that helps organisations navigate uncertainties and maintain focus on their strategic objectives. Ethical behaviour and clear communication build trust and credibility with employees, customers, and stakeholders, essential for maintaining positive relationships and fostering loyalty. Effective resource management and strategic planning lead to improved efficiency and productivity, allowing organisations to achieve their goals more effectively. A culture of continuous learning and collaborative leadership fosters innovation, encouraging creativity and the exchange of ideas, driving continuous improvement and keeping the organisation competitive. Understanding and applying fundamental principles supports sustainable growth, providing a strong foundation that enables organisations to achieve long-term success and resilience.

Leaders who adhere to fundamental principles can navigate changes and uncertainties with agility, ensuring the organisation remains responsive to evolving market conditions and emerging opportunities. A strong focus on fundamental principles contributes to a positive organisational culture where employees feel valued, respected, and motivated to contribute, leading to higher engagement and job satisfaction. By upholding ethical standards and promoting clear communication, leaders model responsible behaviour, enhancing the organisation's reputation and fostering a culture of accountability and integrity. Organisations that prioritise fundamental principles are more resilient and capable of withstanding challenges, with the consistent application of these principles building a solid foundation that supports long-term success and growth.

CULTIVATING PATIENCE & FORBEARANCE

The knowledge of that unchanging rule produces a (grand) capacity and forbearance, and that capacity and forbearance lead to a community (of feeling with all things).

Patience and forbearance are critical qualities for strategic leaders. Recognising that meaningful change and growth take time allows leaders to approach challenges with a calm and composed mindset. This patience fosters a supportive and understanding work environment, where employees feel valued and motivated to contribute their best efforts.

Lao Tzu's passage highlights the critical qualities of patience and forbearance in leadership. Recognising that meaningful change and growth take time allows leaders to approach challenges with a calm and composed mindset. This patience not only helps leaders navigate complexities but also fosters a supportive and understanding work environment where employees feel valued and motivated to contribute their best efforts.

Leaders should understand that significant progress and transformation do not happen overnight; by acknowledging that change requires time, they can avoid the frustration and anxiety that often accompany unrealistic expectations, helping maintain focus on long-term goals rather than short-term gains. A calm and composed mindset enables leaders to make thoughtful and rational decisions, even in the face of challenges, allowing them to step back, assess situations comprehensively, and consider all possible outcomes before taking action, leading to more effective problem-solving and decision-making. Embracing the concept of incremental progress helps leaders stay motivated and positive, celebrating small victories and acknowledging gradual improvements to maintain momentum and encourage their teams to persist in their efforts.

Patience fosters empathy and understanding, enabling leaders to better understand their team members' perspectives, needs, and challenges, building trust and strengthening relationships within the organisation. A supportive environment is built on open communication, so leaders should create opportunities for team members to express their thoughts, ideas, and concerns without fear of judgment or retribution, encouraging collaboration and innovation. When providing feedback, patience is essential, so leaders should offer constructive feedback that is specific, actionable, and delivered with empathy, helping employees understand their areas for improvement and feel supported in their growth journey.

When employees feel valued and understood, they are more likely to be motivated and engaged, as patience and forbearance in leadership create an environment where employees feel confident in their abilities and motivated to contribute their best efforts. A patient and composed approach to challenges builds resilience within the organisation, with employees learning to navigate setbacks and difficulties with a positive attitude, knowing their leaders are supportive and understanding. Patience allows for more thorough and thoughtful problem-solving, as leaders who take the time to explore all options and consider different perspectives are more likely to find innovative and effective solutions. A supportive environment fosters strong team cohesion, where employees who feel understood and appreciated are more likely to collaborate effectively and support one another, leading to a more cohesive and productive team.

Incorporating mindfulness practices, such as meditation and deep breathing exercises, helps leaders cultivate patience and maintain a calm mindset, enhancing self-awareness and reducing stress, enabling them to approach challenges with composure. Leaders should set realistic expectations for themselves and their teams, acknowledging that change takes time and progress may be gradual, helping to maintain a positive outlook and avoid unnecessary pressure. Regular reflection allows leaders to assess their progress, understand their challenges, and refine their strategies, staying grounded and maintaining a long-term perspective. Promoting a growth mindset within the organisation encourages employees to view challenges as opportunities for learning and development, with leaders emphasising the value of perseverance and continuous improvement.

Organisations that prioritise patience and forbearance are more likely to achieve sustainable growth, as this approach ensures that changes and improvements are well-considered and aligned with long-term goals. A culture of patience and understanding fosters a positive work environment where employees feel valued and supported, leading to higher levels of engagement and job satisfaction. Patience allows leaders to navigate uncertainties and adapt to changes with agility, maintaining a calm and composed mindset to respond to emerging opportunities and challenges effectively. Leaders who embody patience and forbearance build resilience within their teams, enabling the organisation to withstand setbacks and continue progressing towards its goals.

DEVELOPING NOBLE CHARACTER & LEADERSHIP

> *From this community of feeling comes a kingliness of character; and he who is king-like goes on to be heaven-like. In that likeness to heaven he possesses the Tao.*

Lao Tzu's wisdom highlights the importance of developing noble character traits, such as integrity, humility, and empathy, in leadership. By embodying these qualities, leaders can inspire and positively influence their teams. This 'kingliness of character' creates a sense of trust and respect, enabling leaders to guide their organisations effectively and ethically.

Integrity is the foundation of trust and ethical behaviour, with leaders who are honest, transparent, and consistent in their actions and decisions, upholding ethical standards and aligning their actions with their words to create a trustworthy environment. Humble leaders recognise their limitations and value the contributions of others, being open to feedback and willing to admit mistakes, fostering a culture of collaboration and mutual respect by acknowledging they do not have all the answers and relying on their team's expertise. Empathy involves understanding and sharing the feelings of others, allowing leaders to connect with their team members on a deeper level, showing genuine concern for their well-being, building strong relationships, creating a supportive environment, and enhancing team morale.

Noble character traits are best demonstrated through actions, so leaders should model integrity, humility, and empathy in their daily interactions, setting a positive example to inspire their teams to adopt similar behaviours and attitudes. Trust is earned through consistent, ethical behaviour, so leaders should be transparent in their communication, deliver on their promises, and act with integrity, fostering loyalty and commitment to empower teams to achieve their best. Creating an environment where open dialogue is encouraged promotes understanding and collaboration, so leaders should actively listen to their team members, value their input, and address concerns with empathy and fairness, strengthening relationships and enhancing team dynamics.

Recognising and celebrating the contributions of team members fosters a sense of value and appreciation, so leaders should regularly highlight individual and team achievements, reinforcing the importance of each person's role in the organisation's success. Inclusive leadership ensures all team members feel valued and respected, so leaders should promote diversity and inclusivity, creating an environment where different perspectives are welcomed and leveraged for collective success. Investing in the growth and development of team members demonstrates a leader's commitment to their well-being and success, so leaders should offer opportunities for training, mentorship, and career advancement, supporting their team's professional journey.

Leaders who embody noble character traits inspire and motivate their teams, leading to higher levels of engagement and performance, as employees are more likely to go above and beyond when they feel supported and valued. A leadership style grounded in integrity, humility, and empathy fosters a positive organisational culture that attracts and retains top talent, enhances job satisfaction, and drives overall success. Ethical and principled leadership ensures that decisions are made with long-term sustainability in mind, creating a stable and resilient organisation capable of navigating challenges and seizing opportunities. Organisations led by noble leaders enjoy a strong reputation for ethical behaviour and excellence, enhancing relationships with customers, partners, and stakeholders, and contributing to the organisation's growth and influence.

Regular self-reflection helps leaders assess their character traits and identify areas for improvement, so they should take time to reflect on their actions, seek feedback, and make a conscious effort to embody noble qualities. Engaging in mentorship and coaching relationships provides valuable insights and guidance, allowing leaders to learn from experienced mentors who exemplify noble character traits and gain inspiration and practical advice for their leadership journey. Committing to continuous learning ensures that leaders stay informed and adaptable, so they should seek out opportunities for professional development, attend workshops, and read extensively to enhance their understanding of ethical and effective leadership. Leaders should establish and promote ethical practices within the organisation, setting clear expectations, providing training on ethical behaviour, and addressing any breaches of integrity promptly and fairly.

Teams led by noble leaders are more resilient and capable of overcoming challenges, as the strong relationships and trust built through noble character traits enable teams to work together effectively in any situation. Leaders with noble character can navigate uncertainties with strategic agility, ensuring decisions are aligned with the organisation's core values and long-term goals through their ethical and empathetic approach. A focus on noble character fosters a positive organisational climate, where employees feel connected to a larger purpose and are more likely to experience job satisfaction and fulfillment. Organisations that prioritise noble leadership traits are better positioned for sustainable growth, with these qualities providing a strong foundation that supports long-term success and resilience.

ENSURING LONG-TERM SUSTAINABILITY

> *Possessed of the Tao, he endures long; and to the end of his bodily life, is exempt from all danger of decay.*

Lao Tzu's passage underscores the importance of focusing on long-term sustainability for enduring success. Leaders should make decisions that ensure the organisation's viability and resilience over time, rather than prioritising short-term gains. This involves strategic planning, risk management, and continuous improvement to adapt to changing conditions and seize new opportunities.

Ensuring that the organisation's vision and mission are aligned with long-term sustainability goals is crucial, so leaders should regularly revisit and refine these guiding statements to reflect the organisation's commitment to enduring success and resilience. Setting clear, long-term goals provides direction and focus for the organisation, so leaders should develop strategic plans that outline the steps needed to achieve these goals, including milestones and timelines, maintaining momentum and ensuring alignment with the organisation's vision. Engaging in scenario planning allows leaders to anticipate various future states and develop strategies to address potential challenges and opportunities, ensuring the organisation is prepared for different outcomes and can adapt quickly to changing conditions.

Effective risk management begins with identifying potential risks that could impact the organisation's long-term sustainability, so leaders should conduct thorough risk assessments to identify internal and external threats, including economic fluctuations, technological changes, and regulatory shifts. Once risks are identified, leaders should develop strategies to mitigate them, such as diversifying revenue streams, investing in new technologies, or strengthening internal controls, proactively addressing risks to reduce their impact and enhance the organisation's resilience. Continuous monitoring and regular review of risk management strategies are essential, so leaders should establish mechanisms to track risks and their mitigation efforts, making adjustments as needed to ensure ongoing effectiveness.

Continuous improvement relies on a culture that values innovation and creativity, so leaders should encourage employees to experiment with new ideas, embrace change, and seek out opportunities for improvement, driving ongoing growth and development. Reflecting on past experiences, both successes and failures, provides valuable insights for continuous improvement, so leaders should facilitate regular debriefs and post-action reviews to capture lessons learned and apply them to future initiatives. Supporting ongoing education and skill development for employees ensures that the organisation remains competitive and capable of adapting to new challenges, so leaders should provide access to training programmes, workshops, and other learning opportunities.

Long-term sustainability requires agility and flexibility, so leaders should develop strategies that allow the organisation to pivot quickly in response to changing conditions, such as adopting agile methodologies, streamlining decision-making processes, and fostering a responsive culture. Engaging with stakeholders, including employees, customers, and partners, helps leaders stay informed about emerging trends and needs, with regular communication and collaboration ensuring the organisation remains relevant and can quickly adapt to market shifts. Adopting sustainable practices in operations and decision-making supports long-term viability, with leaders considering environmental, social, and governance (ESG) factors in their strategies to promote sustainability and ethical behaviour throughout the organisation.

Organisations that focus on long-term sustainability are more resilient and stable, as prioritising strategic planning, risk management, and continuous improvement enables them to withstand challenges and thrive over time. A commitment to long-term sustainability enhances the organisation's reputation among stakeholders, making customers, employees, and investors more likely to support and remain loyal to organisations that demonstrate responsible and forward-thinking behaviour. Continuous improvement and a culture of innovation drive ongoing growth and development, positioning organisations to identify and seize new opportunities and stay competitive in a dynamic market. Long-term sustainability supports sustainable growth by ensuring the organisation's efforts are aligned with its vision and goals, leading to consistent progress and long-term success.

Conducting regular strategic reviews allows leaders to assess progress towards long-term goals and make necessary adjustments, involving key stakeholders and considering both internal and external factors. Diversifying revenue streams reduces reliance on a single source of income and enhances financial stability, so leaders should explore new markets, products, and services to create multiple revenue channels. Adopting agile practices, such as iterative development and frequent feedback loops, enhances the organisation's ability to respond to changes by promoting flexibility and continuous improvement. Strong governance practices ensure accountability and transparency, so leaders should establish clear policies, roles, and responsibilities to support ethical behaviour and effective decision-making.

Organisations that prioritise long-term sustainability experience consistent growth by focusing on strategic planning, risk management, and continuous improvement, ensuring ongoing progress and development. A commitment to long-term sustainability fosters a positive organisational culture, where employees feel connected to a larger purpose and are more likely to be engaged and motivated. Leaders who emphasise long-term sustainability can navigate uncertainties with strategic agility, ensuring the organisation remains responsive to emerging opportunities and challenges. Focusing on sustainability strengthens relationships with stakeholders, as customers, employees, and investors appreciate the organisation's commitment to responsible behaviour and long-term success.

CHAPTER 17 – OWNERSHIP

Chapter 17 of the *Tao Te Ching* explores different leadership styles and the relationship between leaders and their followers. It emphasises the importance of trust, humility, and subtle guidance. Here's how these teachings can be applied to modern-day strategic management:

LEADING WITH SUBTLETY & TRUST

> *In the highest antiquity, (the people) did not know that there were (their rulers).*

Lao Tzu's passage emphasises that the most effective leaders are those whose influence is so subtle and seamless that their presence is hardly noticed. In modern strategic management, leaders should aim to create systems and cultures where employees feel empowered and capable of operating independently. When leadership is too heavy-handed or overt, it can stifle creativity and initiative. Instead, by building trust and providing subtle guidance, leaders can foster an environment where employees feel responsible and motivated to contribute their best.

Empowering employees with autonomy and trust is crucial for fostering a sense of ownership and responsibility, so leaders should delegate decision-making authority and trust their team members to manage their tasks effectively, encouraging initiative and innovation as employees feel confident in their abilities and motivated to take on new challenges. While subtle influence is important, leaders should also provide clear expectations and goals to ensure that employees understand their roles and responsibilities, allowing them to work independently towards shared objectives, with regular feedback and check-ins reinforcing these expectations and providing opportunities for guidance. Providing employees with the necessary resources and support enables them to succeed independently, so leaders should ensure that their team has access to the tools, training, and information needed to perform their duties effectively, helping build confidence and competence.

Trust is built through consistent and reliable behaviour, so leaders should be dependable in their actions and decisions, ensuring they follow through on commitments and maintain transparency, fostering a sense of security and trust within the team. Encouraging open communication helps build trust and transparency, creating an environment where team members feel comfortable sharing their thoughts, ideas, and concerns, which fosters collaboration and mutual respect as employees know their voices are heard and valued. Recognising and celebrating the contributions of team members reinforces trust and appreciation, so leaders should regularly highlight individual and team achievements, expressing gratitude for their efforts, which fosters a positive and supportive culture.

Providing subtle guidance through mentorship and coaching helps employees develop their skills and confidence, so leaders should offer constructive feedback and support, guiding team members in their professional growth without micromanaging, empowering employees to learn and improve independently. Encouraging employees to solve problems independently fosters critical thinking and innovation, so leaders should provide opportunities for team members to tackle challenges and develop solutions, offering guidance and support as needed, helping employees build problem-solving skills and confidence. Subtle influence can also involve facilitating collaboration and teamwork, so leaders should create opportunities for cross-functional projects and collaborative efforts, encouraging team members to work together and share their expertise, enhancing creativity and collective success.

When employees feel empowered and trusted, they are more likely to take initiative and propose new ideas, fostering an environment of autonomy and trust that drives innovation and continuous improvement. Empowered employees are more engaged and motivated, feeling a sense of ownership and responsibility for their work, leading to higher levels of productivity and job satisfaction. Subtle influence and trust build strong team cohesion, as employees who feel supported and trusted by their leaders are more likely to collaborate effectively and support one another. A leadership style grounded in subtle influence and trust supports sustainable growth by fostering an environment where employees can thrive independently, ensuring the long-term success and resilience of the organisation.

Effective delegation involves assigning tasks and responsibilities based on employees' strengths and capabilities, trusting team members to manage their work and providing the necessary support and resources for success. Encouraging experimentation and risk-taking fosters innovation, so leaders should create a safe space where employees feel comfortable exploring new ideas and approaches without fear of failure. Feedback should be specific, actionable, and delivered with empathy, as leaders offer guidance and support to help employees learn and grow, reinforcing a culture of continuous improvement. Holding employees accountable for their work fosters a sense of responsibility and ownership, so leaders should set clear expectations, monitor progress, and provide regular feedback to ensure accountability.

Teams led by subtle and trust-building leaders are more resilient and capable of overcoming challenges, with strong relationships and trust developed through this leadership style enabling effective teamwork in any situation. Leaders who emphasise subtle influence and trust can navigate uncertainties with strategic agility, ensuring the organisation remains responsive to emerging opportunities and challenges. A focus on subtle influence and trust fosters a positive organisational culture where employees feel connected to a larger purpose, leading to higher job satisfaction and fulfillment. Organisations that prioritise subtle influence and trust are better positioned for sustainable success, as these qualities provide a strong foundation supporting long-term growth and resilience.

BUILDING & MAINTAINING TRUST

Thus it was that when faith (in the Tao) was deficient (in the rulers) a want of faith in them ensued (in the people).

Lao Tzu's passage emphasises that trust is the cornerstone of effective leadership. When leaders act with integrity and consistency, they build trust within their teams. Conversely, if leaders are inconsistent or fail to uphold their principles, they lose the trust of their employees, leading to disengagement and lack of motivation. Strategic leaders should prioritise transparency, honesty, and reliability to build and maintain trust within their organisations.

Leaders who are honest and transparent in their communications build a foundation of trust by sharing information openly, admitting mistakes, and providing clear and truthful updates about the organisation's status, fostering a culture of trust and openness. Consistency in actions and decisions is crucial for building trust, so leaders should ensure their behaviours align with their words and principles; when employees see that leaders consistently uphold their values and commitments, trust is reinforced. Upholding high ethical standards is essential for maintaining trust, so leaders should act with integrity, making decisions that are fair, just, and in line with the organisation's values, as ethical behaviour sets a positive example and builds credibility.

Clear and transparent communication helps build trust by ensuring employees are well-informed and understand the reasoning behind decisions, so leaders should provide regular updates, share strategic plans, and encourage open dialogue. An open door policy encourages employees to approach leaders with questions, concerns, and feedback, fostering a sense of trust and inclusion as employees feel their voices are heard and valued. Transparency involves sharing both the challenges and successes of the organisation, so leaders should communicate the realities of the business environment, including obstacles and achievements, to create a balanced and honest narrative.

Reliable leaders follow through on their promises and commitments, building confidence and trust as employees need to know they can depend on their leaders to deliver on their word. Consistency in leadership style and decision-making reinforces trust, with leaders maintaining a steady approach and providing clear guidance and support regardless of the circumstances, creating a sense of security and predictability. Providing regular feedback and recognition helps build trust by showing that leaders are engaged and attentive, acknowledging the efforts and contributions of their team members, offering constructive feedback, and celebrating achievements.

Trust leads to higher levels of employee engagement, as when employees trust their leaders, they are more likely to be motivated, committed, and enthusiastic about their work, driving productivity and performance. Trust fosters collaboration and teamwork, with employees who trust their leaders and colleagues more likely to share ideas, seek input, and work together effectively, enhancing problem-solving and innovation. A culture of trust boosts employee morale, as employees feel valued, respected, and supported, leading to a positive and productive work environment. Trust is a fundamental component of a strong organisational culture, with leaders who prioritise trust creating a culture of integrity, respect, and accountability, supporting long-term success.

Leaders should model the behaviour they wish to see in their teams, acting with integrity, being transparent, and demonstrating reliability to set a positive example and inspire trust in others. Creating opportunities for open dialogue and feedback builds trust, so leaders should facilitate regular team meetings, one-on-one check-ins, and anonymous feedback channels to encourage honest communication. Supporting employees by providing the necessary resources, training, and support shows that leaders are invested in their success, fostering trust and confidence. Leaders should also acknowledge and learn from their mistakes, as admitting errors and taking responsibility demonstrates humility and accountability, reinforcing trust.

Trust leads to sustainable relationships within the organisation, as employees who trust their leaders are more likely to stay, reducing turnover and fostering long-term loyalty. Trust builds resilient teams that can navigate challenges and adapt to change, with strong relationships and open communication enabling teams to work together effectively in any situation. Leaders who prioritise trust can navigate uncertainties with strategic agility, as trust fosters open communication and collaboration, ensuring the organisation remains responsive to emerging opportunities and challenges. A focus on trust fosters a positive organisational climate, where employees feel connected to a larger purpose and are more likely to experience job satisfaction and fulfillment.

VALUING HUMILITY & MODESTY

> How irresolute did those (earliest rulers) appear, showing (by their reticence) the importance which they set upon their words!

Lao Tzu's passage emphasises the importance of humility and modesty in leadership. Humility is a key trait of effective leaders, as it fosters an inclusive and collaborative work environment. Leaders should avoid the temptation to dominate conversations or impose their views. Instead, they should listen actively and value the input of others. By demonstrating humility and restraint, leaders can create a culture where employees feel empowered to share their ideas and take ownership of their work, leading to greater innovation and productivity.

Active listening involves fully engaging with the speaker, giving undivided attention, and showing genuine interest in their thoughts and ideas, so leaders should practise this during meetings and one-on-one interactions to ensure employees feel heard and valued. Asking open-ended questions encourages deeper discussions and allows employees to express their ideas fully; leaders should use questions that invite elaboration, such as 'Can you tell me more about that?' or 'What do you think we should do next?' This approach fosters open dialogue and demonstrates a leader's willingness to listen and learn. Reflecting on what has been said and providing constructive feedback shows that leaders are actively listening and considering employees' input, so they should acknowledge contributions, offer insights, and express appreciation for the ideas shared.

Leaders should create inclusive spaces where all team members feel comfortable sharing their ideas, promoting a culture of respect and inclusivity where diverse perspectives are valued and encouraged, fostering creativity and collaboration for better problem-solving and innovation. Acknowledging and celebrating the contributions of team members reinforces the value of their input, so leaders should regularly recognise and reward employees for their ideas and efforts, both publicly and privately, boosting morale and motivating employees to continue contributing. Trusting employees with responsibilities and allowing them to take ownership of their work demonstrates a leader's confidence in their abilities, so delegating tasks and projects empowers employees and encourages them to take initiative and develop their skills.

Humble leaders acknowledge their mistakes and take responsibility for their actions, setting a positive example for the team and fostering a culture of continuous improvement. They actively seek feedback from their team members, recognising they do not have all the answers, and by inviting input and considering diverse perspectives, they can make more informed decisions and strengthen relationships with employees. Instead of dominating conversations or seeking personal recognition, leaders should focus on the collective success of the team and the organisation, demonstrating humility by shining the spotlight on others and celebrating their achievements.

An inclusive and collaborative environment encourages employees to share their ideas freely, leading to greater innovation as valued and heard employees are more likely to contribute creative solutions and improvements. Empowered and respected employees are more motivated to perform at their best, with humble leadership fostering a positive work environment resulting in higher productivity and job satisfaction. Humility and modesty build trust and respect within the team, as leaders who listen actively and value the input of others create a sense of unity and collaboration, enhancing team cohesion and effectiveness. Organisations led by humble leaders are more likely to achieve sustainable growth, as prioritising the well-being and development of their team creates a strong foundation for long-term success.

Regular self-reflection helps leaders assess their behaviour and identify areas for improvement, so they should take time to reflect on their interactions and consider how to demonstrate greater humility and modesty. Creating channels for open communication, such as suggestion boxes, regular team meetings, and anonymous feedback surveys, allows employees to share ideas and feedback without fear of judgment. Leaders should promote and celebrate team achievements rather than individual successes, reinforcing the value of collaboration and highlighting the importance of collective efforts. Seeking opportunities to learn from others, whether through mentorship, networking, or professional development, shows a commitment to growth and humility by continuously expanding their knowledge and skills.

A culture of humility and modesty fosters a positive organisational climate where employees feel valued and respected, attracting and retaining top talent, and contributing to the organisation's overall success. Teams led by humble leaders are more resilient and capable of overcoming challenges, with strong relationships and trust enabling effective teamwork in any situation. Leaders who emphasise humility and modesty can navigate uncertainties with strategic agility, ensuring the organisation remains responsive to emerging opportunities and challenges. Organisations that prioritise humility and modesty in leadership are better positioned for sustainable success, as these qualities provide a strong foundation supporting long-term growth and resilience.

FOSTERING A SENSE OF OWNERSHIP

Their work was done and their undertakings were successful, while the people all said, 'We are as we are, of ourselves!'

Lao Tzu's wisdom underscores the importance of empowering employees to take ownership of their work. Effective leaders understand that when employees feel valued and have the autonomy to make decisions, they are more engaged and motivated. By delegating responsibilities and trusting their teams to deliver results, strategic leaders can foster a sense of pride and commitment, driving overall organisational success.

Regularly recognising and appreciating employee contributions is crucial for fostering a sense of ownership, so leaders should acknowledge the efforts and achievements of their team members, both publicly and privately, boosting morale and reinforcing the value of each individual's work. Providing constructive feedback and opportunities for development shows employees that their growth is important, so leaders should offer regular feedback, highlight strengths and areas for improvement, and support their team members in pursuing professional development opportunities, fostering a sense of ownership and commitment. Involving employees in decision-making processes ensures that their voices are heard and valued, so leaders should seek input from their team members on key decisions and encourage collaborative discussions, fostering a sense of ownership and responsibility for the outcomes.

Delegating responsibilities and trusting employees to manage their tasks independently is key to fostering a sense of ownership, so leaders should clearly define roles and expectations, provide the necessary resources, and allow team members the autonomy to make decisions, empowering employees to take initiative and ownership of their work. An empowering leadership style focuses on enabling and supporting employees rather than controlling them, so leaders should adopt a coaching and mentoring approach, providing guidance and support while allowing employees the freedom to innovate and solve problems, building confidence and fostering a sense of ownership. Holding employees accountable for their work reinforces the importance of ownership, so leaders should set clear expectations, monitor progress, and provide regular feedback, encouraging accountability to help employees understand the impact of their work and foster a sense of responsibility and pride.

A positive work environment where employees feel valued, respected, and supported enhances engagement and motivation, so leaders should promote a culture of collaboration, open communication, and mutual respect, creating a space where employees are motivated to contribute their best efforts. Encouraging innovation and creativity empowers employees to take ownership of their ideas and projects, so leaders should create opportunities for team members to experiment with new approaches and solutions, providing the freedom to explore and innovate, fostering a sense of ownership and pride in their work. Aligning individual goals with organisational values and mission helps employees see the larger purpose of their work, so leaders should communicate the organisation's vision and values clearly, helping employees understand how their contributions align with and support these goals, fostering a sense of ownership and commitment.

Employees who feel a sense of ownership are more engaged and motivated, taking pride in their work and going above and beyond to achieve success. Empowered employees are more productive as they take initiative and responsibility for their tasks, driving overall organisational success and efficiency. A culture of ownership fosters innovation and creativity, with empowered employees more likely to contribute innovative solutions and improvements. Ownership also fosters a sense of unity and collaboration within the team, as employees who feel responsible for their work are more likely to support one another and work together effectively. Organisations that foster a sense of ownership among their employees are better positioned for sustainable growth, as this empowerment creates a strong foundation for long-term success and resilience.

Setting clear goals and expectations provides direction and focus for employees, so leaders should set specific, measurable, achievable, relevant, and time-bound (SMART) goals to ensure employees understand what is expected of them. Ensuring that employees have the necessary resources and support to succeed is crucial, so leaders should provide access to tools, training, and information, removing obstacles that hinder progress. Creating opportunities for collaboration and teamwork fosters a sense of ownership, so leaders should promote cross-functional projects and encourage team members to share ideas and work together. Regularly celebrating successes, both big and small, reinforces the value of ownership, so leaders should acknowledge and celebrate milestones and achievements, recognising the contributions of their team members.

A culture of ownership fosters a positive and sustainable organisational climate, where employees feel connected to a larger purpose and are more likely to experience job satisfaction and fulfillment. Teams that take ownership of their work are more resilient and capable of overcoming challenges, with strong relationships and trust enabling effective teamwork in any situation. Leaders who foster a sense of ownership can navigate uncertainties with strategic agility, ensuring the organisation remains responsive to emerging opportunities and challenges. Organisations that prioritise ownership among their employees are better positioned for long-term success, with this sense of ownership providing a strong foundation for sustainable growth and resilience.

CHAPTER 18 – SUPERFICIALITY

Chapter 18 of the *Tao Te Ching* explores the consequences of losing alignment with the Tao and highlights the emergence of artificial virtues and disorder. These teachings can provide valuable insights for modern-day strategic management:

ALIGNING WITH CORE PRINCIPLES & VALUES

> *When the Great Tao (Way or Method) ceased to be observed, benevolence and righteousness came into vogue.*

Lao Tzu's passage highlights the importance of staying true to core principles and values. When organisations stray from their foundational values and mission, they may attempt to compensate with artificial measures and superficial virtues. Leaders should ensure that all actions and decisions are aligned with the core values of the organisation. This alignment fosters authenticity, integrity, and trust.

Core values are the fundamental beliefs that guide an organisation's behaviour and decision-making, so leaders should clearly define these values and ensure they are communicated consistently throughout the organisation. Core values might include integrity, excellence, innovation, respect, and teamwork. The mission and vision statements articulate the organisation's purpose and long-term aspirations, so leaders should ensure that these statements are aligned with the core values and guide the organisation's strategic planning and daily operations. Regularly revisiting and refining these statements helps maintain focus and alignment. Leaders should incorporate core values into the decision-making process, evaluating options and strategies through the lens of the organisation's values to ensure choices support the mission and vision, fostering ethical behaviour and consistency.

Leaders should model integrity by acting with honesty, transparency, and fairness, making ethical decisions, being truthful in communications, and treating others with respect, which sets a powerful example for employees and builds a culture of trust and accountability. Consistency between words and actions reinforces integrity, so leaders should ensure their behaviours align with the organisation's values and commitments, creating a stable and trustworthy environment where employees feel confident in their leaders' reliability. Trust is built through consistent, ethical behaviour, so leaders should prioritise transparency in their actions and decisions, keeping employees informed and engaged, fostering a positive work environment where employees feel valued and motivated to contribute.

Authentic leadership involves being genuine and true to oneself while aligning with the organisation's values, avoiding superficial measures or presenting a façade, as authenticity builds credibility and fosters genuine connections with employees. Ethical practices are grounded in core values and principles, so leaders should ensure the organisation's policies, procedures, and practices reflect these values, including promoting ethical behaviour, addressing unethical conduct, and maintaining high standards of integrity. Superficial virtues are often adopted to mask a lack of true alignment with core values, so leaders should focus on genuine adherence to values rather than engaging in performative actions, reinforcing the organisation's commitment to its principles.

Alignment with core principles and values builds trust and loyalty among employees, customers, and stakeholders, as people are more likely to support and remain committed to an organisation that consistently upholds its values. A culture grounded in core values fosters a positive and cohesive work environment, where employees feel connected to a larger purpose and are more likely to be engaged, motivated, and satisfied with their work. Value-based decision-making ensures that choices are consistent and aligned with the organisation's mission and vision, enhancing strategic clarity and supporting long-term success. Organisations that stay true to their core values are better positioned for sustainable growth, as ethical behaviour, authenticity, and integrity provide a strong foundation for enduring success and resilience.

Leaders should regularly communicate the organisation's values to employees through meetings, internal communications, and training sessions, ensuring values remain top of mind and integrated into daily operations. Evaluating employees based on their alignment with core values reinforces their importance, so leaders should include value-based criteria in performance evaluations and recognise employees who exemplify the organisation's principles. Promoting ethical leadership at all levels involves providing training on ethical behaviour, establishing clear expectations, and addressing deviations from the organisation's values. Organisational policies should reflect and support core values, so leaders should review and update policies regularly to ensure they promote ethical behaviour, respect, and accountability.

A focus on core values fosters a positive organisational climate where employees feel valued and respected, attracting and retaining top talent and contributing to the organisation's overall success. Teams that are aligned with core values are more resilient and capable of overcoming challenges, with strong relationships and trust developed through value-based leadership enabling effective teamwork in any situation. Leaders who prioritise core values can navigate uncertainties with strategic agility, ensuring decisions are made with long-term sustainability in mind, supporting the organisation's resilience. Organisations that consistently align with their core principles and values are better positioned for long-term success, as these values provide a strong foundation supporting sustainable growth and resilience.

AVOIDING SUPERFICIAL MEASURES

Then appeared wisdom and shrewdness, and there ensued great hypocrisy.

Lao Tzu's passage warns against the perils of superficial measures and artificial virtues, which can lead to hypocrisy and mistrust within an organisation. Leaders should avoid implementing policies or practices that merely appear virtuous on the surface but lack genuine substance. Instead, they should focus on creating authentic and meaningful strategies that reflect the true purpose and values of the organisation. This approach builds credibility and trust among employees and stakeholders.

Superficial measures often manifest as performative actions intended to create an illusion of virtue without genuine commitment, such as token diversity initiatives, empty sustainability promises, and insincere employee recognition programmes; leaders should be wary of adopting measures that serve more as PR stunts than genuine efforts. Policies and practices that are implemented with great fanfare but lack sustained effort and follow-through are superficial, so leaders must ensure their initiatives are backed by long-term plans, resources, and genuine commitment. Inconsistent behaviour, such as preaching work-life balance while encouraging excessive overtime, creates a sense of hypocrisy, so leaders should strive for consistency between their words and actions to maintain credibility.

Authentic strategies are grounded in the organisation's core values and mission, so leaders should ensure that all initiatives align with these foundational principles, fostering a sense of purpose and integrity within the organisation. Authenticity requires genuine commitment from leadership, so leaders should invest time, resources, and effort into initiatives that reflect the organisation's values, signalling to employees and stakeholders that the organisation's actions are more than just window dressing. Open and transparent communication builds trust and credibility, so leaders should be honest about the organisation's goals, challenges, and progress, fostering a culture of trust and accountability.

Ethical behaviour is the cornerstone of trust, so leaders should ensure all organisational practices are ethical and fair, including treating employees with respect, engaging in fair business practices, and maintaining high standards of integrity. Trust is built through consistent behaviour, so leaders should ensure their actions consistently reflect the organisation's values and commitments, reinforcing trust and credibility. Involving employees and stakeholders in decision-making processes fosters a sense of ownership and trust, so leaders should seek input from diverse perspectives and make decisions collaboratively, enhancing the authenticity of the organisation's actions.

Meaningful strategies require long-term planning and sustained effort, so leaders should develop comprehensive plans with clear goals, milestones, and timelines, ensuring initiatives are not just short-term fixes but contribute to long-term success. Investing in the development and growth of employees demonstrates commitment to the organisation's values, so leaders should provide opportunities for training, mentorship, and career advancement, fostering a culture of continuous improvement. Adopting sustainable practices reflects a genuine commitment to ethical and responsible behaviour, so leaders should prioritise sustainability in their operations, considering environmental, social, and governance (ESG) factors in their strategies.

Authentic actions build trust and loyalty among employees and stakeholders, as people are more likely to support and remain committed to an organisation that demonstrates genuine commitment to its values. A culture grounded in authenticity and integrity fosters a positive and cohesive work environment, where employees feel connected to a larger purpose and are more likely to be engaged, motivated, and satisfied with their work. Organisations that prioritise authenticity and ethical behaviour enjoy a strong reputation for credibility and trustworthiness, attracting top talent, loyal customers, and strategic partners. Avoiding superficial measures supports sustainable success, as genuine and meaningful strategies provide a strong foundation for long-term growth and resilience.

Regularly auditing organisational practices to ensure alignment with core values helps identify and eliminate superficial measures, so leaders should assess whether initiatives genuinely reflect the organisation's values and make necessary adjustments. Engaging with employees, customers, and other stakeholders provides valuable insights into the authenticity of the organisation's actions, so leaders should seek feedback and involve stakeholders in shaping and refining initiatives. Leaders should promote ethical leadership at all levels of the organisation by providing training on ethical behaviour, establishing clear expectations, and addressing any deviations from the organisation's values. Setting realistic and achievable goals ensures initiatives are grounded in reality, so leaders should avoid overpromising and focus on delivering tangible results that reflect genuine effort and commitment.

A focus on authenticity and integrity fosters a positive organisational climate where employees feel valued and respected, attracting and retaining top talent and contributing to the organisation's overall success. Teams that are aligned with authentic and meaningful strategies are more resilient and capable of overcoming challenges, with strong relationships and trust developed through genuine commitment enabling effective teamwork in any situation. Leaders who prioritise authenticity can navigate uncertainties with strategic agility, ensuring decisions are made with long-term sustainability in mind, supporting the organisation's resilience. Organisations that consistently avoid superficial measures and focus on genuine strategies are better positioned for long-term success, with these values providing a strong foundation supporting sustainable growth and resilience.

MAINTAINING HARMONY & UNITY

When harmony no longer prevailed throughout the six kinships, filial sons found their manifestation; when the states and clans fell into disorder, loyal ministers appeared.

Lao Tzu's passage highlights that disorder within an organisation often leads to reactive measures and the emergence of individuals who strive to restore order. To prevent this, strategic leaders should prioritise maintaining harmony and unity within their teams. By fostering open communication, collaboration, and a sense of belonging, leaders can address issues proactively and create a cohesive work environment. This approach prevents the need for reactive measures and ensures smooth operations.

Open and transparent communication is the foundation of harmony and unity, so leaders should ensure that information flows freely within the organisation by providing regular updates on goals, progress, and challenges, building trust and keeping everyone aligned with the organisation's mission and vision. Active listening involves fully engaging with team members, understanding their perspectives, and responding thoughtfully, so leaders should practise this in meetings and interactions, showing genuine interest in employees' thoughts and concerns, encouraging a culture where everyone feels heard and valued. Establishing feedback mechanisms allows employees to share their ideas and concerns without fear of judgment, so leaders should create channels for both formal and informal feedback, such as suggestion boxes, regular check-ins, and anonymous surveys, ensuring that issues are identified and addressed proactively.

Team building activities strengthen relationships and foster a sense of unity, so leaders should organise regular team-building exercises, such as workshops, retreats, and social events, to encourage collaboration and camaraderie among employees. Encouraging cross-functional projects promotes collaboration across different departments, so leaders should create opportunities for employees to work together on initiatives requiring diverse skill sets and perspectives, enhancing problem-solving and innovation. Establishing shared goals aligns team members' efforts towards a common purpose, so leaders should clearly define the organisation's objectives and involve employees in setting and achieving these goals, fostering a shared vision, unity, and collective responsibility.

An inclusive culture ensures that all employees feel valued and respected, so leaders should promote diversity and inclusion by celebrating different backgrounds, experiences, and viewpoints, fostering a sense of belonging and enriching the organisational culture. Regularly recognising and celebrating employees' contributions reinforces their sense of belonging, so leaders should acknowledge individual and team achievements, expressing appreciation for their efforts, which boosts morale and motivation. A supportive work environment where employees feel safe to express themselves and take risks is essential for unity, so leaders should encourage open dialogue, provide support for professional development, and address any issues promptly and fairly.

Proactively addressing potential issues before they escalate maintains harmony, so leaders should monitor team dynamics and address any signs of conflict or dissatisfaction early, preventing issues from festering and disrupting the work environment. Effective conflict resolution involves addressing disagreements constructively and finding mutually beneficial solutions, so leaders should facilitate open discussions, mediate conflicts impartially, and promote a culture where conflicts are seen as opportunities for growth and understanding. Fostering a culture of continuous improvement ensures the organisation remains agile and responsive to change, so leaders should encourage employees to identify areas for improvement and implement changes that enhance efficiency and effectiveness.

A harmonious and united team is more productive, as employees who feel connected and supported are more motivated to contribute their best efforts, leading to higher levels of performance. Collaboration and open communication foster innovation, with valued and included employees more likely to share creative ideas and solutions, driving continuous improvement and growth. Maintaining harmony and unity strengthens team cohesion, as employees who trust and respect one another work together more effectively, enhancing overall team performance. A positive work environment where employees feel a sense of belonging and purpose reduces turnover, with leaders who prioritise harmony and unity creating a loyal and committed workforce, thereby reducing recruitment and training costs.

Holding regular team meetings ensures that communication remains open and everyone stays aligned with the organisation's goals, so leaders should use these meetings to share updates, discuss challenges, and celebrate successes. Implementing initiatives that enhance employee engagement fosters a sense of connection and commitment, so leaders should consider programmes such as wellness activities, professional development opportunities, and employee resource groups. Providing tools and technologies that facilitate collaboration enhances teamwork, so leaders should invest in platforms that enable seamless communication and project management, making it easier for employees to work together. Establishing recognition programmes that reward teamwork and collaboration reinforces the importance of unity, so leaders should celebrate collaborative efforts and recognise employees who contribute to a positive and harmonious work environment.

Focusing on harmony and unity fosters a sustainable organisational culture where employees feel valued and respected, attracting and retaining top talent and contributing to the organisation's overall success. Teams that maintain harmony and unity are more resilient and capable of overcoming challenges, with strong relationships and trust enabling effective teamwork in any situation. Leaders who prioritise harmony and unity can navigate uncertainties with strategic agility, ensuring decisions are made with long-term sustainability in mind, supporting the organisation's resilience. Organisations that consistently prioritise harmony and unity are better positioned for long-term success, with these values providing a strong foundation supporting sustainable growth and resilience.

CHAPTER 19 – GOVERNANCE

Chapter 19 of the *Tao Te Ching* encourages renouncing superficial wisdom, benevolence, and contrivances to embrace simplicity and authenticity. Here's how these teachings can be applied to modern-day strategic management:

EMBRACING SIMPLICITY & AUTHENTICITY

If we could renounce our sageness and discard our wisdom, it would be better for the people a hundredfold.

Lao Tzu's wisdom emphasises the importance of simplicity and authenticity in leadership. In strategic management, prioritising simplicity and authenticity over ostentatious displays of intelligence and wisdom creates a more transparent and efficient organisation. By focusing on clear, straightforward strategies and genuine actions, leaders can reduce complexity and foster trust among employees and stakeholders.

Leaders should develop strategies that are simple and easy to understand by clearly defining objectives, setting achievable goals, and outlining actionable steps, as simple strategies are more likely to be embraced and effectively implemented by the team. Simplifying organisational processes enhances efficiency and reduces the likelihood of errors, so leaders should regularly review and streamline workflows, eliminating unnecessary steps and bureaucracy to improve productivity and make it easier for employees to navigate their tasks. Clear and concise communication reduces misunderstandings and ensures that everyone is on the same page, so leaders should avoid jargon and complex language, opting for straightforward and direct communication to make information more accessible and actionable.

Authentic leaders are true to themselves and transparent in their actions, building credibility and trust within the organisation by being genuine and honest. Acting with honesty and integrity is crucial for authenticity, so leaders should be truthful in their communications, admit mistakes, and take responsibility for their actions, fostering a culture of trust and accountability. Consistency between words and actions reinforces authenticity, so leaders should ensure their behaviours align with their stated values and commitments, with transparency in decision-making and actions further building trust and credibility.

Decision-making processes should be straightforward and involve only the necessary stakeholders, avoiding overcomplication with excessive analysis or too many people; clear criteria and streamlined processes make decision-making more efficient and effective. Delegating authority to team members reduces the bottleneck of central decision-making and empowers employees to take ownership of their tasks, so leaders should trust their team's capabilities and provide them with the autonomy to make decisions within their areas of responsibility. Leveraging technology to automate routine tasks and streamline operations reduces complexity, so leaders should invest in tools and systems that enhance productivity and simplify workflows, allowing employees to focus on more strategic and value-added activities.

Open and honest communication fosters trust within the organisation, so leaders should provide regular updates, share important information, and create opportunities for employees and stakeholders to ask questions and provide feedback. Actively engaging with stakeholders, including employees, customers, and partners, builds trust and strengthens relationships, so leaders should seek input, listen to concerns, and involve stakeholders in decision-making processes to ensure actions and strategies align with the needs and expectations of all parties.

Recognising and celebrating the contributions of team members reinforces their value and builds trust, so leaders should acknowledge individual and team achievements, expressing appreciation for their efforts, which boosts morale and motivation.

Simplified strategies and processes enhance organisational efficiency, allowing employees to focus on their tasks without unnecessary complexity, leading to higher productivity and better outcomes. Authentic and straightforward leadership fosters trust and loyalty among employees and stakeholders, as people are more likely to support and remain committed to an organisation that consistently acts with integrity and transparency. Clear and concise communication reduces misunderstandings and ensures alignment with the organisation's goals, enhancing collaboration and collective effort. A culture grounded in simplicity and authenticity fosters a positive and cohesive work environment, where employees feel connected to a larger purpose and are more likely to be engaged, motivated, and satisfied with their work.

Leaders should break down complex objectives into simple, achievable goals, making it easier for employees to understand and work towards the organisation's vision. Regularly reviewing processes and strategies helps identify areas for simplification, so leaders should encourage continuous improvement by seeking feedback from employees and making necessary adjustments. Providing leadership development programmes that emphasise authenticity and integrity helps cultivate genuine leaders, so leaders should receive training on ethical behaviour, transparent communication, and effective decision-making. Promoting a culture of openness and honesty encourages employees to be authentic in their interactions, so leaders should model these behaviours and create an environment where employees feel safe to express themselves.

A focus on simplicity and authenticity fosters a sustainable organisational culture where employees feel valued and respected, attracting and retaining top talent and contributing to the organisation's overall success. Teams that embrace simplicity and authenticity are more resilient and capable of overcoming challenges, with strong relationships and trust developed through these principles enabling effective teamwork in any situation. Leaders who prioritise simplicity and authenticity can navigate uncertainties with strategic agility, ensuring decisions are made with long-term sustainability in mind and supporting the organisation's resilience. Organisations that consistently embrace simplicity and authenticity are better positioned for long-term success, as these values provide a strong foundation supporting sustainable growth and resilience.

ENCOURAGING GENUINE RELATIONSHIPS & ETHICAL BEHAVIOUR

> *If we could renounce our benevolence and discard our righteousness, the people would again become filial and kindly.*

Lao Tzu's passage highlights the dangers of superficial benevolence and righteousness, which can lead to inauthentic behaviours and relationships. Leaders should strive to encourage genuine relationships and ethical behaviour by leading by example. This means being honest, fair, and transparent in all interactions. By fostering a culture of integrity, leaders can build a supportive and collaborative work environment.

Leaders should prioritise honesty and transparency in their communications and actions by being truthful about the organisation's challenges and successes, sharing information openly, and admitting mistakes, as transparent leadership builds trust and encourages employees to be open and honest as well. Fair and impartial decision-making is crucial for maintaining ethical standards, so leaders should ensure their decisions are based on objective criteria and not influenced by personal biases or favouritism, fostering a sense of justice and respect within the team. Consistency between words and actions is essential for leading by example, so leaders should ensure their behaviours align with the values and principles they advocate, reinforcing the importance of ethical behaviour and building credibility.

Trust is the foundation of genuine relationships, so leaders should take deliberate steps to build trust with their team members by being reliable, keeping promises, and showing genuine concern for their well-being, fostering open communication and collaboration. Listening actively and empathetically to team members shows that their opinions and feelings are valued, so leaders should create opportunities for employees to share their thoughts, ideas, and concerns without fear of judgment, strengthening relationships and promoting a supportive work environment. Promoting teamwork and collaboration helps build strong relationships among employees, so leaders should create an environment where collaboration is encouraged and diverse perspectives are welcomed, with team-building activities and collaborative projects fostering camaraderie and mutual respect.

Leaders should establish and communicate clear ethical standards and expectations by developing a code of conduct that outlines acceptable behaviours and practices, with regular training on ethical behaviour to ensure employees understand and adhere to these standards. Recognising and rewarding ethical behaviour reinforces its importance, so leaders should highlight examples of ethical decision-making and actions within the organisation, celebrating employees who demonstrate integrity and fairness. Promptly addressing unethical behaviour is crucial for maintaining a culture of integrity, so leaders should have mechanisms in place to report and investigate unethical conduct and take appropriate corrective actions to ensure ethical standards are upheld.

Genuine relationships and ethical behaviour build trust and loyalty among employees and stakeholders, leading to greater support and commitment for an organisation that consistently demonstrates integrity and fairness. A culture grounded in these principles fosters a positive and cohesive work environment, where employees feel connected to a larger purpose and are more likely to be engaged, motivated, and satisfied with their work. Trust and mutual respect enhance collaboration and teamwork, as valued and supported employees are more likely to share ideas, seek input, and work together effectively, driving innovation and problem-solving. Organisations that prioritise these values are better positioned for sustainable success, as ethical practices and strong relationships provide a stable foundation for long-term growth and resilience.

Leaders should model ethical behaviour in their actions and decisions by being transparent, fair, and consistent, as well as showing respect and empathy towards others. Establishing open channels of communication allows employees to share their thoughts and concerns freely, so leaders should encourage feedback and ensure that employees feel heard and valued. Developing and implementing ethical guidelines and policies provides a framework for expected behaviour, so leaders should ensure these guidelines are communicated clearly and reinforced regularly. Promoting a culture of collaboration and mutual respect enhances relationships and ethical behaviour, so leaders should create opportunities for teamwork and recognise collaborative efforts.

Focusing on genuine relationships and ethical behaviour fosters a sustainable organisational culture where employees feel valued and respected, attracting and retaining top talent and contributing to the organisation's overall success. Teams built on trust and mutual respect are more resilient and capable of overcoming challenges, with strong relationships and ethical standards enabling effective teamwork in any situation. Leaders who prioritise genuine relationships and ethical behaviour can navigate uncertainties with strategic agility, ensuring decisions are made with long-term sustainability in mind and supporting the organisation's resilience. Organisations that consistently encourage genuine relationships and ethical behaviour are better positioned for long-term success, as these values provide a strong foundation supporting sustainable growth and resilience.

FOCUSING ON LONG-TERM VALUE OVER SHORT-TERM GAINS

If we could renounce our artful contrivances and discard our (scheming for) gain, there would be no thieves nor robbers.

Lao Tzu's passage underscores the dangers of focusing on short-term gains at the expense of long-term value. Strategic leaders should prioritise long-term value creation rather than engaging in schemes or tactics that may offer quick profits but ultimately harm the organisation's reputation and sustainability. By prioritising ethical practices and long-term goals, leaders can build a more stable and resilient organisation.

Leaders should prioritise ethical decision-making that aligns with the organisation's core values and mission by evaluating the long-term impact of decisions and avoiding actions that might offer immediate benefits but compromise the organisation's integrity, as ethical decisions build trust and credibility essential for long-term success. Implementing sustainable practices ensures the organisation's operations are environmentally and socially responsible, so leaders should prioritise sustainability in their strategies, considering the long-term impact on the environment, society, and stakeholders, as sustainable practices contribute to the organisation's reputation and resilience. Innovation drives long-term growth and competitiveness, so leaders should invest in research and development, fostering a culture of creativity and continuous improvement to stay ahead of industry trends and adapt to changing market conditions.

Quick fixes and short-term schemes may provide immediate benefits but often come with long-term consequences, so leaders should resist the temptation to pursue quick profits at the expense of the organisation's sustainability, focusing instead on strategies that deliver lasting value. Transparent operations build trust with stakeholders and prevent the pitfalls of short-term schemes, so leaders should be open about the organisation's goals, challenges, and progress, ensuring all actions are aligned with long-term objectives to foster accountability and trust. Incentive structures should be aligned with long-term goals rather than short-term performance metrics, so leaders should design compensation and reward systems that encourage employees to focus on sustainable growth and ethical behaviour, ensuring everyone in the organisation works towards common long-term objectives.

Strategic planning should focus on long-term goals and sustainability, with leaders developing comprehensive plans that outline clear objectives, milestones, and timelines to ensure the organisation remains focused on its mission and vision. Effective risk management involves identifying and mitigating potential risks that could impact the organisation's long-term success, so leaders should conduct thorough risk assessments and develop strategies to address potential threats, enhancing resilience and stability. A culture of continuous improvement ensures the organisation remains agile and responsive to change, so leaders should encourage employees to identify areas for improvement and implement changes that enhance efficiency and effectiveness, driving long-term success and innovation.

Organisations that prioritise long-term value and ethical practices enjoy a strong reputation among stakeholders, attracting top talent, loyal customers, and strategic partners, contributing to growth and success. Long-term value creation supports sustainable growth, allowing organisations to achieve consistent progress and resilience in the face of challenges. Ethical behaviour and transparency build trust and loyalty among employees, customers, and stakeholders, making people more likely to support and remain committed to an organisation that demonstrates integrity and long-term thinking. Investing in innovation and continuous improvement provides a competitive advantage, positioning organisations to stay ahead of industry trends and adapt to changing market conditions.

Leaders should develop a clear and compelling long-term vision for the organisation, communicating it regularly and integrating it into all strategic planning and decision-making processes. Ethical leadership should be promoted at all levels of the organisation, with leaders modelling ethical behaviour, providing training on ethical practices, and establishing clear expectations for conduct. Leaders should prioritise sustainability in their operations, considering environmental, social, and governance (ESG) factors in their strategies, as this commitment supports long-term success and resilience. Incentive structures should be designed to reward long-term performance and ethical behaviour, ensuring that compensation and rewards align with the organisation's mission and vision. Encouraging a culture of innovation and continuous improvement drives long-term value, so leaders should create opportunities for employees to experiment with new ideas, embrace change, and contribute to the organisation's growth.

Focusing on long-term value fosters a sustainable organisational culture where employees feel valued and respected, attracting and retaining top talent and contributing to the organisation's overall success. Teams that prioritise long-term value are more resilient and capable of overcoming challenges, with strong relationships and ethical standards enabling them to work together effectively in any situation. Leaders who prioritise long-term value can navigate uncertainties with strategic agility, ensuring decisions are made with long-term sustainability in mind, supporting the organisation's resilience. Organisations that consistently focus on long-term value creation are better positioned for long-term success, as these values provide a strong foundation supporting sustainable growth and resilience.

SIMPLIFYING GOVERNANCE & PROCESSES

> *Those three methods (of government)... made these names their want of worth to veil; But simple views, and courses plain and true Would selfish ends and many lusts eschew.*

Lao Tzu's passage highlights the benefits of adopting simple and straightforward approaches to governance and processes. Simplifying governance and processes can lead to more effective management by reducing unnecessary layers of bureaucracy and complexity. Leaders should strive to implement clear and plain policies, which can create a more agile and responsive organisation. This clarity helps in reducing misunderstandings and fostering a culture of accountability.

Simplified governance structures allow organisations to respond more quickly to changes in the market or internal dynamics by removing bureaucratic barriers, enabling decisions to be made and implemented more swiftly, keeping the organisation agile and competitive. Streamlining processes and eliminating unnecessary steps enhances efficiency, allowing employees to focus on their core tasks without being bogged down by redundant procedures, leading to increased productivity and better use of resources. Clear and straightforward policies improve transparency within the organisation, making it easier for employees to understand the rules and expectations, fostering an environment of trust and openness.

Strategies for Simplifying Governance & Processes

Eliminating Redundancies: Leaders should conduct thorough reviews of existing processes to identify and eliminate redundancies. This involves examining each step of a process to determine its necessity and value. By removing redundant tasks, organisations can streamline operations and improve efficiency.

Empowering Decision-Making: Decentralising decision-making authority empowers employees and reduces the bottleneck of central governance. Leaders should delegate decision-making powers to team members at various levels, allowing for quicker and more informed decisions. This empowerment fosters a sense of ownership and accountability.

Implementing Clear Policies: Developing clear and concise policies helps reduce complexity. Leaders should ensure that policies are easy to understand and implement. This includes using plain language, avoiding jargon, and providing practical guidelines. Clear policies provide a consistent framework for decision-making and actions.

Utilising Technology: Leveraging technology to automate routine tasks and streamline processes enhances efficiency. Leaders should invest in digital tools and platforms that facilitate communication, project management, and data analysis. Technology can simplify governance by providing real-time insights and reducing manual efforts.

Clear expectations help employees understand their roles and responsibilities, so leaders should communicate expectations explicitly and provide regular feedback to ensure alignment, fostering accountability and performance. Encouraging employees to take ownership of their tasks and decisions promotes accountability, so leaders should trust their team members to manage their responsibilities and support them in their efforts, motivating employees to deliver their best work. Recognising and celebrating the contributions of team members reinforces accountability, so leaders should acknowledge individual and team achievements, expressing appreciation for their efforts, which boosts morale and encourages continued excellence.

Simplifying governance and processes reduces complexity, making it easier for employees to navigate their tasks and responsibilities, fostering a more efficient and productive work environment. A streamlined organisation can respond more quickly to changes and challenges, with simplified governance structures enabling swift decision-making and implementation, keeping the organisation agile and adaptable. Clear and straightforward processes promote collaboration, as employees who understand the rules and expectations can work together more effectively towards common goals, enhancing innovation and problem-solving. Simplified governance also fosters a culture of accountability, as clear policies and empowered decision-making encourage employees to take responsibility for their actions and outcomes, leading to higher levels of performance and trust.

Regular process audits help identify areas for simplification, as leaders assess existing processes, gather feedback from employees, and implement changes to enhance efficiency and clarity. Involving employees in the simplification process ensures that their insights and perspectives are considered, so leaders should create opportunities for employees to share their ideas and suggestions for improving governance and processes. Providing training on new and simplified processes helps employees adapt to changes, so leaders should offer comprehensive training programmes that equip employees with the skills and knowledge needed to navigate simplified governance structures. Continuous monitoring and adjustment ensure that simplification efforts remain effective, so leaders should track the impact of changes, gather feedback, and make necessary adjustments to maintain efficiency and alignment with organisational goals.

Simplifying governance fosters a sustainable organisational culture where employees feel empowered and valued, attracting and retaining top talent and contributing to the organisation's overall success. Teams that operate within simplified governance structures are more resilient and capable of overcoming challenges, as the clarity and accountability developed through this focus enable them to work together effectively in any situation. Leaders who prioritise simplicity can navigate uncertainties with strategic agility, ensuring that decisions are made with long-term sustainability in mind and supporting the organisation's resilience. Organisations that consistently simplify governance and processes are better positioned for long-term success, as these values provide a strong foundation supporting sustainable growth and resilience.

CHAPTER 20 – INDIVIDUALITY

Chapter 20 of the *Tao Te Ching* explores themes of simplicity, humility, and the rejection of superficial learning and conformity. These teachings can provide valuable insights for modern-day strategic management:

EMBRACING SIMPLICITY & REDUCING COMPLEXITY

When we renounce learning we have no troubles.

Lao Tzu's wisdom highlights the importance of embracing simplicity and reducing complexity in strategic management. Simplifying processes and avoiding unnecessary complexity can lead to better outcomes. Leaders should focus on clear and straightforward strategies, avoiding the pitfalls of overcomplicating their plans and operations. By embracing simplicity, organisations can improve efficiency and reduce the stress and confusion that often come with overly complex systems.

Simplified processes are more efficient, allowing employees to complete their work more quickly and with fewer errors, leading to higher productivity and better use of resources. Reduced complexity alleviates stress and confusion for employees, making it easier for them to understand their tasks and responsibilities, enhancing job satisfaction. Simple and clear communication ensures everyone in the organisation is on the same page, fostering better collaboration and alignment by avoiding jargon and overly complex language. Simplified processes and strategies also enable organisations to respond more quickly to changes and challenges, with streamlined decision-making and minimal bureaucracy, allowing leaders to implement changes swiftly and keep the organisation agile and adaptable.

Leaders should set clear and achievable objectives and goals that are specific, measurable, and aligned with the organisation's mission and vision, providing direction and focus for employees to understand what they need to achieve. Simplifying processes involves eliminating unnecessary steps and redundancies, with leaders conducting regular reviews of existing workflows to identify areas for improvement, enhancing efficiency and reducing the likelihood of errors. Leveraging technology to automate routine tasks and streamline operations simplifies workflows, so leaders should invest in digital tools and platforms that facilitate communication, project management, and data analysis, reducing complexity and enhancing productivity. Decentralising decision-making authority empowers employees and reduces the bottleneck of central governance, so leaders should trust their team members to make decisions within their areas of responsibility, fostering a sense of ownership and accountability.

Leaders should communicate their strategies using plain language, avoiding jargon and overly complex terminology to ensure all employees understand the organisation's goals and their roles in achieving them, thereby reducing misunderstandings and fostering alignment. Organisations should focus on their core competencies and avoid diversifying into areas that add unnecessary complexity, concentrating on their strengths to deliver better value and maintain a clear strategic direction. Regularly reviewing and adjusting strategies ensures they remain relevant and effective, so leaders should gather feedback from employees and stakeholders to identify areas for improvement and make necessary adjustments, keeping strategies simple and aligned with organisational goals.

Fostering a Culture of Simplicity

Encouraging open dialogue and feedback helps identify areas where complexity can be reduced, so leaders should create opportunities for employees to share their ideas and suggestions for simplifying processes and improving efficiency. Recognising and celebrating efforts to simplify processes reinforces the importance of simplicity, so leaders should acknowledge and reward employees who contribute to streamlining workflows and reducing complexity. Leaders should model simplicity in their actions and decisions, demonstrating clear and straightforward approaches to problem-solving and decision-making, setting a positive example for employees to follow.

Simplified processes and strategies support sustainable growth by ensuring the organisation operates efficiently and effectively, enabling it to scale and adapt to changes more easily. Teams that operate within simplified structures are more resilient and capable of overcoming challenges, as clarity and efficiency developed through simplicity enable them to work together effectively in any situation. Simplicity fosters a culture of innovation by reducing the cognitive load on employees and freeing up time for creative thinking, allowing them to focus on developing innovative solutions and ideas. Leaders who prioritise simplicity can navigate uncertainties with strategic agility, as simplified processes allow for quicker decision-making and implementation, keeping the organisation responsive to emerging opportunities and challenges.

VALUING AUTHENTICITY OVER FLATTERY

The (ready) 'yes,' and (flattering) 'yea;'—Small is the difference they display.

Lao Tzu's passage emphasises that there is little difference between ready agreement and flattery, both of which can be detrimental to leadership and organisational growth. Leaders should value authentic feedback over flattery and sycophancy. Encouraging honest and constructive feedback from team members helps identify real issues and opportunities for improvement. This approach creates a culture of trust and continuous improvement, where employees feel safe to express their true opinions without fear of retribution.

Leaders should create safe spaces where employees feel comfortable sharing their thoughts and opinions by fostering an environment of psychological safety, ensuring team members know they can speak up without fear of negative consequences. An open door policy encourages employees to approach leaders with feedback and concerns, so leaders should make themselves accessible and approachable to demonstrate they value and welcome input from their team members. Implementing regular feedback mechanisms, such as surveys, suggestion boxes, and one-on-one meetings, provides structured opportunities for employees to share their insights, and leaders should actively seek feedback and show commitment to listening and learning.

Leaders should recognise and appreciate honest feedback, even when it is critical, as acknowledging the value of constructive criticism reinforces their openness to different perspectives and commitment to improvement. By modelling authenticity through open and transparent communication, including admitting mistakes, sharing challenges, and being honest about the organisation's status, leaders set a positive tone for the entire organisation. Flattery and sycophancy should be discouraged to prevent a toxic culture where employees feel compelled to agree with leaders rather than express their true opinions, so leaders should emphasise the importance of honest feedback and make it clear that flattery is neither expected nor rewarded.

Trust is built through transparency and honesty, with leaders being transparent in their decision-making processes, sharing the reasoning behind their choices and the potential impact on the organisation, fostering trust and credibility. Empowering employees by involving them in decision-making processes and giving them a voice in shaping the organisation builds trust, so leaders should seek input from team members on key decisions and demonstrate that their feedback is valued and considered. Following through on feedback shows that leaders are committed to making improvements based on employee input, so leaders should communicate the actions taken in response to feedback and the outcomes achieved, reinforcing the value of honest feedback.

Authentic feedback provides leaders with valuable insights that can improve decision-making by giving them a clear understanding of real issues and opportunities within the organisation, enabling more informed and effective decisions. Honest feedback fosters innovation by encouraging employees to share their ideas and suggestions for improvement, promoting creativity and problem-solving, and driving continuous improvement. Valuing authenticity strengthens relationships between leaders and employees, making team members more likely to be engaged and committed to the organisation's success when their opinions are respected and valued. Organisations that prioritise authentic feedback over flattery are better positioned for sustainable growth, as this commitment to continuous improvement and ethical behaviour supports long-term success and resilience.

Leaders should establish multiple channels for feedback, including anonymous options, to ensure that all employees feel comfortable sharing their insights, and regularly solicit feedback through surveys, focus groups, and suggestion boxes to encourage open communication. Providing training on giving and receiving constructive feedback helps employees develop the skills needed for honest and respectful communication, so leaders should offer workshops and resources that teach effective feedback techniques. Recognising and celebrating constructive criticism by highlighting examples of how feedback has led to positive changes reinforces the value of honest input and encourages employees to continue sharing their insights. Developing action plans based on feedback demonstrates that leaders are committed to making meaningful changes, so leaders should outline specific steps to address the issues raised and communicate progress regularly.

A focus on authenticity fosters a positive organisational culture where employees feel valued and respected, attracting and retaining top talent and contributing to the organisation's overall success. Teams that value authentic feedback are more resilient and capable of overcoming challenges, as strong relationships and trust developed through this focus enable them to work together effectively in any situation. Leaders who prioritise authenticity can navigate uncertainties with strategic agility, as honest feedback provides the insights needed to make informed decisions, keeping the organisation responsive to emerging opportunities and challenges. Organisations that consistently value authentic feedback are better positioned for long-term success, as these values provide a strong foundation that supports sustainable growth and resilience.

UNDERSTANDING THE RANGE OF PERSPECTIVES

> *What all men fear is indeed to be feared; but how wide and without end is the range of questions (asking to be discussed)!*

Lao Tzu's passage emphasises the vast range of perspectives and concerns that exist within any organisation. Strategic leaders should recognise this diversity and actively acknowledge and address these varied viewpoints. By doing so, leaders can make more informed and balanced decisions. This inclusivity fosters a culture of respect and collaboration, where everyone's input is valued.

Leaders should actively listen to a variety of voices within the organisation by seeking input from employees at all levels, departments, and backgrounds to gain a comprehensive understanding of the issues at hand. Creating opportunities for open dialogue encourages employees to share their thoughts and concerns, so leaders should facilitate forums, town hall meetings, and discussion groups where team members can express their viewpoints freely and without fear of judgment. Recognising and valuing all contributions, regardless of their source, fosters an inclusive environment, ensuring everyone feels heard and appreciated, and their input is considered in decision-making processes.

Inclusive decision-making involves considering a range of perspectives before arriving at a conclusion, so leaders should involve diverse stakeholders in the decision-making process to ensure different viewpoints are represented and considered. Addressing varied viewpoints often means balancing competing interests, so leaders should strive to find solutions that consider the needs and concerns of different groups, aiming for decisions that are fair and equitable. Providing context and clarity about decisions is important when addressing diverse perspectives, so leaders should explain the rationale behind their choices, highlighting how different viewpoints were considered and how the decision aligns with the organisation's goals.

Considering a range of perspectives leads to more informed decision-making, as leaders who take into account diverse viewpoints are better equipped to understand the complexities of issues and develop well-rounded solutions. Inclusivity fosters a culture of collaboration and mutual respect, enhancing problem-solving and innovation as employees feel their input is valued and are more likely to support one another. Employees who feel heard and respected are more engaged and motivated, with inclusivity boosting morale and job satisfaction by providing a sense of belonging and purpose. An inclusive culture strengthens the overall organisational culture, creating a positive work environment where everyone feels valued and empowered to contribute, as leaders prioritise diversity and inclusion.

Leaders should implement various feedback mechanisms, such as surveys, suggestion boxes, and regular check-ins, to gather input from employees and provide structured opportunities for them to share their views. Building diverse teams ensures a variety of perspectives in discussions and decision-making, so leaders should prioritise diversity in hiring and team composition, considering factors like gender, ethnicity, experience, and expertise. Inclusive meetings should be facilitated by setting ground rules for respectful dialogue, actively encouraging quieter team members to speak up, and addressing any dominance by more vocal participants. Providing training on diversity, equity, and inclusion helps employees understand the importance of varied perspectives and navigate differences constructively, so leaders should offer workshops and resources that promote inclusivity and respect.

Teams that value diverse perspectives are more resilient and adaptable, with varied viewpoints and experiences enabling them to navigate challenges and find innovative solutions. Leaders who prioritise inclusivity can navigate uncertainties with strategic agility, as the comprehensive understanding gained from diverse perspectives ensures well-informed and aligned decisions with long-term goals. Inclusivity supports sustainable growth by fostering a culture of respect, collaboration, and continuous improvement, positioning organisations that value diversity for long-term success and resilience. A focus on inclusivity creates a positive organisational climate where employees feel valued and respected, attracting and retaining top talent and contributing to the organisation's overall success.

PRACTISING HUMILITY & EMPATHY

> *The multitude of men look satisfied and pleased; as if enjoying a full banquet, as if mounted on a tower in spring. I alone seem listless and still, my desires having as yet given no indication of their presence.*

Lao Tzu's passage reflects the virtue of humility, suggesting that true leaders do not seek to exalt themselves or display their desires prominently. Humility and empathy are key traits for effective leadership. Leaders should remain aware of their own limitations and be empathetic towards the experiences and challenges of their team members. By demonstrating humility, leaders can build stronger, more supportive relationships within their organisation.

Humble leaders recognise and acknowledge their limitations, understanding they do not have all the answers and are open to learning from others, which fosters a culture of continuous improvement and encourages employees to share their knowledge and expertise. Admitting mistakes is a powerful demonstration of humility, as leaders take responsibility for their errors and view them as opportunities for growth and learning, building trust and setting a positive example for the team. Actively seeking feedback from team members, humble leaders value different perspectives and are open to constructive criticism, showing they value their employees' opinions and are committed to personal and organisational growth. Recognising and sharing credit for successes with the team is a hallmark of humility, with leaders highlighting the contributions of their team members and celebrating collective achievements, reinforcing the importance of collaboration and fostering a sense of unity and belonging.

Empathetic leaders take the time to understand the experiences and challenges of their team members by actively listening to their concerns, asking open-ended questions, and showing genuine interest in their well-being, thereby providing better support and guidance. Compassionate actions, such as offering support during difficult times, demonstrating patience, and showing kindness, are integral to empathetic leadership, creating an environment where employees feel valued and cared for, fostering a positive and supportive work culture. Recognising that each team member is unique and may require different approaches to leadership, empathetic leaders tailor their leadership style to meet the individual needs of their employees, enhancing engagement, motivation, and performance. Promoting work-life balance is also an essential aspect of empathetic leadership, with leaders encouraging employees to take breaks, set boundaries, and prioritise their well-being, preventing burnout and ensuring employees remain healthy and productive.

Humility and empathy build stronger, more supportive relationships within the organisation, as employees who feel understood and valued are more likely to trust their leaders and collaborate effectively. This engagement leads to higher levels of productivity, job satisfaction, and overall performance. A culture of humility and empathy fosters innovation by encouraging employees to share their ideas and take risks, contributing creative solutions and improvements. Humble and empathetic leadership creates a positive organisational culture where employees feel respected and appreciated, attracting and retaining top talent and contributing to the organisation's long-term success.

Leaders should practise active listening by giving their full attention to team members during conversations, making eye contact, nodding, and asking clarifying questions to show engagement and interest. They should offer support by providing resources, guidance, and assistance when needed, demonstrating empathy and helping employees overcome challenges. Regular reflection on their leadership style, seeking feedback, identifying areas for improvement, and making necessary adjustments is crucial for demonstrating greater humility and empathy. Additionally, leaders should create a safe space for open and honest dialogue where employees feel comfortable sharing their thoughts and concerns, encouraging transparency and fostering trust.

Teams led by humble and empathetic leaders are more resilient and capable of overcoming challenges, as the strong relationships and trust developed through these traits enable teams to work together effectively in any situation. Leaders who prioritise humility and empathy can navigate uncertainties with strategic agility, ensuring the organisation remains responsive to emerging opportunities and challenges. Organisations that prioritise humility and empathy in leadership are better positioned for sustainable growth, as these qualities provide a strong foundation that supports long-term success and resilience. A focus on humility and empathy fosters a positive organisational climate where employees feel valued and respected, attracting and retaining top talent and contributing to the organisation's overall success.

EMBRACING INDIVIDUALITY & NON-CONFORMITY

Ordinary men look bright and intelligent, while I alone seem to be benighted. They look full of discrimination, while I alone am dull and confused.

Lao Tzu's passage highlights the importance of individuality and non-conformity. In strategic management, recognising and valuing these traits can lead to innovative solutions and fresh ideas. Encouraging diverse thinking and allowing team members to express their unique perspectives enriches the organisational environment. Leaders should create a culture where non-conformity is celebrated and where employees feel free to explore new approaches.

Leaders should create a safe environment where employees feel comfortable expressing their unique perspectives and ideas by promoting a culture of psychological safety, ensuring team members know they can speak up without fear of judgment or retribution. Recognising and valuing diversity in all its forms—backgrounds, experiences, skills, and viewpoints—enhances creativity and innovation, so leaders should actively seek to build diverse teams and encourage input from all members. Encouraging curiosity and a willingness to explore new ideas fosters diverse thinking, so leaders should promote a culture of learning and curiosity, where questioning the status quo and seeking new knowledge are encouraged and rewarded.

Promoting creative freedom is essential for fostering innovation, so leaders should provide opportunities for team members to experiment with new ideas, take risks, and learn from failures. Recognising and celebrating unique contributions reinforces the value of non-conformity, so leaders should highlight examples of how diverse perspectives have led to successful outcomes, showcasing the importance of thinking differently. Removing barriers that stifle creativity and non-conformity is crucial, so leaders should eliminate unnecessary bureaucracy and create flexible processes that allow employees to pursue innovative solutions.

Embracing individuality and non-conformity leads to enhanced innovation, as employees who feel free to express their unique ideas are more likely to contribute creative solutions and improvements. Diverse perspectives enhance problem-solving capabilities, with teams that value non-conformity able to approach challenges from multiple angles, leading to more robust and effective solutions. Employees who feel their individuality is valued and that they can be their authentic selves at work are more engaged and motivated, driving higher levels of productivity and job satisfaction. A culture that celebrates individuality and non-conformity fosters a positive and inclusive work environment, attracting and retaining top talent and contributing to the organisation's long-term success.

Leaders should encourage open dialogue and the sharing of diverse ideas by creating forums, brainstorming sessions, and workshops where employees can discuss their thoughts and collaborate on innovative solutions. Providing resources such as time, funding, and tools for innovation enables employees to pursue their creative ideas, so leaders should support initiatives that encourage experimentation and exploration. Offering flexibility in how employees approach their work fosters creativity and non-conformity, allowing team members to choose methods and strategies that work best for them within the framework of organisational goals. Recognising and rewarding creativity and unique contributions reinforces the value of non-conformity, so leaders should celebrate successes resulting from innovative thinking and highlight the impact of diverse perspectives.

Embracing individuality and non-conformity fosters a sustainable organisational culture where employees feel valued and respected, attracting and retaining top talent and contributing to the organisation's overall success. Teams that value diverse thinking and non-conformity are more resilient and adaptable, as varied perspectives and experiences enable them to navigate challenges and find innovative solutions. Leaders who prioritise individuality and non-conformity can navigate uncertainties with strategic agility, ensuring that diverse thinking informs decisions and aligns them with long-term goals. Organisations that consistently embrace individuality and non-conformity are better positioned for long-term success, as these values provide a strong foundation that supports sustainable growth and resilience.

FOSTERING A SENSE OF PURPOSE & CONNECTION

> *(Thus) I alone am different from other men, but I value the nursing-mother (the Tao).*

Lao Tzu's passage highlights the significance of valuing foundational principles, such as the Tao, which serves as a guiding force. Leaders should foster a sense of purpose and connection to the core values and mission of the organisation. By aligning their actions with these foundational principles, leaders can create a cohesive and motivated team. This shared sense of purpose helps guide the organisation through challenges and drives collective success.

Leaders should clearly define the organisation's core values and mission, providing a foundation for decision-making and actions, ensuring everyone understands the organisation's purpose and goals. Regularly communicating the organisation's vision and how it aligns with its values and mission reinforces a sense of purpose, with leaders sharing stories, examples, and successes that illustrate the organisation's impact and highlight how each team member's contributions support this vision. Aligning individual goals with organisational goals helps employees see the direct link between their work and the organisation's success, so leaders should work with employees to set personal and professional goals that align with the organisation's mission, fostering a sense of ownership and motivation.

A collaborative environment fosters a sense of connection among team members, so leaders should encourage teamwork, open communication, and mutual support, which help build relationships and a sense of belonging within the organisation. Recognising and celebrating employees' contributions reinforces their sense of connection to the organisation, so leaders should acknowledge individual and team achievements, expressing appreciation for their efforts, boosting morale, and strengthening the bond between employees and the organisation. Providing opportunities for employees to engage with the organisation's mission and values strengthens their connection, so leaders should create initiatives such as volunteer programmes, team-building activities, and professional development opportunities that align with the organisation's core principles and allow employees to actively contribute.

Leaders should ensure their decisions consistently reflect the organisation's core values and mission, reinforcing the importance of these principles and building trust among employees. Consistent decision-making demonstrates a commitment to the organisation's foundational principles. Ethical leadership involves making decisions that are fair, transparent, and aligned with the organisation's values, with leaders modelling ethical behaviour and setting clear expectations for conduct, fostering a culture of integrity and trust. Regular reflection on the organisation's values and mission helps ensure actions remain aligned with these principles, and leaders should encourage continuous improvement by seeking feedback, assessing progress, and making necessary adjustments to stay true to the organisation's core values.

A strong sense of purpose and connection increases employee engagement, as understanding the organisation's mission and seeing how their work contributes to its success motivates and commits employees to their roles. This shared sense of purpose fosters collaboration and teamwork, with connected employees more likely to work together effectively, driving collective success. A focus on purpose and connection strengthens the overall organisational culture, as leaders who prioritise these elements create a positive and cohesive work environment where employees feel valued and empowered. A shared sense of purpose helps guide the organisation through challenges, making employees more resilient and capable of navigating difficulties together, united by a common mission and values.

Leaders should regularly review and communicate the organisation's values and mission to ensure they remain relevant and aligned with the organisation's goals, keeping these principles at the forefront of employees' minds. Transparent communication helps build trust and reinforces the organisation's values, so leaders should provide regular updates on progress, challenges, and successes to keep employees informed and engaged. Involving employees in decision-making processes and strategic planning fosters a sense of ownership and connection, so leaders should seek input from team members and involve them in shaping the organisation's direction. Offering professional development opportunities that align with the organisation's values and mission supports employees' growth and reinforces their connection to the organisation, so leaders should invest in training, mentorship, and career advancement programmes.

Fostering a sense of purpose and connection creates a sustainable organisational culture where employees feel valued and respected, attracting and retaining top talent and contributing to the organisation's overall success. Teams united by a shared purpose and connection are more resilient and capable of overcoming challenges, as strong relationships and trust developed through this focus enable them to work together effectively in any situation. Leaders who prioritise purpose and connection can navigate uncertainties with strategic agility, ensuring that decisions are made with long-term sustainability in mind and supporting the organisation's resilience. Organisations that consistently foster a sense of purpose and connection are better positioned for long-term success, as these values provide a strong foundation that supports sustainable growth and resilience.

CHAPTER 21 – CREATIVITY & INNOVATION

Chapter 21 of the *Tao Te Ching* explores the profound, elusive, and enduring nature of the Tao, which serves as the source of all things. Here's how these teachings can be applied to modern-day strategic management:

EMBRACING THE SOURCE OF CREATIVITY & INNOVATION

The grandest forms of active force from Tao come, their only source.

Lao Tzu's passage emphasises that the greatest forms of active force and creativity originate from the Tao, the fundamental source. In strategic management, leaders should recognise and tap into these fundamental sources of creativity and innovation within their organisation. By fostering an environment where new ideas can flourish, leaders can drive continuous improvement and breakthrough innovations. This involves encouraging a culture of experimentation and openness to new perspectives.

Leaders should create an environment that encourages experimentation and exploration by allowing employees to try new approaches, take risks, and learn from failures, promoting a culture where experimentation is valued and stimulating creativity and innovation. Providing necessary resources such as time, funding, and tools supports creative efforts, so leaders should ensure employees have access to what they need to pursue their innovative ideas and projects, fostering a culture of continuous improvement. Designing flexible workspaces that accommodate different working styles enhances creativity, so leaders should create work environments that inspire creativity and collaboration, offering spaces for both focused work and group brainstorming sessions.

Building diverse teams that include individuals with different backgrounds, experiences, and viewpoints enhances creativity, so leaders should prioritise diversity in hiring and team composition, recognising that varied perspectives drive innovative thinking. Open communication channels that facilitate the sharing of ideas and feedback are essential for fostering creativity, so leaders should create forums, meetings, and digital platforms where employees can freely exchange their thoughts and collaborate on innovative solutions. Recognising and celebrating unique ideas reinforces the value of diverse thinking, so leaders should highlight examples of how new perspectives have led to successful innovations, showcasing the importance of thinking differently.

Embracing creativity and innovation leads to continuous improvement, as employees encouraged to explore new ideas and approaches are more likely to identify opportunities for enhancing processes, products, and services. A culture that values creativity can drive breakthrough innovations, fostering an environment where new perspectives are welcomed and leaders can spur the development of groundbreaking solutions that set the organisation apart from its competitors. Employees who feel their creative ideas are valued and supported are more engaged and motivated, leading to higher levels of productivity and job satisfaction. Organisations that prioritise creativity and innovation are better positioned to stay ahead of industry trends and adapt to changing market conditions, ensuring long-term success and resilience.

Leaders should implement structured programmes that encourage idea generation, such as hackathons, innovation labs, and brainstorming sessions, providing employees with dedicated time and space to develop and share their creative ideas. Offering training and development opportunities that focus on creativity and innovation skills helps employees enhance their creative thinking abilities, so leaders should provide workshops, courses, and resources that support creative skill development. Encouraging cross-functional collaboration brings together diverse perspectives and expertise, creating opportunities for employees from different departments to work together on innovative projects and initiatives. Recognising and rewarding employees for their innovative contributions reinforces the value of creativity, so leaders should celebrate successful innovations and provide incentives, such as bonuses, promotions, or public recognition, for creative efforts.

Embracing creativity and innovation fosters a sustainable organisational culture where employees feel valued and empowered, attracting and retaining top talent and contributing to the organisation's overall success. Teams that prioritise creativity and innovation are more resilient and adaptable, as diverse perspectives and experiences enable them to navigate challenges and find innovative solutions. Leaders who embrace creativity and innovation can navigate uncertainties with strategic agility, ensuring the organisation remains responsive to emerging opportunities and challenges. Organisations that consistently prioritise creativity and innovation are better positioned for long-term success, as these values provide a strong foundation that supports sustainable growth and resilience.

VALUING INTANGIBLE ASSETS

Eluding sight, eluding touch, the forms of things all in it crouch; Eluding touch, eluding sight, there are their semblances, all right.

Lao Tzu's passage emphasises the significance of intangible aspects that cannot be seen or touched directly but are essential to the essence of things. In strategic management, intangible assets such as company culture, employee engagement, and brand reputation play a crucial role in a business's success. Leaders should prioritise and nurture these intangible assets, even though they may not be immediately visible or quantifiable. By doing so, they can build a strong foundation for sustainable growth and long-term success.

A positive work environment where employees feel valued, respected, and supported is essential for a strong company culture, so leaders should promote values such as collaboration, respect, and integrity, creating a workplace where employees thrive. Open communication channels that facilitate honest and transparent dialogue are critical for a healthy company culture, so leaders should encourage employees to share their ideas, feedback, and concerns, fostering a culture of trust and mutual respect. Regularly recognising and celebrating employee achievements reinforces a positive company culture, so leaders should acknowledge individual and team successes, expressing appreciation for their contributions and boosting morale and motivation.

Offering opportunities for professional development and career advancement enhances employee engagement, so leaders should invest in training, mentorship, and development programmes that support employees' growth and aspirations. Empowering employees by involving them in decision-making processes and giving them autonomy over their work fosters engagement, so leaders should trust their team members to take ownership of their tasks and provide the necessary support and resources. Promoting work-life balance is crucial for employee engagement and well-being, so leaders should encourage employees to set boundaries, take breaks, and prioritise their health and well-being, helping prevent burnout and ensuring a motivated and productive workforce.

Consistency in brand messaging and actions builds a strong brand reputation, so leaders should ensure that the organisation's values and mission are reflected in all communications, marketing efforts, and customer interactions, fostering trust and credibility. Providing exceptional customer experiences enhances brand reputation, so leaders should prioritise customer satisfaction by delivering high-quality products and services and addressing customer needs promptly and effectively. Engaging with the community through social responsibility initiatives and partnerships also enhances brand reputation, so leaders should involve the organisation in community activities, demonstrating a commitment to social and environmental responsibility.

A strong company culture and engaged employees lead to higher retention rates, as employees who feel valued and connected to the organisation are more likely to stay, reducing turnover and recruitment costs. Engaged employees are more productive and motivated, contributing more effectively to the organisation's success. A positive brand reputation fosters customer loyalty, with customers who trust and believe in the brand more likely to remain loyal and advocate for the organisation, driving long-term growth. Intangible assets provide a strong foundation for sustainable growth, so by nurturing company culture, employee engagement, and brand reputation, leaders can ensure the organisation's long-term success and resilience.

Regularly assessing the company culture through surveys, focus groups, and interviews helps identify strengths and areas for improvement, enabling leaders to gather employee feedback and make necessary adjustments. Implementing initiatives that enhance employee engagement, such as wellness programmes, recognition schemes, and development opportunities, fosters a positive work environment aligned with the organisation's values and goals. Developing and adhering to brand guidelines ensures consistency in brand messaging and actions, with comprehensive guidelines outlining the organisation's values, mission, and voice to align all communications with these principles. Measuring the impact of efforts to nurture intangible assets provides valuable insights, so leaders should establish key performance indicators (KPIs) to track employee engagement, customer satisfaction, and brand reputation, using this data to inform strategies and improvements.

Valuing intangible assets fosters a sustainable organisational culture where employees feel valued and respected, attracting and retaining top talent and contributing to the organisation's overall success. Teams that are engaged and connected to the organisation's mission are more resilient and capable of overcoming challenges, as strong relationships and trust developed through this focus enable them to work together effectively in any situation. Leaders who prioritise intangible assets can navigate uncertainties with strategic agility, as a strong company culture, engaged employees, and a positive brand reputation provide a solid foundation for making informed and effective decisions. Organisations that consistently value and nurture intangible assets are better positioned for long-term success, as these values provide a strong foundation that supports sustainable growth and resilience.

UNDERSTANDING THE DEPTH & COMPLEXITY OF BUSINESS DYNAMICS

Profound it is, dark and obscure; Things' essences all there endure.

Lao Tzu's passage highlights the profound and complex nature of things, suggesting that understanding these depths is essential. In strategic management, leaders should appreciate the depth and complexity of business dynamics. This involves understanding the underlying forces and trends that shape the market and the organisation. By gaining deep insights into these factors, leaders can make more informed and strategic decisions, navigating uncertainties with confidence.

Leaders should regularly analyse market trends to understand the current and future state of the industry, studying economic indicators, consumer behaviour, technological advancements, and competitive dynamics to stay informed, anticipate changes, and adapt their strategies accordingly.

Analysing the competitive landscape helps leaders understand their organisation's position relative to competitors by identifying key players, their strengths and weaknesses, and their strategies, allowing leaders to develop strategies that leverage their organisation's unique strengths and opportunities. Recognising key industry drivers, such as regulatory changes, technological innovations, and economic shifts, is crucial for strategic planning, enabling leaders to identify these drivers, assess their potential impact on the organisation, proactively address challenges, and capitalise on opportunities.

Understanding the organisation's internal capabilities, including resources, skills, and competencies, is essential for strategic decision-making, so leaders should conduct regular assessments to identify strengths and areas for improvement, aligning strategies with the organisation's capabilities. Evaluating the organisational culture, including values, behaviours, and norms, is crucial for ensuring alignment with the organisation's goals, as a strong and supportive culture fosters collaboration, innovation, and resilience. Regularly monitoring performance metrics provides insights into the organisation's effectiveness and efficiency, so leaders should establish key performance indicators (KPIs) to track progress and identify areas for improvement, supporting informed decision-making and continuous improvement.

Deep insights into business dynamics enable leaders to make informed and strategic decisions by understanding market trends, competitive landscape, and organisational capabilities, allowing them to develop well-rounded strategies that drive success. Understanding the depth and complexity of business dynamics allows leaders to identify and mitigate potential risks, enhancing the organisation's resilience and ability to navigate uncertainties with a proactive approach to risk management. Appreciating business dynamics fosters strategic agility, as leaders who understand the underlying forces shaping the market and organisation can quickly adapt to changes and seize emerging opportunities. A thorough understanding of business dynamics supports sustainable growth, aligning strategies with market trends and organisational capabilities to achieve long-term success and resilience.

Regular market research helps leaders stay informed about industry trends and consumer behaviour, so they should invest in research tools and resources, and engage with industry experts to gain comprehensive insights. Engaging with stakeholders, including employees, customers, suppliers, and partners, provides valuable perspectives on business dynamics, so leaders should seek input to understand their needs, expectations, and concerns. Leveraging data analytics tools enables leaders to analyse large volumes of data and identify patterns and trends, so they should invest in advanced analytics capabilities to gain deeper insights and support data-driven decision-making. Participating in industry networks and forums provides opportunities to exchange knowledge and insights with peers, so leaders should actively engage in industry associations, conferences, and events to stay updated on the latest developments and best practices.

Teams that understand the depth and complexity of business dynamics are more resilient and capable of overcoming challenges, as the insights gained from this understanding enable them to work together effectively and navigate uncertainties. Leaders who appreciate business dynamics can navigate uncertainties with strategic agility, ensuring that decisions are made with long-term sustainability in mind and supporting the organisation's resilience. Organisations that prioritise understanding business dynamics are better positioned for sustainable growth, as these insights provide a strong foundation that supports continuous improvement and long-term success. A focus on understanding business dynamics fosters a positive organisational culture where employees feel informed and empowered, attracting and retaining top talent and contributing to the organisation's overall success.

EMBRACING TIMELESS PRINCIPLES

Now it is so; 'twas so of old. Its name—what passes not away; So, in their beautiful array, Things form and never know decay.

Lao Tzu's passage emphasises the enduring nature of certain principles that remain unchanged and continuously relevant. In modern business, timeless principles such as integrity, resilience, and adaptability are crucial for long-term success. Leaders should integrate these enduring principles into their strategies and actions. By doing so, they can ensure that their organisation remains strong and resilient, capable of withstanding challenges and seizing opportunities over time.

Integrity involves a steadfast commitment to ethical practices, so leaders should ensure that all business operations align with ethical standards and values, including fair treatment of employees, honest communication with stakeholders, and adherence to legal and regulatory requirements. Transparent and honest communication builds trust with employees, customers, and stakeholders, so leaders should be open about the organisation's goals, challenges, and successes, fostering a culture of trust and accountability. Consistency between words and actions reinforces integrity, so leaders should ensure their behaviours align with the values and commitments they advocate, building credibility and reinforcing the importance of integrity within the organisation.

Resilience is built on a strong foundation of core values, resources, and capabilities, so leaders should invest in building a robust organisational infrastructure that can withstand challenges and adapt to changes, including financial stability, a skilled workforce, and effective processes. A growth mindset fosters resilience by encouraging employees to view challenges as opportunities for learning and development, so leaders should promote a culture that values continuous improvement and adaptability, empowering employees to embrace change and seek solutions. Proactive risk management involves developing contingency plans to address potential challenges, so leaders should identify potential risks and develop strategies to mitigate their impact, enhancing the organisation's ability to navigate uncertainties and maintain stability.

Adaptability involves a willingness to embrace change and explore new opportunities, so leaders should foster a culture of innovation where employees feel encouraged to experiment with new ideas and approaches, driving continuous improvement and keeping the organisation competitive. Agile decision-making processes enable the organisation to respond quickly to changes in the market or internal dynamics, so leaders should streamline decision-making processes, empowering employees to make informed decisions and take action swiftly. Continuous learning and development are essential for adaptability, so leaders should provide opportunities for employees to enhance their skills and knowledge through training, workshops, and professional development programmes, ensuring the organisation remains agile and capable of adapting to new challenges.

Integrating timeless principles into strategies and actions supports sustainable growth by providing a strong foundation through ethical practices, resilience, and adaptability, enabling the organisation to thrive in the long term. A commitment to integrity builds trust and credibility with employees, customers, and stakeholders, fostering loyalty and long-term relationships that drive the organisation's success. A resilient and adaptable organisation is better positioned to navigate challenges and seize opportunities, leading to improved performance and competitiveness in the market. Embracing timeless principles also fosters a positive organisational culture where employees feel valued and empowered, attracting and retaining top talent and contributing to the organisation's overall success.

Leaders should establish and communicate clear core values that reflect timeless principles such as integrity, resilience, and adaptability, guiding decision-making and actions within the organisation. Embedding these core values in organisational policies and procedures ensures they are consistently upheld, so leaders should regularly review and update policies to align with the organisation's values and goals. Offering ethics training programmes helps employees understand the importance of integrity and ethical behaviour, so leaders should provide resources and training that emphasise ethical decision-making and conduct. Leaders should also promote a culture of continuous improvement by encouraging employees to seek innovative solutions and embrace change, creating opportunities for learning, experimentation, and feedback.

Embracing timeless principles fosters a sustainable organisational culture where employees feel valued and respected, attracting and retaining top talent and contributing to the organisation's overall success. Teams that prioritise integrity, resilience, and adaptability are more resilient and capable of overcoming challenges, as the strong relationships and trust developed through these principles enable them to work together effectively in any situation. Leaders who integrate timeless principles can navigate uncertainties with strategic agility, ensuring that decisions are made with long-term sustainability in mind and supporting the organisation's resilience. Organisations that consistently embrace timeless principles are better positioned for long-term success, as these values provide a strong foundation that supports sustainable growth and resilience.

RECOGNISING THE INTERCONNECTEDNESS OF ALL THINGS

How know I that it is so with all the beauties of existing things? By this (nature of the Tao).

Lao Tzu's passage emphasises the interconnectedness of all things, a fundamental principle of the Tao. Leaders should recognise the interconnectedness of all aspects of the organisation. This holistic perspective helps in understanding how different elements influence each other and contribute to the overall success. By fostering collaboration and synergy among various departments and teams, leaders can create a more cohesive and effective organisation.

Leaders should adopt holistic thinking, considering the organisation as an interconnected system by understanding how decisions in one area can impact others and recognising the interdependencies between different functions, processes, and teams. Conducting systemic analysis helps identify the relationships and interactions between various elements of the organisation, so leaders should use tools such as systems thinking, process mapping, and network analysis to visualise these connections and understand their implications. Recognising interdependencies within the organisation is crucial for effective decision-making, so leaders should consider how changes in one area might affect others, balancing different needs and priorities to avoid unintended consequences and ensure that all parts of the organisation work together harmoniously.

Creating cross-functional teams encourages collaboration and leverages diverse perspectives, so leaders should bring together employees from different departments to work on projects and initiatives, fostering a culture of teamwork and mutual respect. Open communication channels facilitate the sharing of information and ideas across the organisation, so leaders should establish forums, meetings, and digital platforms that enable employees to connect and collaborate, breaking down silos and promoting transparency. Setting shared goals and objectives aligns the efforts of different departments and teams towards a common purpose, so leaders should ensure that everyone understands the organisation's vision and how their contributions support its achievement, fostering a sense of unity and collective responsibility.

A holistic perspective enhances decision-making by providing a comprehensive understanding of the organisation's dynamics, allowing leaders to make more informed and balanced decisions considering the broader impact of their actions. Collaboration and synergy drive innovation by bringing together diverse skills and perspectives, enabling employees to generate creative solutions and new ideas that contribute to the organisation's growth. Recognising and leveraging interdependencies can improve efficiency by optimising processes and resource allocation, helping leaders streamline workflows, reduce redundancies, and enhance overall productivity. Fostering a culture of collaboration and interconnectedness strengthens the organisational culture, making employees who feel connected to their colleagues and the organisation's mission more engaged, motivated, and committed to its success.

Leaders should implement systems thinking approaches to understand the organisation as an interconnected system, using tools such as causal loop diagrams, process mapping, and scenario planning to visualise relationships and interactions. Designing collaborative workspaces that facilitate interaction and teamwork can enhance synergy, so leaders should create physical and virtual environments that support collaboration, like open-plan offices, project rooms, and digital collaboration platforms. Promoting interdepartmental projects encourages employees to work together across functions, so leaders should identify opportunities for cross-functional collaboration and create project teams that leverage diverse expertise. Encouraging knowledge sharing and continuous learning fosters a culture of interconnectedness, so leaders should provide opportunities for employees to share their expertise through training sessions, workshops, and knowledge-sharing platforms.

Recognising interconnectedness fosters a sustainable organisational culture where employees feel valued and respected, attracting and retaining top talent and contributing to the organisation's overall success. Teams that understand and leverage interconnectedness are more resilient and capable of overcoming challenges, as strong relationships and collaboration developed through this focus enable them to work together effectively in any situation. Leaders who prioritise interconnectedness can navigate uncertainties with strategic agility, ensuring decisions are made with long-term sustainability in mind and supporting the organisation's resilience. Organisations that consistently recognise and leverage interconnectedness are better positioned for long-term success, as these values provide a strong foundation that supports sustainable growth and resilience.

CHAPTER 22 – TRANSFORMATION

Chapter 22 of the *Tao Te Ching* emphasises the power of humility, simplicity, and non-striving. Here's how these teachings can be applied to modern-day strategic management:

EMBRACING TRANSFORMATION & FLEXIBILITY

The partial becomes complete; the crooked, straight; the empty, full; the worn out, new.

Lao Tzu's passage emphasises the dynamic nature of transformation, where everything has the potential to evolve and change. In strategic management, leaders should recognise and embrace the potential for transformation and growth. This involves being flexible and adaptable, allowing for change and improvement. By seeing potential in every situation and individual, leaders can foster an environment where continuous development and innovation thrive. This mindset encourages resilience and the ability to turn challenges into opportunities.

Leaders should identify and acknowledge the potential for growth in their organisation by evaluating current capabilities, recognising areas for improvement, and setting ambitious but achievable goals, inspiring a culture of continuous development. A growth mindset encourages individuals to view challenges as opportunities for learning and development, so leaders should promote this mindset by encouraging employees to take on new challenges, embrace failures as learning experiences, and continuously seek ways to improve. Innovation is a key driver of transformation, so leaders should create an environment that encourages creativity and experimentation by providing resources, support, and opportunities for employees to explore new ideas and develop innovative solutions.

Flexibility involves the ability to adapt to changing circumstances, so leaders should be open to new information, willing to adjust plans as needed, and responsive to emerging trends and challenges, ensuring the organisation remains agile and resilient. Empowering teams with the autonomy to make decisions and take action fosters flexibility, so leaders should delegate authority, trust their team members, and provide the necessary support, allowing teams to respond quickly to changes and seize opportunities. Streamlining processes and eliminating unnecessary bureaucracy enhances organisational flexibility, so leaders should regularly review and optimise workflows to ensure they are efficient and adaptable, enabling quicker decision-making and implementation.

A culture of transformation and flexibility builds organisational resilience, continuously evolving and adapting the organisation to navigate challenges and uncertainties better. Embracing transformation and flexibility drives innovation and continuous improvement, as empowered employees explore new ideas and adapt to change, contributing to innovative solutions and enhanced performance. Employees who see opportunities for growth and feel supported in their development are more engaged and motivated, leading to higher levels of productivity and job satisfaction. Organisations that prioritise transformation and flexibility gain a competitive advantage by staying agile and responsive to market changes, enabling them to capitalise on emerging opportunities and maintain their relevance in a dynamic environment.

Practical Strategies for Embracing Transformation & Flexibility

Setting Clear Goals and Milestones: Leaders should set clear, achievable goals and milestones that align with the organisation's vision. These goals provide direction and motivation for continuous development and transformation.

Encouraging Risk-Taking: Encouraging calculated risk-taking fosters a culture of innovation. Leaders should support employees in taking risks, experimenting with new ideas, and learning from failures. This approach promotes creativity and adaptability.

Investing in Development: Investing in employee development through training, mentorship, and professional growth opportunities supports transformation. Leaders should provide resources and support for employees to enhance their skills and capabilities.

Creating a Flexible Work Environment: A flexible work environment that accommodates different working styles and preferences enhances adaptability. Leaders should offer flexible work arrangements, such as remote work options and flexible hours, to support employees' needs.

Regularly Reviewing and Adjusting Strategies: Leaders should regularly review and adjust strategies based on new information and changing circumstances. This ongoing assessment ensures that the organisation remains aligned with its goals and responsive to emerging trends.

Embracing transformation and flexibility fosters a sustainable organisational culture where employees feel valued and respected, attracting and retaining top talent and contributing to the organisation's overall success. Teams that prioritise transformation and flexibility are more resilient and capable of overcoming challenges, as strong relationships and trust developed through this focus enable them to work together effectively in any situation. Leaders who embrace transformation and flexibility can navigate uncertainties with strategic agility, ensuring that decisions are made with long-term sustainability in mind and supporting the organisation's resilience. Organisations that consistently prioritise transformation and flexibility are better positioned for long-term success, as these values provide a strong foundation that supports sustainable growth and resilience.

PRACTISING HUMILITY

> *He whose (desires) are few gets them; he whose (desires) are many goes astray.*

Lao Tzu's passage emphasises the virtue of humility and the dangers of excessive ambition. Leaders should cultivate humility by focusing on essential goals and avoiding the pitfalls of excessive ambition. By setting realistic and meaningful objectives, leaders can maintain clarity and direction. Humility helps leaders remain grounded and focused on the well-being of their teams and organisation, rather than personal gains.

Leaders should set realistic and achievable objectives that align with the organisation's mission and values, providing clear direction and helping to prioritise efforts. By focusing on essential goals, leaders can avoid being overwhelmed by excessive ambitions and maintain a clear sense of purpose. Prioritising outcomes that have a meaningful impact on the organisation and its stakeholders helps maintain focus, so leaders should identify the key results that drive success and allocate resources accordingly, ensuring efforts are directed towards initiatives that truly matter. Excessive ambition can lead to distractions and a loss of focus, so leaders should be mindful of their goals and avoid pursuing initiatives that do not align with the organisation's core values and objectives, maintaining clarity and direction.

Humble leaders recognise their own limitations and seek input from others, acknowledging that they do not have all the answers and valuing the expertise and perspectives of their team members. By fostering a culture of collaboration, leaders can make better-informed decisions. Active listening is a key component of humility, so leaders should listen attentively to the concerns and ideas of their team members, showing genuine interest and respect to build trust and encourage open communication. Admitting mistakes and taking responsibility for them is a powerful demonstration of humility, and leaders should view mistakes as learning opportunities and be transparent about their errors, fostering a culture of continuous improvement and resilience. Humble leaders also share credit for successes with their teams, recognising the contributions of team members and celebrating collective achievements, reinforcing the importance of collaboration and building a sense of community.

Humility fosters stronger relationships within the organisation, as employees who feel respected and valued by humble leaders are more likely to trust and support them, enhancing collaboration and teamwork. This humility creates an environment where employees feel comfortable expressing their ideas and taking risks, leading to enhanced engagement, productivity, and innovation. Humility also allows leaders to make better-informed decisions by considering diverse perspectives and seeking input from others, leading to more balanced and effective decision-making. A culture of humility promotes respect, trust, and collaboration, with leaders who model humility setting a positive example for their teams and fostering a supportive and cohesive work environment.

Leaders should actively seek feedback from their team members and act on it, demonstrating that they value input and are committed to continuous improvement. Modelling humility in their actions and decisions, including being transparent, admitting mistakes, and sharing credit, sets a positive example and encourages their teams to adopt similar behaviours. Offering opportunities for professional and personal development supports humility by recognising the potential for growth in every individual, so leaders should provide resources and support for employees to enhance their skills and capabilities. Promoting a culture of respect where diverse perspectives are valued involves creating an inclusive environment where everyone feels heard and appreciated.

Practising humility fosters a sustainable organisational culture where employees feel valued and respected, attracting and retaining top talent and contributing to the organisation's overall success. Teams that embrace humility are more resilient and capable of overcoming challenges, as strong relationships and trust developed through this focus enable them to work together effectively in any situation. Leaders who practise humility can navigate uncertainties with strategic agility, ensuring that decisions are made with long-term sustainability in mind and supporting the organisation's resilience. Organisations that consistently prioritise humility are better positioned for long-term success, as these values provide a strong foundation that supports sustainable growth and resilience.

AVOIDING SELF-DISPLAY & SELF-ASSERTION

> He is free from self-display, and therefore he shines; from self-assertion, and therefore he is distinguished; from self-boasting, and therefore his merit is acknowledged; from self-complacency, and therefore he acquires superiority.

Lao Tzu's passage underscores the virtue of humility and the pitfalls of self-display and self-assertion. Effective leaders do not seek to display their power or assert their dominance. Instead, they lead by example and let their actions speak for themselves. By avoiding self-promotion and focusing on the collective good, leaders earn genuine respect and admiration from their teams. This approach fosters a culture of mutual respect and collaboration, where the focus is on achieving shared goals.

Leaders who demonstrate integrity through their actions earn the trust and respect of their teams, as integrity involves being honest, transparent, and consistent in decision-making and behaviour, setting a positive standard for others to follow. Humble leaders take responsibility for their actions and decisions, including mistakes, fostering a culture of trust and openness where team members feel safe to admit errors and learn from them, and reinforcing the leader's commitment to the team's success. Empathetic leaders understand and consider the perspectives and feelings of their team members, building strong relationships and creating an inclusive environment where everyone feels valued and heard, which helps leaders make more informed and compassionate decisions.

Leaders who prioritise team achievements over personal recognition foster a collaborative culture, celebrating collective successes and acknowledging the contributions of team members, which reinforces the importance of teamwork and shared goals and helps build a sense of unity and collective responsibility. Humble leaders promote the talents and successes of their team members rather than seeking personal acclaim, highlighting the strengths and accomplishments of others to build confidence and morale within the team, and demonstrating a commitment to the development and growth of the team. Remaining grounded and modest helps leaders avoid the pitfalls of self-complacency, maintaining a balanced perspective, being open to feedback, and continuously seeking ways to improve, which helps leaders stay focused on the organisation's mission and goals.

Leaders who avoid self-display and self-assertion earn genuine respect and admiration from their teams, as this respect is based on the leader's actions, integrity, and commitment to the collective good rather than on self-promotion. A culture of mutual respect and collaboration is fostered when leaders focus on shared goals rather than personal gains, making team members more likely to work together effectively and support one another. Employees are more engaged and motivated when they work with humble leaders who prioritise the team's success, leading to higher levels of productivity and job satisfaction. Leaders who focus on the collective good and avoid self-promotion build a strong foundation for sustainable success, ensuring that the organisation's achievements are based on genuine collaboration and shared efforts.

Leaders should practise humility in their daily interactions and decisions by being open to feedback, admitting mistakes, and showing appreciation for the contributions of others, as humility sets a positive example and fosters a culture of respect. Encouraging open dialogue and feedback helps leaders stay grounded and connected to their team members, so they should create opportunities for team members to share their thoughts, ideas, and concerns, fostering a culture of transparency and trust. Regularly celebrating team successes reinforces the importance of collective achievements, so leaders should highlight the contributions of team members and recognise their efforts in achieving shared goals. Offering development opportunities for team members demonstrates a commitment to their growth and success, so leaders should support professional development through training, mentorship, and career advancement programmes.

Avoiding self-display and self-assertion fosters a sustainable organisational culture where employees feel valued and respected, attracting and retaining top talent and contributing to the organisation's overall success. Teams that prioritise mutual respect and collaboration are more resilient and capable of overcoming challenges, as strong relationships and trust developed through this focus enable them to work together effectively in any situation. Leaders who avoid self-display and self-assertion can navigate uncertainties with strategic agility, ensuring decisions are made with long-term sustainability in mind and supporting the organisation's resilience. Organisations that consistently prioritise humility and collaboration are better positioned for long-term success, as these values provide a strong foundation that supports sustainable growth and resilience.

ENCOURAGING NON-STRIVING & NATURAL FLOW

It is because he is thus free from striving that therefore no one in the world is able to strive with him.

Lao Tzu's passage highlights the profound wisdom in the concept of non-striving, or *Wú Wéi* (無為/无为), which means allowing things to unfold naturally without forcing outcomes. In strategic management, this approach encourages a more organic and adaptive way of working, where leaders guide and support their teams without micromanaging. By creating an environment where employees feel empowered to take initiative and make decisions, leaders can foster innovation and creativity.

Leaders should allow projects and initiatives to progress naturally without imposing rigid controls or deadlines, trusting the process and giving teams the space to develop and execute their ideas, fostering a sense of ownership and reducing stress. Embracing non-striving requires leaders to let go of the need to control every detail, focusing instead on providing guidance and support, allowing teams to find their own path to success, encouraging autonomy and building confidence within the team. Flexibility is a key component of non-striving, so leaders should be open to adapting plans and strategies based on new information and changing circumstances, ensuring that the organisation remains responsive and agile in the face of uncertainties.

Empowering employees to take initiative and make decisions fosters a sense of ownership and accountability, so leaders should delegate authority and trust their team members to manage their tasks independently, encouraging creativity and innovation. A culture of experimentation supports non-striving by allowing employees to explore new ideas and approaches, so leaders should create an environment where it is safe to take risks and learn from failures, driving continuous improvement and innovation. Collaboration enhances the natural flow of ideas and solutions, so leaders should promote teamwork and create opportunities for cross-functional collaboration, leveraging diverse perspectives to develop more comprehensive and innovative solutions.

Non-striving fosters a culture of creativity and innovation by empowering employees to explore and experiment, making them more likely to develop innovative solutions that drive the organisation's success. Allowing things to unfold naturally reduces the pressure and stress associated with rigid controls and deadlines, leading to reduced stress and burnout, and resulting in higher levels of job satisfaction and well-being. An adaptive approach to work enhances problem-solving capabilities by remaining open to new information and adjusting plans as needed, enabling teams to navigate challenges more effectively and find innovative solutions. A culture of empowerment and collaboration strengthens team dynamics, as employees who feel trusted and valued are more likely to support one another and work together towards shared goals.

Leaders should set clear goals that provide direction while allowing flexibility in how they are achieved, ensuring that teams have a sense of purpose while retaining the freedom to adapt and innovate. Providing the necessary resources and support helps teams succeed without micromanagement, so leaders should ensure that employees have access to the tools, information, and guidance they need to achieve their goals. Building a culture of trust is essential for non-striving, so leaders should demonstrate trust in their team members by delegating responsibilities and encouraging independent decision-making, fostering a sense of ownership and accountability. Recognising and celebrating successes, both big and small, reinforces the value of non-striving, so leaders should acknowledge the achievements of their teams and celebrate milestones, creating a positive and motivating work environment.

Embracing non-striving and natural flow fosters a sustainable organisational culture where employees feel valued and respected, attracting and retaining top talent and contributing to the organisation's overall success. Teams that prioritise non-striving and natural flow are more resilient and capable of overcoming challenges, as strong relationships and trust developed through this focus enable them to work together effectively in any situation. Leaders who embrace non-striving and natural flow can navigate uncertainties with strategic agility, ensuring that decisions are made with long-term sustainability in mind and supporting the organisation's resilience. Organisations that consistently prioritise non-striving and natural flow are better positioned for long-term success, as these values provide a strong foundation that supports sustainable growth and resilience.

ACHIEVING REAL COMPLETION THROUGH SIMPLICITY

That saying of the ancients that 'the partial becomes complete' was not vainly spoken:—all real completion is comprehended under it.

Lao Tzu's passage underscores the profound wisdom in the idea that 'the partial becomes complete.' This concept highlights the value of simplicity and focusing on core principles. In strategic management, leaders should aim to simplify processes and eliminate unnecessary complexities. By focusing on what truly matters and ensuring that all actions are aligned with the organisation's core values, leaders can achieve sustainable success and true fulfillment.

Leaders should regularly review and streamline workflows to eliminate unnecessary steps and redundancies, enhancing efficiency and productivity by allowing employees to focus on high-impact tasks. Reducing bureaucracy is crucial, as excessive bureaucracy can hinder progress and innovation, so leaders should strive to reduce bureaucratic barriers by decentralising decision-making and empowering employees, promoting agility and responsiveness. Simplifying processes also involves prioritising core activities that align with the organisation's mission and values, so leaders should focus resources and efforts on activities that drive value and support the organisation's strategic goals, ensuring alignment with core principles and avoiding distractions.

Clear and concise communication reduces misunderstandings and ensures alignment with the organisation's objectives, so leaders should avoid jargon and overly complex language, opting for straightforward and transparent communication to foster collaboration and cohesion within the team. Setting realistic and achievable goals helps maintain focus and direction, so leaders should define clear objectives aligned with the organisation's mission and values, breaking down complex goals into manageable tasks to ensure steady progress and avoid overwhelming their teams. Simplified decision-making processes enhance efficiency and effectiveness, so leaders should establish clear criteria for decision-making and empower employees to make informed choices, reducing delays and promoting a culture of accountability and trust.

Consistency between actions and core values reinforces the organisation's integrity and credibility, so leaders should ensure that all decisions and behaviours reflect the organisation's principles, building trust and fostering a strong organisational culture. Ethical practices are fundamental to achieving real completion through simplicity, so leaders should prioritise ethical behaviour in all aspects of the organisation, from business operations to employee interactions, supporting long-term success and sustainability. Regularly reflecting on the organisation's actions and their alignment with core values helps maintain focus and direction, so leaders should encourage continuous improvement by seeking feedback, assessing outcomes, and making necessary adjustments, ensuring the organisation remains true to its principles.

Simplifying processes and aligning actions with core values support sustainable success by focusing on what truly matters, enabling organisations to achieve consistent progress and long-term growth. Simplified workflows and decision-making processes enhance efficiency and productivity, allowing employees to focus on high-value tasks and improve performance and outcomes. Employees are more engaged and motivated in a clear, focused, and supportive environment, as simplified processes and clear communication reduce stress and enhance job satisfaction. A culture of simplicity and alignment with core values fosters a positive and cohesive work environment, where employees feel connected to the organisation's mission and are more likely to contribute to its success.

Leaders should regularly conduct process audits to identify areas for simplification by gathering input from employees, analysing workflows, and implementing improvements to streamline operations. Clear policies that reflect the organisation's core values provide a framework for consistent decision-making and actions, so leaders should develop and communicate policies that promote simplicity and ethical behaviour. Open communication channels facilitate transparency and collaboration, so leaders should create opportunities for employees to share their ideas, feedback, and concerns, fostering a culture of trust and mutual respect. Offering training and support helps employees embrace simplicity and align their actions with the organisation's values, so leaders should provide resources and guidance to ensure that employees understand and can implement simplified processes effectively.

Achieving real completion through simplicity fosters a sustainable organisational culture where employees feel valued and respected, attracting and retaining top talent and contributing to the organisation's overall success. Teams that prioritise simplicity and alignment with core values are more resilient and capable of overcoming challenges, as strong relationships and trust developed through this focus enable them to work together effectively in any situation. Leaders who embrace simplicity and focus on core principles can navigate uncertainties with strategic agility, ensuring that decisions are made with long-term sustainability in mind and supporting the organisation's resilience. Organisations that consistently prioritise simplicity and alignment with core values are better positioned for long-term success, as these values provide a strong foundation that supports sustainable growth and resilience.

CHAPTER 23 — SPONTANEITY

Chapter 23 of the *Tao Te Ching* emphasises the importance of spontaneity, moderation, alignment with the Tao, and the influence of faith. Here's how these teachings can be applied to modern-day strategic management:

EMBRACING SPONTANEITY & MODERATION

> *Abstaining from speech marks him who is obeying the spontaneity of his nature. A violent wind does not last for a whole morning; a sudden rain does not last for the whole day.*

Lao Tzu's passage highlights the importance of spontaneity, suggesting that natural processes should be allowed to unfold without interference. In strategic management, leaders should recognise the value of spontaneity and create environments where creativity and innovation can emerge naturally. This involves trusting the process and allowing ideas to develop organically, without forcing outcomes.

Leaders should trust the natural progression of projects and initiatives by providing guidance and support while allowing teams the freedom to explore and experiment, fostering a sense of ownership and encouraging innovative thinking. Creating a safe environment where employees feel comfortable taking risks and expressing their ideas is essential for spontaneity, so leaders should promote a culture of psychological safety, where team members are not afraid to fail and learn from their experiences, driving creativity and innovation. Flexibility allows for the natural flow of ideas and solutions, so leaders should avoid rigid structures and processes that stifle creativity, encouraging adaptive thinking and the willingness to pivot when necessary, enhancing problem-solving and innovation.

Leaders should avoid pushing their teams to constant extremes, as sustained high pressure can lead to burnout, and strive for a balanced approach that promotes both high performance and employee health by maintaining moderation in workload and expectations. Moderation also includes promoting a healthy work-life balance by encouraging employees to take breaks, set boundaries, and prioritise their well-being, preventing burnout and ensuring that employees remain motivated and productive. Setting realistic and achievable goals helps maintain moderation, so leaders should define clear objectives that challenge their teams without overwhelming them, ensuring steady progress and sustained success by setting manageable targets.

Embracing spontaneity fosters a culture of creativity and innovation, as employees who feel free to explore and experiment are more likely to develop innovative solutions that drive the organisation's success. Moderation helps maintain sustained productivity by preventing burnout and ensuring that employees remain motivated and engaged, supporting long-term performance and well-being with a balanced approach to workload and expectations. Allowing natural processes to unfold enhances problem-solving capabilities, as teams can navigate challenges more effectively and find innovative solutions by remaining open to new ideas and adapting to changing circumstances. A culture that values spontaneity and moderation fosters a positive and supportive work environment, where employees who feel trusted and respected are more likely to collaborate effectively and contribute to the organisation's success.

Encouraging open dialogue fosters spontaneity by allowing employees to share their ideas and feedback freely, so leaders should create opportunities for meaningful conversations and brainstorming sessions. Providing autonomy empowers employees to take initiative and make decisions, as leaders should delegate responsibilities and trust their team members to manage tasks independently, promoting creativity and ownership. Implementing flexible work arrangements supports both spontaneity and moderation, with leaders offering options such as remote work, flexible hours, and compressed workweeks to accommodate different working styles and preferences. Recognising and rewarding employees who demonstrate a balanced approach to work reinforces the value of moderation, so leaders should celebrate achievements that result from steady progress and sustainable practices.

Embracing spontaneity and moderation fosters a sustainable organisational culture where employees feel valued and respected, attracting and retaining top talent and contributing to the organisation's overall success. Teams that prioritise spontaneity and moderation are more resilient and capable of overcoming challenges, as strong relationships and trust developed through this focus enable them to work together effectively in any situation. Leaders who embrace spontaneity and moderation can navigate uncertainties with strategic agility, ensuring that decisions are made with long-term sustainability in mind and supporting the organisation's resilience. Organisations that consistently prioritise spontaneity and moderation are better positioned for long-term success, as these values provide a strong foundation that supports sustainable growth and resilience.

LEADING WITH CONSISTENCY & ALIGNMENT

Therefore when one is making the Tao his business, those who are also pursuing it, agree with him in it, and those who are making the manifestation of its course their object agree with him in that; while even those who are failing in both these things agree with him where they fail.

Lao Tzu's passage highlights the power of aligning actions and decisions with core principles. Leaders who demonstrate consistency and alignment create a sense of purpose within the organisation. When leaders are clear about their values and goals, they naturally attract and align with others who share the same vision. This alignment fosters a cohesive and motivated team, working towards common objectives. Even when challenges arise, a shared sense of purpose helps in navigating difficulties together.

Leaders should clearly define and communicate the organisation's core values, which serve as guiding principles for all actions and decisions, ensuring everyone is aligned and working towards a common purpose, providing a foundation for consistency and integrity. Setting clear and achievable goals helps maintain consistency and focus, so leaders should ensure the organisation's goals are aligned with its mission and values, and by clearly defining objectives, guide the organisation towards its vision and create a sense of purpose. Leaders should model consistent behaviour by aligning their actions with the organisation's core values and goals, demonstrating integrity, fairness, and commitment in all interactions, setting a positive example, and reinforcing the importance of alignment.

Regularly communicating the organisation's vision and mission helps ensure alignment among team members, fostering a sense of unity and shared responsibility by sharing stories, successes, and progress towards the organisation's goals and highlighting how individual contributions support the larger purpose. Engaging stakeholders in the decision-making process helps align their interests with the organisation's goals, as leaders should seek input and feedback from employees, customers, and partners, ensuring their perspectives are considered, which builds trust and fosters alignment. Aligning incentives with the organisation's goals and values reinforces the importance of consistency and alignment, so leaders should design compensation and reward systems that encourage behaviours and actions that support the organisation's mission, motivating employees to contribute to shared objectives.

A strong team culture that values consistency and alignment helps navigate challenges, so leaders should foster a supportive environment where team members feel connected to the organisation's mission and to each other, enhancing resilience through trust and collaboration. Open communication is essential for navigating challenges, so leaders should create channels for transparent and honest dialogue, allowing team members to share their concerns and ideas, fostering a culture of problem-solving and continuous improvement. Providing the necessary support and resources helps teams overcome challenges, so leaders should ensure that employees have access to the tools, training, and guidance they need to succeed, reinforcing the organisation's commitment to its values and goals.

Consistency and alignment build trust and credibility within the organisation, as employees who see their leaders acting in accordance with core values are more likely to trust and respect them, fostering loyalty and long-term commitment. Employees who understand and align with the organisation's vision and values are more engaged and motivated, leading to higher levels of productivity and job satisfaction, driving the organisation's success. Alignment fosters collaboration and teamwork, as when everyone is working towards common goals, team members are more likely to support each other and work together effectively, enhancing innovation and problem-solving. A focus on consistency and alignment supports sustainable success, as by maintaining alignment with core values and goals, organisations can navigate uncertainties and achieve long-term growth.

Leaders should develop and regularly communicate a clear vision statement that reflects the organisation's core values and goals, serving as a guiding beacon for all actions and decisions. Regular check-ins with team members help ensure alignment and address any misalignments, so leaders should hold team meetings, one-on-one sessions, and feedback loops to discuss progress, challenges, and alignment with the organisation's mission. Providing training on the organisation's values and goals helps employees understand their importance and how to incorporate them into their daily work, so leaders should offer workshops, seminars, and resources that reinforce these principles. Recognising and rewarding behaviour that aligns with the organisation's values and goals reinforces their importance, so leaders should celebrate examples of consistent and aligned actions, highlighting their impact on the organisation's success.

Leading with consistency and alignment fosters a sustainable organisational culture where employees feel valued and respected, attracting and retaining top talent and contributing to the organisation's overall success. Teams that prioritise consistency and alignment are more resilient and capable of overcoming challenges, as strong relationships and trust developed through this focus enable them to work together effectively in any situation. Leaders who prioritise consistency and alignment can navigate uncertainties with strategic agility, ensuring decisions are made with long-term sustainability in mind, supporting the organisation's resilience. Organisations that consistently prioritise consistency and alignment are better positioned for long-term success, as these values provide a strong foundation that supports sustainable growth and resilience.

BUILDING & SUSTAINING TRUST

Hence, those with whom he agrees as to the Tao have the happiness of attaining to it... (But) when there is not faith sufficient (on his part), a want of faith (in him) ensues (on the part of the others).

Lao Tzu's passage highlights the pivotal role of trust in leadership. Trust is a fundamental component of effective leadership. Leaders who demonstrate faith in their teams and consistently uphold their commitments build strong trust and loyalty. Conversely, if leaders lack faith in their own principles or fail to demonstrate reliability, it leads to mistrust and disengagement among employees. Building and sustaining trust requires leaders to be transparent, consistent, and supportive.

Demonstrating faith in teams involves empowering employees to take initiative and make decisions, trusting them to manage their tasks independently while providing the necessary support and resources, which builds confidence and fosters a sense of ownership and accountability. Providing autonomy allows employees to explore their creativity and innovate, so leaders should delegate responsibilities and avoid micromanaging, showing trust in their team's abilities. Autonomy encourages employees to take risks and learn from their experiences, driving growth and development. Recognising and celebrating the contributions of team members reinforces trust and appreciation, so leaders should acknowledge individual and team achievements and express gratitude for their efforts, boosting morale and strengthening the bond between leaders and employees.

Reliability is a cornerstone of trust, so leaders should consistently follow through on their commitments and promises by meeting deadlines, fulfilling obligations, and delivering on expectations, thereby building credibility and trust within the organisation. Transparent communication fosters trust by ensuring that employees are informed and aware of important developments, so leaders should communicate openly and honestly about the organisation's goals, challenges, and successes, promoting a culture of trust and mutual respect. Admitting mistakes and taking responsibility for them demonstrates integrity and humility, so leaders should be transparent about errors and view them as opportunities for learning and improvement, fostering a culture of continuous improvement and resilience.

Consistency between words and actions reinforces trust, so leaders should ensure their behaviours align with their stated values and commitments, building credibility and trust over time, and creating a stable and supportive environment. Providing support and resources helps employees succeed and feel valued, so leaders should be approachable and available to offer guidance, assistance, and encouragement, fostering a sense of security and trust within the team. Encouraging feedback and actively listening to employees' concerns and ideas fosters trust and collaboration, so leaders should create opportunities for open dialogue and demonstrate that they value input from their team members, building trust and fostering a positive organisational culture.

Trust leads to increased engagement and motivation among employees, as those who trust their leaders and feel trusted in return are more committed to their work and the organisation's success, driving higher levels of productivity and performance. Trust fosters collaboration and teamwork, with employees who trust each other and their leaders more likely to work together effectively and support one another, enhancing problem-solving and innovation. A culture of trust and transparency also improves employee retention, as employees who feel valued and trusted are more likely to stay with the organisation, reducing turnover and associated costs. Building and sustaining trust supports long-term success, providing a foundation that ensures the organisation can navigate challenges and uncertainties with resilience and adaptability.

Leaders should set clear expectations and goals for their team members, ensuring everyone understands their roles and responsibilities, which promotes accountability and trust. Regular feedback helps employees understand their progress and areas for improvement, so leaders should provide constructive feedback and recognise achievements, fostering a culture of continuous development and trust. A safe and inclusive environment where employees feel comfortable expressing their ideas and concerns fosters trust, so leaders should promote psychological safety and create opportunities for open dialogue. Leaders should also model trustworthy behaviour by demonstrating integrity, reliability, and transparency, setting a positive standard and encouraging employees to adopt similar behaviours.

Building and sustaining trust fosters a sustainable organisational culture where employees feel valued and respected, attracting and retaining top talent and contributing to the organisation's overall success. Teams that prioritise trust are more resilient and capable of overcoming challenges, as strong relationships and trust developed through this focus enable them to work together effectively in any situation. Leaders who prioritise trust can navigate uncertainties with strategic agility, ensuring decisions are made with long-term sustainability in mind, supporting the organisation's resilience. Organisations that consistently prioritise trust are better positioned for long-term success, as these values provide a strong foundation that supports sustainable growth and resilience.

PRACTISING THOUGHTFUL COMMUNICATION

Abstaining from speech marks him who is obeying the spontaneity of his nature.

Lao Tzu's passage highlights the virtue of thoughtful communication, suggesting that one should choose words carefully and avoid unnecessary or impulsive speech. In strategic management, leaders should practise thoughtful communication to ensure that their interactions remain clear, purposeful, and effective. Thoughtful communication helps in reducing misunderstandings and promotes a culture of respect and consideration.

Leaders should aim for clarity and precision in their communication by conveying messages in a straightforward manner without ambiguity, ensuring that everyone understands the intended message and reducing the likelihood of misunderstandings and confusion. Impulsive speech can lead to misunderstandings and unintended consequences, so leaders should take a moment to think before they speak, ensuring that their words are measured and appropriate for the situation, helping to maintain a professional and respectful tone. Thoughtful communication involves focusing on key messages and avoiding unnecessary details, so leaders should prioritise the most important information and present it concisely to keep communication effective and to the point.

Before communicating, leaders should set clear intentions for their messages, considering the desired outcome and the best way to achieve it, to ensure interactions are meaningful and productive, aligning with the organisation's goals and values. Active listening is a crucial component of thoughtful communication, where leaders listen attentively to others, showing genuine interest and respect, helping in understanding different perspectives and fostering a culture of openness and collaboration. Thoughtful communication also includes providing constructive feedback that is specific, actionable, and supportive, encouraging improvement and growth rather than criticism, which helps build trust and foster a positive work environment.

Leaders should encourage open dialogue and create a safe space for employees to share their thoughts and concerns, promoting an inclusive environment where everyone feels valued and heard, which fosters mutual respect and collaboration. They should model respectful behaviour in all interactions by using polite language, acknowledging others' contributions, and showing appreciation, setting a positive example and encouraging thoughtful communication. Thoughtful communication is also essential in addressing conflicts and resolving issues, so leaders should approach conflicts with a calm and composed demeanour, seeking to understand all sides before offering solutions, helping to find common ground and maintain harmony within the team through diplomatic communication.

Thoughtful communication minimises misunderstandings by ensuring that messages are clear and precise, reducing the potential for confusion and errors and leading to more effective interactions and decision-making. A culture of thoughtful communication fosters collaboration and teamwork, as team members who feel respected and understood are more likely to work together effectively and support each other, enhancing problem-solving and innovation. Thoughtful communication also builds trust and respect within the organisation, with employees experiencing respectful and considerate interactions more likely to trust their leaders and feel valued, enhancing loyalty and long-term commitment. Practising thoughtful communication contributes to a positive organisational culture, where leaders prioritise clear, purposeful, and respectful communication, creating an environment where employees feel supported and motivated to contribute their best efforts.

Leaders should take a moment to reflect before responding to ensure their words are thoughtful and appropriate, avoiding impulsive speech and maintaining professionalism. Encouraging feedback and input from team members fosters a culture of open communication, so leaders should create opportunities for employees to share their ideas and perspectives, demonstrating that their voices are valued. Offering training on effective communication skills helps employees develop their ability to communicate thoughtfully, so leaders should provide resources and workshops focusing on active listening, constructive feedback, and respectful interactions. Recognising and celebrating examples of thoughtful communication reinforces its importance, so leaders should acknowledge team members who demonstrate clear, purposeful, and respectful communication, highlighting its positive impact on the organisation.

Practising thoughtful communication fosters a sustainable organisational culture where employees feel valued and respected, attracting and retaining top talent and contributing to the organisation's overall success. Teams that prioritise thoughtful communication are more resilient and capable of overcoming challenges, as strong relationships and trust developed through this focus enable them to work together effectively in any situation. Leaders who practise thoughtful communication can navigate uncertainties with strategic agility, ensuring decisions are made with long-term sustainability in mind and supporting the organisation's resilience. Organisations that consistently prioritise thoughtful communication are better positioned for long-term success, as these values provide a strong foundation that supports sustainable growth and resilience.

CHAPTER 24 – OVER-ASSERTION

Chapter 24 of the *Tao Te Ching* emphasises the pitfalls of arrogance and self-promotion, advocating for humility and authentic leadership. Here's how these teachings can be applied to modern-day strategic management:

AVOIDING ARROGANCE & SELF-PROMOTION

> *He who stands on his tiptoes does not stand firm; he who stretches his legs does not walk (easily).*

Lao Tzu's passage warns against the pitfalls of arrogance and self-promotion, suggesting that overreaching or trying too hard to appear superior can lead to instability and a lack of authenticity. In strategic management, leaders should avoid arrogance and self-promotion to maintain stability and authenticity. By staying true to their values and maintaining a humble approach, they can build a strong foundation for their leadership.

Arrogance and self-promotion can lead to instability in leadership, as leaders who focus on projecting an image of superiority may neglect essential aspects of their role, such as supporting their team and making informed decisions, undermining their credibility and effectiveness. When leaders engage in self-promotion, they often sacrifice authenticity, as overemphasising personal achievements and abilities can create a disconnect with team members, who may perceive the leader as insincere, whereas authentic leadership builds trust and respect. Arrogance can erode trust within the organisation, as employees are more likely to trust leaders who are humble, transparent, and genuinely interested in their well-being, while leaders who prioritise self-promotion over genuine connection risk alienating their team members.

Humble leaders recognise that their success is a collective effort and give credit to their team members, acknowledging contributions, admitting mistakes, and showing gratitude, fostering a positive and supportive work environment. Authentic leaders stay true to their core values and principles, maintaining consistency between words and actions, which reinforces integrity and builds credibility, ensuring that decisions and behaviours align with the organisation's mission and values. Building genuine relationships with team members requires openness and empathy, so leaders should take the time to understand their perspectives, provide support, and show genuine interest in their well-being, enhancing collaboration and trust.

Leaders who avoid arrogance and self-promotion earn the trust and respect of their team members, as this trust is based on the leader's authenticity, humility, and commitment to the team's success. Humble and authentic leadership fosters collaboration and teamwork, with employees more likely to support and work effectively with leaders who value their contributions and prioritise collective success. Genuine and grounded leaders increase engagement and motivation among employees, leading to higher levels of productivity and job satisfaction, driving the organisation's success. Avoiding arrogance and self-promotion supports sustainable leadership, as leaders who remain humble and true to their values build a strong foundation for long-term success, resilience, and adaptability.

Leaders should regularly reflect on their behaviour and motivations to ensure that they are acting with humility and authenticity, as this self-reflection helps them stay grounded and aligned with their values. Encouraging feedback from team members provides valuable insights into how the leader is perceived, so leaders should be open to constructive criticism and use it to improve their leadership style and approach. Recognising and celebrating the achievements of team members should be a priority, as this focus on collective success reinforces the importance of teamwork and reduces the emphasis on individual self-promotion. Leaders should also model the behaviours and values they expect from their team members by demonstrating humility, authenticity, and integrity, setting a positive example and encouraging others to follow suit.

Avoiding arrogance and self-promotion fosters a sustainable organisational culture where employees feel valued and respected, attracting and retaining top talent and contributing to the organisation's overall success. Teams that prioritise humility and authenticity are more resilient and capable of overcoming challenges, as strong relationships and trust developed through this focus enable them to work together effectively in any situation. Leaders who avoid arrogance and self-promotion can navigate uncertainties with strategic agility, ensuring decisions are made with long-term sustainability in mind, supporting the organisation's resilience. Organisations that consistently prioritise humility and authenticity are better positioned for long-term success, as these values provide a strong foundation that supports sustainable growth and resilience.

LEADING WITH HUMILITY & AUTHENTICITY

> *He who displays himself does not shine; he who asserts his own views is not distinguished; he who vaunts himself does not find his merit acknowledged; he who is self-conceited has no superiority allowed to him.*

Lao Tzu's passage emphasises the importance of humility and the pitfalls of self-promotion and conceit. In strategic management, humility is a key trait for effective leadership. Leaders who avoid self-promotion and focus on the collective success of their team are often more respected and admired. By acknowledging the contributions of others and leading by example, leaders can foster a culture of collaboration and mutual respect. This authenticity helps in building trust and credibility within the organisation.

Leaders should prioritise the success of their team over individual recognition by celebrating collective achievements and acknowledging the efforts of all team members, creating a supportive environment where everyone feels valued and motivated. Humble leaders share credit for successes and highlight the contributions of others, reinforcing the importance of collaboration and demonstrating that they value the input and efforts of their team, which builds morale and fosters a sense of unity. Leaders should downplay their own achievements and avoid seeking personal acclaim, directing attention to the accomplishments of the team and the organisation to ensure the focus remains on collective goals and foster a culture of mutual respect.

Authentic leaders demonstrate integrity through their actions and decisions, being honest, transparent, and consistent in their behaviour, which sets a positive example for their team and builds credibility and trust. Humble leaders are approachable and open to feedback, actively listening to their team members and creating an environment where everyone feels comfortable sharing their ideas and concerns, fostering open communication and collaboration. Authentic leaders admit their mistakes and take responsibility for their actions, demonstrating humility and commitment to continuous improvement, fostering a culture of learning and resilience.

Leaders should encourage teamwork and collaboration by creating opportunities for team members to work together on projects and initiatives, fostering a sense of shared purpose and ensuring that everyone understands their role in achieving collective goals. An inclusive environment where diverse perspectives are valued enhances collaboration and mutual respect, so leaders should promote inclusivity by ensuring that all team members have a voice and are encouraged to contribute, driving innovation and creativity. Regularly recognising and celebrating the contributions of team members reinforces the value of collaboration, so leaders should acknowledge individual and team achievements, expressing appreciation for their efforts to boost morale and foster a positive work environment.

Consistency between words and actions is essential for building trust and credibility, so leaders should ensure that their behaviour aligns with their stated values and commitments, reinforcing integrity and reliability. Transparent communication fosters trust by ensuring everyone is informed and aware of important developments, so leaders should communicate openly and honestly about the organisation's goals, challenges, and successes, promoting a culture of trust and mutual respect. Leaders who support the development and growth of their team members build trust and credibility by providing opportunities for professional development, mentorship, and career advancement, demonstrating their investment in the success of their team.

Leaders who prioritise humility and authenticity earn the trust and respect of their team members based on their genuine commitment to the team's success and well-being rather than self-promotion. A culture of humility and authenticity fosters collaboration and teamwork, as employees are more likely to support and work effectively with leaders who value their contributions and prioritise collective success. Employees are more engaged and motivated when they work with humble and authentic leaders, leading to higher levels of productivity and job satisfaction, driving the organisation's success. Humility and authenticity support sustainable leadership, as leaders who remain true to their values and prioritise the well-being of their team build a strong foundation for long-term success, resilience, and adaptability.

Leaders should regularly reflect on their behaviour and motivations to ensure they are acting with humility and authenticity, as this self-reflection helps them stay grounded and aligned with their values. Encouraging feedback from team members provides valuable insights into how the leader is perceived, so leaders should be open to constructive criticism and use it to improve their leadership style and approach. Prioritising recognising and celebrating team achievements reinforces the importance of teamwork and reduces the emphasis on individual self-promotion, as leaders should focus on collective success. By demonstrating humility, authenticity, and integrity, leaders set a positive example and encourage others to follow suit, modelling the behaviours and values they expect from their team members.

Leading with humility and authenticity fosters a sustainable organisational culture where employees feel valued and respected, attracting and retaining top talent and contributing to the organisation's overall success. Teams that prioritise humility and authenticity are more resilient and capable of overcoming challenges, as strong relationships and trust developed through this focus enable them to work together effectively in any situation. Leaders who embrace humility and authenticity can navigate uncertainties with strategic agility, ensuring decisions are made with long-term sustainability in mind and supporting the organisation's resilience. Organisations that consistently prioritise humility and authenticity are better positioned for long-term success, as these values provide a strong foundation that supports sustainable growth and resilience.

AVOIDING OVER-ASSERTION

He who asserts his own views is not distinguished.

Lao Tzu's passage highlights the importance of avoiding over-assertion in leadership. Strategic leaders should avoid over-assertion of their views. Instead, they should encourage open dialogue and listen to diverse perspectives. This approach fosters a culture of inclusivity and innovation, where new ideas are welcomed and valued. By being open to feedback and willing to adapt, leaders can make more informed and effective decisions.

Over-assertion of one's views can stifle innovation within the organisation by dominating conversations and imposing ideas, discouraging employees from sharing their own thoughts and suggestions, which limits creativity and hinders the development of innovative solutions. It can erode trust between leaders and their teams, as employees may feel that their opinions are undervalued or ignored, leading to disengagement and a lack of motivation. Trust, built on mutual respect and open communication, is undermined by over-assertion, which also hinders collaboration and teamwork. When team members feel that their input is not valued, they are less likely to engage in collaborative efforts, reducing the effectiveness of the team and the quality of outcomes.

Leaders should foster an inclusive environment where diverse perspectives are welcomed and valued, creating opportunities for all team members to share their ideas and contribute to discussions, promoting a sense of belonging and encouraging active participation. Active listening is essential for encouraging open dialogue, so leaders should listen attentively to their team members, showing genuine interest in their perspectives, and acknowledging and validating others' ideas, even if they differ from the leader's own views. Leaders should facilitate constructive discussions that allow for the free exchange of ideas by creating a safe space for open dialogue, setting ground rules for respectful communication, and encouraging critical thinking, leading to more informed and balanced decisions.

Leaders should actively solicit feedback from their team members on various aspects of the organisation, including leadership style, processes, and strategies, as this feedback provides valuable insights and helps leaders understand different perspectives. Being receptive to criticism is a hallmark of effective leadership, so leaders should view criticism as an opportunity for growth and improvement, being open to feedback and willing to adapt to enhance their effectiveness and build stronger relationships with their team. Flexibility in adapting strategies based on feedback and changing circumstances is crucial, so leaders should be willing to revise their plans and approaches when new information or insights emerge, ensuring that decisions remain relevant and effective.

Encouraging open dialogue and valuing diverse perspectives fosters innovation, as employees who feel comfortable sharing their ideas contribute a wider range of creative solutions and improvements to the organisation. A culture of inclusivity and open communication increases employee engagement and motivation, with team members who feel heard and valued more likely to be committed to their work and the organisation's success. Leaders who listen to diverse perspectives and are open to feedback make more informed and effective decisions, considering various viewpoints and potential impacts to achieve better outcomes. Avoiding over-assertion and fostering open dialogue contribute to a positive organisational culture, where employees experience respectful and inclusive communication, enhancing their sense of connection and loyalty to the organisation.

Leaders should create opportunities for diverse voices to be heard through brainstorming sessions, team meetings, and feedback loops, encouraging a wide range of perspectives and ideas. Establishing ground rules for discussions ensures communication remains respectful and productive, promoting active listening, encouraging constructive feedback, and discouraging dominance by any single voice. Regularly seeking input from team members on key decisions and initiatives fosters a culture of open communication, with leaders using surveys, suggestion boxes, and one-on-one meetings to gather feedback. Modelling open-mindedness by demonstrating a willingness to consider different viewpoints and adapt ideas sets a positive example and encourages others to do the same.

Avoiding over-assertion fosters a sustainable organisational culture where employees feel valued and respected, attracting and retaining top talent and contributing to the organisation's overall success. Teams that prioritise open dialogue and inclusivity are more resilient and capable of overcoming challenges, as strong relationships and trust developed through this focus enable them to work together effectively in any situation. Leaders who avoid over-assertion can navigate uncertainties with strategic agility, ensuring decisions are made with long-term sustainability in mind and supporting the organisation's resilience. Organisations that consistently prioritise open dialogue and inclusivity are better positioned for long-term success, as these values provide a strong foundation that supports sustainable growth and resilience.

CHAPTER 25 - ADAPTABILITY

Chapter 25 of the *Tao Te Ching* delves into the concept of the Tao as the source of all existence, emphasising its greatness, constancy, and the interconnection of all things. Here's how these teachings can be applied to modern-day strategic management:

RECOGNISING THE IMPORTANCE OF A CLEAR & GUIDING VISION

There was something undefined and complete, coming into existence before Heaven and Earth.

Lao Tzu's passage highlights the significance of an undefined yet complete vision that predates all existence. In strategic management, leaders should recognise the importance of having a clear and guiding vision for their organisation. This vision, though it may start as an abstract idea, serves as the foundation for all strategies and actions. It provides a sense of direction and purpose that aligns the efforts of the entire organisation.

A compelling vision statement encapsulates the core purpose and future aspirations of the organisation, and leaders should articulate a vision that inspires and motivates employees, conveying a clear and compelling picture of the organisation's desired future state. The vision should align with the organisation's core values and principles, ensuring that it is grounded in the organisation's identity and culture, providing a consistent and authentic guide for decision-making and actions. Involving stakeholders in the vision-setting process fosters a sense of ownership and commitment, so leaders should engage employees, customers, partners, and other key stakeholders to gather diverse perspectives and build a shared vision that resonates with everyone.

Strategic goals translate the vision into actionable objectives, so leaders should define clear, measurable, and achievable goals that align with the vision, providing a roadmap for the organisation and helping track progress towards the desired future state. Effective communication of the vision is essential for alignment and engagement, and leaders should consistently share the vision with all members of the organisation using various channels and formats to reinforce its importance, ensuring everyone understands and supports the vision. Empowering teams to take ownership of the vision and contribute to its realisation is crucial, so leaders should provide the necessary resources, support, and autonomy for teams to implement strategies and achieve goals that align with the vision, fostering innovation and accountability.

A clear and guiding vision provides a unified direction for the organisation, aligning the efforts of all team members towards a common goal, fostering collaboration and coherence, and enhancing the organisation's ability to achieve its objectives and adapt to changes. A compelling vision inspires and motivates employees by giving them a sense of purpose and meaning in their work, making them more engaged and committed when they understand how their contributions support the larger vision. It serves as a guide for decision-making, helping leaders evaluate options and make choices that align with the organisation's long-term goals, ensuring decisions are consistent with the organisation's values and aspirations. Additionally, a guiding vision provides stability and direction during times of change and uncertainty, helping the organisation stay focused on its long-term goals while adapting to evolving circumstances, ensuring sustained progress and growth.

Leaders should conduct vision workshops to engage stakeholders in defining and refining the vision, providing a collaborative space for brainstorming, discussion, and alignment, ensuring that the vision reflects diverse perspectives and collective aspirations. Regularly reviewing and updating the vision ensures its relevance and alignment with changing circumstances, as leaders should assess progress, gather feedback, and make necessary adjustments to keep the vision current and impactful. Vision champions are individuals who advocate for and promote the vision within the organisation, so leaders should identify and empower vision champions at various levels to reinforce the vision and drive its implementation across teams and departments. Integrating the vision into daily activities and practices reinforces its importance, so leaders should ensure that the vision is reflected in performance evaluations, project planning, and other organisational processes, embedding the vision into the organisational culture.

A clear and guiding vision fosters a sustainable organisational culture where employees feel valued and aligned with the organisation's purpose, attracting and retaining top talent and contributing to the organisation's overall success. Teams aligned with a clear vision are more resilient and capable of overcoming challenges, as strong relationships and trust developed through this focus enable them to work together effectively in any situation. Leaders who prioritise a clear vision can navigate uncertainties with strategic agility, ensuring decisions are made with long-term sustainability in mind and supporting the organisation's resilience. Organisations that consistently prioritise a clear and guiding vision are better positioned for long-term success, providing a strong foundation that supports sustainable growth and resilience.

EMBRACING FLEXIBILITY & ADAPTABILITY

How still it was and formless, standing alone, and undergoing no change, reaching everywhere and in no danger (of being exhausted)!

Lao Tzu's passage emphasises the formlessness and adaptability of the Tao, highlighting the importance of flexibility in leadership. Strategic leaders should create adaptable frameworks that allow the organisation to respond to changing circumstances and evolving market conditions. This adaptability ensures that the organisation remains resilient and can navigate uncertainties effectively.

Adaptability allows organisations to respond quickly to changes in the market, whether it is shifts in consumer preferences, technological advancements, or economic fluctuations, by adjusting their strategies and operations to stay competitive and relevant. The business environment is often unpredictable, with unexpected challenges and opportunities arising, and adaptable organisations are better equipped to navigate these uncertainties, making informed decisions that ensure long-term success and sustainability. Flexibility fosters a culture of innovation by encouraging employees to explore new ideas and approaches, empowering them to experiment and innovate, which drives continuous improvement and growth.

Agile planning involves creating flexible strategies that can be adjusted as needed, and leaders should implement agile methodologies, such as iterative planning and regular reviews, to ensure strategies remain relevant and effective in a changing environment. Decentralised decision-making empowers employees at all levels to make decisions that align with the organisation's goals, enhancing responsiveness and allowing the organisation to adapt quickly to emerging challenges and opportunities. Scenario planning involves anticipating potential future scenarios and developing strategies to address them, so leaders should create multiple scenarios based on different assumptions and identify actions that can be taken in each case, enhancing the organisation's ability to adapt to various outcomes.

A culture of continuous learning supports adaptability by encouraging employees to develop new skills and knowledge, so leaders should provide opportunities for training, mentorship, and professional development, fostering a growth mindset within the organisation. Open communication channels facilitate the sharing of ideas and feedback, enhancing the organisation's adaptability, so leaders should encourage transparent and honest dialogue, creating an environment where employees feel comfortable expressing their thoughts and concerns. Recognising and rewarding employees who demonstrate flexibility reinforces its importance, so leaders should celebrate examples of adaptability and highlight how flexible approaches have led to successful outcomes.

Adaptable organisations are more resilient in the face of challenges; by remaining flexible and responsive, they can quickly adjust their strategies and operations to overcome obstacles and seize opportunities. Flexibility supports sustained growth by allowing organisations to continuously improve and innovate, keeping them ahead of industry trends and maintaining their competitive edge. Employees who work in a flexible and adaptive environment are more engaged and motivated, which leads to higher levels of productivity and job satisfaction, driving the organisation's success. Flexible organisations also make more informed and effective decisions by considering diverse perspectives and being open to new information, ensuring that decisions align with the organisation's long-term goals and values.

Leaders should implement agile methodologies, such as Scrum and Kanban, to enhance flexibility in planning and execution, as these methodologies promote iterative development, regular feedback, and continuous improvement. Cross-functional collaboration brings together diverse perspectives and expertise, enhancing the organisation's adaptability, so leaders should create opportunities for employees from different departments to work together on projects and initiatives. Regularly reviewing and adjusting strategies ensures they remain relevant and effective, so leaders should conduct periodic assessments of their plans and make necessary adjustments based on new information and changing circumstances. Fostering a culture of innovation involves encouraging experimentation and risk-taking, and leaders should provide the necessary resources and support for employees to explore new ideas and approaches.

Embracing flexibility and adaptability fosters a sustainable organisational culture where employees feel valued and respected, attracting and retaining top talent and contributing to the organisation's overall success. Teams that prioritise flexibility and adaptability are more resilient and capable of overcoming challenges, as strong relationships and trust developed through this focus enable them to work together effectively in any situation. Leaders who embrace flexibility and adaptability can navigate uncertainties with strategic agility, ensuring decisions are made with long-term sustainability in mind and supporting the organisation's resilience. Organisations that consistently prioritise flexibility and adaptability are better positioned for long-term success, as these values provide a strong foundation that supports sustainable growth and resilience.

ACKNOWLEDGING THE INTERCONNECTEDNESS OF ALL THINGS

> Therefore the Tao is great; Heaven is great; Earth is great; and the (sage) king is also great. In the universe there are four that are great, and the (sage) king is one of them.

Lao Tzu's passage emphasises the interconnectedness of all things, highlighting the greatness of the Tao, Heaven, Earth, and the sage king. Leaders should recognise the interconnectedness of all aspects of their organisation and its environment. This holistic perspective helps in understanding how different elements influence each other and contribute to overall success. By fostering collaboration and synergy among various departments and teams, leaders can create a more cohesive and effective organisation.

Leaders should adopt holistic thinking, considering the organisation as an interconnected system, understanding how decisions in one area can impact other areas and recognising the interdependencies between different functions, processes, and teams. Conducting systemic analysis helps identify the relationships and interactions between various elements of the organisation, and leaders should use tools such as systems thinking, process mapping, and network analysis to visualise these connections and understand their implications. Recognising interdependencies within the organisation is crucial for effective decision-making, as leaders should consider how changes in one area might affect others and strive to balance different needs and priorities, helping avoid unintended consequences and ensuring that all parts of the organisation work together harmoniously.

Creating cross-functional teams encourages collaboration and leverages diverse perspectives, as leaders should bring together employees from different departments to work on projects and initiatives, fostering a culture of teamwork and mutual respect. Open communication channels facilitate the sharing of information and ideas across the organisation, so leaders should establish forums, meetings, and digital platforms that enable employees to connect and collaborate, breaking down silos and promoting transparency. Setting shared goals and objectives aligns the efforts of different departments and teams towards a common purpose, ensuring everyone understands the organisation's vision and how their contributions support its achievement, fostering a sense of unity and collective responsibility.

A holistic perspective enhances decision-making by providing a comprehensive understanding of the organisation's dynamics, allowing leaders who recognise interconnectedness to make more informed and balanced decisions while considering the broader impact of their actions. Collaboration and synergy drive innovation by bringing together diverse skills and perspectives, enabling employees to generate creative solutions and new ideas that contribute to the organisation's growth. Recognising and leveraging interdependencies can improve efficiency by optimising processes and resource allocation, with leaders who understand how different elements interact streamlining workflows, reducing redundancies, and enhancing overall productivity. Fostering a culture of collaboration and interconnectedness strengthens the organisational culture, as employees who feel connected to their colleagues and the organisation's mission are more engaged, motivated, and committed to its success.

Leaders should implement systems thinking approaches to understand the organisation as an interconnected system, using tools such as causal loop diagrams, process mapping, and scenario planning to visualise relationships and interactions. Designing collaborative workspaces that facilitate interaction and teamwork can enhance synergy, so leaders should create physical and virtual environments that support collaboration, such as open-plan offices, project rooms, and digital collaboration platforms. Promoting interdepartmental projects encourages employees to work together across functions, so leaders should identify opportunities for cross-functional collaboration and create project teams that leverage diverse expertise. Encouraging knowledge sharing and continuous learning fosters a culture of interconnectedness, so leaders should provide opportunities for employees to share their expertise through training sessions, workshops, and knowledge-sharing platforms.

Recognising interconnectedness fosters a sustainable organisational culture where employees feel valued and respected, attracting and retaining top talent and contributing to the organisation's overall success. Teams that understand and leverage interconnectedness are more resilient and capable of overcoming challenges, as the varied perspectives and experiences within the team enable them to navigate challenges and find innovative solutions. Leaders who prioritise interconnectedness can navigate uncertainties with strategic agility, ensuring decisions are made with long-term sustainability in mind and supporting the organisation's resilience. Organisations that consistently recognise and leverage interconnectedness are better positioned for long-term success, providing a strong foundation that supports sustainable growth and resilience.

CULTIVATING A GREAT & ENDURING PRESENCE

Great, it passes on (in constant flow). Passing on, it becomes remote. Having become remote, it returns.

Lao Tzu's passage emphasises the continuous and enduring nature of greatness, suggesting that true impact extends beyond immediate presence and returns to influence the future. In strategic management, leaders should focus on building long-term value and sustainability, ensuring that their strategies and actions have lasting impact. By prioritising long-term goals over short-term gains, leaders can create a legacy of excellence and resilience.

Leaders should develop strategies that prioritise sustainability and long-term value creation, considering the long-term impact of decisions on the organisation, stakeholders, and the environment, ensuring the organisation remains resilient and capable of adapting to future challenges. Core values serve as the foundation for long-term success, and leaders should ensure their actions and decisions align with the organisation's core values, reinforcing a consistent and authentic approach that builds trust and credibility, supporting sustained growth and excellence. Investing in the development and well-being of employees is crucial for long-term value creation, so leaders should provide opportunities for professional growth, support work-life balance, and foster a positive organisational culture, as engaged and motivated employees contribute to the organisation's long-term success.

Visionary goals provide a long-term perspective and guide the organisation's efforts towards sustainable success, so leaders should articulate clear and inspiring goals that reflect the organisation's mission and aspirations, driving continuous improvement and innovation. While short-term gains are important, leaders should balance them with long-term objectives, making decisions that support immediate needs without compromising the organisation's future potential, ensuring steady progress towards long-term goals. Resilience is a key component of long-term success, so leaders should build resilience into their strategies and operations to withstand and adapt to disruptions and challenges, developing contingency plans, fostering a culture of adaptability, and investing in sustainable practices.

Leaders who demonstrate commitment to long-term value and sustainability set a positive example for their teams, embodying the organisation's values and prioritising long-term goals, which inspires others to follow suit and fosters a culture of excellence and integrity. Innovation is essential for maintaining a competitive edge and achieving long-term success, so leaders should create an environment that encourages creativity and experimentation, supporting employees in developing and implementing innovative solutions, driving continuous improvement and growth. Recognising and celebrating achievements, both big and small, reinforces the importance of long-term goals and sustained efforts, as leaders should acknowledge the contributions of their teams and highlight how their work supports the organisation's long-term vision, boosting morale and motivation.

By prioritising long-term value and sustainability, organisations can achieve sustainable growth, ensuring they remain competitive and relevant while adapting to changing market conditions and opportunities. Organisations that focus on long-term goals and sustainable practices build a strong reputation for excellence and integrity, attracting top talent, loyal customers, and strategic partners, contributing to overall success. This focus enhances resilience by building a strong foundation and fostering a culture of adaptability, enabling organisations to navigate uncertainties and challenges confidently. Leaders who prioritise long-term goals create a lasting legacy of excellence, inspiring future generations and ensuring the organisation continues to thrive and contribute positively to society.

Leaders should implement long-term planning processes that align with the organisation's vision and goals by setting strategic priorities, developing action plans, and regularly reviewing progress to ensure alignment with long-term objectives. Promoting a culture of sustainability involves integrating sustainable practices into all aspects of the organisation's operations, encouraging resource efficiency, environmental stewardship, and social responsibility. Continuous improvement is essential for achieving long-term success, so leaders should support ongoing learning and development, encouraging employees to seek new knowledge and skills to drive innovation and excellence. Building strong relationships with stakeholders, including employees, customers, suppliers, and the community, supports long-term value creation, so leaders should engage with stakeholders, seek their input, and collaborate on initiatives that contribute to mutual success.

Cultivating a great and enduring presence fosters a sustainable organisational culture where employees feel valued and aligned with the organisation's purpose, attracting and retaining top talent and contributing to overall success. Teams that prioritise long-term value and sustainability are more resilient and capable of overcoming challenges, as strong relationships and trust developed through this focus enable them to work together effectively in any situation. Leaders who prioritise long-term goals can navigate uncertainties with strategic agility, ensuring decisions are made with long-term sustainability in mind, supporting the organisation's resilience. Organisations that consistently prioritise long-term value and sustainability are better positioned for long-term success, providing a strong foundation that supports sustainable growth and resilience.

ALIGNING WITH FUNDAMENTAL PRINCIPLES

Man takes his law from the Earth; the Earth takes its law from Heaven; Heaven takes its law from the Tao. The law of the Tao is its being what it is.

Lao Tzu's passage emphasises the hierarchical flow of principles from the Tao to Heaven, Earth, and ultimately to man. Strategic leaders should align their actions with these fundamental principles and values. These core principles serve as a compass, guiding decision-making and ensuring that the organisation remains true to its mission. By adhering to these values, leaders can build a strong and ethical foundation for the organisation.

Leaders should begin by identifying the core values that define the organisation's identity and mission, ensuring these values reflect the organisation's purpose, ethical standards, and long-term goals, providing a foundation for all actions and decisions. A value statement articulates these core principles and their importance, and leaders should communicate this statement clearly and consistently so all members understand and embrace these values, reinforcing the organisation's commitment to its principles. Involving stakeholders in defining core principles fosters a sense of ownership and commitment, so leaders should engage employees, customers, partners, and other key stakeholders to gather diverse perspectives and ensure the values resonate with everyone.

Core principles should serve as a compass for decision-making, with leaders evaluating options and making choices based on how well they align with the organisation's values, ensuring consistency, integrity, and ethical behaviour in all actions. Ethical guidelines provide a framework for applying these principles in various situations, so leaders should establish clear guidelines outlining acceptable behaviours and practices to help employees navigate ethical dilemmas and make informed decisions. Accountability reinforces adherence to core principles, so leaders should create mechanisms for monitoring and evaluating actions and decisions to ensure alignment with the organisation's values, fostering a culture of responsibility and trust.

Integrity is the cornerstone of a strong and ethical foundation, so leaders should model integrity through their actions and decisions by demonstrating honesty, transparency, and consistency, which sets a positive example and builds credibility and trust within the organisation. Encouraging ethical behaviour at all levels involves creating an environment where employees feel empowered to speak up, report concerns, and act in accordance with the organisation's values, contributing to a positive organisational culture and long-term success. Supporting social responsibility extends the organisation's commitment to its values beyond its operations, so leaders should engage in initiatives that promote social and environmental well-being, demonstrating a commitment to the greater good and enhancing the organisation's reputation and impact.

Adhering to core principles builds trust and credibility with employees, customers, and stakeholders, fostering loyalty and long-term relationships based on consistent commitment to values. These principles provide a clear framework for decision-making, helping leaders evaluate options and make ethical, consistent choices aligned with the organisation's mission and long-term goals. Focusing on core principles fosters a positive organisational culture where employees feel valued and respected, attracting and retaining top talent and contributing to overall success. Organisations that prioritise fundamental principles are better positioned for sustainable success, ensuring they remain resilient, adaptable, and capable of achieving long-term growth by building a strong and ethical foundation.

Leaders should regularly review and update the organisation's core values to ensure their relevance and alignment with changing circumstances, keeping them current and impactful. Integrating core principles into organisational policies and procedures ensures they are consistently upheld, with regular reviews and updates to align with the organisation's values and goals. Offering ethics training programmes helps employees understand the importance of core principles and how to apply them in their daily work, emphasising ethical decision-making and conduct. Recognising and celebrating ethical behaviour reinforces the importance of core principles, with leaders highlighting examples of integrity and ethical conduct to showcase their positive impact on the organisation.

Aligning with fundamental principles fosters a sustainable organisational culture where employees feel valued and respected, attracting and retaining top talent and contributing to overall success. Teams that prioritise core principles are more resilient and capable of overcoming challenges, as strong relationships and trust developed through this focus enable them to work together effectively in any situation. Leaders who align with fundamental principles can navigate uncertainties with strategic agility, ensuring decisions are made with long-term sustainability in mind and supporting the organisation's resilience. Organisations that consistently prioritise fundamental principles are better positioned for long-term success, providing a strong foundation that supports sustainable growth and resilience.

CHAPTER 26 – STILLNESS & REFLECTION

Chapter 26 of the *Tao Te Ching* offers profound insights on the importance of gravity, stillness, and rootedness in leadership and decision-making. Here's how these teachings can be applied to modern-day strategic management:

EMBRACING THE POWER OF STILLNESS & REFLECTION

Gravity is the root of lightness; stillness, the ruler of movement.

Lao Tzu's passage emphasises the profound power of stillness and reflection, suggesting that gravity and stillness serve as the foundation for lightness and movement. In strategic management, leaders should recognise the power of stillness and reflection. Taking time to pause, reflect, and consider the broader picture can lead to more informed and effective decisions. Leaders who cultivate a practice of mindfulness and reflection can navigate challenges with greater clarity and composure. This stillness serves as a foundation for thoughtful action and strategic planning.

Stillness and reflection provide leaders with the opportunity to gather and analyse information, consider different perspectives, and evaluate potential outcomes, ensuring well-considered and strategic choices. Taking time to reflect helps leaders gain clarity on their goals, values, and priorities, enabling them to focus on what truly matters and align their actions with the organisation's mission, leading to more effective and purposeful leadership. Mindfulness practices help leaders manage stress and maintain emotional composure, cultivating inner calm to respond to challenges and uncertainties with greater resilience and steadiness, enhancing their ability to lead with confidence and empathy. Reflection also allows leaders to see the bigger picture, identifying long-term opportunities and risks, enabling proactive planning and decision-making, ensuring the organisation remains adaptable and forward-thinking.

Leaders should incorporate mindfulness practices, such as meditation, deep breathing, and mindful walking, into their daily routines to help quiet the mind, reduce stress, and enhance focus and clarity. Setting aside dedicated time for reflection is essential for thoughtful leadership, so leaders should schedule regular moments of stillness and contemplation, whether through journaling, solitary walks, or quiet contemplation, to process experiences and gain insights. Creating a reflective culture within the organisation involves encouraging team members to take time for contemplation and providing opportunities for group reflection, such as debrief sessions and reflective meetings, fostering continuous learning and improvement. Reflection should also include seeking diverse perspectives from team members and stakeholders, engaging in active listening and open dialogue to consider different viewpoints and insights, which enriches the reflection process and leads to more comprehensive decision-making.

Integrating reflection into the strategic planning process ensures decisions are well-considered and aligned with long-term goals, so leaders should incorporate reflective practices into planning sessions, allowing time for thoughtful discussion and analysis. Effective leadership requires balancing action with stillness, so while decisive action is important, leaders should also recognise the value of pausing and reflecting before making significant decisions, enhancing the quality of their actions and ensuring alignment with strategic objectives. Reflection should be an ongoing practice that supports continuous improvement, so leaders should regularly review and assess their decisions, actions, and outcomes, identifying areas for growth and development, driving innovation and excellence through this iterative process.

Leaders should establish daily mindfulness routines that incorporate practices such as meditation, deep breathing, and mindful observation to create a foundation of calm and clarity for effective leadership. Regular reflection breaks scheduled throughout the day provide opportunities to step back, process information, and gain new perspectives, enhancing focus and decision-making. Encouraging reflective practices within teams through activities such as after-action reviews, reflective discussions, and learning circles promotes a culture of collective learning and improvement. Providing quiet spaces within the workplace supports mindfulness and reflection, as leaders should design environments that offer areas for solitude and contemplation, allowing employees to take a break from the busyness of work and recharge.

Embracing stillness and reflection fosters a sustainable organisational culture where employees feel valued and supported, attracting and retaining top talent and contributing to overall success. Teams that prioritise stillness and reflection are more resilient and capable of overcoming challenges, as strong relationships and trust developed through this focus enable them to work together effectively in any situation. Leaders who embrace stillness and reflection can navigate uncertainties with strategic agility, ensuring decisions are made with long-term sustainability in mind, supporting the organisation's resilience. Organisations that consistently prioritise stillness and reflection are better positioned for long-term success, providing a strong foundation that supports sustainable growth and resilience.

STAYING GROUNDED & FOCUSED

> Therefore a wise prince, marching the whole day, does not go far from his baggage waggons.

Lao Tzu's passage underscores the value of staying grounded and focused. In strategic management, effective leaders understand the importance of staying grounded and focused, even when pursuing ambitious goals. By keeping close to their 'baggage wagons'—the core values, resources, and support systems of their organisation—leaders ensure that they remain connected to what truly matters. This grounding helps in maintaining stability and consistency, preventing the organisation from being swayed by fleeting opportunities or distractions.

Core values serve as the foundation of the organisation, and leaders should continuously remind themselves and their teams of these values to ensure all actions and decisions align with them, building a strong organisational culture and maintaining integrity. Clear communication of core values reinforces their importance, so leaders should regularly share stories, examples, and successes that highlight the organisation's values in action, embedding them into daily operations and decision-making processes. Leaders should use core values as a compass for decision-making, evaluating options based on how well they align with the organisation's values to ensure decisions are ethical, consistent, and reflective of the organisation's principles.

Effective use of resources is crucial for maintaining focus and achieving goals, so leaders should ensure resources are allocated efficiently and support strategic priorities, helping to avoid wastage and enhance productivity. Support systems provide the necessary infrastructure for success, so leaders should invest in developing robust support systems, including technology, processes, and human resources, enabling the organisation to operate smoothly and adapt to changes effectively. Engaging stakeholders, including employees, customers, and partners, strengthens the organisation's support network, so leaders should foster strong relationships with stakeholders, seeking their input and collaboration to enhance trust and ensure the organisation is well-supported in its endeavours.

Ambitious goals are important, but they should be balanced with practicality, so leaders should set realistic and achievable targets to ensure the organisation remains grounded and focused, preventing overreach and maintaining steady progress. Distractions can derail progress and lead to inefficiencies, so leaders should remain vigilant and avoid being swayed by fleeting opportunities or trends that do not align with the organisation's core values and goals, ensuring efforts are directed towards meaningful and strategic objectives. Consistency is key to building trust and credibility, so leaders should ensure their actions and decisions are consistent with the organisation's mission and values, fostering stability and reinforcing the organisation's commitment to its principles.

Staying grounded and focused builds trust and credibility within the organisation, as employees and stakeholders are more likely to trust leaders who demonstrate consistency and adherence to core values, fostering loyalty and long-term commitment. A grounded approach enhances decision-making by ensuring choices are aligned with the organisation's values and long-term goals, leading to more informed and strategic decisions that support sustainable success. Grounded and focused organisations are more resilient in the face of challenges, maintaining stability and consistency to navigate uncertainties and adapt to changes effectively, ensuring sustained progress and growth. Staying grounded and focused also fosters a positive organisational culture where employees feel valued and supported, attracting and retaining top talent and contributing to overall success.

Leaders should regularly review and reflect on the organisation's core values to ensure they remain relevant and impactful, keeping these values at the forefront of decision-making and actions. Incorporating reflection practices, such as mindfulness and contemplation, helps leaders stay grounded by providing opportunities to pause, consider the bigger picture, and realign with core values. Setting clear priorities ensures efforts are focused on what truly matters, so leaders should establish strategic priorities that align with the organisation's goals and values, guiding their actions and decisions. Open communication channels facilitate transparency and collaboration, so leaders should create opportunities for team members to share their thoughts, feedback, and concerns, fostering a culture of mutual respect and support.

Staying grounded and focused fosters a sustainable organisational culture where employees feel valued and respected, attracting and retaining top talent and contributing to overall success. Teams that prioritise staying grounded and focused are more resilient and capable of overcoming challenges, as strong relationships and trust developed through this focus enable them to work together effectively in any situation. Leaders who stay grounded and focused can navigate uncertainties with strategic agility, ensuring decisions are made with long-term sustainability in mind and supporting the organisation's resilience. Organisations that consistently prioritise staying grounded and focused are better positioned for long-term success, providing a strong foundation that supports sustainable growth and resilience.

EXERCISING PATIENCE & RESTRAINT

> *Although he may have brilliant prospects to look at, he quietly remains (in his proper place), indifferent to them.*

Lao Tzu's passage emphasises the virtue of exercising patience and restraint, even when presented with attractive prospects. Leaders should exercise patience and restraint, even when presented with tempting opportunities. Rather than rushing into action or being swayed by short-term gains, strategic leaders assess the situation thoroughly and make deliberate choices that align with long-term objectives. This disciplined approach ensures sustainable success and avoids unnecessary risks.

Patience allows leaders to thoroughly assess opportunities before making decisions by gathering relevant information, analysing potential outcomes, and considering the broader impact on the organisation, ensuring decisions are well-informed and strategically sound. Exercising patience helps leaders avoid impulsive actions that may lead to negative consequences, as taking the time to reflect and deliberate allows for more thoughtful and effective choices, preventing hasty decisions driven by short-term desires. Patience also enables leaders to balance short-term opportunities with long-term goals by evaluating how these opportunities align with the organisation's strategic objectives, ensuring actions support sustainable success.

Restraint involves maintaining a disciplined approach to decision-making and actions by setting clear criteria for evaluating opportunities and adhering to these guidelines, ensuring consistency and alignment with the organisation's mission and values. It helps leaders stay focused on core priorities, avoiding distractions and diversions, so they can concentrate on what truly matters and direct their efforts towards achieving strategic goals, enhancing productivity and effectiveness. Restraint is also essential for managing risks and avoiding unnecessary exposures, as leaders should carefully assess potential risks and take a measured approach to mitigate them, ensuring the organisation remains stable and resilient.

Exercising patience and restraint leads to more informed decision-making, as leaders who thoroughly assess opportunities and consider long-term implications are better equipped to make strategic choices that drive success. A disciplined approach ensures sustainable success by aligning actions with long-term objectives, helping leaders navigate uncertainties and achieve consistent progress towards their goals. Leaders who exercise patience and restraint build trust and credibility within the organisation, as employees and stakeholders are more likely to trust leaders who demonstrate thoughtful and deliberate decision-making, fostering loyalty and long-term commitment. By avoiding impulsive actions and managing risks effectively, leaders can minimise potential negative outcomes, enhancing the organisation's stability and resilience and ensuring sustained growth and success.

Leaders should establish clear criteria for evaluating opportunities and making decisions, including defining key factors such as alignment with strategic goals, potential risks, and resource requirements, to provide a structured approach to decision-making. Incorporating reflection practices, such as mindfulness and contemplation, helps leaders exercise patience and restraint by providing opportunities to pause, consider different perspectives, and make deliberate choices. Regularly reviewing long-term goals helps leaders stay focused and aligned with their strategic objectives, assessing progress, identifying potential distractions, and making necessary adjustments to stay on track. Encouraging open dialogue with team members and stakeholders facilitates thoughtful decision-making, as leaders should seek input, listen to different viewpoints, and consider diverse perspectives, enriching the decision-making process and enhancing overall effectiveness.

Exercising patience and restraint fosters a sustainable organisational culture where employees feel valued and respected, attracting and retaining top talent and contributing to overall success. Teams that prioritise patience and restraint are more resilient and capable of overcoming challenges, as strong relationships and trust developed through this focus enable them to work together effectively in any situation. Leaders who exercise patience and restraint can navigate uncertainties with strategic agility, ensuring decisions are made with long-term sustainability in mind and supporting the organisation's resilience. Organisations that consistently prioritise patience and restraint are better positioned for long-term success, providing a strong foundation that supports sustainable growth and resilience.

AVOIDING IMPULSIVENESS & SUPERFICIALITY

How should the lord of a myriad chariots carry himself lightly before the kingdom? If he do act lightly, he has lost his root (of gravity); if he proceed to active movement, he will lose his throne.

Lao Tzu's passage warns against impulsiveness and superficiality, suggesting that such behaviour can undermine a leader's effectiveness and credibility. Leaders should avoid making hasty decisions or acting without proper consideration. By maintaining a sense of gravity and thoughtfulness in their actions, leaders can uphold their authority and the trust of their teams. This careful and deliberate approach prevents missteps and strengthens the leader's position.

Impulsiveness can lead to inconsistency in decision-making, undermining a leader's credibility as hasty decisions without thorough consideration risk errors that erode trust and respect among team members. Impulsive actions can create instability within the organisation, with rapid, unplanned changes disrupting workflows, confusing employees, and leading to inefficiencies, making stability crucial for maintaining a productive and cohesive work environment. Additionally, focusing on short-term gains or acting superficially can cause leaders to lose sight of long-term goals, as impulsive decisions may provide immediate benefits but can have detrimental effects on the organisation's strategic objectives and sustainability.

Thoughtful leaders take the time to gather information, analyse options, and consider potential outcomes before making decisions, ensuring choices are well-informed and align with the organisation's values and long-term goals. A sense of gravity and thoughtfulness helps leaders maintain consistency in their actions and decisions, building trust and credibility as team members know they can rely on their leaders to act with integrity and foresight. Thoughtful actions demonstrate that leaders care about the impact of their decisions on the organisation and its members, fostering trust and respect, and strengthening the leader's position and enhancing team cohesion.

Practical Strategies for Avoiding Impulsiveness & Superficiality

Implementing Reflection Practices: Leaders should incorporate reflection practices, such as mindfulness and contemplation, into their daily routines. These practices provide opportunities to pause, consider the bigger picture, and make deliberate choices.

Establishing Decision-Making Frameworks: A structured decision-making framework helps leaders evaluate options methodically. This includes defining criteria for decision-making, weighing pros and cons, and considering long-term implications. A clear framework supports thoughtful and consistent decisions.

Seeking Diverse Perspectives: Engaging diverse perspectives enhances the decision-making process. Leaders should seek input from team members, stakeholders, and experts to gather a wide range of insights. This collaborative approach enriches the analysis and leads to more balanced decisions.

Prioritising Long-Term Goals: Leaders should prioritise long-term goals over short-term gains. This involves aligning decisions with the organisation's strategic objectives and considering the broader impact on the organisation's sustainability and growth.

Regularly Reviewing Outcomes: Regularly reviewing the outcomes of decisions helps leaders learn from their experiences and improve their decision-making process. Leaders should assess the effectiveness of their choices, identify areas for improvement, and make necessary adjustments.

Thoughtful and deliberate actions build credibility and trust within the organisation, as employees and stakeholders are more likely to trust leaders who demonstrate consistency, integrity, and consideration in their decisions. Maintaining a sense of gravity and thoughtfulness fosters stability and cohesion within the organisation, creating a positive work environment where employees feel secure and supported. A thoughtful approach to decision-making ensures choices are informed and strategic, with leaders who take the time to analyse options and consider long-term implications making better decisions that support the organisation's success. Avoiding impulsiveness and superficiality supports sustainable success, as leaders who prioritise thoughtful and deliberate actions ensure the organisation remains focused on its long-term goals and values, driving sustained growth and resilience.

Avoiding impulsiveness and superficiality fosters a sustainable organisational culture where employees feel valued and respected, attracting and retaining top talent and contributing to overall success. Teams that prioritise thoughtfulness are more resilient and capable of overcoming challenges, as strong relationships and trust developed through this focus enable them to work together effectively in any situation. Leaders who avoid impulsiveness and superficiality can navigate uncertainties with strategic agility, ensuring decisions are made with long-term sustainability in mind and supporting the organisation's resilience. Organisations that consistently prioritise thoughtfulness are better positioned for long-term success, providing a strong foundation that supports sustainable growth and resilience.

CHAPTER 27 – BUREAUCRACY

Chapter 27 of the *Tao Te Ching* underscores the subtleties of skillful action and the importance of mutual respect between those of different skill levels. Here's how these teachings can be applied to modern-day strategic management:

PRACTISING SUBTLETY & PRECISION

> *The skilful traveller leaves no traces of his wheels or footsteps; the skilful speaker says nothing that can be found fault with or blamed.*

Lao Tzu's passage emphasises the value of subtlety and precision, suggesting that effective actions and communications should be unobtrusive and faultless. In strategic management, leaders should aim to be subtle and precise in their actions and communications. This means making decisions and implementing strategies in a way that is effective but unobtrusive. Subtlety in leadership allows for smoother operations and minimises friction. Precision ensures that actions are well thought out and executed without unnecessary complications.

Subtlety involves taking effective actions that do not draw unnecessary attention or cause disruption, so leaders should implement strategies in a manner that seamlessly integrates with existing processes and minimises resistance, fostering cooperation and smooth operations. Subtle leaders influence others without dominating or overpowering them by guiding and supporting team members while allowing them to take ownership of their tasks, inspiring and motivating their teams without imposing their will. Subtlety in leadership helps build trust and respect within the organisation, as leaders who act with discretion and consideration are more likely to earn the trust of their team members, enhancing collaboration and fostering a positive organisational culture.

Precision requires leaders to make well-thought-out decisions based on thorough analysis and understanding by gathering relevant information, considering various perspectives, and evaluating potential outcomes to minimise errors and ensure strategic alignment. Precision in communication involves conveying messages clearly and concisely, so leaders should articulate their ideas and expectations in a straightforward manner, avoiding ambiguity and confusion, ensuring everyone understands their roles and responsibilities, enhancing efficiency and effectiveness. Precision also requires attention to detail in planning and execution, so leaders should ensure all aspects of a strategy or project are carefully considered and addressed, preventing oversights and enhancing the quality of outcomes.

Practical Strategies for Practising Subtlety & Precision

Implementing Seamless Strategies: Leaders should implement strategies in a way that integrates smoothly with existing processes. This involves understanding the current workflow, identifying potential points of resistance, and making adjustments to ensure a seamless transition.

Exercising Discretion: Leaders should exercise discretion in their actions and communications. This means being mindful of the timing, context, and impact of their decisions. By acting with discretion, leaders can avoid unnecessary disruptions and maintain harmony within the organisation.

Developing Clear Communication Plans: Leaders should develop clear communication plans that outline the key messages, methods, and frequency of communication. This ensures that information is conveyed effectively and consistently, minimising misunderstandings and confusion.

Conducting Thorough Analysis: Leaders should conduct thorough analysis before making decisions. This involves collecting and analysing data, consulting with experts, and considering potential risks and benefits. A comprehensive analysis ensures that decisions are based on sound reasoning and evidence.

Paying Attention to Details: Leaders should pay close attention to details in planning and execution. This includes reviewing plans and documents for accuracy, monitoring progress, and addressing any issues that arise. Attention to detail enhances the quality and success of initiatives.

Practising subtlety and precision ensures smoother operations by minimising disruptions and resistance, allowing the organisation to function efficiently and harmoniously. Leaders who exercise subtle influence can inspire and motivate their teams without imposing their will, fostering a sense of ownership and autonomy among team members, leading to higher engagement and productivity. Precision in communication ensures that everyone understands their roles, responsibilities, and expectations, minimising misunderstandings and enhancing collaboration and efficiency. Precision in planning and execution leads to higher quality outcomes, as leaders who pay attention to detail and make well-thought-out decisions can achieve better results and avoid costly mistakes. Subtle and precise leaders earn the trust and respect of their team members, fostering a positive organisational culture, enhancing collaboration, and contributing to long-term success.

Practising subtlety and precision fosters a sustainable organisational culture where employees feel valued and respected, attracting and retaining top talent and contributing to overall success. Teams that prioritise subtlety and precision are more resilient and capable of overcoming challenges, as strong relationships and trust developed through this focus enable them to work together effectively in any situation. Leaders who practise subtlety and precision can navigate uncertainties with strategic agility, ensuring decisions are made with long-term sustainability in mind and supporting the organisation's resilience. Organisations that consistently prioritise subtlety and precision are better positioned for long-term success, providing a strong foundation that supports sustainable growth and resilience.

STREAMLINING PROCESSES & REDUCING BUREAUCRACY

> *The skilful reckoner uses no tallies; the skilful closer needs no bolts or bars, while to open what he has shut will be impossible; the skilful binder uses no strings or knots, while to unloose what he has bound will be impossible.*

Lao Tzu's passage emphasises the effectiveness of simplicity and the power of skillful actions that do not rely on excessive measures. Leaders should focus on streamlining processes and reducing unnecessary bureaucracy. This involves creating efficient systems that do not rely on excessive controls or documentation. By simplifying operations, leaders can enhance productivity and reduce the burden on their teams. This approach fosters a more agile and responsive organisation.

Streamlined processes eliminate unnecessary steps and reduce the time required to complete tasks, increasing efficiency and allowing employees to focus on high-impact activities, enhancing overall productivity. Simplified operations enable organisations to respond more quickly to changes and opportunities, making them more agile and better able to adapt to market shifts, customer needs, and competitive pressures, ensuring sustained success. Reducing bureaucracy lessens the administrative burden on employees, creating a more satisfying work environment that leads to higher morale and job satisfaction. Additionally, streamlined processes often result in cost savings by eliminating waste and optimising resource use, allowing the organisation to allocate resources more effectively and invest in strategic initiatives.

Strategies for Streamlining Processes

Identifying Bottlenecks: Leaders should identify bottlenecks and inefficiencies in current processes. This involves conducting a thorough analysis of workflows, gathering input from employees, and pinpointing areas where improvements are needed. Addressing these bottlenecks streamlines operations and enhances productivity.

Implementing Automation: Automation can significantly reduce manual tasks and streamline operations. Leaders should explore opportunities to automate repetitive processes, such as data entry, reporting, and approvals. Implementing automation tools frees up employees to focus on more strategic and creative tasks.

Simplifying Approval Processes: Excessive approval layers can slow down decision-making and hinder progress. Leaders should simplify approval processes by delegating authority and empowering employees to make decisions within defined parameters. This approach accelerates workflow and fosters a sense of ownership and accountability.

Eliminating Redundant Documentation: Redundant documentation adds unnecessary complexity and consumes valuable time. Leaders should review and streamline documentation requirements, ensuring that only essential information is collected and recorded. This simplification reduces the administrative burden on employees.

Standardising Procedures: Standardising procedures enhances consistency and efficiency across the organisation. Leaders should develop clear guidelines and best practices for common tasks, providing employees with a framework to follow. Standardisation reduces variability and ensures that processes are executed smoothly.

A culture of continuous improvement encourages employees to identify and implement process enhancements, so leaders should create an environment where employees feel empowered to suggest and test new ideas, driving ongoing optimisation and efficiency. Collaboration between departments and teams enhances the effectiveness of process improvements, so leaders should facilitate cross-functional collaboration, allowing employees to share insights and work together to streamline operations, leading to more comprehensive and successful improvements. Training and support are essential for successful process improvements, so leaders should provide employees with the necessary skills and resources to implement new processes and tools, ensuring they remain proficient and confident in their roles. Recognising and rewarding employees who contribute to process improvements reinforces the importance of efficiency, so leaders should celebrate successes and acknowledge the efforts of individuals and teams who drive positive change, motivating employees to continue seeking ways to enhance operations.

Streamlining processes and reducing bureaucracy fosters a sustainable organisational culture where efficiency and innovation are valued, attracting and retaining top talent and contributing to overall success. Teams that prioritise efficiency are more resilient and capable of overcoming challenges, as strong relationships and trust developed through streamlined operations enable them to work together effectively in any situation. Leaders who focus on streamlining processes can navigate uncertainties with strategic agility, ensuring decisions are made with long-term sustainability in mind and supporting the organisation's resilience. Organisations that consistently streamline processes and reduce bureaucracy are better positioned for long-term success, providing a strong foundation that supports sustainable growth and resilience.

VALUING & RETAINING TALENT

In the same way the sage is always skilful at saving men, and so he does not cast away any man; he is always skilful at saving things, and so he does not cast away anything.

Lao Tzu's passage emphasises the value of skillfully preserving and nurturing people and resources. Effective leaders recognise the value of their team members and strive to retain talent. This means investing in employee development, providing support, and creating opportunities for growth. Leaders should avoid discarding employees who may be struggling and instead focus on nurturing their potential. This approach not only enhances loyalty and retention but also fosters a culture of continuous improvement.

Leaders should offer training and learning opportunities that align with employees' roles and career aspirations, including workshops, courses, certifications, and mentorship programmes, to help employees develop new skills, stay engaged, and contribute more effectively to the organisation. Encouraging employees to set and pursue professional growth goals demonstrates a commitment to their development, so leaders should support them in identifying their career aspirations and provide guidance and resources to help achieve these goals, fostering motivation and dedication. Clear career advancement paths provide employees with a roadmap for their professional development within the organisation, so leaders should outline the steps and requirements for promotion and advancement, offering opportunities for employees to progress in their careers, enhancing retention and loyalty through transparent career paths.

Regular feedback helps employees understand their strengths and areas for improvement, so leaders should provide constructive feedback that is specific, actionable, and supportive, fostering a culture of continuous development. Supporting employee well-being is essential for retention and productivity, so leaders should create a work environment that promotes physical, mental, and emotional well-being, including offering flexible work arrangements, access to wellness programmes, and a supportive workplace culture. Recognising and appreciating employees' contributions reinforces their value to the organisation, so leaders should celebrate successes, acknowledge hard work, and express gratitude for employees' efforts, boosting morale and strengthening the connection between employees and the organisation.

When employees struggle, leaders should take the time to understand the underlying issues by having open and empathetic conversations to identify any challenges or obstacles that may be affecting performance, helping employees get back on track. Leaders should provide additional support and resources, such as personalised coaching, additional training, or adjustments to workload, to help struggling employees improve and realise their potential. Creating a safe and supportive environment for growth encourages employees to take risks and learn from their mistakes, promoting a culture where it is acceptable to fail and learn, fostering resilience and continuous improvement.

Valuing and investing in employees' development enhances their loyalty to the organisation, as employees who feel supported and appreciated are more likely to stay long-term, reducing turnover and associated costs. Employees who see opportunities for growth and feel valued are more engaged and motivated, leading to higher levels of productivity and job satisfaction, driving the organisation's success. A focus on employee development and support fosters a positive organisational culture, attracting and retaining top talent and contributing to the organisation's overall success and reputation. Nurturing employees' potential and supporting their growth fosters a culture of continuous improvement, as employees committed to their development are more likely to innovate, adapt, and contribute to the organisation's long-term success.

Leaders should implement comprehensive development programmes that offer a range of learning opportunities, including technical training, leadership development, and soft skills enhancement. Regular check-ins with employees help maintain open lines of communication and provide opportunities for feedback and support, so leaders should schedule one-on-one meetings to discuss progress, address concerns, and offer guidance. Recognition programmes that celebrate employee achievements reinforce their value to the organisation, so leaders should develop formal and informal recognition initiatives that acknowledge individual and team contributions. Mentorship programmes pair employees with experienced mentors who can offer guidance and support, so leaders should facilitate these relationships to help employees navigate their career paths and develop their skills.

Valuing and retaining talent fosters a sustainable organisational culture where employees feel valued and respected, attracting and retaining top talent and contributing to the organisation's overall success. Teams that prioritise employee development and support are more resilient and capable of overcoming challenges, as strong relationships and trust developed through this focus enable them to work together effectively in any situation. Leaders who value and retain talent can navigate uncertainties with strategic agility, ensuring decisions are made with long-term sustainability in mind and supporting the organisation's resilience. Organisations that consistently prioritise valuing and retaining talent are better positioned for long-term success, providing a strong foundation that supports sustainable growth and resilience.

FOSTERING MUTUAL RESPECT & COLLABORATION

> *Therefore the man of skill is a master (to be looked up to) by him who has not the skill; and he who has not the skill is the helper of (the reputation of) him who has the skill.*

Lao Tzu's passage highlights the importance of mutual respect and collaboration between individuals of different skill levels. In a harmonious and productive work environment, mutual respect between team members of different skill levels is essential. Leaders should encourage collaboration and mentorship, where experienced employees guide and support those who are still developing their skills. This reciprocal relationship benefits both parties and strengthens the overall team dynamic.

Mutual respect involves recognising and valuing the diverse skills and contributions of all team members, with leaders emphasising the unique strengths each individual brings to the team, fostering an inclusive and appreciative culture. Respecting team members as equals, regardless of their skill level or experience, is crucial, and leaders should promote a culture where everyone's voice is heard and valued, creating an environment of equality and fairness. Mutual respect builds trust within the team, and when team members respect and support each other, they are more likely to collaborate effectively and share ideas openly, enhancing communication and strengthening team cohesion.

Leaders should create opportunities for team members to interact and collaborate by organising team projects, cross-functional initiatives, and collaborative meetings, which foster a sense of community and encourage knowledge sharing. Mentorship programmes pair experienced employees with those still developing their skills, so leaders should facilitate these relationships by providing guidance and support for both mentors and mentees, enhancing learning and fostering a culture of continuous improvement. Knowledge sharing is essential for collaboration, so leaders should encourage employees to share their expertise and insights with the team, creating a culture of collective learning that benefits everyone and strengthens the team's overall capabilities.

Mutual respect and collaboration enhance team dynamics by fostering a positive and supportive work environment, leading to team members working together effectively and supporting each other's growth. Collaborative teams are more innovative, as individuals with diverse skills and perspectives come together to generate creative solutions and new ideas, driving the organisation's success and competitiveness. Teams that collaborate effectively and respect each other's contributions achieve higher levels of performance, leading to better problem-solving, increased efficiency, and higher productivity. A culture of mutual respect and collaboration strengthens the organisation's overall culture, attracting and retaining top talent and contributing to the organisation's long-term success.

Leaders should implement team-building activities that promote interaction and collaboration, helping team members build relationships, understand each other's strengths, and develop trust. Providing collaborative tools and platforms enhances communication and teamwork, so leaders should invest in technology that supports collaboration, such as project management software, communication apps, and shared workspaces. Open communication is key to mutual respect and collaboration, so leaders should create channels for transparent and honest dialogue, encouraging team members to share their thoughts, ideas, and feedback. Recognising and rewarding collaborative efforts reinforces their importance, so leaders should celebrate successful collaboration and acknowledge the contributions of team members who foster mutual respect and teamwork. Training programmes on collaboration skills help employees develop the abilities needed for effective teamwork, so leaders should offer workshops and resources on communication, conflict resolution, and teamwork.

Fostering mutual respect and collaboration creates a sustainable organisational culture where employees feel valued and respected, attracting and retaining top talent and contributing to overall success. Teams that prioritise mutual respect and collaboration are more resilient and capable of overcoming challenges, as strong relationships and trust developed through this focus enable them to work together effectively in any situation. Leaders who foster mutual respect and collaboration can navigate uncertainties with strategic agility, ensuring decisions are made with long-term sustainability in mind and supporting the organisation's resilience. Organisations that consistently prioritise mutual respect and collaboration are better positioned for long-term success, providing a strong foundation that supports sustainable growth and resilience.

LEADING WITH HUMILITY & RECOGNISING CONTRIBUTIONS

> *If the one did not honour his master, and the other did not rejoice in his helper, an (observer), though intelligent, might greatly err about them. This is called 'The utmost degree of mystery.'*

Lao Tzu's passage underscores the importance of humility and mutual recognition in leadership. Leaders should lead with humility, recognising the contributions of all team members. By honouring the expertise of skilled employees and appreciating the efforts of those still learning, leaders create a culture of respect and gratitude. This approach fosters a positive and inclusive environment where everyone feels valued and motivated to contribute their best.

Humble leaders show genuine respect for their team members' skills and contributions by acknowledging the expertise of experienced employees and valuing the efforts of those still developing their abilities, fostering a sense of dignity and worth. Humility involves admitting mistakes and taking responsibility for them, demonstrating integrity and transparency and setting a positive example for the team, which encourages a culture of learning and improvement. Humble leaders also seek input and feedback from their team members, recognising that diverse perspectives can enhance decision-making and lead to better outcomes, fostering a collaborative and inclusive environment by valuing others' opinions.

Recognising and celebrating achievements, both big and small, reinforces the value of individual and collective contributions, so leaders should regularly acknowledge successes and express gratitude for employees' hard work and dedication, boosting morale and motivation. Constructive feedback helps employees understand their strengths and areas for improvement, so leaders should provide specific, actionable feedback that supports growth and development, demonstrating a commitment to helping employees succeed. Leaders should create opportunities for employees to develop their skills and advance in their careers, including access to training, mentorship, and challenging projects, fostering a sense of investment and loyalty by supporting employees' growth.

Collaboration enhances team dynamics and fosters mutual respect, so leaders should encourage team members to work together, share ideas, and support each other, leading to more innovative solutions and stronger relationships. Inclusivity ensures that all team members feel valued and respected, regardless of their background or experience, so leaders should promote an inclusive environment where everyone has a voice and an opportunity to contribute, driving engagement and creativity. A culture of gratitude reinforces the importance of recognising contributions, so leaders should model gratitude by expressing appreciation for employees' efforts and encouraging team members to do the same, strengthening bonds and enhancing the overall work environment.

Leading with humility and recognising contributions builds trust and loyalty among team members, making employees more likely to remain committed to an organisation where they feel valued and respected. Recognition and appreciation boost employee engagement and motivation, as acknowledged contributions lead to higher dedication and productivity. A positive and inclusive environment leads to improved performance, with teams that collaborate effectively and support each other achieving higher levels of productivity and success. Humility and recognition contribute to a strong organisational culture where employees feel a sense of belonging and purpose, attracting and retaining top talent, and driving long-term success.

Leaders should implement formal and informal recognition programmes that celebrate employees' achievements, including awards, shout-outs in meetings, and written notes of appreciation. Regular check-ins with employees provide opportunities for feedback and recognition, so leaders should schedule one-on-one meetings to discuss progress, address concerns, and offer support. Mentorship programmes pair experienced employees with those still developing their skills, and leaders should facilitate these relationships to support learning and growth. Encouraging peer recognition fosters a culture of mutual respect and appreciation, so leaders should create platforms where employees can acknowledge each other's contributions, such as online recognition boards or team meetings.

Leading with humility and recognising contributions fosters a sustainable organisational culture where employees feel valued and respected, attracting and retaining top talent and contributing to overall success. Teams that prioritise humility and recognition are more resilient and capable of overcoming challenges, as strong relationships and trust developed through this focus enable them to work together effectively in any situation. Leaders who lead with humility and recognise contributions can navigate uncertainties with strategic agility, ensuring decisions are made with long-term sustainability in mind and supporting the organisation's resilience. Organisations that consistently prioritise humility and recognition are better positioned for long-term success, providing a strong foundation that supports sustainable growth and resilience.

CHAPTER 28 – NON-VIOLENCE

Chapter 28 of the *Tao Te Ching* emphasises the importance of embracing both strength and softness, humility, and the power of simplicity. Here's how these teachings can be applied to modern-day strategic management:

BALANCING STRENGTH & SOFTNESS

Who knows his manhood's strength, Yet still his female feebleness maintains; As to one channel flow the many drains, All come to him, yea, all beneath the sky.

Lao Tzu's passage highlights the importance of balancing strength and softness, suggesting that true leadership embodies both assertiveness and empathy. In strategic management, leaders should balance assertiveness with empathy. This means being strong and decisive when necessary, while also being compassionate and understanding. By embracing both strength and softness, leaders can create a more inclusive and supportive work environment. This balance helps in building trust and fostering collaboration among team members.

Strength in leadership involves making assertive and confident decisions, so leaders should be decisive, taking charge of situations and providing clear direction to ensure the organisation moves forward with purpose and clarity. Strong leaders uphold their authority by setting clear expectations and holding team members accountable, establishing boundaries, enforcing policies, and ensuring standards are met, which fosters respect and order within the team. Strength also involves driving performance and achieving results, so leaders should set ambitious goals, motivate their teams, and push for excellence, inspiring team members to strive for their best and contributing to the organisation's success.

Softness in leadership involves showing empathy and understanding towards team members by listening to their concerns, offering support, and demonstrating compassion, which creates a sense of psychological safety and fosters a supportive work environment. It is also about building strong, trusting relationships by investing time in getting to know employees, understanding their strengths and aspirations, and providing encouragement, which enhances collaboration and loyalty. Inclusive leaders value and respect diverse perspectives, creating an environment where everyone feels welcome and valued, promoting inclusivity, encouraging open dialogue, and ensuring all voices are heard, which drives innovation and creativity.

Balancing strength and softness builds trust and respect among team members, as employees appreciate leaders who are both assertive and compassionate, demonstrating integrity and care, enhancing team cohesion and collaboration. A balance of assertiveness and empathy improves communication within the team, with leaders who are clear and confident in their messaging, while being open and understanding, fostering effective and transparent communication, preventing misunderstandings, and enhancing teamwork. Employees are more engaged and motivated when they feel supported and challenged, as leaders who balance strength and softness create an environment where team members are encouraged to take risks, innovate, and perform at their best, driving productivity and job satisfaction. A balance of strength and softness also enhances the team's resilience and adaptability, providing stability and direction through strong leadership, while empathetic leadership offers support and flexibility, equipping the team to navigate challenges and adapt to change effectively.

Practical Strategies for Balancing Strength & Softness

Leading with Authenticity: Authentic leaders are genuine in their actions and communications, embodying both strength and softness. Leaders should be true to themselves, demonstrating their strengths while also showing vulnerability and empathy. Authenticity fosters trust and respect.

Practising Active Listening: Active listening involves fully engaging with team members' concerns and feedback. Leaders should practise active listening by giving their full attention, asking clarifying questions, and responding thoughtfully. This practice demonstrates empathy and fosters strong relationships.

Setting Clear Expectations: Setting clear expectations provides direction and structure for the team. Leaders should communicate their expectations clearly and consistently, ensuring that everyone understands their roles and responsibilities. Clear expectations maintain order and drive performance.

Providing Support and Resources: Leaders should provide the necessary support and resources to help team members succeed. This includes offering guidance, training, and tools that enable employees to perform at their best. Supportive leadership demonstrates care and fosters a positive work environment.

Encouraging Feedback and Reflection: Encouraging feedback and reflection helps leaders continuously improve their balance of strength and softness. Leaders should seek feedback from their team members, reflect on their actions, and make adjustments as needed. This continuous improvement enhances leadership effectiveness.

Balancing strength and softness fosters a sustainable organisational culture where employees feel valued and respected, attracting and retaining top talent and contributing to overall success. Teams that prioritise a balance of strength and softness are more resilient and capable of overcoming challenges, as strong relationships and trust developed through this focus enable them to work together effectively in any situation. Leaders who balance strength and softness can navigate uncertainties with strategic agility, ensuring decisions are made with long-term sustainability in mind and supporting the organisation's resilience. Organisations that consistently prioritise a balance of strength and softness are better positioned for long-term success, providing a strong foundation that supports sustainable growth and resilience.

PRACTISING HUMILITY & MODESTY

> *Who knows how white attracts, Yet always keeps himself within black's shade,*
> *The pattern of humility displayed, Displayed in view of all beneath the sky.*

Lao Tzu's passage highlights the virtue of humility, suggesting that true wisdom and leadership come from recognising one's own limitations and maintaining modesty. Humility is a key trait for effective leadership. Leaders should recognise their own limitations and be open to learning from others. By practising humility, leaders can create a culture where employees feel valued and respected. This approach encourages open communication and continuous improvement, as team members are more likely to share their ideas and feedback.

Humble leaders acknowledge that they do not have all the answers and are open to admitting their imperfections, fostering trust and authenticity by showing that they are human and approachable. Recognising their limitations, they actively seek advice and feedback from their team members, demonstrating a willingness to learn and grow and empowering employees to contribute their expertise and perspectives. Humility involves learning from mistakes and viewing them as opportunities for growth, so leaders who admit their errors and take responsibility set a positive example for their teams, encouraging a culture of continuous learning and improvement.

Humble leaders recognise and value the contributions of all team members by acknowledging their skills, efforts, and achievements, fostering a sense of belonging and respect within the organisation. A culture of humility promotes open communication, so leaders should create an environment where team members feel safe to express their ideas, opinions, and concerns without fear of judgment, enhancing collaboration and innovation. Humble leaders also ensure that all voices are heard and respected, regardless of background or experience, promoting inclusivity and fostering a diverse and dynamic work environment where everyone feels valued and empowered to contribute.

Practising humility builds trust and loyalty among team members, as employees are more likely to trust and remain committed to leaders who are genuine, respectful, and open to learning from others. When employees feel valued and respected, they are more engaged and motivated, as humble leadership creates a positive work environment where team members are encouraged to share their ideas and take initiative. Humble leaders make better decisions by incorporating diverse perspectives and feedback, ensuring that decisions are well-informed and consider the needs and insights of all stakeholders. A culture of humility supports continuous improvement, encouraging leaders and team members alike to learn from their experiences, seek feedback, and strive for excellence, which drives the organisation's success.

Leaders should model humility through their actions and interactions, including admitting mistakes, seeking feedback, and showing appreciation for others' contributions, as leading by example sets the tone for the entire organisation. They should create opportunities for employees to provide input and share their ideas, such as regular feedback sessions, brainstorming meetings, and suggestion boxes, demonstrating that they value their team members' insights. Recognising and celebrating employees' contributions reinforces their value to the organisation, so leaders should regularly acknowledge individual and team achievements and express gratitude for their hard work and dedication. Investing in employee development shows that leaders are committed to their team members' growth, offering training, mentorship, and opportunities for career advancement, which fosters a culture of continuous learning.

Practising humility fosters a sustainable organisational culture where employees feel valued and respected, attracting and retaining top talent and contributing to overall success. Teams that prioritise humility are more resilient and capable of overcoming challenges, as strong relationships and trust developed through this focus enable them to work together effectively in any situation. Leaders who practise humility can navigate uncertainties with strategic agility, ensuring decisions are made with long-term sustainability in mind and supporting the organisation's resilience. Organisations that consistently prioritise humility are better positioned for long-term success, providing a strong foundation that supports sustainable growth and resilience.

EMBRACING SIMPLICITY & AUTHENTICITY

The simple child again, free from all stains.

Lao Tzu's passage highlights the virtue of simplicity and authenticity, likening it to the innocence and purity of a child. Leaders should strive to maintain simplicity and authenticity in their actions and decisions. This involves being transparent and honest with their teams, and avoiding unnecessary complexity. By keeping things simple and straightforward, leaders can ensure that everyone is aligned and understands the organisation's goals and objectives.

Simplicity in communication involves conveying messages in a clear and straightforward manner, avoiding jargon, complex language, and unnecessary details to ensure everyone understands key messages, goals, and expectations. Simplifying processes and procedures enhances efficiency and reduces the administrative burden on employees, so leaders should identify and eliminate unnecessary steps, creating streamlined workflows that are easy to follow, enhancing productivity and minimising frustration. Simplicity also involves focusing on what truly matters and avoiding distractions, so leaders should set clear priorities and guide their teams to concentrate on high-impact activities, helping the organisation achieve its strategic objectives and prevent resource wastage.

Authentic leaders are transparent and honest in their interactions, sharing information openly, admitting mistakes, and being truthful about challenges and opportunities, which builds trust and fosters a culture of integrity. Authenticity means staying true to the organisation's core values and principles, with leaders aligning their actions and decisions with these values, demonstrating consistency and integrity, thereby reinforcing the organisation's mission and building credibility. Authentic leaders also encourage team members to be themselves and express their ideas and opinions freely, creating an inclusive environment where diversity is valued and everyone feels safe to contribute, driving creativity and innovation through authentic expression.

Simplicity and authenticity enhance alignment within the organisation by ensuring clear and straightforward communication, so everyone understands the organisation's goals and objectives, fostering a sense of unity and collective purpose. Authenticity builds trust and respect among team members, as employees appreciate leaders who are transparent, honest, and true to their values, strengthening relationships and enhancing collaboration. Simplicity improves efficiency by reducing complexity and streamlining processes, enabling employees to focus on high-impact activities, enhancing productivity and effectiveness. A culture of simplicity and authenticity fosters a positive work environment where employees feel valued and respected, leading to higher levels of engagement, motivation, and job satisfaction, and attracting and retaining top talent.

Leaders should communicate clearly and regularly with their teams using simple language, providing updates, and ensuring everyone is informed about key developments, as regular communication keeps everyone aligned and engaged. They should regularly review processes and identify opportunities for simplification by eliminating unnecessary steps, automating repetitive tasks, and creating clear guidelines to enhance efficiency and reduce frustration. Leaders should model authentic behaviour by being transparent, honest, and true to their values, admitting mistakes, sharing successes, and demonstrating integrity to set a positive example for the entire organisation. Encouraging open dialogue fosters authenticity and inclusivity, so leaders should create opportunities for team members to share their ideas, opinions, and feedback, enhancing collaboration and driving innovation. Setting clear priorities and expectations helps maintain focus and alignment, so leaders should define key goals and objectives, provide clear guidance, and ensure everyone understands their roles and responsibilities.

Embracing simplicity and authenticity fosters a sustainable organisational culture where employees feel valued and respected, attracting and retaining top talent and contributing to overall success. Teams that prioritise simplicity and authenticity are more resilient and capable of overcoming challenges, as strong relationships and trust developed through this focus enable them to work together effectively in any situation. Leaders who embrace simplicity and authenticity can navigate uncertainties with strategic agility, ensuring decisions are made with long-term sustainability in mind and supporting the organisation's resilience. Organisations that consistently prioritise simplicity and authenticity are better positioned for long-term success, providing a strong foundation that supports sustainable growth and resilience.

LEADING WITH INTEGRITY & RESILIENCE

Who knows how glory shines, Yet loves disgrace, nor e'er for it is pale; Behold his presence in a spacious vale, To which men come from all beneath the sky.

Lao Tzu's passage emphasises the importance of maintaining integrity and resilience, even in the face of challenges. Effective leaders demonstrate integrity by staying true to their values and principles. This approach inspires confidence and loyalty within their teams. Resilience helps leaders navigate setbacks and maintain a positive outlook, which is crucial for sustaining long-term success.

Leaders who demonstrate integrity consistently adhere to their core values and principles, even when faced with difficult decisions or challenging situations, reinforcing their credibility and building trust within the organisation. Integrity involves being honest and transparent in all interactions, so leaders should communicate openly with their teams, sharing information truthfully and admitting mistakes when they occur, fostering a culture of trust and accountability. Leaders with integrity lead by example, modelling the behaviours and attitudes they expect from their team members, demonstrating fairness, respect, and ethical behaviour in all actions, setting a positive standard for the entire organisation.

Resilient leaders are adaptable and able to navigate change effectively, being flexible and open to new ideas while adjusting strategies and plans when necessary, ensuring the organisation can respond to evolving circumstances and challenges. Resilience is also characterised by maintaining a positive outlook, even in the face of setbacks, so leaders should stay optimistic and focused on finding solutions rather than dwelling on problems, motivating the team and encouraging perseverance. Resilient leaders view challenges as opportunities for growth and learning, analysing setbacks to identify lessons and improvements, using these experiences to strengthen the organisation and fostering continuous improvement and resilience.

Leaders who demonstrate integrity and resilience inspire confidence and loyalty among team members, as employees are more likely to trust and remain committed to leaders who uphold their values and navigate challenges with grace. Integrity and resilience contribute to stronger team cohesion, with leaders who model ethical behaviour and maintain a positive outlook fostering a supportive and collaborative work environment, enhancing teamwork and productivity. Integrity ensures that decisions are made ethically and transparently, while resilience enables leaders to adapt and respond to changing circumstances, leading to informed and effective decision-making that supports the organisation's long-term success. Integrity and resilience are key to sustaining long-term success, as leaders who uphold their values and navigate challenges effectively build a strong foundation for the organisation's growth and resilience, supporting sustained performance and achievement.

Leaders should communicate the organisation's core values clearly and consistently, integrating them into all aspects of the organisation from decision-making processes to employee performance evaluations, reinforcing the importance of integrity. Supporting employees in developing resilience is essential, so leaders should offer resources such as training, mentorship, and wellness programmes to help employees build resilience and cope with stress, fostering a resilient and empowered workforce. Open dialogue fosters transparency and trust, so leaders should create channels for honest communication, encouraging team members to share their ideas, concerns, and feedback, ensuring everyone feels heard and valued. Recognising and celebrating examples of integrity and resilience reinforces their importance, so leaders should highlight and reward employees who demonstrate ethical behaviour and perseverance, motivating others to embody these values. Leaders should foster a positive organisational culture that promotes integrity and resilience, creating an environment where employees feel safe to take risks, learn from mistakes, and support each other, enhancing overall performance and well-being.

Leading with integrity and resilience fosters a sustainable organisational culture where employees feel valued and respected, attracting and retaining top talent and contributing to overall success.

Teams that prioritise integrity and resilience are more resilient and capable of overcoming challenges, as strong relationships and trust developed through this focus enable them to work together effectively in any situation. Leaders who lead with integrity and resilience can navigate uncertainties with strategic agility, ensuring decisions are made with long-term sustainability in mind and supporting the organisation's resilience. Organisations that consistently prioritise integrity and resilience are better positioned for long-term success, providing a strong foundation that supports sustainable growth and resilience.

FOSTERING A COLLABORATIVE & INCLUSIVE ENVIRONMENT

All come to him, yea, all beneath the sky.

Lao Tzu's passage underscores the significance of creating a welcoming and inclusive environment where diverse perspectives are valued. Leaders should create an environment where collaboration and inclusivity are prioritised. This involves encouraging diverse perspectives and ensuring that all team members feel welcome and included. By fostering a sense of community, leaders can enhance creativity and innovation, leading to better outcomes for the organisation.

Embracing diversity means recognising the unique contributions that individuals from different backgrounds bring to the team, so leaders should actively seek to include people with varied experiences, skills, and viewpoints, as this diversity enriches decision-making and problem-solving. Leaders should create safe spaces where team members feel comfortable sharing their ideas and perspectives without fear of judgment or retaliation, fostering an open and respectful environment where all voices are heard and valued. Open dialogue is essential for collaboration, so leaders should encourage team members to engage in meaningful conversations, listen actively, and respect differing opinions, fostering mutual understanding and enhancing team cohesion.

Leaders should implement policies and practices that promote inclusivity, ensuring equal opportunities for all employees, providing accommodations when needed, and addressing any biases or barriers within the organisation. Celebrating differences and promoting cultural awareness can enhance inclusivity, so leaders should organise events, training sessions, and activities that highlight diverse cultures, traditions, and perspectives, fostering a sense of belonging and appreciation for diversity. Ensuring that all team members have equal access to opportunities for growth and development is crucial for inclusivity, so leaders should create pathways for career advancement, offer mentorship programmes, and provide resources that support the development of all employees.

Collaboration thrives in an environment where teamwork is encouraged, so leaders should promote team-based projects, cross-functional initiatives, and collaborative problem-solving sessions to strengthen relationships and enhance collective creativity. Knowledge sharing is vital for effective collaboration, and leaders should create platforms and opportunities for team members to share their expertise, insights, and best practices, driving innovation and improving overall performance. Trust is the foundation of collaboration, so leaders should foster trust by being transparent, reliable, and supportive, ensuring team members are more likely to collaborate effectively and achieve common goals.

A collaborative and inclusive environment stimulates creativity and innovation, as diverse perspectives lead to unique ideas and solutions, driving the organisation's ability to innovate and stay competitive. Teams that embrace diversity and collaboration are better equipped to solve complex problems, with the combination of different viewpoints and expertise resulting in more comprehensive and effective solutions. Inclusivity and collaboration boost employee engagement and satisfaction, as when employees feel valued and included, they are more motivated, committed, and productive, contributing to the organisation's success. A culture that prioritises collaboration and inclusivity is more resilient and adaptable, attracting and retaining top talent, fostering long-term growth and success.

Leaders should design physical and virtual workspaces that facilitate collaboration, such as open-plan offices, shared workspaces, and digital collaboration platforms, encouraging interaction and teamwork. Implementing diversity training helps raise awareness and build skills for inclusive behaviour, so leaders should offer training sessions that educate employees about unconscious bias, cultural competence, and inclusive practices. Employee resource groups (ERGs) provide a platform for individuals with common interests or backgrounds to connect and support each other, so leaders should support ERGs and encourage their formation, enhancing inclusivity and community. Recognising and rewarding collaborative efforts reinforces their importance, so leaders should celebrate successful team projects, highlight collaborative achievements, and provide incentives for teamwork.

Fostering a collaborative and inclusive environment creates a sustainable organisational culture where employees feel valued and respected, attracting and retaining top talent and contributing to overall success. Teams that prioritise collaboration and inclusivity are more resilient and capable of overcoming challenges, as strong relationships and trust developed through this focus enable them to work together effectively in any situation. Leaders who foster collaboration and inclusivity can navigate uncertainties with strategic agility, ensuring decisions are made with long-term sustainability in mind and supporting the organisation's resilience. Organisations that consistently prioritise collaboration and inclusivity are better positioned for long-term success, providing a strong foundation that supports sustainable growth and resilience.

UTILISING RESOURCES WISELY & EFFICIENTLY

The unwrought material, when divided and distributed, forms vessels.

Lao Tzu's passage emphasises the potential of raw materials when they are wisely divided and utilised. Strategic leaders should focus on utilising resources wisely and efficiently. This means allocating resources where they are most needed and ensuring that they are used effectively. By doing so, leaders can maximise the potential of their teams and achieve organisational goals more efficiently.

Efficient resource allocation begins with identifying the key needs of the organisation, so leaders should conduct thorough assessments to determine where resources can have the most significant impact, understanding the organisation's strategic goals and the specific requirements of different departments and projects. Once key needs are identified, leaders should prioritise high-impact areas for resource allocation, ensuring resources are directed towards initiatives that contribute most significantly to the organisation's success, maximising return on investment and achieving strategic objectives. Resource allocation should also balance short-term needs with long-term goals, ensuring that immediate operational requirements are met while investing in initiatives that support long-term growth and sustainability, fostering both stability and innovation.

Effective resource utilisation involves optimising the use of available resources by implementing processes and technologies that enhance efficiency and reduce waste, adopting best practices, streamlining workflows, and leveraging automation where appropriate. Leaders should cultivate a culture of resourcefulness within the organisation by encouraging employees to think creatively and find innovative solutions to challenges, ensuring the organisation makes the most of its available assets and capabilities. Continuous monitoring of resource utilisation is essential for maintaining efficiency, so leaders should regularly review resource allocation and usage, identifying areas for improvement and making necessary adjustments to ensure resources are used effectively and aligned with evolving needs.

Human resources are among the most valuable assets of any organisation, so leaders should recognise and utilise the unique talents and skills of their team members by assigning tasks and responsibilities that align with employees' strengths and providing opportunities for professional growth. Investing in training and development enhances employees' capabilities and improves overall performance, so leaders should offer continuous learning opportunities, including workshops, courses, and mentorship programmes, as well-developed employees contribute more effectively to the organisation's goals. Effective utilisation of human resources requires fostering collaboration and teamwork, so leaders should create an environment where employees can work together, share knowledge, and support each other, enhancing productivity and driving innovation.

Wise and efficient resource utilisation maximises the potential of both material and human resources, ensuring the organisation operates at its highest capacity and achieves its strategic objectives. Efficient resource allocation and utilisation enhance productivity by directing resources towards high-impact areas, with streamlined processes and optimised workflows enabling employees to focus on their core responsibilities and deliver results more effectively. Efficient resource utilisation often results in cost savings by reducing waste and improving efficiency, allowing leaders to allocate savings towards strategic investments that support the organisation's growth and innovation. Organisations that utilise resources wisely and efficiently achieve improved overall performance, as effective resource allocation supports the successful execution of projects, initiatives, and day-to-day operations, driving the organisation's success.

Leaders should conduct regular assessments to evaluate the organisation's resource needs and usage, identifying key areas for investment, monitoring resource utilisation, and adjusting allocation as necessary. Adopting best practices for resource management enhances efficiency and effectiveness, so leaders should stay informed about industry standards and incorporate proven strategies into their resource allocation processes. Technology can significantly enhance resource utilisation, and leaders should invest in tools and systems that support efficient resource management, such as project management software, data analytics, and automation technologies. Promoting a culture of efficiency involves encouraging employees to adopt resourceful and sustainable practices, providing training on efficient workflows, recognising and rewarding resourceful behaviour, and creating an environment that values optimisation.

Utilising resources wisely and efficiently fosters a sustainable organisational culture where efficiency and effectiveness are valued, attracting and retaining top talent and contributing to overall success. Teams that prioritise wise and efficient resource utilisation are more resilient and capable of overcoming challenges, as strong relationships and trust developed through this focus enable them to work together effectively in any situation. Leaders who utilise resources wisely and efficiently can navigate uncertainties with strategic agility, ensuring decisions are made with long-term sustainability in mind and supporting the organisation's resilience. Organisations that consistently prioritise wise and efficient resource utilisation are better positioned for long-term success, providing a strong foundation that supports sustainable growth and resilience.

IMPLEMENTING NON-VIOLENT & ETHICAL MEASURES

The sage, when employed, becomes the Head of all the Officers (of government); and in his greatest regulations he employs no violent measures.

Lao Tzu's passage highlights the importance of employing non-violent and ethical measures in leadership. Leaders should implement policies and practices that are ethical and non-violent. This involves making decisions that are fair and just, and avoiding any actions that could harm employees or stakeholders. By prioritising ethical behaviour, leaders can build a strong foundation of trust and integrity within the organisation.

Ethical leaders prioritise fairness and justice in all their decisions and actions, treating all employees and stakeholders with respect, ensuring equal opportunities, and making decisions based on merit and ethical principles. Ethical behaviour involves being transparent and accountable, openly communicating decisions and the reasoning behind them, and taking responsibility for their actions, which builds trust and reinforces integrity. Ethical leaders also avoid actions that could cause harm to employees, stakeholders, or the community, making decisions that consider the well-being and safety of all individuals affected and prioritising measures that promote positive outcomes.

Non-violent leaders promote peaceful conflict resolution by fostering a culture where conflicts are addressed through dialogue, mediation, and negotiation rather than aggression or coercion, building stronger relationships and a more harmonious work environment. Collaboration is a key component of non-violent leadership, so leaders should encourage teamwork and cooperation, creating an environment where employees work together to achieve common goals, minimising conflict and enhancing collective success. Non-violent measures also include supporting ethical practices across all organisational activities, so leaders should establish and enforce policies that promote ethical behaviour, such as anti-discrimination, anti-harassment, and fair labour practices, ensuring a safe and respectful workplace.

Implementing ethical and non-violent measures builds trust and integrity within the organisation, as employees and stakeholders are more likely to trust leaders who act with fairness, transparency, and accountability, enhancing loyalty and commitment. Ethical and non-violent practices also enhance the organisation's reputation, attracting top talent, customers, and partners, and contributing to long-term success. A commitment to ethics and non-violence fosters a positive work environment where employees feel safe, respected, and valued, boosting morale, engagement, and productivity. Ethical and non-violent leadership supports sustainable success by building a strong foundation of trust, integrity, and respect, driving long-term growth and resilience, and ensuring the organisation's continued success.

Practical Strategies for Implementing Non-Violent & Ethical Measures

Developing Ethical Policies: Leaders should develop and enforce policies that promote ethical behaviour and non-violence. This includes codes of conduct, anti-discrimination policies, and guidelines for respectful communication. Clear policies provide a framework for ethical behaviour.

Providing Training and Education: Training and education are essential for fostering ethical and non-violent behaviour. Leaders should offer training programmes that educate employees about ethical standards, conflict resolution, and the importance of non-violence. Ongoing education reinforces these values.

Creating Open Communication Channels: Open communication channels facilitate transparency and accountability. Leaders should create opportunities for employees to voice their concerns, provide feedback, and report unethical behaviour without fear of retaliation. This openness promotes trust and integrity.

Recognising and Rewarding Ethical Behaviour: Recognising and rewarding employees who demonstrate ethical and non-violent behaviour reinforces these values. Leaders should celebrate examples of ethical decision-making and peaceful conflict resolution, motivating others to follow suit.

Leading by Example: Leaders should model ethical and non-violent behaviour in all their actions and decisions. This includes demonstrating fairness, transparency, and accountability, as well as promoting peaceful conflict resolution. Leading by example sets the tone for the entire organisation.

Implementing ethical and non-violent measures fosters a sustainable organisational culture where employees feel valued and respected, attracting and retaining top talent and contributing to overall success. Teams that prioritise ethics and non-violence are more resilient and capable of overcoming challenges, as the strong relationships and trust developed through this focus enable them to work together effectively in any situation. Leaders who prioritise ethical and non-violent measures can navigate uncertainties with strategic agility, ensuring decisions are made with long-term sustainability in mind and supporting the organisation's resilience. Organisations that consistently prioritise ethical and non-violent measures are better positioned for long-term success, providing a strong foundation that supports sustainable growth and resilience.

CHAPTER 29 – NON-INTERFERENCE

Chapter 29 of the *Tao Te Ching* emphasises the importance of non-interference, moderation, and aligning with the natural course of things. Here's how these teachings can be applied to modern-day strategic management:

EMBRACING NON-INTERFERENCE & TRUSTING THE PROCESS

> *If any one should wish to get the kingdom for himself, and to effect this by what he does, I see that he will not succeed. The kingdom is a spirit-like thing, and cannot be got by active doing. He who would so win it destroys it; he who would hold it in his grasp loses it.*

Lao Tzu's passage suggests the importance of non-interference and trusting natural processes. In strategic management, this means avoiding micromanaging and forcing outcomes. Leaders should create an environment where their teams can thrive independently. By providing guidance and support without excessive control, leaders can foster innovation, creativity, and a sense of ownership among employees.

Micromanaging can stifle creativity and innovation, as excessive control over every aspect of the team's work limits employees' ability to think freely and come up with creative solutions; creativity flourishes in an environment where individuals have the autonomy to explore new ideas. Constant oversight and control can reduce employees' motivation and engagement, as team members who feel their contributions are not valued or trusted may become disengaged and less committed to their work; trust and autonomy are key drivers of motivation. Micromanaging can also increase stress and lead to burnout, with employees who are constantly monitored and pressured to meet stringent expectations experiencing higher levels of stress and fatigue; a more relaxed and trusting environment promotes well-being and productivity.

Trusting the process involves empowering teams to take ownership of their work by delegating responsibilities and giving employees the autonomy to make decisions within their areas of expertise, fostering a sense of ownership and accountability. While non-interference is important, leaders should still provide guidance and support when needed, offering resources, mentorship, and feedback to help employees succeed, which helps teams feel confident and capable without micromanaging. Trusting the process also means encouraging experimentation and allowing for mistakes, so leaders should create a safe environment where employees can try new approaches and learn from failures, driving innovation and continuous improvement.

Innovation thrives in a flexible environment where employees have the freedom to explore new ideas, so leaders should promote flexibility by allowing flexible work hours, remote work options, and the freedom to experiment with different methods. Collaboration enhances creativity and innovation, so leaders should encourage team members to work together, share ideas, and collaborate on projects, leading to more diverse and innovative solutions. Recognising and celebrating innovative ideas and achievements reinforces their importance, so leaders should highlight and reward employees who contribute creative solutions and breakthroughs, motivating others to innovate.

By fostering an environment of autonomy and trust, leaders can enhance creativity and innovation, as employees who feel empowered to explore new ideas and approaches are more likely to develop innovative solutions. Trusting the process and avoiding micromanagement increases employee engagement, with team members having the autonomy to make decisions and take ownership of their work, leading to higher motivation and commitment to their roles. Providing autonomy and support fosters a sense of ownership among employees, as team members who feel trusted and empowered are more likely to take initiative, be accountable, and contribute to the organisation's success. A trusting and supportive work environment also reduces stress and burnout, with employees who feel valued and respected experiencing higher levels of well-being and job satisfaction.

Leaders should delegate responsibilities and empower team members to take ownership of their tasks by assigning clear roles and providing the autonomy to make decisions within those roles. Setting clear objectives and providing autonomy to achieve them ensures alignment while fostering creativity, so leaders should outline the desired outcomes and allow employees the freedom to determine the best approach to achieve them. Leaders should offer support and resources to help employees succeed, including access to training, tools, and mentorship, empowering employees to perform at their best without micromanaging. Open communication fosters trust and transparency, so leaders should create channels for regular feedback, discussions, and idea-sharing, ensuring employees feel heard and valued.

Embracing non-interference and trusting the process fosters a sustainable organisational culture where employees feel valued and respected, attracting and retaining top talent and contributing to overall success. Teams that prioritise autonomy and trust are more resilient and capable of overcoming challenges, as the strong relationships and trust developed through this focus enable them to work together effectively in any situation. Leaders who embrace non-interference and trust the process can navigate uncertainties with strategic agility, ensuring decisions are made with long-term sustainability in mind and supporting the organisation's resilience. Organisations that consistently prioritise non-interference and trust the process are better positioned for long-term success, providing a strong foundation that supports sustainable growth and resilience.

UNDERSTANDING THE CYCLICAL NATURE OF BUSINESS

The course and nature of things is such that
What was in front is now behind;
What warmed anon we freezing find.
Strength is of weakness oft the spoil;
The store in ruins mocks our toil.

Lao Tzu's passage highlights the inherent cyclicality in the nature of things. This principle applies to the business world as well. Leaders should recognise the cyclical nature of business and be prepared for changes and fluctuations. Success and failure are often part of a larger cycle, and understanding this can help leaders remain resilient and adaptable. By staying flexible and anticipating shifts, leaders can better navigate challenges and capitalise on new opportunities.

Economic cycles consist of periods of growth (expansions) and decline (recessions), influenced by factors such as market demand, consumer confidence, and global economic conditions, so leaders should be aware of these cycles and how they impact their industry. Market trends often follow cyclical patterns influenced by consumer behaviour, technological advancements, and competitive dynamics, so leaders should stay informed about market trends and anticipate shifts to position their organisations advantageously. Industry-specific cycles can affect business performance, so leaders should monitor industry changes, such as regulatory developments, technological innovations, and shifts in consumer preferences, to identify potential opportunities and threats.

Resilience involves building adaptive strategies that can withstand fluctuations, so leaders should develop flexible plans that allow for adjustments based on changing circumstances, ensuring the organisation can navigate both prosperous and challenging times. A resilient culture, characterised by agility, innovation, and a positive mindset, should be fostered by encouraging employees to embrace change, experiment with new ideas, and learn from failures, equipping the organisation to bounce back from setbacks. Financial resilience is crucial for navigating business cycles, so leaders should ensure that the organisation maintains strong financial health by managing cash flow, reducing debt, and building reserves, providing a buffer during downturns.

Flexibility involves being open to change and willing to adapt, so leaders should cultivate a mindset that embraces new opportunities and is not resistant to change, allowing the organisation to pivot quickly in response to shifts. Innovation is a key driver of flexibility, so leaders should encourage employees to think creatively and develop innovative solutions to challenges, enabling the organisation to stay competitive and capitalise on emerging trends. Agile practices enhance flexibility by promoting iterative development and continuous improvement, so leaders should implement agile methodologies that allow for quick adjustments and responsive decision-making, ensuring the organisation can adapt to evolving market conditions.

Recognising the cyclical nature of business enables proactive decision-making, allowing leaders to anticipate changes and prepare for fluctuations, making informed decisions that position the organisation for success. Understanding business cycles enhances the organisation's resilience by building adaptive strategies and fostering a resilient culture, ensuring the organisation can withstand and recover from challenges. Embracing flexibility and innovation fosters strategic agility, with leaders who are open to change and willing to adapt navigating uncertainties and capitalising on new opportunities, ensuring long-term success. By understanding and navigating business cycles, leaders can achieve sustained growth through proactive planning, financial health, and adaptive strategies, ensuring the organisation continues to thrive regardless of economic conditions.

Leaders should conduct regular market research to stay informed about economic conditions, market trends, and industry changes, as this research provides valuable insights that inform strategic planning and decision-making. Developing contingency plans is essential for preparing the organisation for various scenarios, outlining responses to potential challenges such as economic downturns, supply chain disruptions, or competitive threats, ensuring the organisation is ready to act quickly and effectively. Investing in employee development enhances the organisation's resilience and flexibility, with leaders providing training, mentorship, and learning opportunities to equip employees with the skills and mindset needed to navigate change. Building strong partnerships with suppliers, customers, and other stakeholders enhances resilience, so leaders should cultivate relationships that provide support and collaboration during challenging times, strengthening the organisation's ability to adapt and thrive.

Understanding and navigating business cycles fosters a sustainable organisational culture where employees feel valued and respected, attracting and retaining top talent and contributing to overall success. Teams that prioritise resilience and flexibility are more capable of overcoming challenges, with strong relationships and trust developed through this focus enabling them to work together effectively in any situation. Leaders who understand and navigate business cycles can navigate uncertainties with strategic agility, ensuring decisions are made with long-term sustainability in mind and supporting the organisation's resilience. Organisations that consistently recognise and navigate business cycles are better positioned for long-term success, providing a strong foundation that supports sustainable growth and resilience.

PRACTISING MODERATION & AVOIDING EXCESS

Hence the sage puts away excessive effort, extravagance, and easy indulgence.

Lao Tzu's passage emphasises the virtue of moderation and the avoidance of excess. Moderation is key to effective leadership. Leaders should avoid excessive effort, extravagance, and indulgence, as these can lead to burnout and inefficiency. Instead, they should focus on sustainable practices that ensure long-term success. This involves setting realistic goals, managing resources wisely, and maintaining a balanced approach to work.

Excessive effort can lead to burnout, negatively impacting both leaders and their teams by reducing productivity, diminishing creativity, and affecting overall well-being. Leaders should encourage a healthy work-life balance and ensure that workloads are manageable to prevent burnout. Instead of working excessively, leaders should focus on working efficiently by prioritising tasks, delegating responsibilities, and utilising resources effectively, which enhances productivity without compromising health and well-being. Setting realistic and attainable goals prevents the strain associated with over-ambitious targets, so leaders should establish clear, achievable objectives that align with the organisation's capacity and resources, motivating and driving sustained progress.

Extravagance in resource utilisation can lead to waste and inefficiency, so leaders should manage resources wisely by allocating them where they are most needed and avoiding unnecessary expenditures, supporting sustainability and cost-effectiveness. A culture of simplicity values practicality over extravagance, so leaders should promote practices that prioritise essential needs and avoid excess, fostering a more mindful and sustainable use of resources. Mindful spending involves careful consideration of expenditures and their impact, so leaders should encourage their teams to adopt a mindful approach to spending, focusing on investments that deliver the greatest value and benefit to the organisation.

Easy indulgence can undermine discipline and productivity, so leaders should model and encourage disciplined behaviours, such as setting boundaries, maintaining focus, and practising self-control, ensuring efforts are directed towards meaningful and productive activities. Delayed gratification involves prioritising long-term benefits over immediate pleasures, so leaders should foster a mindset that values patience and perseverance, understanding that sustained effort and delayed rewards contribute to long-term success. Setting boundaries helps prevent overindulgence and maintains balance, so leaders should establish clear guidelines for work hours, break times, and personal boundaries, ensuring employees remain productive and motivated without feeling overwhelmed.

Practising moderation ensures sustainable success by promoting balanced and mindful practices, allowing leaders who avoid excess and focus on sustainability to create a stable foundation for long-term growth and achievement. Moderation supports the well-being of leaders and their teams by preventing burnout, managing resources wisely, and maintaining discipline, fostering a healthy and positive work environment that enhances overall well-being and satisfaction. Balanced and efficient practices lead to improved productivity, with leaders who prioritise efficiency, mindful spending, and disciplined behaviours ensuring that efforts are directed towards high-impact activities, driving organisational success. A culture of moderation fosters positive values and behaviours, as leaders who model moderation and balance create an environment where employees feel valued, respected, and motivated to contribute their best.

Practical Strategies for Practising Moderation

Encouraging Work-Life Balance: Leaders should encourage work-life balance by promoting flexible work arrangements, setting clear boundaries, and supporting employees' personal and professional needs. A balanced approach enhances well-being and productivity.

Prioritising Tasks and Goals: Leaders should prioritise tasks and set achievable goals that align with the organisation's capacity and resources. This involves identifying high-impact activities and focusing efforts on achieving them efficiently.

Implementing Mindful Resource Management: Mindful resource management involves careful consideration of expenditures and resource allocation. Leaders should adopt practices that prioritise essential needs and avoid wasteful spending.

Promoting Discipline and Self-Control: Leaders should model and promote disciplined behaviours, such as maintaining focus, setting boundaries, and practising self-control. This discipline ensures that efforts are directed towards meaningful and productive activities.

Fostering a Culture of Simplicity: Leaders should foster a culture that values simplicity and mindfulness. This involves promoting practices that prioritise essential needs, avoid excess, and support sustainable use of resources.

Practising moderation fosters a sustainable organisational culture where balanced and mindful practices are valued, attracting and retaining top talent and contributing to overall success. Teams that prioritise moderation are more resilient and capable of overcoming challenges, with strong relationships and trust developed through this focus enabling them to work together effectively in any situation. Leaders who practise moderation can navigate uncertainties with strategic agility, ensuring decisions are made with long-term sustainability in mind and supporting the organisation's resilience. Organisations that consistently prioritise moderation are better positioned for long-term success, providing a strong foundation that supports sustainable growth and resilience.

CHAPTER 30 – RENEWAL

Chapter 30 of the *Tao Te Ching* offers profound insights into the dangers of forceful leadership, the importance of restraint, and the natural cycles of growth and decline. Here's how these teachings can be applied to modern-day strategic management:

AVOIDING FORCEFUL LEADERSHIP

> *He who would assist a lord of men in harmony with the Tao will not assert his mastery in the kingdom by force of arms. Such a course is sure to meet with its proper return.*

Lao Tzu's passage emphasises the futility and counterproductivity of using force to assert authority. In strategic management, leaders should avoid asserting their authority through force or coercion. Instead, they should seek to lead with wisdom and harmony, aligning their actions with the natural flow of the organisation. This approach fosters a culture of respect, collaboration, and mutual trust. Leaders who rely on forceful tactics may achieve short-term success, but they ultimately undermine long-term stability and goodwill.

Forceful leadership can erode trust between leaders and team members by using coercion or intimidation to achieve compliance, creating an environment of fear and resentment that hinders open communication and collaboration. Employees are likely to resist forceful tactics, which can manifest in decreased productivity, low morale, and high turnover rates, as a coercive approach often breeds opposition rather than cooperation. While forceful tactics may yield short-term results, they are unsustainable in the long run as the negative impact on trust, morale, and employee engagement undermines long-term success and organisational stability. Additionally, a culture of coercion stifles innovation and creativity, as employees fear retribution for mistakes or dissenting opinions, making them less likely to take risks or propose new ideas, whereas innovation thrives in an environment where people feel safe to express themselves.

Wisdom in leadership involves leading by example, as leaders should model the behaviours and attitudes they expect from their team members, demonstrating integrity, humility, and respect in all interactions. Harmony is achieved through collaboration and mutual respect, so leaders should encourage teamwork and create opportunities for employees to collaborate on projects, strengthening relationships and enhancing collective problem-solving. Empowering employees involves giving them the autonomy to make decisions and take ownership of their work, with leaders providing guidance and support but allowing team members the freedom to use their skills and expertise, fostering a sense of responsibility and engagement. Practising active listening is a key component of harmonious leadership, so leaders should listen to their team members' ideas, concerns, and feedback with an open mind, building trust and ensuring that everyone feels heard and valued.

Leaders who avoid forceful tactics build trust and respect within the organisation, as employees are more likely to trust and respect leaders who lead with wisdom, fairness, and compassion, enhancing engagement and loyalty. A culture of respect and collaboration boosts morale and productivity, with valued and supported employees being more motivated to contribute their best efforts, leading to increased productivity and job satisfaction. An environment free from coercion fosters innovation and creativity, as employees who feel safe to express their ideas and take risks are more likely to develop innovative solutions and drive the organisation's growth. Avoiding forceful leadership ensures long-term success and stability, with a culture built on trust, respect, and collaboration being more resilient and capable of sustaining growth over time.

Practical Strategies for Avoiding Forceful Leadership

Promoting Open Communication: Leaders should promote open communication by creating channels for feedback, discussions, and idea-sharing. Open communication fosters transparency and trust within the organisation.

Providing Constructive Feedback: Constructive feedback helps employees grow and improve without feeling coerced. Leaders should offer specific, actionable feedback that is supportive and focused on development.

Recognising and Celebrating Achievements: Recognising and celebrating employees' achievements reinforces positive behaviours and builds a culture of appreciation. Leaders should acknowledge individual and team successes, expressing gratitude for their contributions.

Encouraging Employee Involvement: Involving employees in decision-making processes enhances their sense of ownership and engagement. Leaders should seek input and involve team members in discussions about goals, strategies, and initiatives.

Leading with Empathy and Compassion: Empathy and compassion are essential traits for harmonious leadership. Leaders should show genuine care and concern for their team members' well-being, offering support and understanding in times of need.

Avoiding forceful leadership fosters a sustainable organisational culture where employees feel valued and respected, attracting and retaining top talent and contributing to overall success. Teams that prioritise wisdom and harmony are more resilient and capable of overcoming challenges, as strong relationships and trust developed through this focus enable them to work together effectively in any situation. Leaders who avoid forceful tactics can navigate uncertainties with strategic agility, ensuring decisions are made with long-term sustainability in mind and supporting the organisation's resilience. Organisations that consistently avoid forceful leadership are better positioned for long-term success, providing a strong foundation that supports sustainable growth and resilience.

RECOGNISING THE CONSEQUENCES OF AGGRESSIVE STRATEGIES

> *Wherever a host is stationed, briars and thorns spring up. In the sequence of great armies there are sure to be bad years.*

Lao Tzu's passage underscores the adverse effects of aggressive strategies and heavy-handed approaches. Aggressive strategies and heavy-handed approaches often lead to negative consequences, such as resistance, burnout, and disruption. Leaders should be mindful of the long-term impact of their actions and avoid strategies that cause unnecessary harm or conflict. By adopting a more balanced and considerate approach, leaders can create a sustainable and positive environment.

Aggressive strategies often lead to resistance and pushback from employees and stakeholders, creating an environment of tension and opposition that manifests in decreased cooperation, lower morale, and reduced productivity. Heavy-handed approaches can result in burnout and stress among employees, with constant pressure, unrealistic demands, and a lack of support leading to physical and mental exhaustion, affecting individual well-being and reducing overall organisational performance. Aggressive tactics can disrupt the organisational flow and create instability, with frequent changes, high turnover, and conflicts undermining the stability required for sustainable growth, hampering long-term planning and execution.

A balanced approach involves promoting collaboration rather than imposing decisions unilaterally, so leaders should engage with their teams, seek input, and involve them in decision-making processes, fostering a sense of ownership and commitment. Empathy and support are crucial components of balanced leadership, so leaders should understand the needs and concerns of their employees and provide necessary support to help them succeed, including offering resources, guidance, and encouragement. Leaders should set realistic and achievable expectations, understanding the capabilities and limitations of their teams and setting goals that are challenging yet attainable, preventing undue stress and motivating employees to perform their best.

By avoiding aggressive strategies, leaders build trust and respect within the organisation, as employees are more likely to trust leaders who demonstrate fairness, empathy, and consideration, enhancing collaboration and loyalty. A balanced and considerate approach boosts employee engagement, making employees feel valued and supported, motivating them to commit to their work, which leads to increased productivity and job satisfaction. Avoiding aggressive tactics ensures sustainable growth by fostering a positive work environment, reducing turnover, and promoting long-term planning, supporting the organisation's continued success. A considerate leadership style improves overall organisational health, reducing stress and burnout, enhancing morale, and contributing to a healthier and more productive workforce, which attracts and retains top talent.

Practical Strategies for Adopting a Balanced Approach

Encouraging Open Communication: Leaders should encourage open communication by creating channels for feedback, discussions, and idea-sharing. This openness ensures that employees feel heard and valued, fostering a culture of trust and respect.

Providing Adequate Support: Providing adequate support involves offering resources, training, and guidance to help employees succeed. Leaders should ensure that their teams have the tools and support they need to perform their roles effectively.

Recognising and Celebrating Achievements: Recognising and celebrating achievements reinforces positive behaviours and builds a culture of appreciation. Leaders should acknowledge individual and team successes, expressing gratitude for their contributions.

Promoting Work-Life Balance: Promoting work-life balance helps prevent burnout and stress. Leaders should encourage employees to maintain a healthy balance between work and personal life, offering flexible work arrangements and respecting boundaries.

Modelling Balanced Behaviour: Leaders should model balanced behaviour by demonstrating empathy, fairness, and consideration in their actions. This includes setting realistic expectations, practising self-care, and promoting a positive work environment.

Embracing a balanced approach fosters a sustainable organisational culture where employees feel valued and respected, attracting and retaining top talent and contributing to overall success. Teams that prioritise balance and consideration are more resilient and capable of overcoming challenges, with strong relationships and trust enabling them to work together effectively in any situation. Leaders who adopt a balanced approach can navigate uncertainties with strategic agility, ensuring decisions are made with long-term sustainability in mind and supporting the organisation's resilience. Organisations that consistently avoid aggressive strategies and adopt a balanced approach are better positioned for long-term success, providing a strong foundation that supports sustainable growth and resilience.

PRACTISING RESTRAINT & AVOIDING ARROGANCE

A skilful (commander) strikes a decisive blow, and stops. He does not dare (by continuing his operations) to assert and complete his mastery.

Lao Tzu's passage emphasises the value of restraint and the danger of arrogance in leadership. Effective leaders practise restraint and avoid arrogance. They make decisive actions when necessary but do not overextend their efforts or boast about their achievements. By remaining humble and focused, leaders can maintain credibility and respect within their organisation. This restraint also helps in preserving resources and avoiding overreach.

Leaders must be capable of making decisive actions when the situation demands it, which involves assessing the situation, determining the best course of action, and executing it effectively; however, decisive actions should be measured and deliberate, avoiding unnecessary aggression. Overextending efforts can lead to exhaustion of resources and diminished effectiveness, so leaders should recognise the limits of their capabilities and avoid pushing beyond these boundaries, ensuring that resources are used efficiently and sustainably. Resource management is critical for long-term success, and practising restraint helps leaders conserve resources, whether financial, human, or material, ensuring they are available when truly needed, supporting the organisation's sustainability. Knowing when to stop is as important as knowing when to act, so leaders should have the wisdom to cease operations or initiatives when they have achieved their objectives or when further action would be counterproductive, preventing overexertion and maintaining focus on strategic goals.

Humility is a fundamental quality for effective leadership, as leaders should acknowledge their limitations and be open to learning from others, recognising that success is often the result of collective efforts and not just individual achievements. Humble leaders prioritise the success of their team by giving credit to team members and highlighting their contributions, fostering a culture of respect and collaboration. Effective leaders actively seek and listen to feedback, valuing the insights of their team members, which enhances decision-making and fosters continuous improvement. Celebrating successes with humility and recognising the contributions of all involved builds unity and fosters a positive organisational culture, while avoiding boasting about achievements prevents alienating team members and creating resentment.

Leaders who practise restraint and humility earn credibility and respect within the organisation, as employees are more likely to trust and respect leaders who demonstrate modesty and prudence in their actions. Restraint and humility contribute to sustainable success by preventing resource depletion and fostering a supportive work environment, with leaders who avoid overreach and arrogance building a stable foundation for long-term growth and achievement. A humble approach encourages collaboration and teamwork, as leaders who value and acknowledge the contributions of their team members create a culture of mutual respect and cooperation, driving innovation and collective success. Restraint and humility foster a positive organisational culture where employees feel valued and respected, attracting and retaining top talent and enhancing the organisation's overall performance and reputation.

Practical Strategies for Practising Restraint & Avoiding Arrogance

Setting Realistic Goals: Leaders should set realistic and attainable goals that align with the organisation's capacity and resources. This involves understanding the limits of what can be achieved and avoiding overly ambitious targets that strain resources and capabilities.

Encouraging Team Contributions: Recognising and encouraging team contributions fosters a culture of humility and collaboration. Leaders should regularly acknowledge the efforts of their team members and highlight their achievements, creating an environment of mutual respect.

Promoting a Learning Mindset: Leaders should cultivate a mindset of continuous learning and improvement. This involves being open to feedback, seeking new knowledge, and encouraging team members to do the same. A learning mindset fosters humility and adaptability.

Celebrating Success with Modesty: Celebrating successes with modesty reinforces the value of humility. Leaders should acknowledge achievements without boasting, giving credit to all who contributed to the success. This approach builds unity and respect within the team.

Practising Self-Reflection: Regular self-reflection helps leaders remain grounded and aware of their actions. Leaders should take time to reflect on their decisions, behaviours, and their impact on the organisation. This self-awareness fosters humility and restraint.

Practising restraint and humility fosters a sustainable organisational culture where balanced and mindful practices are valued, attracting and retaining top talent and contributing to overall success. Teams that prioritise restraint and humility are more resilient and capable of overcoming challenges, with strong relationships and trust developed through this focus enabling them to work together effectively in any situation. Leaders who practise restraint and humility can navigate uncertainties with strategic agility, ensuring decisions are made with long-term sustainability in mind and supporting the organisation's resilience. Organisations that consistently prioritise restraint and humility are better positioned for long-term success, providing a strong foundation that supports sustainable growth and resilience.

UNDERSTANDING THE NATURAL CYCLES OF GROWTH & DECLINE

> *When things have attained their strong maturity they become old. This may be said to be not in accordance with the Tao: and what is not in accordance with it soon comes to an end.*

Lao Tzu's passage reflects the inevitability of growth and decline within the natural order. Leaders should recognise the natural cycles of growth and decline in business. Every organisation and initiative goes through phases of growth, maturity, and renewal. By understanding these cycles, leaders can plan strategically for the long term, ensuring that the organisation remains adaptable and resilient. This awareness helps in anticipating changes and preparing for the future.

During the growth phase, an organisation or initiative experiences rapid expansion and development, characterised by innovation, increased market share, and building momentum. Leaders should capitalise on opportunities, invest in resources, and drive forward with energy and vision. As organisations reach maturity, growth stabilises, and the focus shifts to maintaining performance and optimising operations, involving refining processes, consolidating gains, and ensuring efficiency. Leaders should concentrate on sustaining success, maintaining customer loyalty, and adapting to changing market conditions. Following maturity, organisations may enter a period of decline if they fail to innovate and adapt; the renewal phase is about reinvention and transformation, where leaders must identify signs of stagnation, embrace change, and seek new opportunities for growth, requiring strategic planning, investment in new technologies, and fostering a culture of continuous improvement.

Understanding the natural cycles of growth and decline helps leaders anticipate changes and challenges by recognising patterns and trends, enabling them to prepare for potential downturns and identify opportunities for renewal, ensuring the organisation remains agile and resilient.

Diversification is a key strategy for mitigating risk and ensuring sustainability, so leaders should invest in a variety of initiatives, markets, and technologies to spread risk and capitalise on multiple growth opportunities, enhancing the organisation's ability to weather fluctuations and sustain growth. Innovation is crucial for renewal and long-term success, so leaders should create an environment that encourages creativity, experimentation, and risk-taking, fostering a culture of innovation that allows organisations to continually reinvent themselves and stay ahead of the competition. Continuous improvement involves regularly assessing and refining processes, products, and services, so leaders should implement systems for feedback, evaluation, and iterative development, ensuring the organisation remains dynamic and responsive to change.

Recognising the natural cycles of growth and decline enhances organisational resilience, enabling leaders to plan strategically, adapt to changes, and navigate challenges more effectively, supporting sustained success. Understanding business cycles allows for proactive adaptation, as leaders can anticipate shifts and make informed decisions to stay ahead of market changes, minimising disruptions and positioning the organisation for continued growth. Awareness of growth and decline cycles fosters strategic agility, allowing leaders to pivot and realign strategies in response to evolving conditions, ensuring competitiveness and innovation. By planning for the long term and embracing renewal, leaders can achieve sustained growth, with an understanding of business cycles helping them invest wisely, innovate continuously, and maintain momentum through changing circumstances.

Leaders should conduct regular assessments of the organisation's performance, market conditions, and industry trends by analysing key metrics, gathering feedback, and identifying areas for improvement, as these regular assessments provide valuable insights for strategic planning. Investing in talent development ensures that the organisation has the skills and capabilities needed to navigate growth and decline, so leaders should provide training, mentorship, and career development opportunities for employees, supporting innovation and adaptability. Creating flexible business models enables organisations to adapt quickly to changing conditions, so leaders should design models that allow for scalability, diversification, and rapid response, ensuring the organisation can pivot and seize new opportunities. Building strong partnerships with suppliers, customers, and other stakeholders enhances resilience, so leaders should cultivate relationships that provide support, collaboration, and mutual benefit, strengthening the organisation's ability to navigate cycles of growth and decline.

Understanding and managing growth and decline cycles fosters a sustainable organisational culture where adaptability and continuous improvement are valued, attracting and retaining top talent and contributing to overall success. Teams that prioritise resilience and adaptability are more capable of overcoming challenges, with strong relationships and trust developed through this focus enabling them to work together effectively in any situation. Leaders who understand growth and decline cycles can navigate uncertainties with strategic agility, ensuring decisions are made with long-term sustainability in mind and supporting the organisation's resilience. Organisations that consistently recognise and navigate growth and decline cycles are better positioned for long-term success, providing a strong foundation that supports sustainable growth and resilience.

CHAPTER 31 – CALM & REPOSE

Chapter 31 of the *Tao Te Ching* discusses the use of force and the attitude towards conflict, emphasising that weapons and war are to be avoided unless absolutely necessary, and that true leaders should approach such situations with sorrow rather than triumph. Here's how these teachings can be applied to modern-day strategic management:

AVOIDING AGGRESSIVE STRATEGIES

> *Now arms, however beautiful, are instruments of evil omen, hateful, it may be said, to all creatures. Therefore they who have the Tao do not like to employ them.*

Lao Tzu's passage highlights the inherent negativity associated with aggressive strategies, even if they appear advantageous on the surface. In strategic management, leaders should avoid aggressive strategies that can cause harm or foster unnecessary conflict. This means steering clear of hostile takeovers, cutthroat competition, and other harmful business practices. Instead, leaders should focus on creating value through collaboration, ethical practices, and sustainable growth. By doing so, they can build positive relationships with stakeholders and create a more harmonious business environment.

Hostile takeovers create an environment of fear and instability, leading to significant disruption within the target organisation, including layoffs, culture clashes, and decreased morale, often prioritising short-term gains over long-term stability and damaging the reputation of both companies involved. Engaging in cutthroat competition fosters an environment of mistrust and animosity, with companies that employ unethical tactics to outmanoeuvre competitors risking damage to relationships with stakeholders, including customers, employees, and partners, leading to a loss of credibility and a negative public image. Harmful business practices, such as exploiting labour, disregarding environmental standards, or engaging in unfair trade practices, can have severe consequences, leading to legal repercussions, protests, and boycotts, ultimately harming the company's bottom line and reputation.

Collaborative strategies emphasise building positive relationships with stakeholders, so leaders should focus on creating partnerships and alliances that benefit all parties involved, achieving shared goals and fostering a supportive business ecosystem. Ethical behaviour is essential for sustainable success, requiring leaders to uphold high standards of integrity, transparency, and fairness in all business dealings, which builds trust and respect among stakeholders and enhances the organisation's reputation. Sustainable growth involves creating value that benefits the organisation, its stakeholders, and the broader community, so leaders should prioritise long-term strategies that promote environmental stewardship, social responsibility, and economic sustainability, ensuring the organisation remains resilient and adaptable to changing conditions.

By avoiding aggressive strategies and focusing on ethical practices, leaders can build trust and loyalty among stakeholders, as employees, customers, and partners are more likely to remain committed to an organisation that values integrity and respect. Companies that prioritise collaboration and ethical behaviour are more likely to enjoy a positive reputation, attracting top talent, loyal customers, and valuable partners, contributing to overall success. Collaboration fosters innovation by bringing together diverse perspectives and expertise, with leaders who encourage teamwork and open communication creating an environment where new ideas can flourish, driving continuous improvement and competitive advantage. Ethical and sustainable practices contribute to long-term stability, with leaders avoiding short-sighted, aggressive tactics to ensure the organisation is well-positioned to navigate challenges and seize opportunities, supporting sustained growth and resilience.

Practical Strategies for Avoiding Aggressive Strategies

Fostering a Collaborative Culture: Leaders should foster a culture of collaboration by encouraging teamwork, open communication, and mutual respect. This involves creating opportunities for employees to work together on projects and initiatives, sharing knowledge and expertise.

Implementing Ethical Policies: Implementing and enforcing ethical policies ensures that the organisation operates with integrity. Leaders should develop codes of conduct, provide ethics training, and establish mechanisms for reporting and addressing unethical behaviour.

Engaging in Stakeholder Dialogue: Engaging in dialogue with stakeholders helps leaders understand their needs, concerns, and expectations. Regular communication fosters trust and collaboration, allowing the organisation to build strong, positive relationships.

Prioritising Sustainability Initiatives: Leaders should prioritise sustainability initiatives that promote environmental, social, and economic well-being. This includes investing in green technologies, supporting community development, and ensuring fair labor practices. Sustainable practices benefit the organisation and its broader ecosystem.

Recognising and Rewarding Ethical Behaviour: Recognising and rewarding employees who demonstrate ethical behaviour reinforces the importance of integrity. Leaders should celebrate examples of ethical decision-making and collaboration, motivating others to follow suit.

Avoiding aggressive strategies fosters a sustainable organisational culture where collaboration and ethical behaviour are valued, attracting and retaining top talent and contributing to overall success. Teams that prioritise ethical behaviour and collaboration are more resilient and capable of overcoming challenges, with strong relationships and trust enabling them to work together effectively in any situation. Leaders who avoid aggressive strategies can navigate uncertainties with strategic agility, ensuring decisions are made with long-term sustainability in mind and supporting the organisation's resilience. Organisations that consistently avoid aggressive strategies and focus on creating value through collaboration and ethical practices are better positioned for long-term success, providing a strong foundation that supports sustainable growth and resilience.

USING FORCE ONLY WHEN ABSOLUTELY NECESSARY

> *Those sharp weapons are instruments of evil omen, and not the instruments of the superior man;—he uses them only on the compulsion of necessity. Calm and repose are what he prizes; victory (by force of arms) is to him undesirable.*

Lao Tzu's passage emphasises the value of using force only when absolutely necessary and as a last resort. Leaders should resort to forceful actions only when absolutely necessary. This could mean making difficult decisions or taking decisive action in times of crisis, but always with the intention of minimising harm and finding the most peaceful resolution possible. Strategic leaders should prioritise calm and measured responses over aggressive tactics.

Forceful actions often escalate conflicts rather than resolve them, provoking retaliation, creating animosity, and leading to prolonged disputes that can cause long-term damage to relationships and hinder collaboration. Using force can undermine trust within the organisation and among stakeholders, as employees and partners may feel threatened or coerced, leading to a breakdown in communication and cooperation, eroding the trust that is fundamental to effective leadership. Aggressive strategies can negatively impact employee morale by creating an environment of fear and uncertainty, resulting in decreased motivation, lower productivity, and higher turnover rates, ultimately harming the organisation's performance. Resorting to force can lead to ethical and legal issues, with leaders who use coercive tactics potentially facing legal challenges, regulatory scrutiny, and damage to their reputation, as ethical leadership requires adherence to principles of fairness, justice, and respect for others.

Before resorting to force, leaders should evaluate all possible alternatives by considering peaceful and constructive solutions, such as negotiation, mediation, and compromise, finding ways to address issues without escalating conflicts. Consensus-building is a key component of measured leadership, so leaders should engage stakeholders in decision-making processes, seeking input and feedback to reach a consensus, fostering a sense of ownership and alignment, and reducing the need for forceful actions. Patience and restraint are essential qualities for effective leadership, as leaders should take the time to understand the situation fully, consider the long-term implications of their actions, and avoid hasty decisions, ensuring that decisions are well-thought-out and balanced. Transparent communication helps prevent misunderstandings and builds trust, so leaders should communicate openly with their teams and stakeholders, explaining the reasons behind their decisions and the steps being taken to address issues, fostering a culture of honesty and respect.

By using force only as a last resort, leaders can maintain peace and stability within the organisation, preventing unnecessary conflicts and promoting a harmonious work environment through peaceful and constructive approaches. Leaders who prioritise calm and measured responses build strong relationships with employees, partners, and stakeholders, nurturing trust and respect through fair and just actions that enhance collaboration and cooperation. Avoiding forceful actions contributes to a positive organisational culture, where leaders who demonstrate empathy, understanding, and restraint create an environment where employees feel valued and respected, boosting morale and engagement. Ethical and measured leadership ensures long-term success by avoiding aggressive tactics and focusing on sustainable solutions, building a strong foundation for the organisation's growth and resilience.

Practical Strategies for Using Force Only When Necessary

Developing Conflict Resolution Skills: Leaders should develop strong conflict resolution skills to address disputes constructively. This includes training in negotiation, mediation, and effective communication. These skills enable leaders to resolve conflicts peacefully and collaboratively.

Implementing Fair Policies: Fair and transparent policies help prevent conflicts and ensure that issues are addressed equitably. Leaders should establish clear guidelines for behaviour, performance, and conflict resolution, ensuring that everyone understands their rights and responsibilities.

Encouraging Open Dialogue: Open dialogue fosters understanding and cooperation. Leaders should create opportunities for employees and stakeholders to voice their concerns, share their perspectives, and engage in constructive discussions. This open communication helps identify and address issues before they escalate.

Promoting Emotional Intelligence: Emotional intelligence is crucial for measured leadership. Leaders should cultivate self-awareness, empathy, and emotional regulation, enabling them to respond calmly and thoughtfully in challenging situations. Emotional intelligence enhances decision-making and relationship-building.

Seeking External Support: In complex or high-stakes situations, seeking external support can be beneficial. Leaders can engage mediators, consultants, or advisors to provide objective perspectives and expertise. External support helps navigate conflicts and find effective solutions.

Using force only when necessary fosters a sustainable organisational culture where fairness, transparency, and respect are valued, attracting and retaining top talent and contributing to overall success. Teams that prioritise calm and measured responses are more resilient and capable of overcoming challenges, with strong relationships and trust enabling them to work together effectively in any situation. Leaders who use force only as a last resort can navigate uncertainties with strategic agility, ensuring decisions are made with long-term sustainability in mind and supporting the organisation's resilience. Organisations that consistently prioritise calm and measured responses are better positioned for long-term success, providing a strong foundation that supports sustainable growth and resilience.

VALUING CALM & REPOSE

> *Calm and repose are what he prizes; victory (by force of arms) is to him undesirable.*

Lao Tzu's passage highlights the importance of valuing calmness and stability over aggressive actions. Leaders should value calmness and stability within their organisation. Creating a work environment that prioritises mental well-being, stress management, and work-life balance can lead to more productive and engaged employees. By fostering a culture of calm and repose, leaders can reduce burnout and improve overall organisational performance.

Mental well-being is crucial for maintaining a productive and healthy workforce, so leaders should implement initiatives that support employees' mental health, such as providing access to counselling services, mental health days, and wellness programmes, demonstrating a commitment to their employees' overall health and happiness. Stress management programmes help employees cope with work-related pressures, so leaders should offer workshops and resources on stress reduction techniques, such as mindfulness, meditation, and time management, equipping employees with the tools to manage stress effectively and maintain a sense of calm. Work-life balance is essential for sustaining employee engagement and productivity, so leaders should encourage flexible work arrangements, such as remote work options, flexible hours, and time off policies, allowing employees to meet personal responsibilities while staying committed to their professional roles.

Open communication fosters a culture of trust and transparency, so leaders should create channels for regular feedback and discussions, allowing employees to voice their concerns and share their ideas, reducing anxiety and promoting a sense of calm and belonging. Leaders should model calm behaviour in their interactions and decision-making, demonstrating patience, composure, and thoughtful responses to set a positive example for the team, encouraging employees to remain calm under pressure. The physical work environment also plays a role in promoting calmness, so leaders should design workspaces that are conducive to relaxation and focus, incorporating elements such as natural light, plants, and comfortable furniture, enhancing employees' well-being and productivity.

By prioritising calmness and stability, leaders can reduce burnout among employees, as a supportive and stress-free work environment prevents physical and mental exhaustion, ensuring employees remain energised and motivated. Calm and focused employees are more productive, as managed stress levels enable them to concentrate on their tasks and perform at their best, with a calm environment minimising distractions and enhancing overall efficiency. Employees who feel valued and supported are more engaged and committed to their work, with a culture of calm and repose fostering loyalty and dedication, leading to higher levels of engagement and job satisfaction. Valuing calmness and stability contributes to a positive organisational culture, where employees are more likely to collaborate, innovate, and support each other in a peaceful and respectful environment, attracting and retaining top talent.

Practical Strategies for Valuing Calm & Repose

Implementing Wellness Programmes: Leaders should implement wellness programmes that focus on mental and physical health. This includes offering fitness classes, wellness challenges, and mental health resources. Wellness programmes promote a holistic approach to well-being.

Offering Flexible Work Arrangements: Flexible work arrangements help employees manage their personal and professional lives. Leaders should offer options such as remote work, flexible hours, and job-sharing arrangements. Flexibility enhances work-life balance and reduces stress.

Providing Training on Stress Management: Training on stress management equips employees with techniques to handle pressure and maintain calmness. Leaders should offer workshops on mindfulness, relaxation techniques, and time management skills. Training empowers employees to manage stress effectively.

Encouraging Breaks and Downtime: Encouraging regular breaks and downtime prevents burnout and maintains energy levels. Leaders should promote the importance of taking breaks, whether it's a short walk, a lunch break, or a vacation. Downtime allows employees to recharge and return to work refreshed.

Recognising and Rewarding Calm Leadership: Recognising and rewarding leaders who demonstrate calm and composed behaviour reinforces its importance. Leaders should highlight examples of calm leadership and provide incentives for maintaining a peaceful and supportive work environment.

Valuing calm and repose fosters a sustainable organisational culture where employees feel valued and respected, attracting and retaining top talent and contributing to overall success. Teams that prioritise calmness and stability are more resilient and capable of overcoming challenges, with strong relationships and trust enabling them to work together effectively in any situation. Leaders who value calm and repose can navigate uncertainties with strategic agility, ensuring decisions are made with long-term sustainability in mind and supporting the organisation's resilience. Organisations that consistently prioritise calmness and stability are better positioned for long-term success, providing a strong foundation that supports sustainable growth and resilience.

REFLECTING ON THE CONSEQUENCES OF ACTIONS

He who delights in the slaughter of men cannot get his will in the kingdom.

Lao Tzu's passage highlights the critical need for leaders to reflect on the consequences of their actions. Leaders should always consider the consequences of their actions. Delighting in aggressive tactics or harsh measures can lead to long-term damage to the organisation's reputation and relationships. Instead, leaders should approach conflict and challenges with empathy and a focus on constructive solutions.

Aggressive tactics, whether in business decisions or interpersonal interactions, can severely damage an organisation's reputation, leading to a loss of trust and credibility that deters customers, partners, and potential talent from associating with the organisation. Such actions strain relationships with employees, stakeholders, and the broader community, fostering an environment of fear and resentment that hinders collaboration, innovation, and overall organisational effectiveness. Trust, fundamental to any successful organisation, is eroded by aggressive tactics, leading to breakdowns in communication, decreased morale, and compromised organisational cohesion. Moreover, harsh measures can result in legal and ethical repercussions, with leaders who disregard ethical considerations or legal standards facing lawsuits, regulatory penalties, and damage to their professional integrity. Ethical leadership, which requires adherence to principles of fairness, justice, and respect for all individuals, is essential to avoid these negative outcomes.

Empathy involves understanding and sharing the feelings of others, so leaders should approach conflicts and challenges with empathy, considering the impact of their decisions on employees, stakeholders, and the community, fostering a supportive and inclusive environment where individuals feel valued and respected. Constructive solutions address problems in a way that promotes growth and positive outcomes, so leaders should prioritise resolving conflicts through dialogue, negotiation, and collaboration, encouraging mutual understanding and paving the way for sustainable solutions. Open dialogue is essential for addressing conflicts and challenges constructively, so leaders should create channels for honest and transparent communication, allowing employees and stakeholders to express their concerns and perspectives, fostering trust and facilitating problem-solving. Fair practices ensure that decisions and actions are just and equitable, so leaders should establish clear policies and procedures that promote fairness and consistency, building credibility and strengthening relationships within the organisation.

By considering the consequences of their actions and avoiding aggressive tactics, leaders can enhance the organisation's reputation, attracting customers, partners, and talent, and contributing to long-term success. Reflecting on the impact of decisions fosters stronger relationships with employees, stakeholders, and the community, with leaders who prioritise empathy and constructive solutions building trust and loyalty, enhancing collaboration and organisational cohesion. Trust is built through consistent and ethical behaviour, and leaders who choose fair and empathetic approaches earn the trust and respect of their team and stakeholders, strengthening communication and cooperation. Ethical and empathetic leadership ensures sustainable success by prioritising constructive solutions and considering the long-term impact of their actions, creating a stable foundation for growth and resilience.

Practical Strategies for Reflecting on Consequences

Conducting Impact Assessments: Leaders should conduct impact assessments before making significant decisions. This involves evaluating the potential effects of actions on various stakeholders and considering ethical implications. Impact assessments provide a comprehensive understanding of the consequences.

Encouraging Feedback: Encouraging feedback from employees and stakeholders helps leaders understand the potential impact of their actions. Leaders should create mechanisms for gathering and incorporating feedback, ensuring that diverse perspectives are considered.

Implementing Ethical Decision-Making Frameworks: Ethical decision-making frameworks guide leaders in evaluating the consequences of their actions. Leaders should establish principles and guidelines that prioritise fairness, transparency, and respect for all individuals.

Promoting Inclusive Leadership: Inclusive leadership values the contributions and perspectives of all team members. Leaders should foster an inclusive environment where everyone feels heard and valued. Inclusive leadership promotes empathy and constructive solutions.

Reflecting on Past Decisions: Reflecting on past decisions provides valuable insights for future actions. Leaders should regularly review the outcomes of their decisions, considering what worked well and what could be improved. Continuous reflection enhances decision-making and ethical leadership.

Reflecting on the consequences of actions fosters a sustainable organisational culture where empathy, fairness, and ethical behaviour are valued, attracting and retaining top talent and contributing to overall success. Teams that prioritise empathy and constructive solutions are more resilient and capable of overcoming challenges, with strong relationships and trust enabling them to work together effectively in any situation. Leaders who reflect on the consequences of their actions can navigate uncertainties with strategic agility, ensuring decisions are made with long-term sustainability in mind and supporting the organisation's resilience. Organisations that consistently prioritise reflecting on consequences and adopting empathetic and constructive approaches are better positioned for long-term success, providing a strong foundation that supports sustainable growth and resilience.

ACKNOWLEDGING THE GRAVITY OF CONFLICT

He who has killed multitudes of men should weep for them with the bitterest grief; and the victor in battle has his place (rightly) according to those rites.

Lao Tzu's passage underscores the profound impact and sorrow associated with conflict. Leaders should acknowledge the gravity of conflict and its impact on all involved. In business, this means recognising the human cost of decisions and striving to mitigate negative effects. Leaders should approach difficult decisions with empathy and compassion, understanding the broader implications for employees, customers, and other stakeholders.

Empathy involves understanding and sharing the feelings of others, so leaders should incorporate empathy into their decision-making processes, considering how their actions will affect employees, customers, and other stakeholders, fostering a supportive and inclusive environment where individuals feel valued and respected. Decisions often have far-reaching consequences, so leaders should think beyond immediate outcomes and consider the long-term implications of their actions, evaluating how actions will impact relationships, morale, and the organisation's reputation over time. While achieving business objectives is important, leaders must balance these goals with the well-being of their stakeholders, making decisions that prioritise people's needs and minimise harm, as ethical leadership requires a commitment to fairness, justice, and respect for all individuals.

Fair practices ensure that decisions and actions are just and equitable, so leaders should establish clear policies and procedures that promote fairness and consistency, building credibility and strengthening relationships within the organisation. Leaders should provide support and resources to help individuals affected by difficult decisions, such as offering counselling services, training programmes, or financial assistance, demonstrating a commitment to the well-being of stakeholders. Open communication helps prevent misunderstandings and builds trust, so leaders should communicate openly with their teams and stakeholders, explaining the reasons behind their decisions and the steps being taken to address issues, fostering a culture of honesty and respect.

Active listening is a key component of empathetic leadership, so leaders should listen to the concerns and perspectives of their stakeholders, including employees, customers, and partners, ensuring that decisions are informed by diverse viewpoints and address the needs of those affected. Compassion involves recognising the struggles and challenges faced by others and responding with kindness and support, so leaders should show compassion during times of conflict or hardship, offering understanding and assistance to those in need. A culture of care prioritises the well-being and dignity of all individuals, so leaders should foster an environment where empathy, respect, and support are core values, enhancing employee engagement, loyalty, and overall organisational performance.

By acknowledging the gravity of conflict and demonstrating empathy, leaders build trust and loyalty among stakeholders, making employees, customers, and partners more likely to remain committed to an organisation that values their well-being. Organisations that prioritise empathy and compassion are more likely to enjoy a positive reputation, attracting top talent, loyal customers, and valuable partners, contributing to overall success. Acknowledging the human cost of decisions and striving to mitigate negative effects enhances organisational resilience, with leaders who approach conflicts with empathy and compassion creating a supportive environment that can adapt and thrive in the face of challenges. Ethical and compassionate leadership ensures sustainable success by considering the broader implications of their actions, building a strong foundation for the organisation's growth and resilience.

Practical Strategies for Acknowledging the Gravity of Conflict

Conducting Impact Assessments: Leaders should conduct impact assessments before making significant decisions. This involves evaluating the potential effects of actions on various stakeholders and considering ethical implications. Impact assessments provide a comprehensive understanding of the consequences.

Encouraging Feedback: Encouraging feedback from employees and stakeholders helps leaders understand the potential impact of their actions. Leaders should create mechanisms for gathering and incorporating feedback, ensuring that diverse perspectives are considered.

Implementing Ethical Decision-Making Frameworks: Ethical decision-making frameworks guide leaders in evaluating the consequences of their actions. Leaders should establish principles and guidelines that prioritise fairness, transparency, and respect for all individuals.

Promoting Inclusive Leadership: Inclusive leadership values the contributions and perspectives of all team members. Leaders should foster an inclusive environment where everyone feels heard and valued. Inclusive leadership promotes empathy and constructive solutions.

Reflecting on Past Decisions: Reflecting on past decisions provides valuable insights for future actions. Leaders should regularly review the outcomes of their decisions, considering what worked well and what could be improved. Continuous reflection enhances decision-making and ethical leadership.

Acknowledging the gravity of conflict fosters a sustainable organisational culture where empathy, fairness, and ethical behaviour are valued, attracting and retaining top talent and contributing to overall success. Teams that prioritise empathy and constructive solutions are more resilient and capable of overcoming challenges, with strong relationships and trust enabling them to work together effectively in any situation. Leaders who acknowledge the gravity of conflict can navigate uncertainties with strategic agility, ensuring decisions are made with long-term sustainability in mind and supporting the organisation's resilience. Organisations that consistently prioritise empathy and compassion in their decision-making are better positioned for long-term success, providing a strong foundation that supports sustainable growth and resilience.

CHAPTER 32 – NATURAL GROWTH

Chapter 32 of the *Tao Te Ching* delves into the profound and unchanging nature of the Tao and its influence when embraced and applied. Here's how these teachings can be applied to modern-day strategic management:

EMBRACING SIMPLICITY & FUNDAMENTALS

> *The Tao, considered as unchanging, has no name. Though in its primordial simplicity it may be small, the whole world dares not deal with (one embodying) it as a minister.*

Lao Tzu's passage emphasises the power and importance of simplicity. In strategic management, leaders should focus on the fundamental principles and simplicity of their vision and strategy. Keeping strategies straightforward and rooted in core values allows for greater clarity and stability. By embracing simplicity, leaders can make their organisations more resilient and adaptable to change.

A clear and simple vision provides a strong foundation for decision-making and strategic planning, helping to align the organisation's efforts and ensure that everyone is working towards the same goals. Core values serve as guiding principles, so leaders should define and uphold these values, integrating them into all aspects of the business to provide a moral compass and foster a sense of unity and purpose among employees. Focusing on essential goals helps avoid distractions and maintain focus on what truly matters, so leaders should prioritise objectives that align with their vision and core values, allowing organisations to allocate resources effectively and achieve meaningful outcomes.

Simplicity enhances organisational resilience by reducing complexity and uncertainty, making strategies easier to implement, monitor, and adapt, allowing organisations to respond quickly to changes and challenges while maintaining stability and continuity. Embracing simplicity makes organisations more adaptable to change, as straightforward strategies rooted in fundamental principles make it easier to pivot and adjust, ensuring competitiveness and innovation. Simple and clear strategies improve communication and understanding within the organisation, with employees more likely to grasp and support initiatives that are easy to comprehend, fostering engagement and alignment and driving collective success. Simplicity also streamlines decision-making processes, enabling leaders to make informed choices more efficiently when strategies are straightforward and goals are well-defined, reducing the risk of confusion and indecision and leading to more effective outcomes.

Practical Strategies for Embracing Simplicity

Articulating a Clear Vision: Leaders should articulate a clear and concise vision that encapsulates the organisation's purpose and direction. This vision should be communicated consistently and reinforced through actions and decisions.

Defining Core Values: Defining and upholding core values is essential for maintaining simplicity. Leaders should identify values that reflect the organisation's identity and integrate them into everyday practices. Core values should guide behaviour and decision-making at all levels.

Prioritising Key Goals: Prioritising key goals helps focus efforts on what is most important. Leaders should set clear objectives that align with their vision and values, and allocate resources to support these priorities. Regularly reviewing and adjusting goals ensures that the organisation stays on track.

Simplifying Processes: Simplifying processes enhances efficiency and reduces complexity. Leaders should streamline workflows, eliminate unnecessary steps, and implement best practices. Simplified processes save time and resources, improving overall performance.

Encouraging Open Communication: Open communication fosters transparency and understanding. Leaders should create channels for regular feedback and discussions, ensuring that everyone is informed and engaged. Open communication promotes collaboration and alignment.

Embracing simplicity fosters a sustainable organisational culture where clarity, efficiency, and core values are prioritised, attracting and retaining top talent and contributing to overall success. Teams that prioritise simplicity and fundamental principles are more resilient and capable of overcoming challenges, with strong relationships and trust enabling them to work together effectively in any situation. Leaders who embrace simplicity can navigate uncertainties with strategic agility, ensuring decisions are made with long-term sustainability in mind and supporting the organisation's resilience. Organisations that consistently prioritise simplicity and core values are better positioned for long-term success, providing a strong foundation that supports sustainable growth and resilience.

LEADING WITH AUTHENTICITY & HUMILITY

If a feudal prince or the king could guard and hold it, all would spontaneously submit themselves to him.

Lao Tzu's passage highlights the natural authority and influence that come from leading with authenticity and humility. Leaders who embody authenticity and humility naturally earn the respect and trust of their teams. By remaining true to their values and leading with humility, leaders create an environment where employees feel valued and inspired to follow. This genuine approach fosters loyalty and alignment within the organisation.

Authentic leaders are guided by their core values and principles, making decisions and taking actions that align with their beliefs, demonstrating consistency and integrity, and building credibility and trust within their organisation. Authenticity involves being genuine and transparent in all interactions, with leaders communicating openly and honestly, sharing both successes and challenges, fostering a culture of trust and mutual respect where employees feel comfortable expressing themselves. Authentic leaders are not afraid to show vulnerability, acknowledging their limitations and mistakes, and being open to feedback and learning, which humanises them and makes them more relatable and approachable to their teams.

Humble leaders prioritise the needs and well-being of their team members, focusing on serving and supporting others rather than seeking personal recognition or power, which fosters a supportive and collaborative environment. Humility involves being open to the ideas and perspectives of others, so leaders should actively listen to their team members, valuing their input and feedback, which enhances decision-making and strengthens relationships. Humble leaders also recognise and celebrate the contributions of their team members, giving credit where it is due and expressing gratitude for their hard work and dedication, fostering a sense of belonging and motivation within the organisation.

By leading with authenticity and humility, leaders build trust and respect within their organisation, as employees are more likely to trust leaders who are genuine, transparent, and humble, enhancing engagement and loyalty and driving collective success. Authentic and humble leadership fosters loyalty and alignment within the organisation, as employees feel valued and inspired to follow leaders who demonstrate integrity and humility, leading to higher levels of commitment and productivity. Authenticity and humility contribute to a positive organisational culture, where leaders create an environment that values openness, respect, and collaboration, attracting and retaining top talent and enhancing overall performance. Leading with authenticity and humility ensures sustainable success by prioritising core values and fostering a supportive environment, building a strong foundation for long-term growth and resilience.

Practical Strategies for Leading with Authenticity & Humility

Articulating Core Values: Leaders should clearly articulate their core values and ensure that they are integrated into all aspects of the organisation. This involves communicating the importance of these values and leading by example.

Practising Transparent Communication: Transparent communication involves being open and honest in all interactions. Leaders should share information about decisions, challenges, and successes, fostering a culture of trust and mutual respect.

Showing Vulnerability: Leaders should not be afraid to show vulnerability. This includes admitting mistakes, seeking feedback, and being open to learning and growth. Vulnerability strengthens connections and makes leaders more relatable.

Prioritising Team Members: Prioritising the needs and well-being of team members is essential for humble leadership. Leaders should focus on serving and supporting others, creating a supportive and collaborative environment.

Recognising and Celebrating Contributions: Leaders should regularly recognise and celebrate the contributions of their team members. This includes giving credit, expressing gratitude, and highlighting individual and team achievements.

Leading with authenticity and humility fosters a sustainable organisational culture where trust, respect, and collaboration are valued, attracting and retaining top talent and contributing to overall success. Teams that prioritise authenticity and humility are more resilient and capable of overcoming challenges, with strong relationships and trust enabling them to work together effectively in any situation. Leaders who embody authenticity and humility can navigate uncertainties with strategic agility, ensuring decisions are made with long-term sustainability in mind and supporting the organisation's resilience. Organisations that consistently prioritise authenticity and humility in leadership are better positioned for long-term success, providing a strong foundation that supports sustainable growth and resilience.

FACILITATING NATURAL GROWTH & HARMONY

> *Heaven and Earth (under its guidance) unite together and send down the sweet dew, which, without the directions of men, reaches equally everywhere as of its own accord.*

Lao Tzu's passage emphasises the importance of allowing natural processes to flourish without excessive interference. Effective leaders create conditions that facilitate natural growth and harmony within their organisations. Rather than micromanaging, they provide the necessary support and resources, allowing their teams to thrive autonomously. This approach encourages innovation and creativity, as employees feel empowered to take initiative and contribute their best.

Trust is a fundamental component of effective leadership, so leaders should trust their team members' abilities and judgment, giving them the autonomy to manage their tasks and make decisions, fostering a sense of responsibility and ownership that motivates employees to perform at their best. Delegation is essential for fostering growth and development within the team, so leaders should delegate tasks based on employees' strengths and expertise, providing them with opportunities to showcase their skills, empowering employees while allowing leaders to focus on strategic priorities. While avoiding micromanagement, leaders should still provide clear guidelines and expectations by setting goals, defining roles, and establishing boundaries, ensuring that employees understand their responsibilities and have a framework within which to operate.

Leaders should ensure that their team members have access to the resources they need to succeed, providing tools, training, and support to help employees achieve their goals, enabling them to work efficiently and effectively. Innovation thrives in an environment where employees feel free to explore new ideas and approaches, so leaders should encourage a culture of experimentation, allowing team members to take risks and learn from failures, driving continuous improvement and competitive advantage. Collaboration enhances creativity and problem-solving, so leaders should create opportunities for team members to work together, share knowledge, and collaborate on projects, promoting the exchange of ideas and fostering a sense of community.

By providing autonomy and encouraging initiative, leaders create an environment where creativity and innovation can flourish, as employees who feel empowered to take risks and explore new ideas are more likely to develop innovative solutions. Empowering employees to take initiative and contribute their best leads to higher levels of engagement and motivation, as team members who feel valued and trusted are more committed to their work and the organisation's success. Organisations that facilitate natural growth and harmony are more resilient to change and challenges, with the autonomy and initiative fostered within the team enabling the organisation to adapt quickly and effectively to evolving circumstances. A harmonious work environment where employees feel supported and empowered leads to improved overall performance, with team members becoming more productive, collaborative, and motivated, driving the organisation's success.

Practical Strategies for Facilitating Natural Growth & Harmony

Setting Clear Goals and Expectations: Leaders should set clear goals and expectations, ensuring that team members understand their roles and responsibilities. This clarity provides a framework within which employees can operate autonomously.

Providing Continuous Support and Feedback: Continuous support and feedback help employees grow and improve. Leaders should offer guidance, mentorship, and constructive feedback to support their team members' development. Regular check-ins and performance reviews provide opportunities for growth and learning.

Creating Opportunities for Collaboration: Leaders should create opportunities for collaboration by organising team projects, brainstorming sessions, and cross-functional initiatives. This collaborative approach fosters the exchange of ideas and enhances problem-solving.

Encouraging Risk-Taking and Experimentation: Encouraging risk-taking and experimentation drives innovation. Leaders should create a safe environment where employees feel comfortable trying new approaches and learning from failures. This culture of experimentation fosters continuous improvement.

Recognising and Celebrating Successes: Recognising and celebrating successes reinforces positive behaviours and motivates employees. Leaders should acknowledge individual and team achievements, expressing gratitude and appreciation for their contributions.

Facilitating natural growth and harmony fosters a sustainable organisational culture where autonomy, collaboration, and innovation are valued, attracting and retaining top talent and contributing to overall success. Teams that prioritise autonomy and collaboration are more resilient and capable of overcoming challenges, with strong relationships and trust enabling them to work together effectively in any situation. Leaders who facilitate natural growth and harmony can navigate uncertainties with strategic agility, ensuring decisions are made with long-term sustainability in mind and supporting the organisation's resilience. Organisations that consistently prioritise natural growth and harmony are better positioned for long-term success, providing a strong foundation that supports sustainable growth and resilience.

RECOGNISING THE POWER OF ACTION

> *As soon as it proceeds to action, it has a name. When it once has that name, (men) can know to rest in it. When they know to rest in it, they can be free from all risk of failure and error.*

Lao Tzu's passage underscores the vital role of action in bringing strategies to life. Strategic leaders understand the importance of taking decisive action. While planning and vision are crucial, it is through action that strategies come to life. Once a strategy is implemented, it provides a foundation for continuous improvement and learning. Leaders should ensure that their actions are aligned with their values and mission, creating a stable and reliable environment.

Vision and planning lay the groundwork for strategic initiatives, but it is the execution that brings these plans to fruition, as leaders must move beyond conceptualisation and take concrete steps to implement their strategies, making this transition from planning to action essential for achieving organisational goals. Once a strategy is put into action, it serves as a basis for continuous improvement, allowing leaders to evaluate the effectiveness of their strategies, identify areas for enhancement, and make necessary adjustments, driving ongoing growth and development.

Leaders should ensure that their actions reflect the organisation's core values, as consistency between actions and values reinforces the organisation's identity and builds credibility, with employees and stakeholders more likely to support initiatives that align with these values. Actions should be guided by the organisation's mission, prioritising initiatives that advance the mission and contribute to its fulfillment, ensuring resources are used effectively and strategically. Aligned actions create a stable and reliable environment, as leaders consistently acting in accordance with their values and mission foster trust and confidence within the organisation, enabling employees to perform at their best and supporting long-term success.

Taking decisive action builds credibility, as leaders who follow through on their plans demonstrate commitment and reliability, strengthening relationships with employees, customers, and stakeholders. Action-oriented leadership promotes accountability, holding leaders and team members accountable for their performance, driving focus and effort towards achieving results. Recognising the power of action empowers teams to take initiative and contribute to the organisation's success, with leaders who encourage action and provide support creating an environment where employees feel capable and motivated to make a difference. Action-oriented strategies drive sustainable growth, ensuring that the organisation remains dynamic and adaptable, supporting long-term resilience and success.

Practical Strategies for Recognising the Power of Action

Setting Clear Objectives: Leaders should set clear, actionable objectives that align with the organisation's vision and mission. This involves defining specific, measurable, achievable, relevant, and time-bound (SMART) goals.

Creating Action Plans: Developing detailed action plans helps translate strategies into tangible steps. Leaders should outline the tasks, timelines, and resources required for implementation. Action plans provide a roadmap for achieving objectives.

Encouraging Initiative: Leaders should encourage employees to take initiative and contribute to the implementation of strategies. This involves fostering a culture of empowerment, where team members feel confident in their abilities and supported in their efforts.

Monitoring Progress: Regularly monitoring progress ensures that actions are aligned with goals and values. Leaders should establish metrics and key performance indicators (KPIs) to track progress and evaluate the effectiveness of their strategies.

Providing Feedback and Support: Continuous feedback and support help teams stay on track and improve their performance. Leaders should offer constructive feedback, celebrate successes, and provide guidance when needed. This support fosters a culture of continuous improvement.

Recognising the power of action fosters a sustainable organisational culture where decisive action, alignment with values, and continuous improvement are prioritised, attracting and retaining top talent and contributing to overall success. Teams that prioritise action and alignment with values are more resilient and capable of overcoming challenges, with strong relationships and trust enabling them to work together effectively in any situation. Leaders who recognise the power of action can navigate uncertainties with strategic agility, ensuring decisions are made with long-term sustainability in mind and supporting the organisation's resilience. Organisations that consistently prioritise action-oriented strategies and alignment with values are better positioned for long-term success, providing a strong foundation that supports sustainable growth and resilience.

CREATING A FLOW OF POSITIVE INFLUENCE

> *The relation of the Tao to all the world is like that of the great rivers and seas to the streams from the valleys.*

Lao Tzu's passage beautifully illustrates the interconnectedness of all things, using the metaphor of great rivers and seas with streams from the valleys. Leaders should aim to create a flow of positive influence throughout their organisation, much like the relationship between great rivers and streams. This means fostering a culture of support, collaboration, and continuous learning. By nurturing this flow, leaders can ensure that their organisation remains dynamic, innovative, and interconnected.

Supportive leadership begins with empathy and understanding, with leaders actively listening to their team members and acknowledging their feelings, concerns, and aspirations, which builds trust and fosters a sense of belonging. Leaders should ensure that employees have access to the resources they need to succeed, including providing tools, training, and support to help them achieve their goals, empowering teams to perform at their best by offering assistance and removing obstacles. Supporting employees in maintaining a healthy work-life balance is crucial for their well-being and productivity, so leaders should promote flexible work arrangements, time-off policies, and wellness programmes, enhancing overall job satisfaction and engagement.

Collaboration thrives when teamwork is encouraged, so leaders should create opportunities for team members to work together on projects and initiatives, enhancing problem-solving, creativity, and innovation. Strong relationships within the organisation are the foundation of effective collaboration, so leaders should foster an environment where team members feel connected and valued, building relationships through team-building activities, social events, and open communication, strengthening the sense of community. Diversity and inclusion enrich collaboration by bringing diverse perspectives and ideas, so leaders should promote an inclusive culture where everyone feels welcome and respected, enhancing creativity and driving better decision-making.

A growth mindset encourages continuous learning and development, so leaders should inspire employees to embrace challenges, learn from failures, and persist in the face of obstacles, fostering resilience and a commitment to personal and professional growth. Continuous learning is supported by access to educational resources and opportunities, so leaders should offer training programmes, workshops, and mentorship opportunities, investing in employee development to enhance skills and foster a culture of lifelong learning. Feedback and reflection are essential for continuous improvement, so leaders should create channels for regular feedback and encourage employees to reflect on their experiences, helping to identify areas for growth and reinforcing a commitment to excellence.

A supportive and collaborative culture increases employee engagement and motivation, as employees who feel valued and empowered are more committed to their work and the organisation's success. Collaboration and continuous learning foster innovation and creativity, with leaders encouraging diverse perspectives and ideas to create an environment where new solutions and breakthroughs can flourish. A flow of positive influence enhances organisational resilience, as supportive relationships, a collaborative spirit, and a commitment to learning enable the organisation to adapt and thrive in the face of challenges. Organisations that prioritise positive influence and interconnectedness achieve better overall performance, with employees becoming more productive, engaged, and satisfied, driving the organisation's success.

Practical Strategies for Creating a Flow of Positive Influence

Implementing Mentorship Programmes: Mentorship programmes support continuous learning and personal growth. Leaders should pair experienced employees with newer team members, fostering knowledge sharing and professional development.

Encouraging Cross-Functional Teams: Cross-functional teams bring together diverse skills and perspectives. Leaders should create opportunities for employees from different departments to collaborate on projects. This approach enhances innovation and strengthens relationships.

Providing Regular Training and Development: Regular training and development opportunities ensure that employees continue to grow and evolve. Leaders should offer courses, workshops, and certification programmes that align with employees' career goals and the organisation's needs.

Promoting Open Communication Channels: Open communication channels foster transparency and trust. Leaders should create platforms for regular feedback, discussions, and idea-sharing. This openness ensures that everyone's voice is heard and valued.

Celebrating Successes and Milestones: Recognising and celebrating successes reinforces positive behaviours and motivates employees. Leaders should highlight individual and team achievements, expressing gratitude and appreciation for their contributions.

Creating a flow of positive influence fosters a sustainable organisational culture where support, collaboration, and continuous learning are prioritised, attracting and retaining top talent and contributing to overall success. Teams that prioritise positive influence and interconnectedness are more resilient and capable of overcoming challenges, with strong relationships and trust enabling them to work together effectively in any situation. Leaders who create a flow of positive influence can navigate uncertainties with strategic agility, ensuring decisions are made with long-term sustainability in mind and supporting the organisation's resilience. Organisations that consistently prioritise positive influence and interconnectedness are better positioned for long-term success, providing a strong foundation that supports sustainable growth and resilience.

CHAPTER 33 – INNER STRENGTH

Chapter 33 of the *Tao Te Ching* offers profound insights into self-awareness, inner strength, contentment, persistence, and the enduring impact of one's actions. Here's how these teachings can be applied to modern-day strategic management:

SELF-AWARENESS & INTELLIGENCE

He who knows other men is discerning; he who knows himself is intelligent.

Lao Tzu's passage highlights the significance of self-awareness and intelligence in effective leadership. In strategic management, self-awareness is a critical quality for effective leadership. Leaders should strive to understand their strengths, weaknesses, motivations, and biases. This self-knowledge allows them to make more informed decisions, build better relationships, and lead with authenticity. Additionally, understanding others and fostering empathy enables leaders to effectively manage and motivate their teams.

Self-aware leaders recognise their strengths and leverage them to achieve organisational goals, understanding their unique skills and capabilities to contribute effectively and lead their teams with confidence, building on what they do best to drive success. Equally important is acknowledging and addressing weaknesses, as leaders should be honest about their limitations and seek opportunities for growth and improvement, fostering a culture of continuous learning and development within the organisation. By addressing weaknesses, leaders can enhance their effectiveness and build a more balanced approach to leadership.

Self-awareness involves understanding what drives and motivates leaders, so they should reflect on their goals, values, and aspirations to gain clarity on their motivations, aligning their actions with their values to ensure that their leadership is purpose-driven. Leaders should also be aware of their biases and how they influence decision-making, as biases can affect judgment and hinder objectivity. By recognising and challenging their biases, leaders can make more fair and equitable decisions, promoting inclusivity and fostering a culture of respect within the organisation.

Emotional intelligence (EQ) is a key component of self-awareness, enabling leaders to understand and manage their emotions, and recognise and influence the emotions of others, which enhances communication, collaboration, and conflict resolution, leading to stronger relationships. Building better relationships requires active listening, so leaders should listen attentively to their team members, valuing their input and feedback, which fosters trust and respect and ensures that everyone feels heard and appreciated. Providing constructive feedback is essential for growth and development, so leaders should offer specific, actionable feedback that supports employees' progress, and by providing feedback with empathy and encouragement, leaders can build stronger, more supportive relationships.

Authentic leadership involves being true to oneself and leading with integrity, embracing one's values, beliefs, and passions to foster trust and credibility, as employees are more likely to follow leaders who are genuine and transparent. Authentic leaders demonstrate consistency in their actions and decisions, aligning their behaviour with their values and principles to create a stable and predictable environment, which reinforces trust and ensures reliability. They also encourage their team members to be authentic by creating a safe and inclusive environment where employees feel comfortable expressing themselves, fostering a culture of openness and innovation.

Empathy is the ability to understand and share the feelings of others, so leaders should cultivate empathy to build stronger connections with their team members, enhancing communication, collaboration, and morale, and creating a positive work environment. Leaders should also recognise and appreciate the unique qualities and perspectives of each team member, valuing diversity and promoting inclusivity, fostering a culture of respect and cooperation. Understanding others' motivations and needs enables leaders to motivate and inspire their teams effectively, aligning their leadership style with the needs of their team members by providing support, encouragement, and recognition, enhancing engagement and driving performance.

Self-aware leaders make more informed and objective decisions by understanding their strengths, weaknesses, motivations, and biases, which leads to better outcomes and strategic success. Self-awareness and empathy enhance relationships within the organisation, as leaders who understand themselves and others can build trust, respect, and collaboration, driving teamwork and organisational cohesion. Leading with authenticity builds trust and credibility, with leaders who are true to themselves and transparent in their actions creating a stable and reliable environment, fostering loyalty and commitment among employees. Understanding and empathising with team members enables leaders to manage and motivate their teams effectively, aligning leadership with the needs of their team to enhance engagement, performance, and overall satisfaction.

Practical Strategies for Developing Self-Awareness & Intelligence

Engaging in Self-Reflection: Regular self-reflection helps leaders gain insight into their strengths, weaknesses, motivations, and biases. Leaders should set aside time for introspection, journaling, and seeking feedback from trusted colleagues.

Seeking Feedback and Mentorship: Seeking feedback from others provides valuable perspectives on areas for improvement. Leaders should encourage honest feedback from peers, mentors, and team members. Mentorship offers guidance and support for personal and professional growth.

Practising Mindfulness: Mindfulness practices, such as meditation and deep breathing, enhance self-awareness and emotional regulation. Leaders should incorporate mindfulness into their daily routines to stay present and centred.

Investing in Personal Development: Continuous learning and development are essential for self-awareness and intelligence. Leaders should pursue opportunities for personal growth, such as attending workshops, reading books, and participating in training programmes.

Cultivating Empathy and Active Listening: Cultivating empathy and active listening improves relationships and communication. Leaders should practise active listening, seeking to understand others' perspectives and emotions. Empathy strengthens connections and fosters a positive work environment.

Developing self-awareness and intelligence fosters a sustainable organisational culture where authenticity, empathy, and continuous improvement are valued, attracting and retaining top talent and contributing to overall success. Teams that prioritise self-awareness and empathy are more resilient and capable of overcoming challenges, with strong relationships and trust enabling them to work together effectively in any situation. Leaders who develop self-awareness and intelligence can navigate uncertainties with strategic agility, ensuring decisions are made with long-term sustainability in mind and supporting the organisation's resilience. Organisations that consistently prioritise self-awareness and intelligence in leadership are better positioned for long-term success, providing a strong foundation that supports sustainable growth and resilience.

INNER STRENGTH & SELF-MASTERY

He who overcomes others is strong; he who overcomes himself is mighty.

Lao Tzu's passage highlights the profound significance of inner strength and self-mastery. True leadership strength comes from within. Leaders who master their own emotions, impulses, and behaviours exhibit greater control and resilience. This inner strength helps leaders navigate challenges with poise and maintain a clear focus on their goals. By cultivating self-discipline and emotional intelligence, leaders can inspire and influence their teams more effectively.

Mastering one's emotions is a cornerstone of self-mastery, as leaders should develop the ability to manage their emotions, especially in stressful or challenging situations, recognising emotional triggers, staying calm, and responding thoughtfully rather than reactively, which enhances decision-making and leadership effectiveness. Impulse control is crucial for maintaining consistency and discipline, so leaders should practise mindfulness and self-awareness to recognise and manage impulsive reactions, taking a moment to pause and reflect before acting to make more deliberate and strategic choices that align with their long-term goals. Consistency in behaviour builds trust and reliability, so leaders should strive to align their actions with their values and principles, demonstrating integrity and dependability, reinforcing their commitment to their mission and inspiring confidence in their team.

Self-discipline begins with setting clear personal goals, with leaders defining specific, measurable, achievable, relevant, and time-bound (SMART) goals for their personal and professional development, providing direction and motivation for continuous growth. Establishing routines and positive habits supports self-discipline, so leaders should create daily practices that promote productivity, well-being, and self-improvement, such as regular exercise, meditation, reading, and time management techniques. Accountability is essential for maintaining self-discipline, so leaders should seek accountability from mentors, peers, or accountability partners who can provide support and feedback, with regular check-ins and progress reviews helping leaders stay on track and committed to their goals.

Self-awareness is the foundation of emotional intelligence, enabling leaders to understand their emotions, strengths, and areas for improvement, which helps them manage their reactions and make informed decisions. Empathy involves understanding and sharing the feelings of others, allowing leaders to connect with their team members and recognise their needs and perspectives, fostering trust, collaboration, and a positive work environment. Social skills encompass the ability to communicate effectively, build relationships, and navigate social complexities, so leaders should develop strong communication skills, active listening, and conflict resolution abilities, enhancing teamwork and organisational cohesion.

Inner strength and self-mastery enhance resilience, enabling leaders to navigate challenges with poise and determination, adapt to change, recover from setbacks, and maintain a positive outlook. Self-disciplined leaders maintain a clear focus on their goals, avoiding distractions and staying committed to their vision, driving strategic decision-making and sustained progress. Leaders who exhibit self-mastery inspire and influence their teams more effectively, managing emotions, demonstrating consistency, and leading with integrity, which motivates others to follow their example. Emotional intelligence and self-awareness improve decision-making by enabling leaders to consider diverse perspectives and respond thoughtfully, leading to more balanced and effective outcomes.

Practical Strategies for Cultivating Inner Strength & Self-Mastery

Engaging in Self-Reflection: Regular self-reflection helps leaders gain insight into their emotions, behaviours, and progress. Leaders should set aside time for introspection, journaling, and seeking feedback from trusted colleagues.

Practising Mindfulness: Mindfulness practices, such as meditation and deep breathing, enhance emotional regulation and self-awareness. Leaders should incorporate mindfulness into their daily routines to stay present and centred.

Setting Boundaries: Setting boundaries helps leaders manage their time and energy effectively. Leaders should establish clear boundaries for work and personal life, ensuring that they allocate time for self-care, family, and personal interests.

Pursuing Continuous Learning: Continuous learning and development are essential for self-mastery. Leaders should pursue opportunities for personal growth, such as attending workshops, reading books, and participating in training programmes.

Building a Support Network: A support network provides encouragement and accountability. Leaders should cultivate relationships with mentors, peers, and friends who can offer guidance, feedback, and support.

Cultivating inner strength and self-mastery fosters a sustainable organisational culture where resilience, self-discipline, and emotional intelligence are valued, attracting and retaining top talent and contributing to overall success. Teams that prioritise inner strength and self-mastery are more resilient and capable of overcoming challenges, with strong relationships and trust enabling them to work together effectively in any situation. Leaders who cultivate inner strength and self-mastery can navigate uncertainties with strategic agility, ensuring decisions are made with long-term sustainability in mind and supporting the organisation's resilience. Organisations that consistently prioritise inner strength and self-mastery in leadership are better positioned for long-term success, providing a strong foundation that supports sustainable growth and resilience.

CONTENTMENT & SATISFACTION

He who is satisfied with his lot is rich.

Lao Tzu's passage highlights the profound importance of contentment and satisfaction. Contentment and satisfaction are essential for sustainable success. Leaders who appreciate what they have and focus on the present are less likely to be driven by relentless ambition or external validation. This mindset fosters a positive work environment and encourages a healthy work-life balance. Leaders who model contentment can inspire their teams to find fulfillment and motivation in their roles.

Leaders who practise gratitude appreciate their achievements, resources, and relationships, helping them stay grounded and positive even in challenging times. By regularly acknowledging the good things in their lives, leaders can maintain a balanced perspective and avoid the pitfalls of excessive ambition. Contentment involves living in the present moment and appreciating what you have now, allowing leaders to enjoy their successes and learn from their experiences. This focus on the here and now reduces stress and anxiety about future uncertainties, enabling leaders to make more thoughtful and deliberate decisions.

While ambition drives progress and growth, it must be balanced with contentment to avoid burnout and dissatisfaction. Leaders who balance ambition with contentment can set realistic goals and appreciate their progress along the way. Additionally, leaders should seek fulfillment from within rather than relying on external validation, as chasing accolades and approval can lead to an unending cycle of comparison and dissatisfaction. By finding contentment in their own values and accomplishments, leaders can cultivate genuine self-worth and confidence.

Leaders who model contentment prioritise the well-being of their team members, promoting work-life balance, encouraging self-care, and providing support for mental health, which enhances employee satisfaction and productivity. Contentment does not mean complacency; leaders should encourage a growth mindset, where team members feel motivated to learn and improve while appreciating their current progress, fostering resilience, innovation, and continuous improvement. Leaders who demonstrate contentment and satisfaction build trust and respect within their teams, as employees are more likely to trust leaders who are genuine and balanced, enhancing collaboration and organisational cohesion.

Leaders who model contentment inspire their teams to find fulfillment in their roles by demonstrating appreciation for their work and achievements, setting a positive example that encourages employees to adopt a similar mindset, leading to greater job satisfaction and motivation. Recognising and celebrating achievements fosters a sense of accomplishment and fulfillment, as leaders regularly acknowledge individual and team successes, expressing gratitude and appreciation, which boosts morale and motivates employees to strive for excellence. Providing opportunities for growth and development helps employees find fulfillment in their roles, with leaders offering training, mentorship, and career advancement opportunities, showing they value their team members' contributions and potential.

Contentment and satisfaction contribute to sustainable success by promoting balance, well-being, and genuine fulfillment, with leaders who appreciate their progress and achievements building a stable foundation for long-term growth and resilience. A culture of contentment and satisfaction fosters positivity and well-being within the organisation, making employees more likely to feel valued, motivated, and engaged, which attracts and retains top talent. Leaders who are content and satisfied are better equipped to navigate challenges with composure and confidence, enhancing their ability to lead effectively in times of uncertainty and change. Contentment and satisfaction strengthen relationships within the organisation, with leaders who demonstrate appreciation and balance building trust and respect with their team members, driving collaboration and organisational cohesion.

Practical Strategies for Cultivating Contentment & Satisfaction

Practising Gratitude: Regularly practising gratitude helps leaders appreciate their achievements and resources. Leaders should take time each day to reflect on what they are thankful for, whether through journaling, meditation, or expressing gratitude to others.

Setting Realistic Goals: Setting realistic and achievable goals promotes contentment by providing a sense of direction and purpose. Leaders should establish goals that align with their values and resources, celebrating progress along the way.

Encouraging Work-Life Balance: Encouraging work-life balance supports employees' well-being and satisfaction. Leaders should promote flexible work arrangements, time-off policies, and wellness programmes. A balanced approach enhances overall job satisfaction and engagement.

Recognising and Celebrating Successes: Regularly recognising and celebrating successes fosters a culture of appreciation. Leaders should highlight individual and team achievements, expressing gratitude and appreciation for their contributions.

Fostering a Positive Mindset: Fostering a positive mindset helps leaders and employees find fulfillment in their roles. Leaders should encourage self-care, mindfulness, and a focus on the present moment. A positive mindset enhances overall well-being and satisfaction.

Cultivating contentment and satisfaction fosters a sustainable organisational culture where balance, well-being, and fulfillment are valued, attracting and retaining top talent and contributing to overall success. Teams that prioritise contentment and satisfaction are more resilient and capable of overcoming challenges, with strong relationships and trust enabling them to work together effectively in any situation. Leaders who cultivate contentment and satisfaction can navigate uncertainties with strategic agility, ensuring decisions are made with long-term sustainability in mind and supporting the organisation's resilience. Organisations that consistently prioritise contentment and satisfaction in leadership are better positioned for long-term success, providing a strong foundation that supports sustainable growth and resilience.

PERSISTENCE & DETERMINATION

He who goes on acting with energy has a (firm) will.

Lao Tzu's passage emphasises the critical role of persistence and determination in achieving long-term success. Persistence and determination are key traits for achieving long-term success. Leaders should maintain a strong will and continue to act with energy and purpose, even in the face of obstacles. This determination helps leaders overcome challenges and stay committed to their vision. By demonstrating persistence, leaders can motivate their teams to persevere and achieve their goals.

Determination begins with setting clear and achievable goals, where leaders define their vision and establish specific, measurable, achievable, relevant, and time-bound (SMART) goals, providing direction and motivation to stay focused and committed. Resilience, the ability to bounce back from setbacks and continue pursuing goals despite difficulties, is essential; leaders should develop a resilient mindset, viewing challenges as opportunities for growth and learning, helping them maintain determination and persist through adversity. A positive attitude is also crucial for maintaining determination; leaders should focus on the positives, celebrate small wins, and stay optimistic about the future, fostering perseverance and inspiring confidence in others.

Leaders should prioritise their physical and mental well-being to stay energised by maintaining a healthy lifestyle, getting regular exercise, eating nutritious food, and ensuring adequate rest, allowing them to approach tasks with vigour and enthusiasm. Acting with purpose means aligning actions with core values and the organisation's mission, ensuring decisions and efforts reflect their values and contribute to their long-term vision, providing a sense of purpose and fulfillment that drives determination. Focus is crucial for effective leadership, so leaders should minimise distractions, prioritise tasks, and concentrate on what truly matters, helping them channel their energy towards meaningful activities that advance their goals.

Challenges are an inevitable part of any journey, so leaders should face obstacles head-on, analysing problems and developing strategies to overcome them, addressing challenges proactively to maintain momentum and progress towards their goals. Failures provide valuable learning experiences, and leaders should embrace them as opportunities to gain insights and improve, refining their strategies and enhancing their chances of success. Overcoming challenges often requires support and collaboration, so leaders should build strong relationships with their teams, seeking input and assistance when needed, as collaborative efforts enhance problem-solving and drive collective success.

Leaders who demonstrate determination inspire their teams to do the same by consistently showing commitment and perseverance, setting a positive example that motivates others to stay focused and work towards shared goals. Encouragement and support boost morale and motivation, so leaders should recognise their team members' efforts, provide positive reinforcement, and offer assistance when needed, helping teams stay resilient and committed. Celebrating milestones and achievements fosters a sense of accomplishment and progress, so leaders should regularly acknowledge individual and team successes, expressing gratitude and appreciation, which reinforces the importance of persistence and motivates teams to continue striving for excellence.

Persistence and determination are essential for achieving long-term success, as leaders who stay committed to their vision and goals can overcome obstacles and drive sustained progress, ensuring the organisation remains focused and resilient. Leaders who exhibit persistence and determination inspire confidence and trust within their teams, with employees more likely to follow and support leaders who demonstrate unwavering commitment and resilience, enhancing collaboration and organisational cohesion. Persistence and determination contribute to organisational resilience, as leaders foster a culture of perseverance, ensuring the organisation can adapt to change and navigate challenges effectively, supporting long-term stability and growth. Persistent leaders are committed to continuous improvement, consistently seeking ways to enhance performance and achieve goals, driving innovation and excellence, and ensuring the organisation remains competitive and dynamic.

Practical Strategies for Cultivating Persistence & Determination

Setting SMART Goals: Leaders should set SMART goals that provide clear direction and motivation. These goals should be specific, measurable, achievable, relevant, and time-bound. SMART goals help leaders stay focused and committed.

Developing a Resilient Mindset: Developing a resilient mindset involves viewing challenges as opportunities for growth. Leaders should cultivate resilience by practising mindfulness, reflecting on experiences, and maintaining a positive outlook.

Prioritising Well-Being: Prioritising physical and mental well-being is essential for staying energised and focused. Leaders should maintain a healthy lifestyle, get regular exercise, and ensure adequate rest. Well-being supports sustained determination and energy.

Building Strong Relationships: Building strong relationships with team members enhances support and collaboration. Leaders should foster trust, communication, and mutual respect within their teams. Strong relationships drive collective perseverance and success.

Seeking Feedback and Learning: Seeking feedback and learning from experiences enhance growth and improvement. Leaders should encourage feedback from peers, mentors, and team members. Continuous learning and adaptation ensure sustained progress and achievement.

Cultivating persistence and determination fosters a sustainable organisational culture where resilience, commitment, and continuous improvement are valued, attracting and retaining top talent and contributing to overall success. Teams that prioritise persistence and determination are more resilient and capable of overcoming challenges, with strong relationships and trust enabling them to work together effectively in any situation. Leaders who cultivate persistence and determination can navigate uncertainties with strategic agility, ensuring decisions are made with long-term sustainability in mind and supporting the organisation's resilience. Organisations that consistently prioritise persistence and determination in leadership are better positioned for long-term success, providing a strong foundation that supports sustainable growth and resilience.

FULFILLING RESPONSIBILITIES & ACHIEVING LONGEVITY

He who does not fail in the requirements of his position, continues long; he who dies and yet does not perish, has longevity.

Lao Tzu's passage emphasises the enduring impact of fulfilling responsibilities with diligence and integrity. Leaders who fulfil their responsibilities with diligence and integrity build a lasting legacy. Consistently meeting the requirements of their position ensures stability and long-term success for the organisation. Additionally, leaders who make a positive impact through their actions and principles leave a lasting influence, even after they are no longer in their role. This enduring impact is a testament to the importance of ethical and responsible leadership.

Effective leadership begins with a clear understanding of the role and its responsibilities, so leaders should familiarise themselves with the expectations, duties, and goals associated with their position to prioritise their efforts and focus on what matters most. Integrity is the cornerstone of responsible leadership, and leaders should uphold ethical standards, make principled decisions, and act with honesty and transparency to build trust and credibility, which are essential for long-term success. Consistently meeting the requirements of the position requires a commitment to excellence, with leaders striving for high standards in their performance and continuously seeking ways to improve and excel, setting a positive example for the entire organisation.

Stability is achieved by building strong foundations within the organisation, focusing on creating robust systems, processes, and structures that support sustainable growth, providing a stable platform for future success. A positive organisational culture enhances stability and long-term success, so leaders should cultivate a culture of respect, collaboration, and continuous improvement, attracting and retaining top talent, and fostering a supportive and engaged workforce. Long-term success requires strategic planning and foresight, with leaders developing and implementing plans that align with the organisation's vision and goals, and by anticipating future challenges and opportunities, they can position the organisation for sustained growth and resilience.

Leaders who embody and promote core values such as integrity, empathy, and excellence leave a lasting legacy that continues to influence the organisation long after they have moved on, shaping the organisation's culture and guiding its actions. Investing in the development of others through mentorship and support ensures a lasting influence, as mentored individuals go on to mentor others, creating a ripple effect of positive impact. Leaders who drive positive change through their actions and principles, whether through innovation, social responsibility, or ethical practices, inspire others to follow their example, extending their positive influence beyond the organisation and contributing to the broader community and industry.

Ethical and responsible leadership builds trust and credibility within the organisation and with external stakeholders, fostering collaboration, loyalty, and engagement. Leaders who act with integrity and fulfil their responsibilities enhance the organisation's reputation, attracting customers, partners, and top talent, contributing to overall success. Responsible leadership ensures sustainable success by promoting stability, resilience, and continuous improvement, creating a strong foundation for enduring growth and achievement. Furthermore, ethical and responsible leadership fosters a positive organisational culture where values, respect, and excellence are prioritised, supporting employee well-being, engagement, and productivity.

Practical Strategies for Fulfilling Responsibilities & Achieving Longevity

Defining Clear Expectations: Leaders should define clear expectations for themselves and their team members. This involves setting specific goals, establishing performance standards, and communicating responsibilities. Clear expectations provide direction and accountability.

Upholding Ethical Standards: Upholding ethical standards requires a commitment to integrity and transparency. Leaders should establish and enforce codes of conduct, provide ethics training, and model ethical behaviour. This commitment to ethics builds trust and credibility.

Fostering Continuous Improvement: Continuous improvement is essential for long-term success. Leaders should encourage a growth mindset, support professional development, and implement processes for feedback and evaluation. This focus on improvement drives excellence and innovation.

Building Strong Relationships: Building strong relationships with employees, stakeholders, and the community enhances influence and impact. Leaders should foster trust, communication, and collaboration, creating a network of support and mutual respect.

Mentoring and Developing Others: Mentoring and developing others ensures a lasting legacy. Leaders should provide guidance, support, and opportunities for growth, helping their team members achieve their potential. This investment in people creates a positive ripple effect.

Fulfilling responsibilities and achieving longevity fosters a sustainable organisational culture where integrity, excellence, and continuous improvement are valued, attracting and retaining top talent and contributing to overall success. Teams that prioritise ethical and responsible leadership are more resilient and capable of overcoming challenges, with strong relationships and trust enabling them to work together effectively in any situation. Leaders who fulfil their responsibilities with diligence and integrity can navigate uncertainties with strategic agility, ensuring decisions are made with long-term sustainability in mind and supporting the organisation's resilience. Organisations that consistently prioritise ethical and responsible leadership are better positioned for enduring success, providing a strong foundation that supports sustainable growth and resilience.

CHAPTER 34 – AUTONOMY

Chapter 34 of the *Tao Te Ching* emphasises the pervasive and selfless nature of the Tao, highlighting the importance of humility, subtlety, and the natural flow of achievements. Here's how these teachings can be applied to modern-day strategic management:

RECOGNISING THE UBIQUITY & INFLUENCE OF CORE PRINCIPLES

All-pervading is the Great Tao! It may be found on the left hand and on the right.

Lao Tzu's passage underscores the omnipresence and profound influence of the Tao, or core principles. In strategic management, leaders should recognise the importance of core principles and values that permeate every aspect of the organisation. These guiding principles serve as the foundation for decision-making, culture, and operations. By consistently aligning actions with these core values, leaders can create a cohesive and resilient organisation that thrives in various circumstances.

Core principles provide a moral compass for ethical decision-making, ensuring leaders' decisions align with values that promote fairness, integrity, and transparency, which builds trust and credibility within the organisation and with external stakeholders. Consistency in decision-making is achieved when grounded in core values, making leaders' actions predictable and reliable, fostering stability and trust among employees, customers, and partners. In complex and uncertain situations, core principles serve as a reference point, guiding leaders' actions and helping them maintain integrity and clarity in decision-making, even when faced with difficult choices.

Core principles define the identity and character of the organisation, articulating what it stands for and aspires to achieve. Leaders should communicate these values clearly and consistently, ensuring they are integrated into all aspects of the organisation, fostering a positive work environment where employees feel connected and committed to their work, enhancing job satisfaction, engagement, and collaboration. Additionally, core principles that prioritise respect, equality, and inclusion create a diverse and inclusive culture, and leaders should ensure these values are reflected in their policies, practices, and interactions, attracting diverse talent and fostering innovation and creativity.

Core principles drive operational excellence by establishing standards of quality and performance, which leaders should embed into their processes, procedures, and performance metrics to ensure consistent and high-quality outcomes. Customer relationships are strengthened when an organisation's actions reflect its core principles, with leaders prioritising values such as honesty, respect, and customer-centricity in their interactions with customers, building trust and loyalty and enhancing satisfaction and retention. Sustainable growth is achieved when core principles guide strategic initiatives, with leaders developing and implementing strategies that align with their values, ensuring growth is ethical, responsible, and long-lasting, supporting the organisation's resilience and long-term success.

A cohesive organisation is built on a shared vision and common values, with leaders ensuring all employees understand and are committed to the organisation's core principles, fostering collaboration, teamwork, and a sense of purpose. Core principles provide a stable foundation for adaptability and resilience, guiding leaders' actions and decisions in the face of change or adversity, enabling the organisation to navigate challenges and seize opportunities. Empowering employees to act in alignment with core principles fosters autonomy and accountability, with leaders encouraging team members to make decisions that reflect the organisation's values, providing guidance and support when needed, enhancing performance and innovation.

Recognising and adhering to core principles enhances trust and credibility within the organisation and with external stakeholders, which is essential for successful leadership as it fosters collaboration, loyalty, and engagement. A culture grounded in core principles promotes a positive and supportive work environment where employees feel valued, motivated, and aligned with the organisation's mission, attracting and retaining top talent. Aligning actions with core principles ensures sustainable success by promoting ethical conduct, operational excellence, and long-term growth, creating a strong foundation for enduring achievement. A cohesive organisation is more effective and resilient, and core principles create a sense of unity and shared purpose, enhancing teamwork and organisational performance.

Practical Strategies for Aligning Actions with Core Principles

Communicating Core Principles: Leaders should communicate core principles clearly and consistently. This involves incorporating these values into the organisation's mission statement, policies, and everyday communications. Clear communication ensures that everyone understands and embraces the organisation's values.

Embedding Values into Policies and Practices: Embedding core principles into organisational policies and practices ensures that these values guide actions and decisions. Leaders should review and update policies to reflect the organisation's values, promoting ethical and responsible behaviour.

Providing Training and Development: Training and development programmes help employees understand and apply core principles in their work. Leaders should offer workshops, courses, and resources that emphasise the importance of values and ethical conduct.

Recognising and Rewarding Value-Driven Behaviour: Recognising and rewarding employees who demonstrate alignment with core principles reinforces their importance. Leaders should highlight examples of value-driven behaviour and provide incentives for ethical and responsible actions.

Encouraging Feedback and Reflection: Encouraging feedback and reflection helps leaders and employees assess their alignment with core principles. Leaders should create opportunities for feedback, discussions, and self-assessment, fostering continuous improvement and alignment.

Recognising the ubiquity and influence of core principles fosters a sustainable organisational culture where values, ethics, and excellence are prioritised, attracting and retaining top talent and contributing to overall success. Teams that prioritise core principles are more resilient and capable of overcoming challenges, with strong relationships and trust enabling them to work together effectively in any situation. Leaders who align actions with core principles can navigate uncertainties with strategic agility, ensuring decisions are made with long-term sustainability in mind and supporting the organisation's resilience. Organisations that consistently prioritise core principles and values are better positioned for long-term success, providing a strong foundation that supports sustainable growth and resilience.

LEADING WITH SELFLESSNESS & HUMILITY

> *All things depend on it for their production, which it gives to them, not one refusing obedience to it. When its work is accomplished, it does not claim the name of having done it.*

Lao Tzu's passage highlights the power and virtue of selfless leadership. Effective leaders understand the power of selfless leadership. They focus on the success of the organisation and their teams rather than seeking personal recognition or accolades. By leading with humility and allowing the achievements to speak for themselves, leaders can foster a culture of collaboration, respect, and shared success. This selflessness creates an environment where everyone feels valued and motivated to contribute their best.

Selfless leaders prioritise collective goals over personal ambitions by aligning their efforts with the organisation's mission and ensuring their actions contribute to the greater good, creating a sense of shared purpose and direction. Selfless leadership also involves actively supporting team members by providing the resources, guidance, and encouragement necessary for their success, demonstrating a commitment to their growth and development and fostering a positive and empowering environment. Recognising and celebrating team achievements, rather than seeking personal accolades, is a hallmark of selfless leadership, as leaders highlight the contributions of team members and acknowledge their successes, reinforcing the value of teamwork and collaboration.

Humility involves recognising that leadership is about serving others rather than seeking personal glory, with humble leaders acknowledging their limitations, seeking input from others, and being open to learning and growth, fostering trust and respect within the organisation. Leaders who share credit for successes build stronger relationships with their teams by attributing achievements to the collective efforts of the team, which motivates team members and strengthens their commitment to the organisation. Humble leaders regularly engage in self-reflection to assess their actions and behaviours, helping them stay grounded, recognise areas for improvement, and align their efforts with their values, enhancing self-awareness and fostering continuous personal development.

Open communication is essential for collaboration and respect, so leaders should create an environment where team members feel comfortable sharing ideas, feedback, and concerns, promoting transparency, trust, and mutual respect. Inclusivity is a key aspect of a respectful and collaborative culture, and leaders should ensure all team members feel valued and included, regardless of their background or position, as promoting diversity and inclusivity enhances creativity and innovation. Selfless leaders facilitate teamwork by encouraging collaboration and cooperation, creating opportunities for team members to work together on projects and initiatives, fostering a sense of unity and shared purpose, which leads to better problem-solving and more innovative solutions.

Empowering employees involves giving them the autonomy and resources to excel in their roles, with leaders trusting their team members to make decisions and take ownership of their work, fostering a sense of responsibility and motivation. Recognising the contributions of all team members reinforces the value of their efforts, with leaders regularly acknowledging individual and team accomplishments, expressing gratitude and appreciation, which boosts morale and encourages continued excellence. Selfless leaders invest in the growth and development of their team members by providing training, mentorship, and career advancement opportunities, supporting professional development to help their teams reach their full potential and achieve long-term success.

Leading with selflessness and humility increases employee engagement, as team members who feel valued and supported are more motivated and committed to their work, driving higher levels of productivity and job satisfaction. Selfless and humble leadership fosters trust and respect within the organisation, with employees more likely to trust leaders who prioritise the collective good and share credit for successes, strengthening relationships and collaboration. A culture of selflessness and humility promotes positivity and collaboration, creating an environment where respect, inclusivity, and shared success are prioritised, attracting and retaining top talent. Selfless and humble leadership ensures sustainable success by promoting collaboration, continuous improvement, and shared goals, creating a strong foundation for long-term achievement by prioritising the well-being and growth of teams.

Practical Strategies for Leading with Selflessness & Humility

Communicating a Shared Vision: Leaders should communicate a shared vision that emphasises collective goals and values. This vision should inspire and unite team members, fostering a sense of shared purpose and direction.

Modelling Humble Behaviour: Leaders should model humble behaviour by acknowledging their limitations, seeking input from others, and sharing credit for successes. This modelling sets a positive example for the entire organisation.

Providing Support and Resources: Leaders should provide the support and resources necessary for their teams to succeed. This includes offering guidance, training, and encouragement, as well as removing obstacles that hinder progress.

Encouraging Collaboration: Encouraging collaboration involves creating opportunities for team members to work together and share ideas. Leaders should facilitate teamwork through projects, brainstorming sessions, and cross-functional initiatives.

Recognising and Celebrating Achievements: Regularly recognising and celebrating achievements fosters a culture of appreciation and shared success. Leaders should highlight the contributions of individual team members and the collective efforts of the team.

Leading with selflessness and humility fosters a sustainable organisational culture where collaboration, respect, and shared success are valued, attracting and retaining top talent and contributing to overall success. Teams that prioritise selflessness and humility are more resilient and capable of overcoming challenges, with strong relationships and trust enabling them to work together effectively in any situation. Leaders who lead with selflessness and humility can navigate uncertainties with strategic agility, ensuring decisions are made with long-term sustainability in mind and supporting the organisation's resilience. Organisations that consistently prioritise selflessness and humility in leadership are better positioned for long-term success, providing a strong foundation that supports sustainable growth and resilience.

EMPOWERING TEAMS & ENCOURAGING AUTONOMY

> *It clothes all things as with a garment, and makes no assumption of being their lord.*

Lao Tzu's passage beautifully illustrates the importance of nurturing and empowering others without exerting control over them. Leaders should empower their teams by providing them with the resources and support they need while allowing them the autonomy to perform their roles. This approach fosters creativity, innovation, and ownership among employees. By stepping back and trusting their teams, leaders enable individuals to take initiative and drive the organisation forward.

Empowerment begins with providing team members with the tools and resources they need to succeed, ensuring they have access to the latest technology, equipment, and information required for their roles, creating a solid foundation for productivity and innovation. Continuous learning and development are crucial, so leaders should invest in training programmes, workshops, and professional development opportunities that enhance employees' skills and knowledge, demonstrating a commitment to their growth and success. While autonomy is important, so is guidance and mentorship, with leaders offering support and advice to help employees navigate challenges and achieve their goals, fostering a culture of learning and development, enabling individuals to reach their full potential.

Trust is the cornerstone of autonomy, so leaders should trust their team members to make decisions and manage their tasks independently, empowering them to take ownership of their work and fostering a sense of responsibility and accountability. Providing autonomy does not mean a lack of direction; leaders should set clear expectations and define goals to ensure alignment with the organisation's vision and objectives, giving employees a framework within which to operate autonomously. Flexibility is key to fostering autonomy, and leaders should offer flexible work arrangements, such as remote work options and flexible hours, to accommodate employees' needs, empowering team members to manage their work-life balance effectively and enhancing overall job satisfaction.

Autonomy fosters a culture of experimentation and innovation, with leaders encouraging employees to explore new ideas, take risks, and experiment with different approaches, driving continuous improvement and creativity. A safe and supportive environment is essential for innovation, so leaders should create a culture where employees feel comfortable sharing their ideas and taking risks without fear of failure or retribution, fostering psychological safety and bold thinking. Recognising and celebrating innovative efforts reinforces the importance of creativity, with leaders acknowledging and rewarding employees who contribute new ideas and drive innovation, motivating others to pursue innovative solutions.

Empowerment involves granting employees the authority to make decisions related to their roles, with leaders delegating decision-making power and trusting employees to act in the organisation's best interest, fostering a sense of ownership and initiative. With autonomy comes accountability, and leaders should encourage employees to take responsibility for their actions and outcomes, driving performance and commitment to achieving their goals. Collaboration enhances ownership and initiative, so leaders should create opportunities for team members to collaborate on projects and share their expertise, fostering a sense of collective ownership and shared success.

Empowerment and autonomy increase employee engagement, as employees who feel trusted and valued are more motivated and committed to their work, driving higher levels of productivity and job satisfaction. Autonomy fosters creativity and innovation by encouraging experimentation and risk-taking, enabling employees to explore new ideas and develop innovative solutions that drive organisational success. Empowered teams are more agile and capable of adapting to change, with autonomy allowing employees to respond quickly to challenges and opportunities, enhancing the organisation's resilience and competitiveness. Empowerment also drives performance and productivity by fostering a sense of ownership and accountability, encouraging employees to take initiative and responsibility for their work, which leads to achieving goals and contributing to the organisation's success.

Practical Strategies for Empowering Teams & Encouraging Autonomy

Communicating Clear Goals and Expectations: Leaders should communicate clear goals and expectations to provide direction while allowing autonomy. This involves defining objectives, performance standards, and desired outcomes.

Offering Continuous Support and Feedback: Continuous support and feedback help employees stay on track and improve their performance. Leaders should provide regular check-ins, constructive feedback, and guidance to support their team members' development.

Encouraging Risk-Taking and Experimentation: Encouraging risk-taking and experimentation drives innovation. Leaders should create a safe environment where employees feel comfortable trying new approaches and learning from failures. This culture of experimentation fosters continuous improvement.

Recognising and Rewarding Achievements: Recognising and rewarding achievements reinforces the importance of autonomy and empowerment. Leaders should celebrate individual and team successes, expressing gratitude and appreciation for their contributions.

Providing Opportunities for Growth: Providing opportunities for growth and development supports empowerment. Leaders should offer training, mentorship, and career advancement opportunities to help employees reach their full potential.

Empowering teams and encouraging autonomy fosters a sustainable organisational culture where creativity, innovation, and ownership are valued, attracting and retaining top talent and contributing to overall success. Teams that prioritise empowerment and autonomy are more resilient and capable of overcoming challenges, with strong relationships and trust enabling them to work together effectively in any situation. Leaders who empower their teams and encourage autonomy can navigate uncertainties with strategic agility, ensuring decisions are made with long-term sustainability in mind and supporting the organisation's resilience. Organisations that consistently prioritise empowerment and autonomy in leadership are better positioned for long-term success, providing a strong foundation that supports sustainable growth and resilience.

EMBRACING SUBTLE & UNDERSTATED INFLUENCE

> All things return (to their root and disappear), and do not know that it is it which presides over their doing so;—it may be named in the greatest things.

Lao Tzu's passage highlights the profound impact of subtle and understated influence. Strategic leaders should embrace a subtle and understated approach to influence. Rather than exerting overt control, they guide and support their teams in a way that allows natural growth and development. This subtle influence helps in creating a positive and sustainable impact without the need for constant oversight or intervention.

Leaders can offer guidance without micromanaging by setting clear goals and providing direction, allowing team members the freedom to determine the best way to achieve those goals, fostering autonomy and empowering employees to take ownership of their work. Subtle influence involves helping team members discover their own strengths and solutions by asking insightful questions, providing resources, and creating opportunities for self-reflection and learning, encouraging individuals to develop their skills and confidence. Leaders can also influence through their own actions and behaviours by exemplifying the values and standards they wish to see in their team, setting a powerful example that often inspires others to emulate the leader's positive qualities more effectively than direct commands.

A supportive environment is essential for natural growth, as leaders should cultivate a culture where employees feel safe to express themselves, take risks, and make mistakes, encouraging creativity and innovation and leading to personal and organisational growth. Collaboration enhances collective growth and development, so leaders should facilitate opportunities for team members to work together, share ideas, and learn from one another, fostering a sense of community and shared success. Continuous learning is a cornerstone of growth, and leaders should promote a culture of lifelong learning by providing access to training, development programmes, and resources, encouraging curiosity and exploration to help employees expand their knowledge and skills.

Subtle influence builds trust and respect within the organisation, as leaders who support and guide without exerting control earn the trust of their team members, strengthening relationships and enhancing collaboration. Empowerment is a key outcome of subtle influence, with leaders providing autonomy and support to empower their teams to take initiative and drive the organisation forward, fostering a sense of ownership and accountability and leading to higher levels of engagement and performance. Subtle and understated influence contributes to sustainable success by promoting natural growth and development, creating a resilient and adaptable organisation that can thrive in various circumstances and achieve long-term goals.

Subtle influence enhances employee engagement by fostering autonomy and empowerment, making employees feel trusted and supported, which increases their motivation and commitment to their work. A supportive environment that encourages natural growth fosters innovation and creativity, as employees with the freedom to explore new ideas and take risks are more likely to develop innovative solutions. Subtle influence also builds resilience by promoting adaptability and continuous learning, creating a dynamic organisation capable of navigating change and overcoming challenges. A culture of subtle and understated influence promotes positivity and respect, with leaders who guide and support without exerting control, creating an environment where employees feel valued and motivated to contribute their best.

Practical Strategies for Embracing Subtle & Understated Influence

Setting Clear Goals and Expectations: Leaders should set clear goals and expectations to provide direction while allowing autonomy. This involves defining objectives, performance standards, and desired outcomes.

Encouraging Self-Reflection and Learning: Encouraging self-reflection and learning helps employees discover their strengths and solutions. Leaders should create opportunities for self-assessment, feedback, and personal development.

Modelling Desired Behaviours: Leaders should model the behaviours and values they wish to see in their team. By leading by example, they set a powerful standard for others to follow.

Facilitating Collaboration and Knowledge Sharing: Facilitating collaboration and knowledge sharing enhances collective growth. Leaders should create opportunities for team members to work together, share ideas, and learn from one another.

Providing Continuous Support and Resources: Continuous support and resources help employees succeed. Leaders should offer guidance, training, and access to necessary tools while allowing autonomy.

Embracing subtle and understated influence fosters a sustainable organisational culture where autonomy, creativity, and respect are valued, attracting and retaining top talent and contributing to overall success. Teams that prioritise subtle influence and autonomy are more resilient and capable of overcoming challenges, with strong relationships and trust enabling them to work together effectively in any situation. Leaders who embrace subtle influence can navigate uncertainties with strategic agility, ensuring decisions are made with long-term sustainability in mind and supporting the organisation's resilience. Organisations that consistently prioritise subtle and understated influence in leadership are better positioned for long-term success, providing a strong foundation that supports sustainable growth and resilience.

ACCOMPLISHING GREAT ACHIEVEMENTS THROUGH HUMILITY

Hence the sage is able (in the same way) to accomplish his great achievements. It is through his not making himself great that he can accomplish them.

Lao Tzu's passage underscores the power of humility in achieving great accomplishments. Leaders who practise humility and do not seek to elevate themselves above others are often able to accomplish great things. By focusing on the collective good and prioritising the organisation's mission, leaders can inspire their teams and achieve lasting success. This humility also builds trust and loyalty, as employees feel that their leader genuinely cares about their well-being and growth.

Humble leaders prioritise the organisation's mission above their personal ambitions, making decisions that align with the organisation's values and goals, ensuring their actions benefit the collective and create a sense of shared purpose and direction. They recognise the importance of each team member's contributions, understanding that great achievements result from collective effort and collaboration, fostering a culture of respect and appreciation by valuing and acknowledging their team's efforts. Encouraging inclusivity, humble leaders create an environment where diverse perspectives and ideas are welcomed and valued, enhancing creativity, innovation, and problem-solving within the organisation.

Humble leaders lead by example, demonstrating the values and behaviours they wish to see in their teams, such as humility, respect, and integrity, thereby inspiring their teams to adopt these qualities and fostering a positive and ethical organisational culture. Practising active listening is a critical component of humble leadership, where leaders listen attentively to their team members, valuing their input and feedback, which shows genuine care for their team's opinions and encourages open communication. Additionally, humble leaders empower their team members by giving them the autonomy and resources to succeed, trusting them to make decisions and take ownership of their work, which fosters a sense of responsibility and motivation, driving higher levels of engagement and performance.

Humble leaders genuinely care about the well-being and growth of their team members, investing in their development, providing support, and celebrating their successes, which builds trust and loyalty as employees feel valued and appreciated. Leaders who share success with their team members build stronger relationships and trust by attributing achievements to the collective efforts of the team, reinforcing the importance of teamwork and collaboration. Transparency is essential for building trust, so humble leaders are open and honest about their decisions and actions, communicating clearly and consistently to ensure their team members are informed and involved, fostering a culture of trust and integrity.

Humility enhances team collaboration by fostering a culture of respect and appreciation, where leaders value their team members' contributions and encourage inclusivity, strengthening teamwork and collective problem-solving. Humble leadership increases employee engagement by creating a supportive and empowering environment, motivating and committing team members to their work. A culture of humility promotes positivity and ethical behaviour, with leaders demonstrating humility and focusing on the collective good, creating an environment where employees feel respected and inspired. Humility ensures sustainable success by promoting collaboration, continuous improvement, and ethical decision-making, with leaders prioritising the organisation's mission and genuinely caring about their team, creating a strong foundation for long-term achievement.

Practical Strategies for Practising Humility in Leadership

Recognising and Celebrating Team Contributions: Leaders should regularly recognise and celebrate the contributions of their team members. This involves expressing gratitude and acknowledging individual and collective achievements.

Encouraging Open Communication: Open communication fosters transparency and trust. Leaders should create opportunities for team members to share their ideas, feedback, and concerns. This open dialogue promotes inclusivity and collaboration.

Providing Support and Resources: Providing support and resources helps team members succeed. Leaders should offer guidance, training, and access to necessary tools, ensuring that their team has what they need to perform their roles effectively.

Practising Self-Reflection: Self-reflection helps leaders stay grounded and aware of their actions. Leaders should regularly reflect on their decisions, behaviours, and their impact on the organisation. This self-awareness fosters humility and continuous improvement.

Leading by Example: Leaders should model the behaviours and values they wish to see in their team. By demonstrating humility, respect, and integrity, leaders set a powerful example for others to follow.

Practising humility fosters a sustainable organisational culture where respect, collaboration, and ethical behaviour are valued, attracting and retaining top talent and contributing to overall success. Teams that prioritise humility and inclusivity are more resilient and capable of overcoming challenges, with strong relationships and trust enabling them to work together effectively in any situation. Leaders who practise humility can navigate uncertainties with strategic agility, ensuring decisions are made with long-term sustainability in mind and supporting the organisation's resilience. Organisations that consistently prioritise humility in leadership are better positioned for long-term success, as these values provide a strong foundation that supports sustainable growth and resilience.

CHAPTER 35 – VISION

Chapter 35 of the *Tao Te Ching* emphasises the power of the Tao, its ability to attract and provide peace, and the enduring value of its simplicity and subtlety. Here's how these teachings can be applied to modern-day strategic management:

CREATING A VISION THAT ATTRACTS & INSPIRES

> *To him who holds in his hands the Great Image (of the invisible Tao), the whole world repairs. Men resort to him, and receive no hurt, but (find) rest, peace, and the feeling of ease.*

Lao Tzu's passage highlights the transformative power of a compelling vision. In strategic management, leaders should craft a compelling vision that attracts and inspires people. This vision should be clear, inclusive, and aligned with the core values of the organisation. When employees resonate with the vision, they are more likely to engage deeply with their work, find a sense of purpose, and contribute to a positive and harmonious work environment. A well-crafted vision brings people together and creates a sense of peace and stability within the organisation.

A compelling vision begins with clarity of purpose, with leaders articulating the organisation's mission, goals, and desired future state in a clear and concise manner, helping employees understand the direction and aspirations of the organisation, providing a sense of purpose and motivation. Inclusivity is essential for creating a vision that resonates with all members of the organisation, ensuring the vision reflects the diverse perspectives and values of the team, fostering a sense of belonging and unity, as employees see themselves as integral parts of the organisation's journey. The vision should be deeply rooted in the organisation's core values, with leaders identifying the principles that define the organisation's identity and ensuring the vision embodies these values, reinforcing the organisation's commitment to its values and guiding decision-making and behaviour.

A compelling vision must be communicated with passion and enthusiasm, as leaders share their vision in a way that inspires and energises their team, creating an emotional connection that motivates employees to embrace the vision and work towards its realisation. A well-crafted vision provides employees with a sense of purpose and meaning in their work, and when team members understand how their contributions align with the organisation's vision, they are more likely to feel fulfilled and motivated, driving engagement and commitment. Leaders should create opportunities for employees to contribute to the vision by involving team members in the planning and implementation of strategic initiatives, ensuring that when employees have a voice and can see the impact of their efforts, they feel more connected to the vision and motivated to succeed.

A compelling vision fosters collaboration and unity within the organisation, with leaders encouraging teamwork and creating opportunities for team members to work together towards common goals, enhancing relationships and creating a harmonious work environment. A vision that prioritises well-being and work-life balance contributes to a positive work environment, with leaders ensuring that the vision includes a commitment to supporting employees' physical, mental, and emotional health, enhancing job satisfaction and overall happiness. Celebrating progress and success reinforces the vision and motivates employees, with leaders regularly acknowledging and celebrating individual and team achievements, expressing gratitude and appreciation, fostering a culture of positivity and recognition.

A compelling vision increases employee engagement by providing a sense of purpose and direction, motivating employees and driving higher levels of productivity and job satisfaction. A shared vision fosters organisational cohesion by aligning the efforts and aspirations of all team members, enhancing collaboration, communication, and overall performance. Rooted in core values, a vision promotes a positive organisational culture, where leaders embody the vision, prioritising respect, inclusivity, and excellence, which attracts and retains top talent. Sustainable success is ensured by a compelling vision that guides strategic decision-making and behaviour, with leaders prioritising the organisation's mission and values, creating a strong foundation for long-term growth and resilience.

Practical Strategies for Creating & Communicating a Compelling Vision

Articulating the Vision Clearly: Leaders should articulate the vision clearly and concisely. This involves defining the organisation's mission, goals, and desired future state, and communicating this vision in a way that is easy to understand and remember.

Engaging Employees in the Vision: Engaging employees in the vision helps create a sense of ownership and commitment. Leaders should involve team members in the development and implementation of the vision, seeking their input and feedback.

Communicating with Passion and Enthusiasm: Leaders should communicate the vision with passion and enthusiasm. This involves sharing stories, examples, and personal experiences that illustrate the vision's importance and impact.

Aligning Actions with the Vision: Leaders should ensure that their actions align with the vision. This involves making decisions and taking actions that reflect the organisation's mission and values, and consistently demonstrating commitment to the vision.

Providing Opportunities for Contribution: Providing opportunities for employees to contribute to the vision fosters a sense of ownership and engagement. Leaders should create platforms for team members to share their ideas, participate in strategic initiatives, and contribute to the organisation's success.

Creating a compelling vision fosters a sustainable organisational culture where purpose, values, and engagement are prioritised, attracting and retaining top talent and contributing to overall success. Teams that resonate with the vision are more resilient and capable of overcoming challenges, with strong relationships and a shared purpose enabling them to work together effectively in any situation. Leaders who create and communicate a compelling vision can navigate uncertainties with strategic agility, ensuring decisions are made with long-term sustainability in mind and supporting the organisation's resilience. Organisations that consistently prioritise a compelling vision are better positioned for long-term success, as this vision provides a strong foundation that supports sustainable growth and resilience.

RECOGNISING THE ENDURING VALUE OF SIMPLICITY

> *Music and dainties will make the passing guest stop (for a time). But though the Tao as it comes from the mouth, seems insipid and has no flavour, though it seems not worth being looked at or listened to, the use of it is inexhaustible.*

Lao Tzu's passage highlights the enduring power of simplicity and subtlety. Leaders should recognise the enduring value of simplicity and subtlety. While flashy and elaborate strategies may grab attention in the short term, it is the simple, well-grounded principles and actions that sustain long-term success. By focusing on the fundamentals and avoiding unnecessary complexity, leaders can ensure that their strategies are robust and adaptable. This simplicity allows for greater clarity and more effective execution.

Simple and well-grounded principles have a lasting impact by being easier to understand, implement, and maintain, ensuring organisational stability and resilience over time, thus supporting long-term success and growth. Simplicity brings clarity and focus to strategic initiatives, with leaders who avoid unnecessary complexity better able to communicate their vision and goals, ensuring alignment and productivity throughout the organisation while reducing confusion. Simple strategies are more adaptable to changing circumstances, allowing leaders to quickly pivot and adjust plans in response to new challenges and opportunities, ensuring the organisation remains competitive and innovative.

Leaders should identify and prioritise the core values and principles that define the organisation's identity, as these values serve as the foundation for decision-making and behaviour, guiding actions and ensuring alignment with its mission. Streamlining processes and procedures reduces complexity and enhances efficiency, with leaders eliminating unnecessary steps and optimising workflows to improve overall performance, saving time and resources for more effective operations. Setting clear and achievable goals provides direction and motivation, with leaders setting specific, measurable, achievable, relevant, and time-bound (SMART) goals that align with the organisation's mission and values, helping to focus efforts and drive progress.

Simplified communication enhances understanding and collaboration, with leaders using clear and concise language, avoiding jargon and unnecessary complexity to ensure messages are easily understood and acted upon. By focusing on key priorities, leaders can avoid spreading themselves too thin, concentrating on the most important initiatives and allocating resources effectively to achieve meaningful outcomes, thus driving strategic success. Embracing minimalism involves prioritising what truly matters and eliminating distractions, with leaders focusing on essential tasks and goals and avoiding unnecessary activities that do not contribute to the organisation's success, enhancing productivity and clarity.

Leaders should develop strategies that are simple yet effective, involving clear objectives, actionable steps, and measurable outcomes, as these strategies are easier to implement and monitor, ensuring successful execution. A culture of simplicity promotes efficiency and clarity throughout the organisation, with leaders encouraging team members to embrace simplicity in their work, focusing on essential tasks and eliminating unnecessary complexity, fostering a supportive and productive work environment. Continuous improvement is essential for maintaining simplicity and effectiveness, so leaders should regularly review and refine processes, seeking opportunities to streamline and optimise workflows, ensuring the organisation remains agile and efficient. Recognising and celebrating successes reinforces the value of simplicity, with leaders highlighting achievements from simple, well-grounded strategies, expressing gratitude and appreciation for team members' efforts, motivating others to embrace simplicity.

Embracing simplicity enhances organisational resilience by promoting clarity, focus, and adaptability, enabling leaders who prioritise simple and well-grounded strategies to navigate uncertainties and challenges more effectively. Simple and effective strategies drive sustainable growth and success by focusing on the fundamentals and avoiding unnecessary complexity, ensuring the organisation remains stable and resilient over time. A culture of simplicity promotes employee engagement by reducing confusion and enhancing productivity, motivating and committing team members to their work when they understand their roles and goals. A focus on simplicity fosters a positive organisational culture where efficiency, clarity, and collaboration are prioritised, attracting and retaining top talent and contributing to overall success.

Practical Strategies for Embracing Simplicity & Subtlety

Articulating Core Values and Principles: Leaders should articulate the organisation's core values and principles, ensuring that they are integrated into all aspects of the business. This clarity provides a strong foundation for decision-making and behaviour.

Streamlining Communication Channels: Streamlined communication channels enhance understanding and collaboration. Leaders should use clear and concise language and ensure that messages are easily accessible and actionable.

Prioritising Key Initiatives: Leaders should prioritise key initiatives that align with the organisation's mission and values. This focus on essential tasks and goals ensures that resources are allocated effectively and meaningful outcomes are achieved.

Implementing Continuous Improvement Processes: Continuous improvement processes help maintain simplicity and effectiveness. Leaders should regularly review and refine workflows, seeking opportunities to streamline and optimise operations.

Recognising and Celebrating Simplicity: Recognising and celebrating simplicity reinforces its value. Leaders should highlight achievements that result from simple and well-grounded strategies, expressing gratitude and appreciation for team members' efforts.

Recognising the enduring value of simplicity fosters a sustainable organisational culture where efficiency, clarity, and collaboration are prioritised, attracting and retaining top talent and contributing to overall success. Teams that prioritise simplicity and clarity are more resilient and capable of overcoming challenges, with strong relationships and trust enabling them to work together effectively in any situation. Leaders who embrace simplicity can navigate uncertainties with strategic agility, ensuring decisions are made with long-term sustainability in mind and supporting the organisation's resilience. Organisations that consistently prioritise simplicity and well-grounded principles are better positioned for long-term success, as these values provide a strong foundation that supports sustainable growth and resilience.

CHAPTER 36 – CHANGE

Chapter 36 of the *Tao Te Ching* emphasises the dynamics of action and reaction, the subtle power of softness, and the prudence of discretion. Here's how these teachings can be applied to modern-day strategic management:

RECOGNISING & MANAGING DYNAMICS OF CHANGE

> *When one is about to take an inspiration, he is sure to make a (previous) expiration; when he is going to weaken another, he will first strengthen him; when he is going to overthrow another, he will first have raised him up; when he is going to despoil another, he will first have made gifts to him:—this is called 'Hiding the light (of his procedure).'*

Lao Tzu's passage highlights the importance of understanding the intricate dynamics of change and the action-reaction relationships that arise. In strategic management, leaders should understand the dynamics of change and action-reaction relationships. This means being aware of how actions can have counteractions and planning accordingly. For example, when implementing a major change, leaders might first build up trust and strength within the team to ensure a smoother transition. Understanding these dynamics helps leaders anticipate challenges and manage them more effectively.

Every action a leader takes can prompt a reaction, so leaders should anticipate potential counteractions and plan strategies to address them, managing resistance and mitigating negative impacts. Recognising that weakening a process or approach might necessitate first strengthening it is crucial, ensuring any reduction in one area is balanced by reinforcement in another. Before implementing significant changes, leaders should focus on building trust and rapport within the team, as this trust forms the foundation for acceptance and cooperation, making team members more likely to support and adapt to changes.

Transparent communication is key to managing change, as leaders should clearly articulate the reasons for the change, the expected benefits, and the potential challenges, which helps build trust and understanding while reducing uncertainty and anxiety. Involving stakeholders in the change process fosters a sense of ownership and collaboration, with leaders seeking input and feedback from team members, customers, and other stakeholders to ensure diverse perspectives are considered and potential issues are identified and addressed. Leaders should also provide the necessary support and resources to help team members navigate the change, including training, tools, and guidance to ensure a smooth transition, demonstrating the leader's commitment to the team's success and well-being.

Strengthening team dynamics before implementing change fosters resilience and adaptability, with leaders focusing on team-building activities, enhancing communication, and creating a supportive environment, ensuring the team is better equipped to handle challenges. Gradual implementation of changes allows time for adjustment and reduces disruption, with leaders planning phased rollouts, starting with pilot programmes or small-scale implementations to identify and address issues early, ensuring a smoother transition. Continuous monitoring and adjustment are essential for successful change management, with leaders regularly assessing progress and impact, seeking feedback, and making necessary adjustments to ensure the change remains aligned with the organisation's goals and values.

Understanding and managing change dynamics enhances organisational resilience, as leaders who anticipate counteractions and plan accordingly can navigate challenges more effectively, ensuring continuity and stability. Transparent communication and stakeholder involvement build trust and collaboration, making team members more likely to support the change and work together towards common goals. Effective change management leads to successful implementation, with leaders providing support, resources, and gradual rollouts to ensure changes are adopted smoothly and deliver the intended benefits. Managing change dynamics supports sustainable growth, with leaders who understand and address the complexities of change driving continuous improvement and innovation, positioning the organisation for long-term success.

Practical Strategies for Recognising & Managing Dynamics of Change

Conducting Impact Assessments: Leaders should conduct impact assessments to anticipate potential counteractions and challenges. This involves analysing the effects of proposed changes on various stakeholders and preparing strategies to address them.

Developing Communication Plans: Clear and transparent communication plans are essential for managing change. Leaders should outline key messages, channels, and timelines for communicating with stakeholders, ensuring that everyone is informed and engaged.

Providing Training and Resources: Training and resources help team members adapt to change. Leaders should offer workshops, courses, and support materials to ensure that employees have the skills and knowledge needed for the transition.

Implementing Gradual Rollouts: Gradual rollouts allow time for adjustment and learning. Leaders should start with pilot programmes or small-scale implementations, gathering feedback and making adjustments before full-scale rollout.

Seeking Continuous Feedback: Continuous feedback is crucial for monitoring the impact of changes. Leaders should create opportunities for team members to share their experiences and provide input, ensuring that issues are identified and addressed promptly.

Recognising and managing the dynamics of change fosters a sustainable organisational culture where resilience, transparency, and collaboration are valued, attracting and retaining top talent and contributing to overall success. Teams that prioritise understanding and managing change dynamics are more resilient and capable of overcoming challenges, with strong relationships and trust enabling them to work together effectively in any situation. Leaders who recognise and manage change dynamics can navigate uncertainties with strategic agility, ensuring decisions are made with long-term sustainability in mind and supporting the organisation's resilience. Organisations that consistently prioritise understanding and managing change dynamics are better positioned for long-term success, providing a strong foundation that supports sustainable growth and resilience.

LEVERAGING THE POWER OF SOFTNESS & FLEXIBILITY

The soft overcomes the hard; and the weak the strong.

Lao Tzu's passage highlights the power of softness and flexibility in overcoming rigidity and strength. Leaders should leverage the power of softness and flexibility in their strategies. Softness, in this context, refers to adaptability, empathy, and resilience. By being flexible and responsive to changing circumstances, leaders can navigate challenges more effectively. This approach also includes empathetic leadership, where understanding and addressing the needs of employees can lead to stronger, more cohesive teams. Flexibility and empathy can often achieve better results than rigid or forceful tactics.

Adaptability is the ability to respond effectively to changing circumstances, with leaders open to new ideas, approaches, and solutions, allowing them to pivot and adjust strategies as needed, ensuring the organisation remains resilient and competitive. Adaptable leaders foster a culture of innovation by encouraging team members to experiment and explore new possibilities, driving continuous improvement and creative problem-solving, enabling their teams to thrive in the face of change. Additionally, adaptable leaders learn from their experiences, using insights gained to inform future decisions, adopting a continuous learning approach that helps leaders and their teams grow and evolve, enhancing their ability to navigate challenges and seize opportunities.

Empathy involves understanding and addressing the needs and concerns of team members, with leaders actively listening to their employees and valuing their perspectives and experiences to foster a supportive and inclusive work environment. Empathetic leaders build strong, trusting relationships with their team members by showing genuine care and concern for their well-being, creating a sense of loyalty and commitment, which enhances collaboration and communication. During times of stress or uncertainty, empathetic leaders provide emotional support by offering encouragement, understanding, and resources to help employees cope with challenges, fostering resilience and well-being.

Resilient leaders promote a growth mindset, encouraging team members to view challenges as opportunities for learning and development, fostering perseverance and adaptability, and enabling the organisation to overcome obstacles and achieve long-term success. A supportive culture is essential for fostering resilience, with leaders creating an environment where employees feel valued, respected, and empowered to take risks, enhancing overall morale and productivity. Recognising the importance of work-life balance, resilient leaders promote flexible work arrangements and encourage self-care, helping employees manage stress and maintain resilience.

Agile practices enhance flexibility and responsiveness, with leaders implementing methodologies that prioritise iterative development, collaboration, and continuous improvement, ensuring the organisation can adapt quickly to changing needs and demands. Flexible leaders empower their team members to make decisions and take ownership of their work, fostering a sense of responsibility and accountability and driving higher levels of engagement and performance. Creating adaptable plans allows for adjustments based on evolving circumstances, with leaders developing strategic plans that include contingency measures and flexibility to pivot as needed, ensuring the organisation remains resilient and proactive.

Leveraging softness and flexibility fosters strong, cohesive teams, as empathetic leadership and adaptability enhance collaboration, communication, and trust, creating a positive and supportive work environment. Flexibility and adaptability drive innovation and creativity by encouraging experimentation and openness to new ideas, fostering a culture of continuous improvement and creative problem-solving. Softness and flexibility also enhance organisational resilience, with leaders who prioritise adaptability and empathy navigating challenges and uncertainties more effectively, ensuring stability and long-term success. Empathetic leadership and flexible practices increase employee engagement by making employees feel valued, supported, and empowered, thus boosting their motivation and commitment to their work.

Practical Strategies for Leveraging Softness & Flexibility

Encouraging Open Communication: Open communication fosters a culture of transparency and trust. Leaders should create opportunities for team members to share their ideas, feedback, and concerns, promoting collaboration and understanding.

Providing Continuous Learning Opportunities: Continuous learning opportunities enhance adaptability and resilience. Leaders should offer training, development programmes, and resources that support professional growth and skill development.

Implementing Flexible Work Arrangements: Flexible work arrangements support work-life balance and well-being. Leaders should offer options such as remote work, flexible hours, and job-sharing arrangements to accommodate employees' needs.

Modelling Empathetic Behaviour: Leaders should model empathetic behaviour by actively listening, showing understanding, and providing support. This modelling sets a positive example for the entire organisation.

Promoting a Culture of Experimentation: A culture of experimentation fosters innovation and creativity. Leaders should encourage team members to explore new ideas, take risks, and learn from failures, promoting continuous improvement.

Leveraging softness and flexibility fosters a sustainable organisational culture where empathy, adaptability, and innovation are valued, attracting and retaining top talent and contributing to overall success. Teams that prioritise softness and flexibility are more resilient and capable of overcoming challenges, with strong relationships and trust enabling them to work together effectively in any situation. Leaders who leverage softness and flexibility can navigate uncertainties with strategic agility, ensuring decisions are made with long-term sustainability in mind and supporting the organisation's resilience. Organisations that consistently prioritise softness and flexibility in leadership are better positioned for long-term success, as these values provide a strong foundation that supports sustainable growth and resilience.

PRACTISING DISCRETION & STRATEGIC TIMING

> *Fishes should not be taken from the deep; instruments for the profit of a state should not be shown to the people.*

Lao Tzu's passage emphasises the critical role of discretion and strategic timing in effective leadership. Discretion and strategic timing are crucial in leadership. Leaders should be mindful of when and how they share information, make decisions, or implement changes. Not all strategies or plans need to be disclosed immediately or fully. By carefully considering the timing and manner of their actions, leaders can avoid unnecessary resistance and ensure that their strategies are more likely to succeed.

Leaders should practise selective disclosure, sharing information on a need-to-know basis to manage sensitive information and prevent unnecessary confusion or concern, maintaining control over the narrative and ensuring clarity. Confidentiality is essential for building trust and maintaining a strategic advantage, with leaders respecting the confidentiality of sensitive information and only sharing it with those who need to know, protecting the organisation's interests and fostering a culture of trust and respect. While transparency is important, it must be balanced with discretion, with leaders being transparent about their intentions and goals while exercising discretion in the details, ensuring team members are informed and engaged without being overwhelmed with unnecessary information.

The timing of decisions can significantly impact their effectiveness, so leaders should consider the broader context and potential consequences before making decisions to ensure they are made when they are most likely to succeed and have the greatest positive impact. Gradual implementation of changes allows time for adjustment and reduces resistance, with leaders planning phased rollouts, starting with pilot programmes or small-scale implementations to identify and address issues early, ensuring a smoother transition. Effective communication requires choosing the right moment to share information, with leaders considering the readiness of their audience and the timing of other events or changes, enhancing understanding and receptivity when sharing information at the right time.

Building trust and rapport within the team is essential for managing resistance to change, with leaders establishing strong relationships with their team members, demonstrating reliability and integrity to form a foundation for acceptance and cooperation during times of change. Clear and compelling explanations help in managing resistance, as leaders articulate the reasons for the change, the expected benefits, and the potential challenges, building trust and understanding while reducing uncertainty and anxiety. Leaders should provide the necessary support and resources to help team members navigate the change, including training, tools, and guidance to ensure a smooth transition, demonstrating their commitment to the team's success and well-being.

Practising discretion and strategic timing enhances trust and credibility within the organisation, as leaders who share information thoughtfully and make decisions strategically build trust and confidence among team members. Strategic timing improves decision-making by ensuring decisions are made when they are most likely to succeed, considering the broader context and potential consequences for more informed and effective choices. Discretion and strategic timing lead to successful change implementation, with leaders phasing changes gradually and choosing the right moment to communicate, ensuring smooth adoption and intended benefits. This practice supports sustainable growth and success, as leaders who carefully manage the timing and manner of their actions drive continuous improvement and innovation, positioning the organisation for long-term achievement.

Practical Strategies for Practising Discretion & Strategic Timing

Assessing Information Sensitivity: Leaders should assess the sensitivity of information before sharing it. This involves considering the potential impact on the organisation and its stakeholders, and deciding who needs to know and when.

Developing Communication Plans: Clear and strategic communication plans are essential for practising discretion and timing. Leaders should outline key messages, channels, and timelines for communicating with stakeholders, ensuring that information is shared thoughtfully and effectively.

Implementing Gradual Rollouts: Gradual rollouts allow time for adjustment and learning. Leaders should start with pilot programmes or small-scale implementations, gathering feedback and making adjustments before full-scale rollout.

Seeking Continuous Feedback: Continuous feedback is crucial for monitoring the impact of decisions and changes. Leaders should create opportunities for team members to share their experiences and provide input, ensuring that issues are identified and addressed promptly.

Balancing Transparency and Discretion: Balancing transparency and discretion requires thoughtful consideration. Leaders should be transparent about their intentions and goals, while also exercising discretion in the details. This balance ensures that team members are informed and engaged without overwhelming them with unnecessary information.

Practising discretion and strategic timing fosters a sustainable organisational culture where trust, transparency, and thoughtful decision-making are valued, attracting and retaining top talent and contributing to overall success. Teams that prioritise discretion and strategic timing are more resilient and capable of overcoming challenges, with strong relationships and trust enabling them to work together effectively in any situation. Leaders who practise discretion and strategic timing can navigate uncertainties with strategic agility, ensuring decisions are made with long-term sustainability in mind and supporting the organisation's resilience. Organisations that consistently prioritise discretion and strategic timing in leadership are better positioned for long-term success, providing a strong foundation that supports sustainable growth and resilience.

CHAPTER 37 – NON-ACTION

Chapter 37 of the *Tao Te Ching* highlights the power of simplicity, non-action, and the natural flow of the Tao. Here's how these teachings can be applied to modern-day strategic management:

EMBRACING NON-ACTION & ALLOWING NATURAL PROCESSES

> *The Tao in its regular course does nothing (for the sake of doing it), and so there is nothing which it does not do.*

Lao Tzu's passage introduces the concept of *Wú Wéi* (無為/无为), often translated as 'non-action' or 'effortless action.' In strategic management, leaders should understand the concept of *Wú Wéi*, which means allowing things to unfold naturally rather than forcing outcomes. This does not mean inaction, but rather taking actions that are in harmony with the natural flow and dynamics of the organisation. By fostering an environment where processes can develop organically, leaders can achieve more sustainable and effective results.

Wú Wéi emphasises actions that align with the natural flow of events and the inherent dynamics of the organisation, with leaders not imposing artificial constraints or forcing outcomes but instead working with the natural tendencies and rhythms of their team and environment. Effortless action involves achieving results with minimal effort by aligning actions with the existing currents and forces, identifying opportunities where efforts can have the most impact without undue strain or resistance. Letting go of control means releasing the need to manage every detail and outcome, with leaders trusting their team's abilities and the natural processes within the organisation, fostering creativity, autonomy, and collaboration.

Allowing processes to develop organically encourages autonomy among team members, with leaders empowering their team to take initiative and make decisions, fostering ownership and accountability and leading to more innovative and effective solutions. Leaders should create conditions that support natural growth and development by providing the necessary resources, training, and support while allowing team members the freedom to explore and experiment, enhancing creativity and problem-solving. Reducing micromanagement aligns with the principles of *Wú Wéi*, with leaders focusing on providing guidance and support without imposing unnecessary control, allowing team members to work more freely and efficiently, resulting in better outcomes.

Actions that align with the organisation's values and goals are more likely to produce sustainable results, so leaders should ensure their strategies and decisions reflect the core principles and mission of the organisation, fostering consistency and integrity. Flexibility and adaptability are key to achieving sustainable results, with leaders being open to adjusting their strategies based on changing circumstances and feedback, ensuring the organisation remains resilient and responsive to new opportunities and challenges. A culture of trust and collaboration supports the principles of *Wú Wéi*, with leaders building strong, trusting relationships with their team members and encouraging open communication and collaboration, enhancing teamwork and collective problem-solving.

Allowing processes to develop organically fosters a culture of innovation and creativity, as team members who are empowered to take initiative and explore new ideas are more likely to develop innovative solutions. Embracing non-action enhances the organisation's resilience and adaptability, with leaders aligning actions with natural dynamics and remaining flexible to ensure the organisation can navigate challenges and seize opportunities effectively. Autonomy and trust increase employee engagement, as valued and empowered team members are more motivated and committed to their work, driving higher levels of productivity and satisfaction. Actions that are in harmony with the organisation's values and natural dynamics lead to sustainable success, as leaders foster an environment where processes can develop organically, creating a strong foundation for long-term growth and achievement.

Practical Strategies for Embracing Non-Action & Allowing Natural Processes

Empowering Team Members: Leaders should empower their team members by providing autonomy and support. This involves giving them the freedom to make decisions and take initiative, fostering a sense of ownership and accountability.

Creating Supportive Conditions: Creating supportive conditions includes providing the necessary resources, training, and guidance. Leaders should ensure that team members have access to the tools and knowledge they need to succeed while allowing them the freedom to explore and innovate.

Reducing Micromanagement: Reducing micromanagement involves focusing on guidance and support rather than control. Leaders should trust their team's abilities and allow them to work independently, intervening only when necessary.

Aligning Actions with Values: Leaders should ensure that their actions and strategies align with the organisation's values and goals. This alignment fosters consistency and integrity, ensuring that efforts are directed towards meaningful and sustainable outcomes.

Embracing Flexibility and Adaptability: Leaders should be open to adjusting their strategies based on changing circumstances and feedback. This flexibility ensures that the organisation remains resilient and responsive to new opportunities and challenges.

Embracing non-action fosters a sustainable organisational culture where autonomy, creativity, and collaboration are valued, attracting and retaining top talent and contributing to overall success. Teams that prioritise non-action and natural processes are more resilient and capable of overcoming challenges, with strong relationships and trust enabling them to work together effectively in any situation. Leaders who embrace non-action can navigate uncertainties with strategic agility, ensuring decisions are made with long-term sustainability in mind and supporting the organisation's resilience. Organisations that consistently prioritise non-action and natural processes in leadership are better positioned for long-term success, providing a strong foundation that supports sustainable growth and resilience.

LEADING WITH SIMPLICITY & CLARITY

> *If princes and kings were able to maintain it, all things would of themselves be transformed by them.*

Lao Tzu's passage emphasises the significant impact of simplicity and clarity in leadership. Simplicity and clarity in leadership can lead to significant transformation within an organisation. Leaders should strive to communicate their vision and values clearly and avoid unnecessary complexity. When leaders maintain a simple and focused approach, it can inspire and guide the entire organisation towards common goals.

A clear vision provides direction and purpose for the organisation, with leaders articulating their vision in a way that is easy to understand and remember, helping employees grasp the organisation's goals and their role in achieving them. Core values serve as guiding principles for the organisation, so leaders should define and communicate these values clearly, ensuring they are integrated into all aspects of the business, providing a moral compass and fostering a sense of unity and purpose among employees. Consistent messaging reinforces the organisation's vision and values, with leaders ensuring their communications align with the organisation's mission and principles, building trust and credibility and enhancing employee engagement and alignment.

Simplified processes and procedures enhance efficiency and reduce confusion, so leaders should eliminate unnecessary steps and focus on optimising workflows to save time and resources, allowing the organisation to operate more effectively. Leaders should focus on key priorities and avoid spreading themselves too thin, concentrating on the most important initiatives to allocate resources effectively and achieve meaningful outcomes, driving strategic success. Clear and concise language enhances understanding and communication, so leaders should avoid jargon and overly complex explanations, ensuring their messages are accessible to all team members, fostering effective collaboration and decision-making.

Leaders who embody simplicity and clarity set a positive example for their team, inspiring others to follow suit and fostering a culture of transparency and integrity. Open communication fosters trust and collaboration, with leaders creating opportunities for team members to share their ideas, feedback, and concerns, promoting transparency and alignment with the organisation's goals. Providing support and guidance helps employees navigate their roles and responsibilities, with leaders offering resources, training, and mentorship to enhance performance and foster a sense of confidence and empowerment.

Simplicity and clarity increase employee engagement by providing a sense of purpose and direction, motivating and committing employees to their work. A shared vision and clear values foster organisational cohesion, with leaders communicating clearly and consistently to create unity and alignment among team members, enhancing collaboration and overall performance. Clear and concise communication improves decision-making by ensuring everyone has the necessary information, while simplified processes and focused priorities enable informed and effective decisions. These qualities ensure sustainable success by promoting efficiency, transparency, and alignment, creating a strong foundation for long-term growth and achievement.

Practical Strategies for Leading with Simplicity & Clarity

Articulating the Vision Clearly: Leaders should articulate the organisation's vision clearly and concisely. This involves defining the mission, goals, and desired future state in a way that is easy to understand and remember.

Defining and Communicating Core Values: Leaders should define the organisation's core values and ensure that they are communicated consistently. These values should be integrated into all aspects of the business, guiding decision-making and behaviour.

Simplifying Processes and Procedures: Simplifying processes and procedures enhances efficiency and reduces confusion. Leaders should eliminate unnecessary steps and optimise workflows to improve overall performance.

Focusing on Key Priorities: Leaders should focus on key priorities that align with the organisation's mission and values. This focus ensures that resources are allocated effectively and meaningful outcomes are achieved.

Using Clear and Concise Language: Clear and concise language enhances communication and understanding. Leaders should avoid jargon and overly complex explanations, ensuring that their messages are accessible to all team members.

Leading with simplicity and clarity fosters a sustainable organisational culture where transparency, efficiency, and alignment are valued, attracting and retaining top talent and contributing to overall success. Teams that prioritise simplicity and clarity are more resilient and capable of overcoming challenges, with strong relationships and trust enabling them to work together effectively in any situation. Leaders who embrace simplicity and clarity can navigate uncertainties with strategic agility, ensuring decisions are made with long-term sustainability in mind and supporting the organisation's resilience. Organisations that consistently prioritise simplicity and clarity in leadership are better positioned for long-term success, providing a strong foundation that supports sustainable growth and resilience.

CULTIVATING AN ENVIRONMENT OF EASE & REST

Simplicity without a name is free from all external aim. With no desire, at rest and still, all things go right as of their will.

Lao Tzu's passage emphasises the value of simplicity and rest in achieving harmony and success. Creating an environment where employees feel at ease and are not constantly driven by external pressures can enhance creativity and productivity. Leaders should focus on fostering a culture of rest and balance, where employees are encouraged to take breaks, maintain a healthy work-life balance, and work in a stress-free environment. This approach can lead to better overall performance and well-being.

Regular breaks are essential for maintaining focus and productivity, so leaders should encourage employees to take short breaks throughout the day to recharge and refresh, preventing burnout and enhancing overall performance. Flexible work arrangements, such as remote work and flexible hours, support work-life balance, with leaders offering these options to accommodate employees' personal needs and preferences, allowing them to manage their time effectively and reducing stress. Time off and vacations are crucial for rest and rejuvenation, so leaders should encourage employees to use their vacation days and take time off when needed, helping them return to work feeling refreshed and motivated.

Comfortable workspaces enhance well-being and productivity, so leaders should ensure that the physical work environment is ergonomically designed and aesthetically pleasing, with comfortable furniture, natural lighting, and greenery contributing to a relaxing atmosphere. Wellness resources support employees' physical and mental health, so leaders should offer access to wellness programmes, such as fitness classes, mental health support, and stress management workshops, promoting overall well-being. Mindfulness practices, such as meditation and deep breathing, help reduce stress and enhance focus, so leaders should encourage employees to incorporate mindfulness into their daily routines, providing quiet spaces for meditation and relaxation to support these practices.

Setting realistic expectations helps reduce pressure and stress, with leaders communicating clear and achievable goals to avoid unrealistic deadlines and workloads, ensuring employees can work effectively without feeling overwhelmed. Open communication fosters a supportive and inclusive culture, where leaders create opportunities for employees to share their ideas, concerns, and feedback, promoting trust and collaboration and enhancing overall well-being. Recognising and celebrating achievements boosts morale and motivation, with leaders regularly acknowledging individual and team successes, expressing gratitude and appreciation, fostering a positive work environment and encouraging continued excellence.

A stress-free environment enhances creativity and innovation, as employees who feel at ease and are not constantly driven by external pressures are more likely to think creatively and develop innovative solutions. Reducing stress and promoting balance improves productivity and performance, with well-rested and supported employees able to focus better and work more efficiently, leading to higher-quality outcomes. A culture of ease and rest increases employee engagement, as employees who feel valued and supported are more motivated and committed to their work, driving higher levels of job satisfaction and retention. Promoting rest and balance enhances overall well-being, with employees who maintain a healthy work-life balance experiencing less stress, better mental and physical health, and greater overall happiness.

Practical Strategies for Cultivating an Environment of Ease & Rest

Encouraging Breaks and Time Off: Leaders should encourage employees to take regular breaks and use their vacation days. This practice helps prevent burnout and promotes rest and rejuvenation.

Implementing Flexible Work Policies: Flexible work policies, such as remote work and flexible hours, support work-life balance. Leaders should offer these options to accommodate employees' personal needs and preferences.

Providing Comfortable Workspaces: Comfortable workspaces enhance well-being and productivity. Leaders should ensure that the physical work environment is ergonomically designed and aesthetically pleasing.

Offering Wellness Programmes: Wellness programmes support employees' physical and mental health. Leaders should offer access to fitness classes, mental health support, and stress management workshops.

Promoting Mindfulness Practices: Mindfulness practices help reduce stress and enhance focus. Leaders should encourage employees to incorporate mindfulness into their daily routines and provide quiet spaces for meditation and relaxation.

Cultivating an environment of ease and rest fosters a sustainable organisational culture where balance, well-being, and creativity are valued, attracting and retaining top talent and contributing to overall success. Teams that prioritise rest and balance are more resilient and capable of overcoming challenges, with strong relationships and trust enabling them to work together effectively in any situation. Leaders who cultivate an environment of ease and rest can navigate uncertainties with strategic agility, ensuring decisions are made with long-term sustainability in mind and supporting the organisation's resilience. Organisations that consistently prioritise rest and balance in leadership are better positioned for long-term success, providing a strong foundation that supports sustainable growth and resilience.

CONCLUSION

As we conclude *The Taoist CEO: Navigating Business with Ancient Wisdom*, it is clear that the ancient wisdom of Lao Tzu's *Tao Te Ching* holds profound relevance for modern business leaders. Through an exploration of Book 1 (chapters 1 to 37), we have uncovered timeless principles that can transform the way we lead, manage, and inspire.

In a world characterised by rapid change and constant demands, the teachings of Lao Tzu offer a refreshing perspective. His advocacy for simplicity, humility, and living in harmony with the natural order provides a blueprint for sustainable success. The concept of *Wú Wéi* (無為/无为), or non-action, teaches us the power of aligning our actions with the natural flow of events, enabling us to achieve more with less effort and greater effectiveness.

Key Takeaways for Modern Business Leaders

- *Embracing Simplicity:* In an era of complexity, the value of simplicity cannot be overstated. Simplifying processes, focusing on essential goals, and reducing unnecessary distractions can enhance clarity, efficiency, and productivity.
- *Cultivating Humility:* Humility in leadership fosters trust, respect, and loyalty. By recognising the contributions of others and leading with empathy and modesty, we can create a more inclusive and supportive organisational culture.
- *Practising Wú Wéi (Non-Action):* Effortless action is about working in harmony with the natural dynamics of our environment. This principle encourages us to be adaptive, responsive, and to avoid forcing outcomes, leading to more innovative and sustainable solutions.
- *Fostering Balance and Harmony:* Balancing the demands of work with the well-being of employees is crucial for long-term success. Promoting work-life balance, supporting mental and physical health, and creating a positive work environment lead to greater engagement and resilience.

As we move forward, the teachings of the *Tao Te Ching* invite us to rethink our approach to leadership and business. By integrating these ancient principles into our modern practices, we can cultivate organisations that are not only successful but also harmonious, ethical, and sustainable. The journey through the *Tao Te Ching* is a continuous one, with each chapter offering deeper insights and opportunities for reflection and growth. As you apply the lessons from this book, I encourage you to remain open to the transformative potential of Lao Tzu's wisdom, embracing the simplicity, humility, and harmony that can guide your leadership and inspire those around you.

This is only the beginning. A sequel will continue this exploration, delving into the remaining chapters 38 to 81 (Book 2) of the *Tao Te Ching* and uncovering further insights for modern business. Together, we will continue to bridge the ancient and the contemporary, fostering a leadership style that is rooted in timeless wisdom and poised for future success. Thank you for joining me on this journey through *The Taoist CEO*. May the principles of Lao Tzu's teachings guide you towards a path of meaningful leadership, profound impact, and lasting fulfillment.

David Leung
Edinburgh, 20 November 2024

APPENDIX – TAO TE CHING BY LAO TZU

THE TAO TEH KING, OR THE TAO AND ITS CHARACTERISTICS

by Lao-Tse

Translated by James Legge

Release date: February 1, 1995
Most recently updated: May 11, 2015
The Project Gutenberg

BOOK 1: CHAPTERS 1–37

CHAPTER 1

1. The Tao that can be trodden is not the enduring and unchanging Tao. The name that can be named is not the enduring and unchanging name.

2. (Conceived of as) having no name, it is the Originator of heaven and earth; (conceived of as) having a name, it is the Mother of all things.

3.
> *Always without desire we must be found,*
> *If its deep mystery we would sound;*
> *But if desire always within us be,*
> *Its outer fringe is all that we shall see.*

4. Under these two aspects, it is really the same; but as development takes place, it receives the different names. Together we call them the Mystery. Where the Mystery is the deepest is the gate of all that is subtle and wonderful.

CHAPTER 2

1. All in the world know the beauty of the beautiful, and in doing this they have (the idea of) what ugliness is; they all know the skill of the skilful, and in doing this they have (the idea of) what the want of skill is.

2. So it is that existence and non-existence give birth the one to (the idea of) the other; that difficulty and ease produce the one (the idea of) the other; that length and shortness fashion out the one the figure of the other; that (the ideas of) height and lowness arise from the contrast of the one with the other; that the musical notes and tones become harmonious through the relation of one with another; and that being before and behind give the idea of one following another.

3. Therefore the sage manages affairs without doing anything, and conveys his instructions without the use of speech.

4. All things spring up, and there is not one which declines to show itself; they grow, and there is no claim made for their ownership; they go through their processes, and there is no expectation (of a reward for the results). The work is accomplished, and there is no resting in it (as an achievement).

> *The work is done, but how no one can see;*
> *'Tis this that makes the power not cease to be.*

CHAPTER 3

1. Not to value and employ men of superior ability is the way to keep the people from rivalry among themselves; not to prize articles which are difficult to procure is the way to keep them from becoming thieves; not to show them what is likely to excite their desires is the way to keep their minds from disorder.

2. Therefore the sage, in the exercise of his government, empties their minds, fills their bellies, weakens their wills, and strengthens their bones.

3. He constantly (tries to) keep them without knowledge and without desire, and where there are those who have knowledge, to keep them from presuming to act (on it). When there is this abstinence from action, good order is universal.

CHAPTER 4

1. The Tao is (like) the emptiness of a vessel; and in our employment of it we must be on our guard against all fulness. How deep and unfathomable it is, as if it were the Honoured Ancestor of all things!

2. We should blunt our sharp points, and unravel the complications of things; we should attemper our brightness, and bring ourselves into agreement with the obscurity of others. How pure and still the Tao is, as if it would ever so continue!

3. I do not know whose son it is. It might appear to have been before God.

CHAPTER 5

1. Heaven and earth do not act from (the impulse of) any wish to be benevolent; they deal with all things as the dogs of grass are dealt with. The sages do not act from (any wish to be) benevolent; they deal with the people as the dogs of grass are dealt with.

2. May not the space between heaven and earth be compared to a bellows?

> *'Tis emptied, yet it loses not its power;*
> *'Tis moved again, and sends forth air the more.*
> *Much speech to swift exhaustion lead we see;*
> *Your inner being guard, and keep it free.*

CHAPTER 6

The valley spirit dies not, aye the same;
The female mystery thus do we name.
Its gate, from which at first they issued forth,
Is called the root from which grew heaven and earth.
Long and unbroken does its power remain,
Used gently, and without the touch of pain.

CHAPTER 7

1. Heaven is long-enduring and earth continues long. The reason why heaven and earth are able to endure and continue thus long is because they do not live of, or for, themselves. This is how they are able to continue and endure.

2. Therefore the sage puts his own person last, and yet it is found in the foremost place; he treats his person as if it were foreign to him, and yet that person is preserved. Is it not because he has no personal and private ends, that therefore such ends are realised?

CHAPTER 8

1. The highest excellence is like (that of) water. The excellence of water appears in its benefiting all things, and in its occupying, without striving (to the contrary), the low place which all men dislike. Hence (its way) is near to (that of) the Tao.

2. The excellence of a residence is in (the suitability of) the place; that of the mind is in abysmal stillness; that of associations is in their being with the virtuous; that of government is in its securing good order; that of (the conduct of) affairs is in its ability; and that of (the initiation of) any movement is in its timeliness.

3. And when (one with the highest excellence) does not wrangle (about his low position), no one finds fault with him.

CHAPTER 9

1. It is better to leave a vessel unfilled, than to attempt to carry it when it is full. If you keep feeling a point that has been sharpened, the point cannot long preserve its sharpness.

2. When gold and jade fill the hall, their possessor cannot keep them safe. When wealth and honours lead to arrogance, this brings its evil on itself. When the work is done, and one's name is becoming distinguished, to withdraw into obscurity is the way of Heaven.

CHAPTER 10

1. When the intelligent and animal souls are held together in one embrace, they can be kept from separating. When one gives undivided attention to the (vital) breath, and brings it to the utmost degree of pliancy, he can become as a (tender) babe. When he has cleansed away the most mysterious sights (of his imagination), he can become without a flaw.

2. In loving the people and ruling the state, cannot he proceed without any (purpose of) action? In the opening and shutting of his gates of heaven, cannot he do so as a female bird? While his intelligence reaches in every direction, cannot he (appear to) be without knowledge?

3. (The Tao) produces (all things) and nourishes them; it produces them and does not claim them as its own; it does all, and yet does not boast of it; it presides over all, and yet does not control them. This is what is called 'The mysterious Quality' (of the Tao).

CHAPTER 11

The thirty spokes unite in the one nave; but it is on the empty space (for the axle), that the use of the wheel depends. Clay is fashioned into vessels; but it is on their empty hollowness, that their use depends. The door and windows are cut out (from the walls) to form an apartment; but it is on the empty space (within), that its use depends. Therefore, what has a (positive) existence serves for profitable adaptation, and what has not that for (actual) usefulness.

CHAPTER 12

1.

Colour's five hues from th' eyes their sight will take;
Music's five notes the ears as deaf can make;
The flavours five deprive the mouth of taste;
The chariot course, and the wild hunting waste
Make mad the mind; and objects rare and strange,
Sought for, men's conduct will to evil change.

2. Therefore the sage seeks to satisfy (the craving of) the belly, and not the (insatiable longing of the) eyes. He puts from him the latter, and prefers to seek the former.

CHAPTER 13

1. Favour and disgrace would seem equally to be feared; honour and great calamity, to be regarded as personal conditions (of the same kind).

2. What is meant by speaking thus of favour and disgrace? Disgrace is being in a low position (after the enjoyment of favour). The getting that (favour) leads to the apprehension (of losing it), and the losing it leads to the fear of (still greater calamity):—this is what is meant by saying that favour and disgrace would seem equally to be feared.

And what is meant by saying that honour and great calamity are to be (similarly) regarded as personal conditions? What makes me liable to great calamity is my having the body (which I call myself); if I had not the body, what great calamity could come to me?

3. Therefore he who would administer the kingdom, honouring it as he honours his own person, may be employed to govern it, and he who would administer it with the love which he bears to his own person may be entrusted with it.

CHAPTER 14

1. We look at it, and we do not see it, and we name it 'the Equable.' We listen to it, and we do not hear it, and we name it 'the Inaudible.' We try to grasp it, and do not get hold of it, and we name it 'the Subtle.' With these three qualities, it cannot be made the subject of description; and hence we blend them together and obtain The One.

2. Its upper part is not bright, and its lower part is not obscure. Ceaseless in its action, it yet cannot be named, and then it again returns and becomes nothing. This is called the Form of the Formless, and the Semblance of the Invisible; this is called the Fleeting and Indeterminable.

3. We meet it and do not see its Front; we follow it, and do not see its Back. When we can lay hold of the Tao of old to direct the things of the present day, and are able to know it as it was of old in the beginning, this is called (unwinding) the clue of Tao.

CHAPTER 15

1. The skilful masters (of the Tao) in old times, with a subtle and exquisite penetration, comprehended its mysteries, and were deep (also) so as to elude men's knowledge. As they were thus beyond men's knowledge, I will make an effort to describe of what sort they appeared to be.

2. Shrinking looked they like those who wade through a stream in winter; irresolute like those who are afraid of all around them; grave like a guest (in awe of his host); evanescent like ice that is melting away; unpretentious like wood that has not been fashioned into anything; vacant like a valley, and dull like muddy water.

3. Who can (make) the muddy water (clear)? Let it be still, and it will gradually become clear. Who can secure the condition of rest? Let movement go on, and the condition of rest will gradually arise.

4. They who preserve this method of the Tao do not wish to be full (of themselves). It is through their not being full of themselves that they can afford to seem worn and not appear new and complete.

CHAPTER 16

1. The (state of) vacancy should be brought to the utmost degree, and that of stillness guarded with unwearying vigour. All things alike go through their processes of activity, and (then) we see them return (to their original state). When things (in the vegetable world) have displayed their luxuriant growth, we see each of them return to its root. This returning to their root is what we call the state of stillness; and that stillness may be called a reporting that they have fulfilled their appointed end.

2. The report of that fulfilment is the regular, unchanging rule. To know that unchanging rule is to be intelligent; not to know it leads to wild movements and evil issues. The knowledge of that unchanging rule produces a (grand) capacity and forbearance, and that capacity and forbearance lead to a community (of feeling with all things). From this community of feeling comes a kingliness of character; and he who is king-like goes on to be heaven-like. In that likeness to heaven he possesses the Tao. Possessed of the Tao, he endures long; and to the end of his bodily life, is exempt from all danger of decay.

CHAPTER 17

1. In the highest antiquity, (the people) did not know that there were (their rulers). In the next age they loved them and praised them. In the next they feared them; in the next they despised them. Thus it was that when faith (in the Tao) was deficient (in the rulers) a want of faith in them ensued (in the people).

2. How irresolute did those (earliest rulers) appear, showing (by their reticence) the importance which they set upon their words! Their work was done and their undertakings were successful, while the people all said, 'We are as we are, of ourselves!'

CHAPTER 18

1. When the Great Tao (Way or Method) ceased to be observed, benevolence and righteousness came into vogue. (Then) appeared wisdom and shrewdness, and there ensued great hypocrisy.

2. When harmony no longer prevailed throughout the six kinships, filial sons found their manifestation; when the states and clans fell into disorder, loyal ministers appeared.

CHAPTER 19

1. If we could renounce our sageness and discard our wisdom, it would be better for the people a hundredfold. If we could renounce our benevolence and discard our righteousness, the people would again become filial and kindly. If we could renounce our artful contrivances and discard our (scheming for) gain, there would be no thieves nor robbers.

2.

Those three methods (of government)
Thought olden ways in elegance did fail
And made these names their want of worth to veil;
But simple views, and courses plain and true
Would selfish ends and many lusts eschew.

CHAPTER 20

1.

When we renounce learning we have no troubles.
The (ready) 'yes,' and (flattering) 'yea;'—
Small is the difference they display.
But mark their issues, good and ill;—
What space the gulf between shall fill?

What all men fear is indeed to be feared; but how wide and without end is the range of questions (asking to be discussed)!

2. The multitude of men look satisfied and pleased; as if enjoying a full banquet, as if mounted on a tower in spring. I alone seem listless and still, my desires having as yet given no indication of their presence. I am like an infant which has not yet smiled. I look dejected and forlorn, as if I had no home to go to. The multitude of men all have enough and to spare. I alone seem to have lost everything. My mind is that of a stupid man; I am in a state of chaos.

Ordinary men look bright and intelligent, while I alone seem to be benighted. They look full of discrimination, while I alone am dull and confused. I seem to be carried about as on the sea, drifting as if I had nowhere to rest. All men have their spheres of action, while I alone seem dull and incapable, like a rude borderer. (Thus) I alone am different from other men, but I value the nursing-mother (the Tao).

CHAPTER 21

The grandest forms of active force
From Tao come, their only source.
Who can of Tao the nature tell?
Our sight it flies, our touch as well.
Eluding sight, eluding touch,
The forms of things all in it crouch;
Eluding touch, eluding sight,
There are their semblances, all right.
Profound it is, dark and obscure;
Things' essences all there endure.
Those essences the truth enfold
Of what, when seen, shall then be told.
Now it is so; 'twas so of old.
Its name—what passes not away;
So, in their beautiful array,
Things form and never know decay.

How know I that it is so with all the beauties of existing things? By this (nature of the Tao).

CHAPTER 22

1. The partial becomes complete; the crooked, straight; the empty, full; the worn out, new. He whose (desires) are few gets them; he whose (desires) are many goes astray.

2. Therefore the sage holds in his embrace the one thing (of humility), and manifests it to all the world. He is free from self-display, and therefore he shines; from self-assertion, and therefore he is distinguished; from self-boasting, and therefore his merit is acknowledged; from self-complacency, and therefore he acquires superiority. It is because he is thus free from striving that therefore no one in the world is able to strive with him.

3. That saying of the ancients that 'the partial becomes complete' was not vainly spoken:—all real completion is comprehended under it.

CHAPTER 23

1. Abstaining from speech marks him who is obeying the spontaneity of his nature. A violent wind does not last for a whole morning; a sudden rain does not last for the whole day. To whom is it that these (two) things are owing? To Heaven and Earth. If Heaven and Earth cannot make such (spasmodic) actings last long, how much less can man!

2. Therefore when one is making the Tao his business, those who are also pursuing it, agree with him in it, and those who are making the manifestation of its course their object agree with him in that; while even those who are failing in both these things agree with him where they fail.

3. Hence, those with whom he agrees as to the Tao have the happiness of attaining to it; those with whom he agrees as to its manifestation have the happiness of attaining to it; and those with whom he agrees in their failure have also the happiness of attaining (to the Tao). (But) when there is not faith sufficient (on his part), a want of faith (in him) ensues (on the part of the others).

CHAPTER 24

He who stands on his tiptoes does not stand firm; he who stretches his legs does not walk (easily). (So), he who displays himself does not shine; he who asserts his own views is not distinguished; he who vaunts himself does not find his merit acknowledged; he who is self-conceited has no superiority allowed to him. Such conditions, viewed from the standpoint of the Tao, are like remnants of food, or a tumour on the body, which all dislike. Hence those who pursue (the course) of the Tao do not adopt and allow them.

CHAPTER 25

1. There was something undefined and complete, coming into existence before Heaven and Earth. How still it was and formless, standing alone, and undergoing no change, reaching everywhere and in no danger (of being exhausted)! It may be regarded as the Mother of all things.

2. I do not know its name, and I give it the designation of the Tao (the Way or Course). Making an effort (further) to give it a name I call it The Great.

3. Great, it passes on (in constant flow). Passing on, it becomes remote. Having become remote, it returns. Therefore the Tao is great; Heaven is great; Earth is great; and the (sage) king is also great. In the universe there are four that are great, and the (sage) king is one of them.

4. Man takes his law from the Earth; the Earth takes its law from Heaven; Heaven takes its law from the Tao. The law of the Tao is its being what it is.

CHAPTER 26

1. Gravity is the root of lightness; stillness, the ruler of movement.

2. Therefore a wise prince, marching the whole day, does not go far from his baggage waggons. Although he may have brilliant prospects to look at, he quietly remains (in his proper place), indifferent to them. How should the lord of a myriad chariots carry himself lightly before the kingdom? If he do act lightly, he has lost his root (of gravity); if he proceed to active movement, he will lose his throne.

CHAPTER 27

1. The skilful traveller leaves no traces of his wheels or footsteps; the skilful speaker says nothing that can be found fault with or blamed; the skilful reckoner uses no tallies; the skilful closer needs no bolts or bars, while to open what he has shut will be impossible; the skilful binder uses

no strings or knots, while to unloose what he has bound will be impossible. In the same way the sage is always skilful at saving men, and so he does not cast away any man; he is always skilful at saving things, and so he does not cast away anything. This is called 'Hiding the light of his procedure.'

2. Therefore the man of skill is a master (to be looked up to) by him who has not the skill; and he who has not the skill is the helper of (the reputation of) him who has the skill. If the one did not honour his master, and the other did not rejoice in his helper, an (observer), though intelligent, might greatly err about them. This is called 'The utmost degree of mystery.'

CHAPTER 28

1.

> Who knows his manhood's strength,
> Yet still his female feebleness maintains;
> As to one channel flow the many drains,
> All come to him, yea, all beneath the sky.
> Thus he the constant excellence retains;
> The simple child again, free from all stains.
>
> Who knows how white attracts,
> Yet always keeps himself within black's shade,
> The pattern of humility displayed,
> Displayed in view of all beneath the sky;
> He in the unchanging excellence arrayed,
> Endless return to man's first state has made.
>
> Who knows how glory shines,
> Yet loves disgrace, nor e'er for it is pale;
> Behold his presence in a spacious vale,
> To which men come from all beneath the sky.
> The unchanging excellence completes its tale;
> The simple infant man in him we hail.

2. The unwrought material, when divided and distributed, forms vessels. The sage, when employed, becomes the Head of all the Officers (of government); and in his greatest regulations he employs no violent measures.

CHAPTER 29

1. If any one should wish to get the kingdom for himself, and to effect this by what he does, I see that he will not succeed. The kingdom is a spirit-like thing, and cannot be got by active doing. He who would so win it destroys it; he who would hold it in his grasp loses it.

2.

> The course and nature of things is such that
> What was in front is now behind;
> What warmed anon we freezing find.
> Strength is of weakness oft the spoil;
> The store in ruins mocks our toil.

Hence the sage puts away excessive effort, extravagance, and easy indulgence.

CHAPTER 30

1. He who would assist a lord of men in harmony with the Tao will not assert his mastery in the kingdom by force of arms. Such a course is sure to meet with its proper return.

2. Wherever a host is stationed, briars and thorns spring up. In the sequence of great armies there are sure to be bad years.

3. A skilful (commander) strikes a decisive blow, and stops. He does not dare (by continuing his operations) to assert and complete his mastery. He will strike the blow, but will be on his guard against being vain or boastful or arrogant in consequence of it. He strikes it as a matter of necessity; he strikes it, but not from a wish for mastery.

4. When things have attained their strong maturity they become old. This may be said to be not in accordance with the Tao: and what is not in accordance with it soon comes to an end.

CHAPTER 31

1. Now arms, however beautiful, are instruments of evil omen, hateful, it may be said, to all creatures. Therefore they who have the Tao do not like to employ them.

2. The superior man ordinarily considers the left hand the most honourable place, but in time of war the right hand. Those sharp weapons are instruments of evil omen, and not the instruments of the superior man;—he uses them only on the compulsion of necessity. Calm and repose are what he prizes; victory (by force of arms) is to him undesirable. To consider this desirable would be to delight in the slaughter of men; and he who delights in the slaughter of men cannot get his will in the kingdom.

3. On occasions of festivity to be on the left hand is the prized position; on occasions of mourning, the right hand. The second in command of the army has his place on the left; the general commanding in chief has his on the right;—his place, that is, is assigned to him as in the rites of mourning. He who has killed multitudes of men should weep for them with the bitterest grief; and the victor in battle has his place (rightly) according to those rites.

CHAPTER 32

1. The Tao, considered as unchanging, has no name.

2. Though in its primordial simplicity it may be small, the whole world dares not deal with (one embodying) it as a minister. If a feudal prince or the king could guard and hold it, all would spontaneously submit themselves to him.

3. Heaven and Earth (under its guidance) unite together and send down the sweet dew, which, without the directions of men, reaches equally everywhere as of its own accord.

4. As soon as it proceeds to action, it has a name. When it once has that name, (men) can know to rest in it. When they know to rest in it, they can be free from all risk of failure and error.

5. The relation of the Tao to all the world is like that of the great rivers and seas to the streams from the valleys.

CHAPTER 33

1. He who knows other men is discerning; he who knows himself is intelligent. He who overcomes others is strong; he who overcomes himself is mighty. He who is satisfied with his lot is rich; he who goes on acting with energy has a (firm) will.

2. He who does not fail in the requirements of his position, continues long; he who dies and yet does not perish, has longevity.

CHAPTER 34

1. All-pervading is the Great Tao! It may be found on the left hand and on the right.

2. All things depend on it for their production, which it gives to them, not one refusing obedience to it. When its work is accomplished, it does not claim the name of having done it. It clothes all things as with a garment, and makes no assumption of being their lord;—it may be named in the smallest things. All things return (to their root and disappear), and do not know that it is it which presides over their doing so;—it may be named in the greatest things.

3. Hence the sage is able (in the same way) to accomplish his great achievements. It is through his not making himself great that he can accomplish them.

CHAPTER 35

1. To him who holds in his hands the Great Image (of the invisible Tao), the whole world repairs. Men resort to him, and receive no hurt, but (find) rest, peace, and the feeling of ease.

2. Music and dainties will make the passing guest stop (for a time). But though the Tao as it comes from the mouth, seems insipid and has no flavour, though it seems not worth being looked at or listened to, the use of it is inexhaustible.

CHAPTER 36

1. When one is about to take an inspiration, he is sure to make a (previous) expiration; when he is going to weaken another, he will first strengthen him; when he is going to overthrow another, he will first have raised him up; when he is going to despoil another, he will first have made gifts to him:—this is called 'Hiding the light (of his procedure).'

2. The soft overcomes the hard; and the weak the strong.

3. Fishes should not be taken from the deep; instruments for the profit of a state should not be shown to the people.

CHAPTER 37

1. The Tao in its regular course does nothing (for the sake of doing it), and so there is nothing which it does not do.

2. If princes and kings were able to maintain it, all things would of themselves be transformed by them.

3. If this transformation became to me an object of desire, I would express the desire by the nameless simplicity.

Simplicity without a name
Is free from all external aim.
With no desire, at rest and still,
All things go right as of their will.

.

www.ingramcontent.com/pod-product-compliance
Lightning Source LLC
Chambersburg PA
CBHW052311220526
45472CB00001B/63